Muscular Christianity

Muscular Christianity

Learning Endurance from the Book of Hebrews

P. G. Mathew

GRACE & GLORY MINISTRIES
Davis, California

© 2010 by P. G. Mathew. Published by Grace and Glory Ministries, Davis, California. Printed in the United States of America. All rights reserved. No part of this book may be reproduced or transmitted in any form or by any means, electronic or mechanical, including photocopying, recording, or by an information storage and retrieval system—except by a reviewer who may quote brief passages in a review to be printed in a magazine, newspaper, or on the Web—without permission in writing from the publisher. For information, please contact Grace and Glory Ministries, gvcc@gracevalley.org.
ISBN: 978-0-9771149-3-1
Library of Congress Control Number: 2010920052
All scripture quotations, unless otherwise indicated, are taken from the HOLY BIBLE, NEW INTERNATIONAL VERSION®, NIV®. Copyright © 1973, 1978, 1984 by International Bible Society. Used by permission of Zondervan. All rights reserved.

Dedication

The Word of God, the Holy Spirit, and the life of faith characterize the life and ministry of my father-in-law Pastor T. K. Thomas (1915–1989) of Pandalam, Kerala, India. I dedicate this book to T. K. Thomas and his wife Mary Nakolakkal, who are examples of the kind of muscular Christianity to which the author of Hebrews calls his believing readers.

When T. K. (Thoppil Kochummen) Thomas was only twenty-one years of age, the Holy Spirit called him to the ministry. God used him to lead many souls to saving faith in Jesus Christ through the clear and powerful preaching of the gospel. Pastor Thomas established over sixty churches in the mission field of Andhra Pradesh, India, including Zion Hall, the church he personally pastored. Moreover, he opened over three hundred villages to the light of the gospel.

Pastor T. K. Thomas

Throughout his life, Pastor Thomas trusted in God to meet his every need, and he personally witnessed many divine healings, divine provisions, and divine protections. He fearlessly and effectively proclaimed the gospel for fifty-three years. In fact, God called this faithful pastor home to glory while he was preaching the gospel to the students of a Bible college.

Throughout history, God has raised up people of faith, as we read about in Hebrews 11, to stand for his truth against both the wicked world and the corrupt church. The Bible speaks of

Abraham, Moses, Gideon, Elijah, Jeremiah, Daniel, and Paul. In the history of the church, God raised up mighty men like Augustine, John Wycliffe, Martin Luther, George Whitefield, J. C. Ryle, C. H. Spurgeon, and Martyn Lloyd-Jones. India has its own legacy of those God raised up to stand boldly for truth, such as the apostle Thomas, Abraham Malpan, and Pandita Ramabai. This heritage includes Pastor T. K. Thomas. It is a heritage in which I myself resolutely stand.

The Man of Faith

The church in South India experienced a tremendous outpouring of the Holy Spirit in the early twentieth century. Pastor Thomas' family was one of many that experienced revival and true conversion. Then God called Pastor Thomas to be a missionary to Andhra Pradesh, and he obeyed and went. Although Andhra Pradesh is a neighboring state to Kerala, its culture and language differed greatly. Unlike Kerala, very little gospel light had penetrated into the Andhra Pradesh region dominated by Hinduism and Islam.

Resolving to know nothing except "Jesus Christ and him crucified," Pastor Thomas evangelized lower-caste untouchables, a group of people many Christians had no interest in reaching. Thomas prayed for and received divine protection as he courageously declared the gospel to hostile Hindus and Muslims. He established Zion Hall, his home church in Warangal, A.P., and faithfully exposited the word of God there for about fifty years. This church became one of the largest local churches in India. Pastor Thomas also served as the General Overseer of the more than sixty churches he established in the region.

Pastor T. K. Thomas and Mrs. Mary Thomas

Zion Hall, Warangal, Andhra Pradesh, India

Like George Müller of Bristol, Pastor Thomas resolved to trust in Jehovah Jireh to meet all his spiritual and physical needs. Unlike many modern missionaries and church leaders, he was not financially supported by any organization. He knew that if God truly called him to the mission field, God would also meet all his needs. As Hudson Taylor used to say, "God's work done in God's way will never lack God's supply." Not only does a truly called missionary or minister not beg for support and tell huge lies, but he even refuses to make others aware of his need. Like Hudson Taylor, Pastor Thomas refused to solicit funds and resolved "to move man, by God, through prayer alone."

The book of Acts guided Pastor T. K. Thomas in his mission work. It should guide all true missionaries. Nowhere in Acts do we see money mentioned in the context of missions. Instead, the focus is on the gospel and the Holy Spirit. In the modern mission model, however, the Holy Spirit has been replaced by money as the *sine qua non* for successful missions, and fundraising as the crucial ability a prospective missionary must demonstrate. We have come a long way from the days of Simon Magus, who wished to buy the Holy Spirit with money (Acts 8). Today money has taken the place of the Holy Spirit altogether. Many modern missionaries and ministers have found that begging for money from gullible people is much easier than earnestly and persistently praying for Holy Spirit-given power, provision, and guidance.

May God raise up many pastors like T. K. Thomas, who feed the sheep with the bread of God's eternal word in the Pentecostal power!

Contents

Dedication v

About the Author xiii

Preface xv

1. The Glory of Jesus 1
   Hebrews 1:1-4

2. Jesus, Superior to Holy Angels 11
   Hebrews 1:4-14

3. The Danger of Drifting 21
   Hebrews 2:1-3

4. The New World Order 31
   Hebrews 2:5-9

5. Jesus, Our Brother and Priest 41
   Hebrews 2:10-18

6. Consider Jesus 53
   Hebrews 3:1-6

7. How to Experience Happiness 63
   Hebrews 3:7-4:11

8. Nowhere to Hide 75
   Hebrews 4:12-13

9. Grace for Living 85
   Hebrews 4:14-16

CONTENTS

10. Jesus, Our Perfect High Priest 97
    Hebrews 5:1–10

11. Muscular Christianity 109
    Hebrews 5:11–14

12. Eternal Security and Eternal Insecurity 119
    Hebrews 6:1–12

13. Cure for Spiritual Laziness. 137
    Hebrews 6:9–12

14. Jesus, Our Anchor of Hope 147
    Hebrews 6:13–20

15. Jesus, Our Eternal Savior. 157
    Hebrews 7:1–28

16. New Covenant Blessings. 171
    Hebrews 8:1–13

17. A Clear Conscience 183
    Hebrews 9:1–14

18. The Blessings of Good Friday 195
    Hebrews 9:15–26

19. The Second Coming of Jesus Christ 209
    Hebrews 9:26b–28

20. Who Can Forgive Sins? 219
    Hebrews 10:1–18

21. Worship of the Saints 229
    Hebrews 10:19–25

22. Warning against Apostasy 239
    Hebrews 10:26–31

23. Saints' Endurance 251
    Hebrews 10:32–39

24. Faith of Our Fathers 265
    Hebrews 11:1–3

CONTENTS

25. Happiness Is Pleasing God 275
    Hebrews 11:4–6

26. Living in the Present by Faith 285
    Hebrews 11:7

27. The Fiery Trial of Our Faith 299
    Hebrews 11:8–22

28. The Faith of Moses 311
    Hebrews 11:23–28

29. The "Foolishness" of Christian Faith 321
    Hebrews 11:29–31

30. By Faith We Live and Die 331
    Hebrews 11:32–40

31. Christian Endurance 341
    Hebrews 12:1–3

32. Our Father's Discipline 351
    Hebrews 12:4–11

33. The Danger of Apostasy 363
    Hebrews 12:12–17

34. New Covenant Worship 375
    Hebrews 12:18–24

35. A Dreadful Warning 387
    Hebrews 12:25–29

36. Brotherly Love 395
    Hebrews 13:1–3

37. Christian Marriage 407
    Hebrews 13:4

38. Key to Happiness: Greed or God? 419
    Hebrews 13:5–6

39. The Christian Minister 431
    Hebrews 13:7–8, 17

xi

Contents

40. The Christian's Sacrifice 441
    Hebrews 13:9–16

41. Living the Resurrection Life 459
    Hebrews 13:20–21

Select Bibliography. 469

About the Author

P. G. Mathew, who holds three graduate degrees in theology from Central and Westminster theological seminaries (USA), is the founder and senior minister of Grace Valley Christian Center in California. Originally a scientist from India, he is also a former professor of Greek and systematic theology and has traveled widely for Christian mission interests. He is the author of *The Normal Church Life* (1 John); *Victory in Jesus* (Joshua); *The Wisdom of Jesus* (The Sermon on the Mount); *The Lawless Church*; and several other titles, including forthcoming commentaries on Romans, Isaiah, Matthew, and Acts. He is also the founder and president of Grace Valley Christian Academy. For more information, visit *www.gracevalley.org*.

Preface

Why study a letter written by an anonymous
author almost 2,000 years ago to a group of Hebrew Christians who were tempted to abandon their faith in Christ and return to the safety of their Jewish religion?

We should study this epistle because we *are* the church of the Hebrews. All who profess Christ have been tempted to quit the life that calls for denying ourselves, taking up the cross, and following Jesus. We may be experiencing persecution, trials, or disappointments, or we may have fallen in love with sin and the things of this world. Perhaps we have lapsed into complacency or sheer laziness in our Christian life. No matter what the cause, we can relate to the Hebrews who needed to be exhorted by their pastor to "persevere so that . . . [we] will receive what he has promised" (Heb. 10:36).

As a pastor for thirty-five years, I speak from experience. I wholeheartedly believe in what the author of this epistle presents to his congregation as the solution. I call it *muscular Christianity*. The author-pastor of our epistle rebuts a glib "once saved, always saved" position that affords a false assurance. We tremble when we read the warnings given to those who do not persevere: "It is impossible for those who have once been enlightened . . . if they fall away, to be brought back to repentance. . . . If we deliberately keep on sinning after we have received the knowledge of the truth, no sacrifice for sins is left" (Heb. 6:4, 6; 10:26). What matters is not our being baptized nor having a history of church attendance, but rather present faith and obedience.

What marvelous incentives we have "to run with perseverance the race marked out for us" (Heb. 12:1). Throughout this letter the Hebrews' pastor placards Jesus—the Son of God who is the

Preface

"radiance of God's glory" (Heb. 1:3) and who became a merciful and faithful high priest who "sacrificed for [our] sins once for all when he offered himself" (Heb. 7:27). This Jesus is superior to angels, to Moses, and to the Levitical priesthood and sacrificial system. It is "impossible for the blood of bulls and goats to take away sins" (Heb. 10:4), but Jesus "entered the Most Holy Place once for all by his own blood, having obtained eternal redemption [for his people]" (Heb. 9:12). Through him we may "approach the throne of grace with confidence, so that we may receive mercy and find grace" (Heb. 4:16). Oh, how foolish to let go of this one, true Savior!

What, then, is the muscular Christianity the pastor is espousing? It is a faith that refuses to let go of God because it sees Jesus (Heb. 2:9) through serious, systematic, devotional study of the Bible, the very word of God. It is a faith that does not flag in the face of opposition because we have learned to "endure hardship as discipline" (Heb. 12:7) given by a loving heavenly Father. It is a faith that does not turn away but seeks to "encourage one another daily" (Heb. 3:13) as vital members of the church.

Today we are surrounded by a moribund, ineffectual Christianity—a Christianity that is morally, spiritually, and intellectually flabby. I invite you to join with me in studying this epistle that calls us up to a virile, victorious faith as we look to Jesus "[who] will appear a second time, not to bear sin, but to bring salvation to those who are waiting for him" (Heb. 9:28).

I thank the members of Grace Valley Christian Center in California, where these sermons were first preached between October 2006 and October 2007. I thank God for my wife Gladys, who has persevered with me in the race marked out for us. I also am grateful for Mr. Gregory Perry, Mr. Matthew Sanders, Mr. Marc Roby, Dr. Lisa Case, and Mrs. Margaret Killeen for their help in preparing this manuscript for publication and Mrs. Lorraine Smith for her work on designing the cover. Soli Deo Gloria!

P. G. Mathew

1
The Glory of Jesus

¹*In the past God spoke to our forefathers through the prophets at many times and in various ways, ²but in these last days he has spoken to us by his Son, whom he appointed heir of all things, and through whom he made the universe. ³The Son is the radiance of God's glory and the exact representation of his being, sustaining all things by his powerful word. After he had provided purification for sins, he sat down at the right hand of the Majesty in heaven. ⁴So he became as much superior to the angels as the name he has inherited is superior to theirs.*

Hebrews 1:1–4

Our God is infinite and personal, yet a God who communicates that we might know him. The epistle to the Hebrews tells us that God has spoken to us finally and fully in his Son, Jesus Christ. Let us, therefore, examine this revelation of God and his Son.

Hebrews is a mystery epistle in that we do not know who wrote it or to whom it was directed. It seems it was written to exhort a congregation of Hellenistic Jewish Christians, possibly in Rome, who were being persecuted for their faith in Jesus Christ. These people were under severe pressure to abandon their confident faith in Jesus and go back to Judaism to avoid further trials. The author encourages them to persevere in their faith until death so that they may obtain better things through Christ, their great high priest. For centuries many people thought Paul wrote Hebrews, but this view is not held by most modern scholars. Only God knows who really wrote it. It appears to have been written before the destruction of the temple in AD 70.

The first four verses are an introduction to the ultimate reality of our communicating, infinite, personal God. Pagan gods are mute idols; the God of the Scriptures is the only true and living God. Through God's gracious revelation, we know who he is, who we are, and what the world around us is really about. Through Christ we understand creation, the fall of man, and God's gracious plan of redemption.

Atheism denies God, pantheism identifies creation with God, and deism denies God's present involvement with creation. Only Christianity teaches that ultimate reality is the triune God who is directing creation to his ultimate purpose. This revelation has been progressive, given to men in two phases. From Moses to Malachi, God promised through the prophets that a Messiah would come. In the second phase, God has spoken to us in his Son. The New Testament is the fulfillment of the Old Testament promise of a Savior. Both are the revelation of God himself.

Paul declares: "All Scripture is God-breathed and is useful for teaching, rebuking, correcting and training in righteousness, so that the man of God may be thoroughly equipped for every good work" (2 Tim. 3:16–17). Peter tells us, "No prophecy of Scripture came about by the prophet's own interpretation. For prophecy never had its origin in the will of man, but men spoke from God as they were carried along by the Holy Spirit" (2 Pet. 1:20–21). The revelation of God in the sacred Scriptures is completely inerrant and totally trustworthy for our faith and life. Let us, then, pay attention to what the Scriptures say about the glory of Jesus, the Son of God.

Jesus Is God's Son

The author states, *"In these last days [God] has spoken to us by his Son"* (Heb. 1:2). The first point is that Jesus Christ is God's eternal Son incarnate, through whom God has spoken to us. Note the phrase, "In these last days." Jesus inaugurated the last days, in which we are now living. This messianic age will continue until Jesus Christ comes again in great glory.

The prophets were men of earth below and sinners just like

us. But the Son, who is from heaven, is eternal God himself. The revelation of God in his Son is full and final; thus, we are to listen to the voice of God in the Scriptures and respond to him obediently, not to seek a fresh, new word. If we long to hear from God, we must listen to the Scriptures. No theologian, philosopher, scientist, or guru can give us a new or different word from God. Any revelation that contradicts the full revelation of God in the Scriptures is not from God, but is an anti-word from the devil himself. The word of God alone can give us everlasting encouragement.

God has spoken finally in his Son, who is God himself. He is the great Prophet, superior to all other prophets through whom God spoke. His Son, however, is more than a prophet; he is our Judge, Creator, and God, whom we must worship: "At the name of Jesus every knee should bow . . . and every tongue confess that Jesus Christ is Lord, to the glory of God the Father" (Phil. 2:10–11).

Creator of All Things

Second, we are told that Christ created all things: *"He has spoken to us by his Son . . . through whom he made the universe"* (Heb. 1:2). We do not live in an impersonal universe. By his command, the Lord Jesus Christ created all things for the Father; therefore, he has a personal interest in his creation. This truth contradicts the Darwinian hypothesis, which is popular today because of its atheistic foundations. The belief that animals, man, and everything else came out of inanimate matter is sheer irrationality.

The writer to the Hebrews tells us that because the Son created the universe, he is the Lord of all history. The apostle John declares, "In the beginning was the Word, and the Word was with God, and the Word was God. He was with God in the beginning. Through him all things were made; without him nothing was made that has been made. In him was life, and that life was the light of men" (John 1:1–4). Paul says, "He is the image of the invisible God, the firstborn over all creation. For by him all things were created: things in heaven and on earth, visible and invisible, whether thrones or powers or rulers or authorities; all things were created by him and for him. He is before all things, and in him all things hold together" (Col. 1:15–17).

Moreover, this Son is the Creator of the new heaven and the new earth (Isa. 65:17). He also makes us new creations. Paul writes, "If anyone is in Christ Jesus, he is a new creation" (2 Cor. 5:17), and, "Neither circumcision nor uncircumcision means anything; what counts is a new creation" (Gal. 6:15).

The Creator-creature distinction is the basis for all sound thought. All creation is the work of Jesus Christ. If so, the Son is almighty and all-wise. In other words, Jesus Christ is God himself.

Heir of All Things

This passage also tells us that God appointed his Son heir of all things: *"He has spoken to us by his Son, whom he appointed heir of all things"* (Heb. 1:2). Jesus Christ already owns all things by virtue of having created them. Because of his successful mediatorial work of our redemption, he is also appointed heir of all things by the Father.

In Psalm 2:8 God says, "Ask of me, and I will make the nations your inheritance, the ends of the earth your possession." The Son owns all things; nothing is excluded. The wonderful thing about this truth is that all who are united to Jesus Christ by faith will also be heirs with him. Hebrews 1:14 asks, "Are not all angels ministering spirits sent to serve those who will inherit salvation?" In Hebrews 6:12, 17 we read: "We do not want you to become lazy, but to imitate those who through faith and patience inherit what has been promised. . . . Because God wanted to make the unchanging nature of his promise very clear to the heirs of what was promised, he confirmed it with an oath."

Paul speaks about this privilege: "Now if we are children, then we are heirs—heirs of God and co-heirs with Christ" (Rom. 8:17). The seventeenth-century theologian John Trapp counseled people to "be married to this heir of all and have all."[1] He pays all our debts and he gives us all his wealth. So Paul writes, "All things are yours, whether Paul or Apollos or Cephas or the world or life or death or the present or the future—all are yours, and you are of Christ, and Christ is of God" (1 Cor. 3:22–23). Jesus came to make poor people rich in him. As Christians, we are rich indeed!

---

1   Quoted by Brown, *Message of Hebrews*, 30.

Radiance of God's Glory

Then we are told that Jesus Christ *"is the radiance of God's glory"* (Heb. 1:3). The Son is light proceeding from the Father, as a beam of light comes from the sun. Jesus is ceaselessly the radiant light of God's glory. This speaks about the oneness of the Son with the Father. The Son is the same in essence as the Father, sharing the nature of God the Father. The Son is God.

The Exact Representation of God

Jesus is *"the exact representation of [God's] being"* (Heb. 1:3). "Exact representation" comes from the Greek word *karaktēr*, which means "true copy." This speaks about the otherness of the Son from the Father. They are distinct persons, yet the Son is the true copy of the Father. He is of the same nature as the Father, yet he is a different person.

We need to understand the glory of our Savior. The apostle John writes, "The Word became flesh and made his dwelling among us. We have seen his glory, the glory of the One and Only, who came from the Father, full of grace and truth. . . . No one has ever seen God, but God the One and Only, who is at the Father's side, has made him known" (John 1:14, 18). Paul also speaks of the glorious divinity of Jesus: "For God was pleased to have all his fullness dwell in him. . . . For in Christ all the fullness of the Deity lives in bodily form" (Col. 1:19; 2:9).

Do you want to know God? Look at Jesus Christ. When Philip said, "Lord, show us the Father and that will be enough for us," Jesus told him, "Don't you know me, Philip, even after I have been among you such a long time? Anyone who has seen me has seen the Father. How can you say, 'Show us the Father'?" (John 14:8–9). In his person and work, Jesus makes the invisible God visible.

He Maintains All Things

"The Son is . . . sustaining all things by his powerful word" (Heb. 1:3). Jesus Christ sustains, maintains, and preserves all

created things by the word of his power. The writer uses a present participle, *pherōn*, indicating that Christ is continuously doing this, directing all creation to its God-ordained goal.

"All things" sustained and maintained by him includes the devil and his demons and all the unbelieving people of the world, who exist because of God's common grace. It includes us—his bride, his body, his church—that he redeemed. It includes all nations and potentates, all idolaters, and false religionists. It includes the smallest particle and the largest star.

By his powerful word Christ created all things, and his word will sustain all things till the end. The continuing stability of the universe is due to him. Jesus keeps his universe "in the hollow of his hand" (Isa. 40:12). He maintains the creation in its being and holds it together (Col. 1:17). When we study creation, we discover his laws. Such discoveries should cause us to praise him.

Not only does Jesus sustain the sparrows and the lilies of the field by his common grace, but he also sustains us, if we have trusted in him, by his special grace. He tells us, "Do not be anxious." The Lord is our shepherd; we shall lack nothing. So fear not; Jesus Christ is bearing us up in being and he shall never fail nor falter. Paul declares that nothing in all creation is "able to separate us from the love of God that is in Christ Jesus our Lord" (Rom. 8:39).

He Provided Purification for Sins

This Son is our great high priest who purifies us from our sins: *"After he had provided purification for sins, he sat down at the right hand of the Majesty in heaven"* (Heb. 1:3). All of a sudden the writer introduces the issue of how God deals with sin. There was creation and the fall; now, thank God, there is redemption.

God is holy, but man became filthy due to his sin and deserves to be destroyed for his stubborn rebellion against his Creator, Owner, and Sustainer. Yet God sent his only Son to make atonement for our sins. Christ came into this world as the sinless Lamb of God to take away the sin of the world. No one else was good enough to deal with our sin and guilt. The Seed of the woman, the Son of Abraham, the Son of David, the virgin-born Jesus, became our great high priest and the perfect sacrificial victim. By his blood shed on the cross, Christ cleanses our consciences and makes us perfect to enjoy fellowship with our perfect God. "He was delivered over to death for our sins and was raised to life for our justification" (Rom. 4:25).

How did Jesus provide purification for our sins? Through his sacrifice of himself. Later in this epistle the author declares, "How much more, then, will the blood of Christ, who through the eternal Spirit offered himself unblemished to God, cleanse our consciences from acts that lead to death, so that we may serve the living God! . . . He has appeared once for all at the end of the ages to do away with sin by the sacrifice of himself" (Heb. 9:14, 26). John also speaks about this: "If we confess our sins, he is faithful and just and will forgive us our sins and purify us from all unrighteousness" (1 John 1:9). As sinners in need of cleansing, we must cry with David, "Have mercy on me, O God, according to your unfailing love; according to your great compassion blot out my transgressions. Wash away all my iniquity and cleanse me from my sin" (Ps. 51:1–2).

Jesus Christ blotted out our sins and now they are gone forever. We can look, but we will not find them. God himself made our consciences as white as snow and put all our sins behind his back (Isa. 1:18; 38:17). That means he does not see them again to judge us, for he judged them in Jesus Christ. Isaiah also says the Lord blotted out our sins and remembers them no more (Isa. 43:25). Jeremiah says God forgave all our sins and wickedness (Jer. 31:34), and Micah says he has trodden our sins underfoot, defeating their power and conquering them (Mic. 7:19). Jesus Christ destroyed sin's power and hurled all our iniquities into the depths of the sea, and they shall not be brought back to be punished again. In Christ we have been cleansed of all the filth of our sin. We have been justified and clothed with the perfect, unimpeachable righteousness of Jesus Christ, which gives us confidence and boldness to approach the throne of God.

Christ's work of atonement was more difficult than his work of creation or sustaining. He created and sustains all things by the word of his power, but the work of redemption required his humiliation, incarnation, death, burial, and resurrection. The wages of our sin is death; Jesus died on the cross in our place and for our sins.

Amazing grace!—how sweet the sound—
that saved a wretch like me!

Away with all ideas of self-esteem! We are filthy sinners, rebels under the wrath of God. Thank God for the Son who provided purification for our sins once for all by his shed blood.

There is no other Savior. Jesus himself declares, "I am the way and the truth and the life. No one comes to the Father except through me" (John 14:6). Notice the exclusivism. There is no salvation except in Christianity. Peter says the same thing: "Salvation is found in no one else, for there is no other name under heaven given to men by which we must be saved" (Acts 4:12). And John tells us, "He who has the Son has life; he who does not have the Son of God does not have life" (1 John 5:12).

He Sat Down at God's Right Hand

"*After he had provided purification for sins, he sat down at the right hand of the Majesty in heaven*" (Heb. 1:3). There were no chairs in the tabernacle or temple. The Aaronic priests of the Old Testament period never sat down because their work was never finished: they had to offer sacrifices daily. But by offering himself as a perfect sacrifice in our behalf to God, Jesus Christ atoned for all our sins. His propitiatory work is done; therefore, he cried out from the cross, "*Tetelestai*—It is finished" (John 10:30). There are no more sacrifices. Jesus Christ was raised from the dead, ascended into the heavens, and is seated in the most honored place because of his mediatorial work in our behalf. He is seated on the right hand of "the Greatness in Heaven," as we read in the Greek. He is our Prophet, Priest, and King.

The author of Hebrews was likely thinking of Psalm 110:1: "The LORD says to my Lord: 'Sit at my right hand until I make your enemies a footstool for your feet.'" It is God's intention to defeat all the enemies of Christ and make them his footstool. Every enemy shall feel the weight of Christ's feet on his neck. Paul also spoke about the authority of this seated Son: "[God] raised him from the dead and seated him at his right hand in the heavenly realms, far above all rule and authority, power and dominion, and every title that can be given, not only in the present age but also in the one to come. And God placed all things under his feet and appointed him to be the head over everything for the church" (Eph. 1:20–22). It is the purpose of the seated Christ to make every unbeliever realize that he is Victor, Conqueror, and King: "For he must reign until he has put all his enemies under his feet" (1 Cor. 15:25).

Even now Christ is ruling. As King of kings and Lord of lords, he defeats all rebels who will not trust in him. As our Priest and King, he also makes intercession before the Father for us.

God Is Speaking to You

Do you desire to have God speak to you personally? Then you must understand that he speaks to us in the Scriptures, as he is doing right now. God has spoken in the past by the prophets; he has spoken in the Messianic age in his Son; he has spoken in the New Testament, written by the apostles; and he speaks today in the Scriptures through his appointed pastors and teachers.

How should we respond to his word? "As the Holy Spirit says: 'Today, if you hear his voice, do not harden your hearts'" (Heb. 3:7–8). We are hearing his voice even now. I pray each of us will repent and believe in Christ, availing ourselves of this great provision of the purification for sins provided by the atonement of Christ. God does not have to speak to anyone; revelation is an act of grace. May we listen to him as he speaks the words of eternal life. If we reject him and his word, we must be aware that his Son is the seated King who will defeat all his enemies. His words that give life will also judge and condemn those who reject him (John 12:48).

God is speaking. I beseech you, by the mercies of God, to believe the Father's revelation in his Son. Heed the heavenly Father's counsel on the Mount of Transfiguration: "This is my Son, whom I love; with him I am well pleased. Listen to him!" (Matt. 17:5). May God help us not to treat Jesus Christ with contempt and unbelief, but to fall down and worship him and be saved.

2
Jesus, Superior to Holy Angels

⁴So he became as much superior to the angels as the name he has inherited is superior to theirs.

⁵For to which of the angels did God ever say,

> "You are my Son;
> today I have become your Father"?

Or again,

> "I will be his Father,
> and he will be my Son"?

⁶And again, when God brings his firstborn into the world, he says,

> "Let all God's angels worship him."

⁷In speaking of the angels he says,

> "He makes his angels winds,
> his servants flames of fire."

⁸But about the Son he says,

> "Your throne, O God, will last for ever and ever,
> and righteousness will be the scepter of your kingdom.
> ⁹You have loved righteousness and hated wickedness;
> therefore God, your God, has set you above your companions
> by anointing you with the oil of joy."

¹⁰He also says,

> "In the beginning, O Lord, you laid the foundations of
>   the earth,
> and the heavens are the work of your hands.

> ¹¹*They will perish, but you remain;*
> *they will all wear out like a garment.*
> ¹²*You will roll them up like a robe;*
> *like a garment they will be changed.*
> *But you remain the same,*
> *and your years will never end."*
>
> ¹³*To which of the angels did God ever say,*
>
> > *"Sit at my right hand*
> > *until I make your enemies*
> > *a footstool for your feet"?*
>
> ¹⁴*Are not all angels ministering spirits sent to serve those who will inherit salvation?*
>
> Hebrews 1:4–14

The book of Hebrews speaks much about angels. In this passage, the writer contrasts the status of these heavenly beings to that of the Lord Jesus Christ and us.

Humans are created inferior to angels in some ways, as we read in Psalm 8:5 ("You made him a little lower than the angels") and Hebrews 2:9 ("But we see Jesus, who was made a little lower than the angels"). Yet as we continue our study of this epistle, we will see that believers in Christ are actually superior to holy angels.

The first three verses of Hebrews 1 describe the supremacy of Jesus Christ, who is the Prophet, Priest, and King forever as well as the Creator, Upholder, and Heir of all things. Verse 4 then declares that Jesus has obtained a name superior to that of angels because he successfully accomplished the redemptive mediatorial work God the Father assigned him. In verses 5 through 14, the author shows the superiority of Jesus to angels through seven scriptural proofs from the Septuagint, the Greek translation of the Old Testament.

Comparing Jesus to Angels

The Jews had a very high view of angels, especially in view of their part in giving the law of Moses: "For if the message spoken by angels was binding . . ." (Heb. 2:2). Angels somehow mediated the law.

Jesus, Superior to Holy Angels

To some unbelieving Jews, Jesus was a blasphemer; to others, he was an angel. But in either case, they would not look upon him as deity. In contrast, these Hebrew Christians believed Jesus is God and worshiped him as Lord, and they were being persecuted for this faith. To avoid persecution, some of these believers were possibly being tempted to abandon their faith in Jesus as Lord and to think of him only as an angel. So the author writes of the supremacy of Christ, proving from the Scriptures that Jesus Christ is superior to angels, that he is God, and that he is to be worshiped.

Because the Bible is God's word, the writer did not have to construct an argument; he could merely quote relevant scriptures to prove his point. He clearly understood that the Old Testament is Christ-centered, as Jesus himself declared: "You diligently study the Scriptures because you think that by them you possess eternal life. These are the Scriptures that testify about me. . . . If you believed Moses, you would believe me, for he wrote about me" (John 5:39, 46). Jesus enlightened the disciples on the road to Emmaus: "And beginning with Moses and all the Prophets, he explained to them what was said in all the Scriptures concerning himself" (Luke 24:27).

What is spoken of Yahweh in the Old Testament is also spoken of our Lord Jesus Christ in the New. The Septuagint translates the Hebrew word *Yahweh* to the Greek *Kurios* (Lord), and many New Testament writers, who were Jewish, attribute the same term to Jesus. For example, Paul declares that we cannot be saved unless we confess *Iēsous Kurios*, "Jesus is Lord" (Rom. 10:9). Paul also applies Isaiah 45:23–24, which speaks about Yahweh, to Jesus in Philippians 2:10–11. Jesus is the Yahweh of the Old Testament.

With this in mind, let us look at seven proofs that Jesus Christ is superior to the holy angels.

1. "Today I Have Become Your Father"

The first proof is from Psalm 2:7: *"For to which of the angels did God ever say, 'You are my Son; today I have become your Father'?"* (Heb. 1:5). What is the answer? To none! The superior name God gave Jesus was "my Son." This statement was applied to the son of David in the psalm, but the reference ultimately points to the antitype Jesus Christ, the Son of David.

This quotation is not speaking about the eternal sonship of Jesus, although Christ is the eternal Son of God. Rather, it refers to his incarnational sonship in time: "*Today* I have become your Father" (italics added). God the Father declared that Jesus was his beloved Son both at his baptism and transfiguration (Matt. 3:17; 17:5), but he particularly declared Christ's sonship by the resurrection. Paul writes about "[God's] Son, who as to his human nature was a descendant of David, and who through the Spirit of holiness was declared with power to be the Son of God by his resurrection from the dead" (Rom. 1:3–4). Paul clearly understood that Psalm 2:7 refers to the resurrection of Christ, as he explained to his listeners at Antioch: "We tell you the good news: What God promised our fathers he has fulfilled for us, their children, by raising up Jesus. As it is written in the second Psalm: 'You are my Son; today I have become your Father'" (Acts 13:32–33).

Because of his successful mediatorial work, Jesus obtained a name superior to all angels: "My Son." No angel ever received this name. This, then, is the first proof the writer gives to show that Jesus Christ is superior to all angels.

2. "He Will Be My Son"

The second proof is a quote from 2 Samuel 7:14: *"I will be his Father, and he will be my Son"* (Heb. 1:5). In its historical context, this quotation refers to the son of David. Ultimately, however, it too has reference to Jesus Christ, and also speaks about the sonship of Christ in time.

Isaiah prophesied, "To us a child is born, to us a son is given, and the government will be on his shoulders. And he will be called Wonderful Counselor, Mighty God, Everlasting Father, Prince of Peace" (Isa. 9:6). The angel told Mary, "He will be great and will be called the Son of the Most High. The Lord God will give him the throne of his father David, and he will reign over the house of Jacob forever; his kingdom will never end" (Luke 1:32–33).

God did not give this promise to an angel, but to his Son, because of his mediatorial work. The throne of David is given to this One who is the Wonderful Counselor, Mighty God, Everlasting Father, Prince of Peace, Son of the Most High, whose kingdom shall never end. Here again the author argues that God's Son is superior to all angels.

3. Angels Worship Him

The third quotation comes from Psalm 97:7 and also probably from Deuteronomy 32:43: *"When God brings his firstborn into the world, he says, 'Let all God's angels worship him'"* (Heb. 1:6). God the Father is speaking authoritatively. We must note that it does not say, "God said" or "It is written," but "God is saying *now*." What is he saying? "Let all God's angels worship him." This is a command to all holy angels, without reference to rank, to cast themselves down before Christ and worship him.

The angels worshiped Jesus at his birth: "Suddenly a great company of the heavenly host appeared with the angel, praising God and saying, 'Glory to God in the highest, and on earth peace to men on whom his favor rests'" (Luke 2:13–14). They are worshiping him even now in heaven, as John reveals: "Then I looked and heard the voice of many angels, numbering thousands upon thousands, and ten thousand times ten thousand. They encircled the throne and the living creatures and the elders. In a loud voice they sang: 'Worthy is the Lamb, who was slain, to receive power and wealth and wisdom and strength and honor and glory and praise!'" (Rev. 5:11–12).

The will of the Father is that all holy angels fall down and worship Jesus Christ as the firstborn of God. "Firstborn" is not speaking about being first in birth order, but about the pre-eminence, sovereignty, and priority of Christ. Those who worship are inferior to the one being worshiped. The Son is superior to these holy angels, who are commanded to worship him.

4. Jesus Creates and Controls Angels

The fourth quotation is from Psalm 104:4 (Ps. 103:4 in the Septuagint): *"In speaking of the angels he says, 'He makes his angels winds, his servants flames of fire'"* (Heb. 1:7). The writer is saying that Jesus is the Creator of angels, who are compared here to storms and lightning—powerful forces created and controlled by him. The point here is simply that Christ is superior to angels because he created and controls them.

5. THE ROYAL KING AND BRIDEGROOM

The fifth quotation is from Psalm 45:6–7: *"But about the Son he says, 'Your throne, O God, will last for ever and ever, and righteousness will be the scepter of your kingdom. You have loved righteousness and hated wickedness; therefore God, your God, has set you above your companions by anointing you with the oil of joy'"* (Heb. 1:8–9). In the original setting, this verse speaks of a royal wedding of a son of David in which the royal bridegroom is addressed. The final reference, however, is not to Solomon, but to Jesus, the Son of David and eternal King.

When we read this quote carefully, we notice that the writer is asserting that Jesus is God: *"Your throne, O God, will last forever and ever"* (Heb. 1:8). We can also translate a phrase from verse 9 from the Septuagint: "Therefore, O God, your God." Twice, then, the Son is addressed as God; at the same time, he is seen worshiping God.

Who is this king who *is* God and yet *worships* God? He is the incarnate Son, the God-man. We are told that this king is altogether righteous in his rule, always doing what is just and right. Certainly this is not speaking of Solomon, but about Jesus Christ.

We are then told that he is anointed with the oil of gladness above his companions. The picture is that of a wedding feast, a joyful celebration symbolized by the "oil of gladness." Before a great party in ancient times, all the guests would be anointed with oil. We find the same idea in Luke 7, when Jesus was invited to a feast by a Pharisee. Because no one washed Jesus' feet, kissed him, or anointed him, he rebuked the Pharisee, saying, "You did not put oil on my head" (Luke 7:46). Note that this is the "oil *of gladness.*" Isaiah prophesied that the Messiah would come "to comfort all who mourn, and provide for those who grieve in Zion—to bestow on them a crown of beauty instead of ashes, the oil of gladness instead of mourning" (Isa. 61:2–3).

This One was anointed above his companions who were seated with him. Who are these companions? They are the church, the bride of Christ. We are Christ's companions! The Hebrews writer later speaks about "bringing many sons to glory" (Heb. 2:10) and says, "We have come to share in Christ" (Heb. 3:14). The royal Son and his companions are seated at this great celebration, having a wonderful time. It is joy unspeakable and full of glory. The apostle John describes this heavenly celebration: "Hallelujah! For our Lord God Almighty reigns. Let us rejoice and be glad and give him glory! For the wedding of the Lamb has come, and his bride has made herself ready" (Rev. 19:6–7). The author, therefore, is declaring that Jesus is superior to all angels because he is God the anointed and righteous King.

6. The Unchanging Creator

Next we read about the immutability of Christ the Creator. In Hebrews 1:10–12, the writer quotes Psalm 102:25–27 (Ps. 101:25–27 in the Septuagint): *"He also says, 'In the beginning, O Lord, you laid the foundations of the earth, and the heavens are the work of your hands. They will perish, but you remain; they will all wear out like a garment. You will roll them up like a robe; like a garment they will be changed. But you remain the same, and your years will never end.'"*

"In the beginning" speaks of the pre-existence of our Lord Jesus Christ. He continues, "In the beginning, O *Lord* . . ." (italics added). This vocative is found not in the Hebrew text, but in the Septuagint, the translation the author was directed by the Holy Spirit to use. Here the author is addressing Christ as Lord. He is Lord eternally (1 Cor. 8:5–6), incarnationally (Luke 2:11), and by virtue of his resurrection (Acts 2:36). Then we read that this pre-existent Lord created heaven and earth (Heb. 1:10). Simply put, he is the Creator of all things.

All creation exists by the sheer will of Christ and is upheld by his powerful word. Eventually, though, it will waste away and perish. Hymnwriter Henry Lyte says,

> Change and decay in all around I see.
> O Thou who changest not, abide with me.

Flux is the only thing that we can count on in this world. The Greek philosopher Heraclitus observed that we cannot enter the same river twice. Yet here we are told that there is One who remains the same. He is dependable, unchanging, and trustworthy: he will fulfill his promises.

In Hebrews 13, the writer declares, "Jesus Christ is the same yesterday and today and forever" (v. 8). What, then, can we conclude? That Christ is superior to angels because he is *before* creation and because he *created* all things. All creation, even angels, will perish if God does not sustain it. Jesus Christ alone never changes.

7. SEATED AT THE RIGHT HAND OF GOD

The seventh quotation comes from Psalm 110:1, a messianic psalm that is the most quoted and alluded-to psalm in the New Testament. The question is put: *"To which of the angels did God ever say, 'Sit at my right hand until I make your enemies a footstool for your feet'?"* (Heb. 1:13). What is the answer? To no angel!

Angels do not sit in the presence of God. The angel Gabriel told Zechariah, "I am Gabriel. *I stand in the presence of God*, and I have been sent to speak to you and to tell you this good news" (Luke 1:19, italics added). Angels stand ever ready to hear and do the will of God.

Psalm 110 speaks of the enthronement of David's Son, who is also David's Lord because of his successful redemptive mission, as we can prove from Hebrews 2:9: "But we see Jesus, who was made a little lower than the angels, now crowned with glory and honor because he suffered death, so that by the grace of God he might taste death for everyone." This special privilege is granted to Christ for his redemptive work. The author also mentions it in Hebrews 12:2: "Let us fix our eyes on Jesus, the author and perfecter of our faith, who for the joy set before him endured the cross, scorning its shame, and *sat down at the right hand* of the throne of God" (italics added; cf. Acts 2:33–35; Eph. 1:20).

No angel can sit at the right hand of God the Father. It is God's Son who is seated in this most honored place, and all his enemies are put under his feet. The commitment of this sovereign King and his Father is to wage war against all who will not put their trust in him. He is the victor, having triumphed over all his enemies by the cross. His death gave him victory over death, sin, hell, the world, and all principalities and powers. He defeated them by his death on the cross and by his resurrection.

Soon all Christ's enemies shall feel the weight of his feet on their necks, an idea we find in the Old Testament. After defeating the kings, Joshua "summoned all the men of Israel and said to the army commanders who had come with him, 'Come here and put your feet on the necks of these kings.' So they came forward and placed their feet on their necks. Joshua said to them, 'Do not be afraid; do not be discouraged. Be strong and courageous. This is what the LORD will do to all the enemies you are going to fight.' Then Joshua struck and killed the kings and hung them on five trees" (Josh. 10:24–26). This demonstrates what will happen to anyone who will not bow before Christ and worship him (cf. Isa. 51:23). So Jesus is superior to the angels, for he alone is the triumphant King, seated on the right hand of God.

Jesus, Superior to the Angels

Who, then, are these angels? They are not fallen angels, but holy angels, sent to serve us: "*Are not all angels ministering spirits sent to serve those who will inherit salvation?*" (Heb. 1:14). These multitudes of holy angels, whom we also read about in Hebrews 12:22, are created by Christ for his everlasting glory and our everlasting joy. They are ever worshiping and serving the Lord Jesus Christ. As the angel said when John fell down to worship him: "Do not do it! I am a fellow servant with you and with your brothers who hold to the testimony of Jesus. Worship God!" (Rev. 19:10).

Unlike the holy angels, the devil seeks worship from us. He even tried to tempt Jesus to worship him, but Jesus responded, "It is written: 'Worship the Lord your God, and serve him only'" (Matt. 4:10).

Though powerful and glorious, these holy angels are, in fact, inferior to Christ and to his saints—to us who are seated already with Christ in heavenly places. They are ever rendering sacred service to the triune God and are sent to serve his people. Though they are invisible, they are working for us by opposing our enemies—the devil, demons, wicked people, false philosophies, sinful impulses, false brothers, and the wicked rulers of this world. They ministered to Jesus at Gethsemane (Luke 22:43) and fed Elijah in the wilderness (1 Kings 19). Several times they helped the apostles (Acts 5:19–20; 8:26; 12:7–11). They will carry us to God when we die (Luke 16:22).

The ministry of angels to us will continue throughout our lives. I believe angels have helped me many times in my life.

They may be invisible to us; yet without our knowing it, they help us even now. Marie Monsen, a Norwegian missionary to north China, tells of how angels intervened when she and other Christians were in serious danger. The enemies saw tall soldiers with shining faces guarding the missionary compound, though the people inside did not see them.[1]

Let us therefore worship Jesus, not angels, for he alone is God. All other religions fail to worship him, although some consider him at best an archangel. But Jesus is the Creator and only Savior and there is no salvation outside of him. This is the exclusivism of Christianity. No one comes to the Father except through his Son. Eternal life is found only in the Son, and one day every knee shall bow and every tongue confess that Jesus is Lord to the glory of God the Father. Jesus is superior to all angels and all other gods.

---

[1] R. Kent Hughes, *Hebrews*, vol. 1, 41–42.

3

The Danger of Drifting

¹*We must pay more careful attention, therefore, to what we have heard, so that we do not drift away.* ²*For if the message spoken by angels was binding, and every violation and disobedience received its just punishment,* ³*how shall we escape if we ignore such a great salvation?*

Hebrews 2:1–3

How do you listen to the word of God? This

passage is speaking about the danger of careless listening when the word is preached. It is a warning against being distracted by creation, being idolatrous, and not paying full attention to our Savior, who is our very life.

The author gives his first warning to his readers in this portion of Scripture. Because of persecution, these Hebrew Christians were tempted to turn their backs on Jesus and his glorious salvation. They had fallen from their first love and had become dull in their minds. Having stopped growing spiritually, they were drifting away from God.

The author warns against such backsliding, commanding them: *"For this reason we must apply our minds to the fullest extent to what we have heard so that we will not drift away"* (Heb. 2:1, author's translation). Notice, this is written to believers. As Christians, we can hear God's word again and again, yet not understand it. We can become so accustomed to it that we fail to truly hear. We must maximally apply our minds to the word of God, just as a driver must pay careful attention to the road if he wants to reach his destination. God is speaking, and we must give him our full attention. Moses declared, "Hear, O Israel, and be careful to obey so that it may go well with you" (Deut. 6:3). If we listen carelessly, it will not go well with us.

God Gives Reasons

In the Greek text, the author begins, *"For this reason..."* (Heb. 2:1). Ours is a reasonable faith and the Bible is a reasonable book given to us by a reasonable God. It is more reasonable to believe that the infinite, personal God created the world out of nothing than to believe that something came out of nothing on its own. It is reasonable to believe in the resurrection of Jesus Christ because God is able to raise the dead to life. It is also reasonable to believe that we ourselves will be raised from the dead.

Throughout the Scriptures, we find the word "therefore." God delights in giving us reasons. Here the author is saying that God himself is speaking to us; *therefore*, we must pay full attention. He speaks about our eternal salvation not through angels or prophets, but through his eternal Son (Heb. 1:1–2), who tells us about our eternal salvation. Therefore, pay more careful attention! The gospel is a matter of life and death because it is the power of God unto salvation. Careless listening leads to drifting into eternal punishment.

Pay Full Attention

We are then told, *"We must pay more careful attention"* to the word of God (Heb. 2:1). The Greek word is *dei*, "ought to." To play golf or not play golf is an optional decision. But whether or not we should listen carefully to the message of the gospel is not optional. We *must* do so if we want to arrive in heaven. If we do not give our fullest attention to the word of God in this life, we will end up in hell, like the rich man of Luke 16.

When we gather to worship, we must focus on the One who ought to be the object of our thoughts. We are called to stretch our minds so that we may understand and believe the word of God, which speaks about our salvation. Many evangelical churches have forsaken thinking for the sake of entertainment.

The Danger of Drifting

This Greek expression tells us that we must give the word of God our full attention *continuously*. Just as we eat food daily, so also we must always be feeding on the spiritual food of God's word. If we do not pay full attention to our doctor's words, we may die before our time. But this is more important. God, our Great Physician, is addressing us concerning our eternal destiny. We must give him our fullest attention so that we will not drift away into a miserable eternity in hell.

The parable of the sower speaks about four kinds of listeners to the word of God (Matt. 13:1–23). The pathway hearer heard the word but paid no attention to it. The devil came and took it away from him, and he was not saved. The stony-heart hearer paid superficial attention, but because he did not understand the cost of discipleship, he never developed any roots. When trials came because of the word, he fell away. He also was not saved. Then there was the thorny-heart hearer, who heard the word, but did not pay full attention to it. He failed to understand that the word of God alone fully satisfies us. His divided heart was drawn away by the worries of this life, the deceitfulness of riches, the desire for things other than God, and the pleasures of this life, until he became fruitless and was choked to death. He also was not saved. But the good-soil, good-heart man heard the word and gave it his fullest attention. Understanding the word, he treasured it and persevered in obeying it until he brought forth fruit. This man alone was saved.

We must pay maximum attention to the word of God. Elsewhere the writer exhorts, "Therefore, holy brothers, who share in the heavenly calling, fix your thoughts on Jesus, the apostle and high priest whom we confess. . . . Let us fix our eyes on Jesus, the author and perfecter of our faith" (Heb. 3:1; 12:2). When we fix our eyes on Jesus, we will be transformed: "And we, who with unveiled faces all behold the Lord's glory, are being transformed into his likeness with ever-increasing glory" (2 Cor. 3:18, author's translation). The purpose of Christ's incarnation was not to make us rich, famous, or powerful, but to bring many sons to glory (Heb. 2:10).

Psalm 1 speaks about the blessing of meditating on the law day and night. Therefore, we must pay full attention when the word is preached. May Christ and his word dwell richly in our hearts so that we may grow in the grace and knowledge of God and be transformed by his truth.

The Danger of Drifting

Next, the author warns us of the danger of drifting: *"We must pay more careful attention . . . so that we do not drift away"* (Heb. 2:1). Carelessness can cost us dearly. The word of God demands the maximum capacity of our renewed minds. We must never come to church to be entertained or to doze off. Church is not an escape from thinking. We must be prepared to think hard so that we may know God and be filled with him.

The author says to pay attention *"so that we will not drift away."* The Greek word *pararēō* means to float past the harbor, to be carried downstream past the landing place. It is as if the pilot of the ship is either drunk or asleep while the ship is carried away by the current. Spiritual inattention will set us adrift to hell, even while we think we are on our way to heaven. *Pararēō* is also used to describe a ring slipping off a finger and being lost forever. There is no standing still in the Christian life. Either we are moving toward God, or we are moving away through inattention and unbelief, only to have Christ tell us on the last day, "Away from me, you evildoers!" (Matt. 7:23).

The writer of Proverbs exhorts, "My son, pay attention to what I say; listen closely to my words. Do not let them out of your sight, keep them within your heart." Why should we pay maximum attention? "For they are life to those who find them and health to a man's whole body" (Prov. 4:20–22).

Greater than the Law of Moses

The writer next uses an argument from lesser to greater: *"For if the message spoken by angels was binding, and every violation and disobedience received its just punishment, how shall we escape if we ignore such a great salvation?"* (Heb. 2:2).

Deuteronomy 33:2 (Septuagint), Acts 7:53, and Galatians 3:19 all indicate that God gave the law to the people of Israel in some sense through the mediation of angels. This law was binding on

The Danger of Drifting

the people, and those who violated it suffered just retribution. For example, when Aaron's sons Nadab and Abihu violated it, God himself killed them before the altar (Lev. 10). When the arrogant Korah rebelled, the earth split open and swallowed him. Not only did God kill Korah, but he also killed 250 of his allies by fire and 14,700 others by a plague (Num. 16). Later, Achan disobeyed God's law, stealing that which belonged to the Lord. Though he dug a hole in his tent to cover it up, God revealed it, and Achan and his entire family were stoned to death and set on fire (Josh. 7). All of these punishments were just, because these people did not pay attention to the law of the covenant Lord. The author posits that if such things happened to those under the law, how can we escape the greater judgment of hell if we despise and neglect the great salvation revealed to us by the Son?

This word "ignore" also appears in Jesus' parable about a lavish feast given by a great king. Many were invited, but the guests despised the invitation: "But they paid no attention and went off—one to his field, another to his business. The rest seized his servants, mistreated them and killed them. The king was enraged. He sent his army and destroyed those murderers and burned their city" (Matt. 22:5–7).

The gospel is a call from heaven. Christ is speaking about our salvation; therefore, we must pay attention. We learn several things about this salvation (*sōtēria*) from the book of Hebrews:

1. Jesus is the author of our salvation.
2. This salvation is eternal.
3. Christ accomplished this salvation by his own death. The Son of God died in our place to accomplish this redemption, which he now offers to all people.
4. When Jesus comes again, we will enjoy this salvation in its fullness.
5. This salvation means death is destroyed for us and we are liberated from our fear of death.
6. This great salvation makes sons of hell into sons of heaven. God's purpose is to bring many sons to glory.
7. This great salvation is necessary for us to draw near to God in worship and be blessed by him.

The argument is that if the message spoken through the angels was binding, how shall we escape if we despise and pay no attention to the word of great salvation spoken by the Son? We find a similar argument in Hebrews 10:

> If we deliberately keep on sinning after we have received the knowledge of the truth, no sacrifice for sins is left, but only a fearful expectation of judgment and of raging fire that will consume the enemies of God. Anyone who rejected the law of Moses died without mercy on the testimony of two or three witnesses. How much more severely do you think a man deserves to be punished who has trampled the Son of God under foot, who has treated as an unholy thing the blood of the covenant that sanctified him, and who has insulted the Spirit of grace? For we know him who said, "It is mine to avenge; I will repay," and again, "The Lord will judge his people." It is a dreadful thing to fall into the hands of the living God. (vv. 26–31)

Messengers of the Gospel

Having established the importance of listening carefully to the gospel, we now want to look at the messengers of the gospel. Who is preaching this great salvation to us?

1. *We know it is not preached to us by angels.* Remember, God told Cornelius to call Peter, not an angel, to bring him the gospel (Acts 10:5). Who, then, is preaching to us?

2. *God the Father preaches to us.* In the New International Version, verse 3 says, "This salvation . . . was first announced *by* the Lord," but it should really be translated, "This salvation . . . was first announced *through* the Lord [Jesus]." God the Father announced it. Peter said the same thing to the household of Cornelius: "You know the message *God sent* to the people of Israel, telling the good news of peace *through Jesus Christ,* who is Lord of all" (Acts 10:36, italics added). We must pay careful attention because God the Father himself is speaking to us about our own great salvation. We must listen to him!

3. *The Lord Jesus preaches to us.* We hear Jesus' preaching throughout the Gospels: "After John was put in prison, Jesus went into Galilee, proclaiming the good news of God. 'The time has come,' he said. 'The kingdom of God is near. Repent and believe the good news!'" (Mark 1:14–15). This salvation was first proclaimed by the Lord, but the majority rejected his word. They

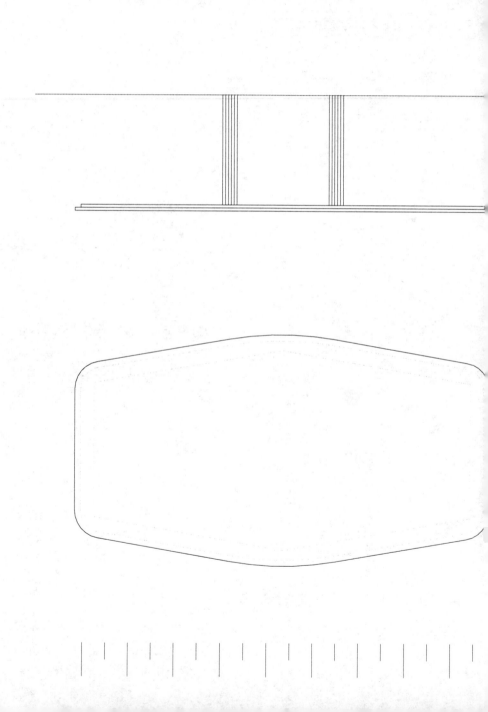

called him a blasphemer and crucified this preacher of good news. "He came to that which was his own, but his own did not receive him" (John 1:11). Yes, some prostitutes believed him, as did the Samaritan woman, some lepers, blind Bartimaeus, the publican Zacchaeus, the eleven apostles, the seventy, the one hundred and twenty, the five hundred, and others. But the majority were so busy that they paid no attention to him. Having ignored Christ's great invitation, they drifted into hell.

This message is spoken to us by the One who is superior to all angels, the Creator of the angels. The eternal Son is speaking. We must acknowledge his person, his dignity, and his authority, for he is greater than all. Though he created us and can justly send us to hell, Jesus now speaks to us in grace and mercy. We must listen to him and pay attention to his word of forgiveness.

4. *The apostles preach to us.* "This salvation, which was first announced by the Lord, *was confirmed to us by those who heard him*" (Heb. 2:3, italics added).

As eyewitnesses of the ministry of Jesus, the apostles attested to his deeds and teachings. And when the apostles spoke by the inspiration of the Spirit, Christ himself was speaking. So the apostles were ambassadors of Christ. The apostle John writes, "That which was from the beginning, which we have heard, which we have seen with our eyes, which we have looked at and our hands have touched—this we proclaim concerning the Word of life" (1 John 1:1). What was the message the apostles proclaimed? "That Christ died for our sins according to the Scriptures, that he was buried, that he was raised on the third day according to the Scriptures and that he appeared" to many (1 Cor. 15:3–8); "He was delivered over to death for our sins and was raised to life for our justification" (Rom. 4:25).

The apostles heard the teachings of Christ and received the Holy Spirit. They saw the miracles Christ performed, including raising the dead, and heard him say that he must die to give his life as a ransom for many. They saw him crucified, dead, and buried. After he rose from the dead, they saw him ascending into heaven. When the Spirit of God came upon them, they went about proclaiming the gospel.

5. "*God also testified to it by signs, wonders and various miracles, and gifts of the Holy Spirit distributed according to his will*" (Heb. 2:4).

Although we are morally obligated to believe the gospel without any miracle, God performed miracles through the apostles to guarantee the authenticity of their words and to encourage us to believe and be saved.

Peter reminded his listeners about these miracles: "Men of Israel, listen to this: Jesus of Nazareth was a man accredited by God to you by miracles, wonders and signs, which God did among you through him, as you yourselves know" (Acts 2:22). The apostles also performed miracles (Acts 9:32–42; 14:3; 19:11–12; 20:9–10; 28:8–9).

The primary purpose of signs, wonders, and various miracles was to authenticate the messenger and the message. Such authentication is not necessary now because we have the complete revelation of the Son in the written word. Many modern miracles result from Satanic powers, as we read in 2 Thessalonians 2:7, 9 and throughout the book of Revelation. Some are the result of psychological manipulation by unscrupulous preachers to get money from gullible people. However, God may perform healings and miracles today. Our compassionate God still hears our prayers and may heal us, in accordance with his sovereign will. But if he does not heal us, we have the comfort of knowing that he has given us eternal life and we shall never perish.

In the final analysis, we do not need any miracles to authenticate that the Bible is the very word of God. God has spoken finally and fully in his Son, and faith comes by hearing this word. It is sheer unbelief that demands signs, wonders, and miracles in addition to the word of God.

6. *The Holy Spirit confirms it.* God pours out his Holy Spirit and various gifts when the gospel is preached (Acts 19:1–6; 1 Cor. 12:1–11). Jesus says, "When the Counselor comes, whom I will send to you from the Father, the Spirit of truth who goes out from the Father, he will testify about me" (John 15:26). Here we see that the Father, the Son, and the Holy Spirit are all involved in the preaching of the gospel. That is why we must pay full attention.

7. *Pastors now preach the gospel.* Since the apostles are dead, pastors are now preaching. They are gifts given by the risen Christ to the church (Eph. 4:11), men appointed by God (1 Cor. 12:28). They are not angels but human beings appointed by Christ. We must not neglect listening to them, because God himself is preaching through these pastors.

We must, therefore, pay fullest attention to the gospel word, for it is preached by the Father, the Son, and the Holy Spirit and by pastors commissioned by the Lord. Hebrews 13:7 says, "Remember your leaders, who spoke the word of God to you." God still uses called, appointed, and gifted human beings to preach the gospel. Careless listening will cause us to drift and float to hell like dead fish.

Conclusion

In conclusion, let me ask you some questions.

1. Are you habitually looking to the word of God that speaks about God's great salvation? Do you pay maximum attention to the word of God when you read it privately? Do you listen carefully when the word is preached in the church? Remember, it is the very word of the triune God. Or do you listen to preachers who will not preach the whole gospel? If so, Jeremiah warns: "The visions of your prophets were false and worthless; they did not expose your sin to ward off your captivity. The oracles they gave you were false and misleading" (Lam. 2:14). If a preacher does not speak about sin and its remedy in Christ, then he is a false preacher. A true preacher will preach the word of God exclusively and completely.

2. Are you drifting away from spiritual things to the deceitfulness of riches, the pleasures of life, and the desire for other things? Are you falling in love with the lust of the flesh, the lust of the eyes, and the pride of life? If so, watch out!

3. Do you take for granted that you are going to heaven because you were baptized and joined a church? If so, consider carefully the words of Jesus to those who assumed they were saved: "I never knew you. Away from me, you evildoers!" (Matt. 7:23). Are you like the first three soils that did not produce any fruit, though they heard the word?

4. Are you like the rich man who expected to go to heaven, yet completely neglected the word and was surprised when he died and went to hell (Luke 16:19–31)? Or are you like the thief on the cross who finally paid attention to Christ, confessed Jesus as Lord in the midst of his pain and suffering, and was given the right to fellowship with him in paradise the same day (Luke 23:40–43)?

I pray that none of us will drift into hell, but will pay maximum attention to God's word, that we may arrive in heaven to spend eternity with our God. May the word of God's grace enter into each one of us to heal, save, strengthen, and comfort us this day.

4
The New World Order

> ⁵*It is not to angels that he has subjected the world to come, about which we are speaking.* ⁶*But there is a place where someone has testified: "What is man that you are mindful of him, the son of man that you care for him?* ⁷*You made him a little lower than the angels; you crowned him with glory and honor* ⁸*and put everything under his feet." In putting everything under him, God left nothing that is not subject to him. Yet at present we do not see everything subject to him.* ⁹*But we see Jesus, who was made a little lower than the angels, now crowned with glory and honor because he suffered death, so that by the grace of God he might taste death for everyone.*
>
> Hebrews 2:5–9

Modern politicians often speak of a new world order, to be established through thriving global trade and its resulting prosperity and peace. In this utopian vision, there will be no war, because war destroys prosperity. Knowledge will increase and all people of the world will love one another. We will all make money, and money will save us all.

Hebrews 2:5–9 does not speak about this type of political world order but about the new world order of Jesus Christ, which is the kingdom of God. In the first four verses of Hebrews 2, the author told us that we must pay our fullest attention to the gospel, which speaks of our great salvation, so that we will not drift away from it. This salvation has to do with the biblical new world order in which the people of God, not angels, rule all creation with Jesus Christ.

Believers have already entered this new world order, which Jesus introduced in these last days. It is the messianic age, the kingdom of God, which began with the first coming of Christ but will manifest itself in greater fullness when Christ comes again. However, even now Christ is seated at the right hand of the Majesty in heaven as King of kings and Lord of lords of the new world order, and we are seated with him. The kingdom of God has invaded into this present age.

In this new world order, we experience the powers of the age to come (Heb. 6:4–5) and the good things associated with it, such as justification, forgiveness of all sins, adoption, and sanctification (Heb. 9:11). The Holy Spirit dwells in us and enlightens us so that we do not remain like pigs, looking only down at the earth. We are enabled to look up to this new world order and all its blessings and see Jesus, crowned with glory and honor. We eagerly await the enduring city that is coming (Heb. 13:14), knowing there is no enduring city here.

How can someone belong to this new world order? It is very simple: Repent and believe on the Lord Jesus Christ. If you have done so, then you are a citizen of Christ's new world order.

Not Subjected to Angels

What do we know about this new world order of Jesus Christ and his people? First, Hebrews 2:5 says that it is not subjected to angels: "*It is not to angels that he has subjected the world to come, about which we are speaking.*"

The Bible indicates that the present world order is under the authority of angels, both good and fallen. We read, "He set the bounds of the people according to the number of angels" (Deut. 32:8, Septuagint). This indicates that the administrations of various nations were parceled out among the number of angelic princes. Daniel also gives us this idea: "Then [the angel] continued, 'Do not be afraid, Daniel. Since the first day that you set your mind to gain understanding and to humble yourself before your God, your words were heard, and I have come in response to them. But the prince of the Persian kingdom resisted me twenty-one days. Then Michael, one of the chief princes, came to help me, because I was detained there with the king of Persia'" (Dan. 10:12–13). Here we see that even fallen angels can be in charge of certain kingdoms. In the same chapter the angel asks, "Do you know why I have come to you? Soon I will return to fight against the prince of Persia, and when I go, the prince of Greece will come; but first I will tell you what is written in the Book of Truth. (No one supports me against them except Michael, your prince)" (Dan. 10:20–21). Later, Daniel is told, "At that time Michael, the great prince who protects your people, will arise" (Dan. 12:1).

Somehow, then, our present world order has been submitted to angels, but the new world order will not be. History tells us that a Dead Sea sect looked forward to two messianic figures: a king and a priest. The priest would be superior to the king, but both would function under the archangel Michael. This particular sect believed that the new world order would be subjected to angels. The author of Hebrews may have been reacting to this particular idea.

Man's Original Destiny

If the world to come is not subjected to angels, we must ask to whom it is subjected. The author tells us that God has subjected it to man: *"You made him a little lower than the angels; you crowned him with glory and honor and put everything under his feet"* (Heb. 2:7–8). The author cites Psalm 8 from the Septuagint as proof of man's original destiny. This psalm speaks of the majesty of God, the utter insignificance of man, and the amazing dignity that God conferred upon man when he created man in his image and likeness.

We first find this idea of man's dominion over creation in Genesis:

> And God said, "Let us make man in our image, in our likeness, and let them rule over the fish of the sea and the birds of the air, over the livestock, over all the earth, and over all the creatures that move along the ground." So God created man in his own image, in the image of God he created him; male and female he created them. God blessed them and said to them, "Be fruitful and increase in number; fill the earth and subdue it. Rule over the fish of the sea and the birds of the air and over every living creature that moves on the ground." (Gen. 1:26–28)

In the Hebrew text of Psalm 8 we read that God made man a little lower than God (*elohim*)—that is, God conferred upon man such dignity that man was accountable only to God. In the Septuagint *elohim* is translated "angels," so we read that God made man a little lower than the angels. God crowned man with glory and honor and put everything under man's sovereignty. Man was to rule the world as God's vicegerent. It appears God's original intention was that man rule not only over this planet earth but over the entire creation, including angels. What great dignity God has conferred upon the little speck of dust called man!

Man's Utter Failure

Man, however, utterly failed to fulfill his God-given destiny: *"Yet at present we do not see everything subject to him"* (Heb. 2:8). The writer sees that something has gone seriously wrong, and man has failed to rule as originally intended by God.

What is the cause of this failure? Sin. Man chose to sin against God's word and so he died. When Adam fell, the whole world fell: "All have sinned and fall short of the glory of God" (Rom. 3:23). Now man is born dead in trespasses and sins. By nature he is an enemy of God and ruled by sin. He is not a master but a slave—a slave to sin, death, and the devil. Instead of being blessed, he is cursed:

> To the woman he said, "I will greatly increase your pains in childbearing; with pain you will give birth to children. Your desire will be for your husband, and he will rule over you." To Adam he said, "Because you listened to your wife and ate from the tree about which I commanded you, 'You must not eat of it,' cursed is the ground because of you; through painful toil you will eat of it all the days of your life. It will produce thorns and thistles for you, and you will eat the plants of the field. By the sweat of your brow you will eat your food until you return to the ground, since from it you were taken; for dust you are and to dust you will return." (Gen. 3:16–19)

Man is not now ruling, and even the most powerful man is a slave to death and decay. Mighty man became mortal, which was not God's original intention. "The wages of sin is death" (Rom. 6:23). Additionally, man's environment suffers because of his sin. Sin is the reason for all thorns, pests, germs, disease, pain, war, and death. Paul compares our current situation with the new world order: "I consider that our present sufferings are not worth comparing with the glory that will be revealed in us. The creation waits in eager expectation for the sons of God to be revealed. For the creation was subjected to frustration, not by its own choice, but by the will of the one who subjected it, in hope that the creation will itself be liberated from its bondage to decay and brought into the glorious freedom of the children of God" (Rom. 8:18–21).

When Adam sinned, man fell from the pinnacle of dignity, losing his glory and becoming pervasively sinful. But the Hebrews writer does not say, "We do not see anything subject to man." Instead, he says, "Yet at present we do not see everything subject to him" (Heb. 2:8). There is a sense of optimism in that statement: there is still hope for fallen man. How can fallen man be restored to his God-intended glory and honor? He needs a redeemer to reconcile him to God.

God's Plan for Man

It was always God's intention that man would rule creation for him. In spite of the Fall, God's plan still stands. In Psalm 8 David speaks of the majesty of God, the greatness of God's heaven, and the utter insignificance of man. David is speaking about man in his fallen condition. Because man fell, he is no longer a ruler but is captive to Satan and death. He deserves to be wiped out from the face of the earth. It would be just for God to send all fallen humans into hell.

Yet God refuses to do this. In God's amazing grace, he has a plan to restore man to even greater glory than Adam ever had before his fall. The writer asks, "*What is man that you are mindful of him, the son of man that you care for him?*" (Heb. 2:6). I would say, "What is sinful, miserable man that you think about him, this wretched being, that you care for him at all?"

The same word for "mindful of" appears also in Hebrews 13:3: "Remember those in prison." It means that we must go and help these people by giving them food, clothing, and fellowship. It is not remembering in a theoretical sense; it is remembering *to help*. Here in chapter 2 the author is saying, "What is sinful man that you, the holy God, should remember him in his lowest estate and come to his aid?" The other word, "care for him," appears in Matthew 25:36: "I needed clothes and you clothed me, I was sick and you *looked after me*" (italics added). It is the same idea—to care for means to go and help someone who is in serious trouble.

In Luke 1 Zechariah says, "Praise be to the Lord, the God of Israel, because he has come and has redeemed his people" (Luke 1:68). God came from heaven in Jesus Christ to our pit to help us out of our misery. He did so "because of the tender mercy of our God, by which the rising sun will come to us from heaven" (Luke 1:78). Though we were in a fallen state of misery, God remembered us and sent his eternal Son to take upon himself human nature to help and save us.

Paradise Lost and Regained

We do not now see man ruling over all the works of God's hand. When we look at man, we see a slave to Satan, sin, and death. We see one who needs a reconciler and restorer. Yet note the words of the writer: *"But we see Jesus, who was made a little lower than the angels, now crowned with glory and honor because he suffered death, so that by the grace of God he might taste death for everyone"* (Heb. 2:9). In Christ, God remembered, cared for, and visited us fallen human beings, and now we have hope. Jesus won for us the paradise that Adam lost.

In Hebrews 1 the author spoke of the superiority of Jesus, especially his deity; now he writes about Jesus' humanity: *"We see Jesus, who was made a little lower than the angels"* (Heb. 2:9). When we see Jesus, we are looking at the Savior of the world: "There is one God and one mediator between God and men, the man Christ Jesus, who gave himself as a ransom for all men" (1 Tim. 2:5). We see the God-man, our perfect substitute and atonement. We see him "who had no sin [made] to be sin for us, so that in him we might become the righteousness of God" (2 Cor. 5:21). We see the Lamb of God who takes away the sin of the world (John 1:29), who died for our sins and was raised for our justification (Rom. 4:25). The author uses the name "Jesus" thirteen times in this epistle.

"*We see Jesus.*" That is in the present tense, which means we are to see Jesus continually. We find the same idea elsewhere: "Therefore, holy brothers, who share in the heavenly calling, fix your thoughts on Jesus. . . . Let us fix our eyes on Jesus, the author and perfecter of our faith" (Heb. 3:1; 12:2). How do we see Jesus? Through faith in the word of God. When we see him, we will experience hope, salvation, and joy. How can we be miserable when we are gazing upon him who is crowned with glory and honor! May God help us to keep on seeing Jesus, who came not to be served but to serve and give his life a ransom for many. Any sinner can look to him and be saved. The answer to our sin problem is seeing Jesus.

Why was Jesus made a little lower than the angels? Because angels cannot die, and we needed someone who could die in our place for our salvation. The Son became incarnate "*so that he might taste death*" (Heb. 2:9). "Taste" here means to experience fully the complete bitterness and pain of eternal death. Jesus Christ suffered death in all its gruesome pain and misery. Not only did he suffer physically, but he also suffered spiritually, as the wrath of God was poured upon him. No one has ever experienced this kind of death. Jesus died our death on the cross and went to hell in our place. What is the implication of Christ's tasting of death for us? Jesus said, "He who believes in me will live, even though he dies; and whoever lives and believes in me will never die" (John 11:25–26). Christ died in our place as our representative and mediator; therefore, we will not die. That is the glory of Christianity.

Christ died his atoning death by the grace of God "*for everyone*" (Heb. 2:9). However, that does not mean there is universal salvation and no one goes to hell. "Everyone" does not mean every human being who has ever lived on the face of the earth. It means everyone without distinction—people of every race who repent and believe in Jesus, our only atonement. In fact, the remaining verses in this passage define "everyone." Hebrews 2:10 begins, "*In bringing many sons to glory.*" So, first, "everyone" means those who are brought to glory. Verse 11 says, "*Both the one who makes men holy and those who are made holy are of the same family.*" Here "everyone" means those who are made holy. Verse 11 continues: "*So Jesus is not ashamed to call them brothers.*" "Everyone" here means brothers of Jesus. Verse 13 says, "*Here am I, and the children God has given me.*" Here "everyone" stands for the children God gave to Jesus Christ to redeem (cf. John 17:6–9). "Everyone" stands also for those people delivered from the fear of death (v. 15), Abraham's descendants (v. 16), and the people of God (v. 17).

So the answer to our sin problem is to see Jesus—crucified, dead, buried, raised from the dead, and crowned with glory and honor. We see Jesus fulfilling what Adam and his descendants failed to do.

We see Jesus as the King of kings and Lord of lords, to whom all creation is subject right now (Heb. 2:9). There are many scriptures that show this. "For he 'has put everything under his feet'" (1 Cor. 15:27); "God placed all things under his feet and appointed him to be head over everything" (Eph. 1:22); "[Christ] has gone into heaven and is at God's right hand—with angels, authorities and powers in submission to him" (1 Pet. 3:22). Jesus himself said, "All authority in heaven and on earth has been given to me" (Matt. 28:18). Because of Jesus' faithfulness in obeying God, especially by his death on the cross, "God exalted him to the highest place and gave him the name that is above every name, that at the name of Jesus every knee should bow, in heaven and on earth and under the earth, and every tongue confess that Jesus Christ is Lord, to the glory of God the Father" (Phil. 2:9–11).

We see Jesus and his new world order. When Jesus entered heaven, we who are united with him by faith entered heaven with him. When he died, we died with him; when he was raised, we were raised with him; when he was seated as Sovereign over all creation, we were also seated with him. In Jesus Christ we have gained the glory and honor that we lost in Adam. Every believer in Christ rules with Christ even now.

If you are unhappy, I counsel you to see Jesus. That will solve your problems. His triumph is your triumph, his rule is your rule, his power is your power, and his position is your position.

Every believer in Christ is ruling with him even now. Yet we wait for the full manifestation of this new world order, where regenerated people will live with Jesus Christ in a new heaven and a new earth, where there is no sin, pain, or death, but only righteousness, peace, and joy in the Holy Spirit. So we pray in anticipation, "Thy kingdom come."

The new world order belongs to us in Christ. We rule over all creation, including angels. Paul tells us, "All things are yours, whether Paul or Apollos or Cephas or the world or life or death or the present or the future—all are yours" (1 Cor. 3:21–22). Later he says, "Do you not know that we will judge angels?" (1 Cor. 6:3). By Christ's death, he has secured dominion for himself and all whom he represents, who are united with him by faith.

I have news for you: I am not looking forward to a new world order created by the political leaders of this world. I am looking forward to the kingdom of God.

Conclusion

The author earlier said, "We must pay more careful attention, therefore, to what we have heard" (Heb. 2:1). Misery, confusion, and fear come when we do not pay full attention to the gospel we have heard. Pay careful attention to this gospel, for it speaks of a new world order where Christ and his people rule over all created realities. In this new order the last word is not death, but everlasting life. Even now God's people are liberated from their fear of death and declare with Paul, "Neither death nor life . . . will be able to separate us from the love of God that is in Christ Jesus our Lord" (Rom. 8:38–39). Because Christ tasted death for us, we shall never die. But only true believers in Jesus Christ belong to this new world order. All enemies of God shall be cast into the lake of fire, which is the second death. It is the destiny of all unbelievers.

Are you part of this new world order? There is only one way to become a member: by faith in Jesus Christ. His triumph can be yours by uniting with him. Therefore, repent and believe on the Lord Jesus, and you shall be saved. The Bible says, "If you confess with your mouth, 'Jesus is Lord,' and believe in your heart that God raised him from the dead, you will be saved" (Rom. 10:9). When you do so, you will be liberated from death, shame, misery, defeat, and slavery to sin, and crowned with glory, honor, and authority.

5

Jesus, Our Brother and Priest

¹⁰*In bringing many sons to glory, it was fitting that God, for whom and through whom everything exists, should make the author of their salvation perfect through suffering.* ¹¹*Both the one who makes men holy and those who are made holy are of the same family. So Jesus is not ashamed to call them brothers.* ¹²*He says, "I will declare your name to my brothers; in the presence of the congregation I will sing your praises."* ¹³*And again, "I will put my trust in him." And again he says, "Here am I, and the children God has given me."* ¹⁴*Since the children have flesh and blood, he too shared in their humanity so that by his death he might destroy him who holds the power of death—that is, the devil—* ¹⁵*and free those who all their lives were held in slavery by their fear of death.* ¹⁶*For surely it is not angels he helps, but Abraham's descendants.* ¹⁷*For this reason he had to be made like his brothers in every way, in order that he might become a merciful and faithful high priest in service to God, and that he might make atonement for the sins of the people.* ¹⁸*Because he himself suffered when he was tempted, he is able to help those who are being tempted.*

Hebrews 2:10–18

There are only two families in the world. Do you belong to the right one? Either we are children of the devil or we belong to God's family, headed by our representative, Jesus Christ. In Hebrews 2:10–18 we discover the good news that for those in God's family, Jesus is our brother, champion, and high priest.

At one time we all belonged to the family of the devil. As sinners, we were slaves to the devil, depravity, and death. Through God's rich mercy, he brought us out of the domain of the devil and into the family of God. There are great privileges associated with God's family; therefore, each of us must make sure we belong to it.

God's Good Plan for Man

The Lord says, "I know the plans I have for you . . . plans to prosper you and not to harm you, plans to give you hope and a future" (Jer. 29:11). When God created man, he gave him authority to rule all creation and dwell in God's presence. Because of the Fall, this good plan of God did not come to fruition, as the author of Hebrews acknowledges: "Yet at present we do not see everything subject to [man]" (Heb. 2:8).

Yet God did not change his mind concerning his eternal plan. Hebrews 2:5 tells us that the world to come is not subjected to angels but to Jesus and all who belong to him. What Adam failed to do, the last Adam did for the members of the family that the Father gave him from all eternity. Hebrews 2:12–13 speaks of this family: *"I will declare your name to my brothers; in the presence of the congregation I will sing your praises. . . . Here am I, and the children God has given me."*

As a result of his perfect obedience to God's will, Jesus was crowned with glory and honor, and all things have been made subject to him (Heb. 2:9). Human sin can never frustrate God's eternal decree to bring many sons to glory (Heb. 2:10). Jesus Christ obeyed his Father and died on the cross for the sins of those whom the Father gave him. He opened up the way of eternal life for all who are called his brothers, even us who trust in him alone for righteousness and forgiveness of all our sins.

Our Sin Problem

Let us consider several points related to this passage. First, we must acknowledge that we have a serious sin problem. When

Adam sinned against God, we sinned in Adam. The Bible says that all are born sinners, all have sinned, and all practice sin daily: "There is no one righteous, not even one. . . . All have sinned and fall short of the glory of God" (Rom. 3:10, 23). The doctrine of total depravity declares that sin is totally pervasive, affecting our mind, will, and feeling.

Because we are unholy by nature, we need someone else to make us holy. That someone is Jesus Christ: "The Son is the radiance of God's glory and the exact representation of his being, sustaining all things by his powerful word. After he had provided purification for sins, he sat down" (Heb. 1:3). We find this theme throughout the book of Hebrews: *"Both the one who makes men holy and those who are made holy are of the same family"* (Heb. 2:11); *"For this reason he had to be made like his brothers in every way, in order that he might become a merciful and faithful high priest in service to God, and that he might make atonement for [our] sins"* (Heb. 2:17); "Unlike the other high priests, he does not need to offer sacrifices day after day, first for his own sins, and then for the sins of the people" (Heb. 7:27); "Then Christ would have had to suffer many times since the creation of the world. But now he has appeared once for all at the end of the ages to do away with sin by the sacrifice of himself. . . . So Christ was sacrificed once to take away the sins of many people" (Heb. 9:26, 28).

Because of our sin problem, the holy God is justly angry with us: "The wrath of God is being revealed from heaven against all the godlessness and wickedness of men" (Rom. 1:18). Sin makes us guilty and liable to punishment, and results in death. God told Adam that he would die because of his sin (Gen. 2:17, 3:19). This was not God's original plan. But the Bible clearly declares, "The wages of sin is death" (Rom. 6:23).

Paul explains the connection between Adam's sin and our death: "Sin entered the world through one man, and death through sin, and in this way death came to all men, because all sinned" (Rom. 5:12). Sickness, death, and judgment all are the results of sin. But there is good news for us: "For since death came through a man, the resurrection of the dead comes also through a man. For as in Adam all die, so in Christ all will be made alive" (1 Cor. 15:21–22). Here we see the two families. Adam's family is now the family of the devil and death; Christ's is the family of life.

"The sting of death is sin" (1 Cor. 15:56). Death has a sting. When we ask unbelievers if they are ready to die, they may say with a smile, "Yes, I know how to die. It is not a problem." Such people are deceived and deceiving.

The first death is physical; the second death is eternal separation from the very presence of God. We read about the first death in Hebrews 9:27: "Just as man is destined to die once, and after that to face judgment." Revelation 21:8 describes the second death: "But the cowardly, the unbelieving, the vile, the murderers, the sexually immoral, those who practice magic arts, the idolaters and all liars—their place will be in the fiery lake of burning sulfur. This is the second death."

In Leviticus God introduced a substitutionary sacrificial system. We may not like the bloodshed in the Bible, but we must marvel at God's grace in accepting an innocent victim in place of those who are guilty and deserving of the death penalty.

But the blood of animals alone cannot truly cleanse us from our sins. We need someone outside of us, yet like us, to help us out of our sin. The Bible speaks of a "kinsman-redeemer"—a close relative who is able and willing to help his needy family (Ruth 2:20). To help with our sin problem, our close relative must be perfect God as well as perfect man, one person in two natures. "There is one God and one mediator between God and men, the man Christ Jesus, who gave himself as a ransom for all men" (1 Tim. 2:5–6). Jesus Christ alone is perfect man and perfect God; therefore, he alone can reconcile us to God.

Through Christ's sacrifice we are brought into the family of God. From all eternity the Father has chosen a group of sinners to belong to his family: *"Both the one who makes men holy and those who are made holy are of the same family"* (Heb. 2:11). We have belonged to this family from all eternity. Paul exclaims, "Praise be to the God and Father of our Lord Jesus Christ, who has blessed us in the heavenly realms with every spiritual blessing in Christ. For he chose us in him before the creation of the world to be holy and blameless in his sight" (Eph. 1:3–4).

In Hebrews 2:12 the writer speaks further of this familial relationship, quoting Psalm 22: *"I will declare your name to my brothers; in the presence of the congregation I will sing your praises."* It appears that Jesus himself meditated on this messianic psalm as he hung on the cross, crying out, "My God, my God, why have you forsaken me?" (Ps. 22:1; cf. Mark 15:34). When God heard the psalmist's prayer, the darkness of the tunnel dispelled, and the psalmist exulted, "I will declare your name to my brothers; in the congregation I will praise you" (Ps. 22:22). The psalmist is speaking of himself, but ultimately this refers to Christ and his church. Because we are Christ's brothers, he has an obligation to redeem us from our degradation, death, and hell, and he has done it (Ps. 22:31).

God's Eternal Plan

What is God's plan for his redeemed people? *"Here am I, and the children God has given me"* (Heb. 2:13). This quote from Isaiah 8 originally referred to Isaiah and the remnant of Israel, but ultimately it has to do with Jesus Christ and us, the children God has given him.

There is a *pactum salutis*, an eternal covenant of salvation, in which the Father chose certain people and gave them to his Son, that he might redeem them in the fullness of time by his death on the cross. Jesus is saying in the quote above, "I will save them and give them eternal life." We are the Father's donation to the Son, our older brother who wants to take care of us. "Christ loved the church and gave himself up for her" (Eph. 5:25).

Jesus referred to this eternal covenant throughout the gospel of John: "All that the Father gives me will come to me, and whoever comes to me I will never drive away. . . . And this is the will of him who sent me, that I shall lose none of all that he has given me" (John 6:37, 39); "My Father, who has given them to me, is greater than all; no one can snatch them out of my Father's hand. I and the Father are one" (John 10:29–30); "For you granted [the Son] authority over all people that he might give eternal life to all those you have given him. . . . I have revealed you to those whom you gave me out of the world. . . . I pray for them. I am not praying for the world, but for those you have given me, for they are yours. . . . Father, I want those you have given me to be with me where I am, and to see my glory, the glory you have given me because you loved me before the creation of the world"

(John 17:2, 6, 9, 24). God achieves his plan of "*bringing many sons to glory*" through Jesus Christ (Heb. 2:10).

Jesus had to become man so that he could redeem us by dying for our sins: "*Since the children have flesh and blood, he too shared in their humanity. . . . For this reason he had to be made like his brothers*" (Heb. 2:14, 17). And Hebrews 2:16 declares, "*For surely it is not angels he helps, but Abraham's descendants.*" The Greek word for "helps" means he grasps us and lifts us out of our trouble. Our elder brother does this for all Abraham's descendants, for us who believe in God as Abraham did.

In eternity the Son agreed to become our redeemer, our Boaz (see Ruth 2:19–20). Revelation 13:8 speaks of the Lamb of God "slain from the creation of the world." He is our blood relative who has the right and responsibility to help us, and he is able and willing to do so. The Immortal became mortal that he may bring life and immortality to us mortals. The transcendent Son became what he was not so that he could identify with us: as a man he wept, slept, hungered and thirsted, experienced pain, and was troubled and tempted in every way. Yet he obeyed God fully and died as the perfect sacrifice for our sins.

The Hebrews writer says Jesus' substitutionary death was an appropriate act of God: "*In bringing many sons to glory, it was fitting that God, for whom and through whom everything exists, should make the author of their salvation perfect through suffering*" (Heb. 2:10). The cross was not accidental; it was based on God's wise, eternal plan. There was no other way for God to satisfy his justice and demonstrate love for sinners. God the Father, therefore, took the initiative to save us. All other ways of salvation are unfitting, human speculations. The way of the cross may be foolishness to the Greeks and a stumbling block to the Jews, but to us who believe, it is the power of God unto salvation (1 Cor. 1:21–25, 30).

Our Merciful and Faithful High Priest

"*For this reason he had to be made like his brothers in every way, in order that he might become a merciful and faithful high priest in service to God*" (Heb. 2:17). Jesus Christ is our merciful and faithful high priest who made propitiation for our sins. Because of sin, the wrath of the holy God is against us. How can we escape? Another must suffer what is due us. This one must be both sinless and able to die.

The Son became man, entering history through the womb of Mary. Hebrews 2:14 says in the Greek that he who was not man entered humanity at a point in time. The eternal Son took upon himself human nature: "The Word became flesh" (John 1:14). The Son was obligated to become our sinless high priest and victim because he belonged to this family from all eternity as our elder brother.

God promised to raise up a faithful high priest (1 Sam. 2:35); this priest came in the person of Jesus. As a faithful high priest, Jesus learned obedience and proved it through his suffering. Unlike Adam, who sinned in paradise, our brother Jesus, the last Adam, obeyed perfectly in a fallen world. He was tempted in every way like us, yet never yielded to temptation. Only the person who never yields to temptation knows its full power. Jesus alone experienced the full power of temptation; therefore, he alone is able to help those who are being tempted.

Not only is Jesus our faithful high priest, but he is also merciful to miserable sinners like us. When the publican cried out for mercy, he went home justified (Luke 18:9–14). Jesus showed mercy to the leper who came to him for healing saying, "If you are willing, you can make me clean" (Mark 1:40). He showed mercy to blind Bartimaeus and to the Syro-Phoenician woman (Matt. 15:21–28; Mark 7:24–30). He showed mercy to the thief on the cross, declaring, "Today you will be with me in paradise" (Luke 23:43).

In understanding the work of Christ as our high priest, consider what happened on the Day of Atonement (see Lev. 16). The Aaronic priest first had to atone for his own sins by sprinkling blood on the mercy seat in the Holy of Holies. He then killed a goat and sprinkled its blood on the mercy seat to make propitiation for the sins of the people. In this way, God's wrath was turned away and the people's sins were forgiven.

Jesus made atonement, not for his sins, but for ours. He did so, not by a beast but through himself as priest, presenting himself as the perfect victim on the cross. By his shed blood, he turned God's wrath away from us. All our sins have been punished in

Jesus. So the writer says, *"For this reason he had to be made like his brothers in every way, in order that he might become a merciful and faithful high priest in service to God, and that he might make atonement for the sins of the people"* (Heb. 2:17).

We must know who we are. If we belong to God's family, we are sons of glory. Paul says, "I consider that our present sufferings are not worth comparing with the glory that will be revealed in us" (Rom. 8:18). He also says that we have already been glorified in Christ, and are waiting for the fullness of glory when Jesus comes again.

Why, then, should we fear? By his death on the cross, Jesus destroyed him who holds the power of death. *"Since the children have flesh and blood, he too shared in their humanity so that by his death he might destroy him who holds the power of death—that is, the devil—and free those who all their lives were held in slavery by their fear of death"* (Heb. 2:14–15). He broke the devil's power and set us free—we who are God's children, who lived in fear of death all our lives. This is true liberation theology. Jesus Christ liberated us from the devil and from the fear of death. Death itself cannot separate us from God because one died for all and therefore all died (2 Cor. 5:14).

Jesus became man to destroy the devil and break his power over us, and remove our fear of death. Why do we become anxious and fearful? The root of all fear is the fear of death. Suppose I go to the doctor and hear that I have cancer. I will suddenly see everything differently. But here we are told that the incarnation of Jesus Christ resulted in the destruction of the devil, who held the power of death over us. We were slaves of this fear all our lives, but the moment we trusted in Christ, we were set free.

Jesus spoke about this in Luke 11: "When a strong man, fully armed, guards his own house, his possessions are safe" (v. 21). The devil is the strong man and we were his possessions. "But when someone stronger attacks and overpowers him, he takes away the armor in which the man trusted and divides up the spoils" (v. 22). Who is the stronger one? Jesus Christ, who bound Satan, destroyed his power, and set his slaves free.

This is illustrated in Isaiah 49, which is probably what Christ was alluding to in Luke 11: "Can plunder be taken from warriors, or captives rescued from the fierce? But this is what the LORD says: 'Yes, captives will be taken from warriors, and plunder retrieved from the fierce. . . . Then all mankind will know that I, the LORD, am your Savior, your Redeemer, the Mighty One of Jacob'" (Isa. 49:24–26). The plunder is the people of God held captive by Satan.

Paul writes, "The sting of death is sin, and the power of sin is the law." As sinners, we are guilty of transgressing God's law and subject to death. We need someone to keep the law in our place. "But thanks be to God! He gives us the victory through our Lord Jesus Christ" (1 Cor. 15:56–57). The Son of David defeated our Goliath, dealing the deathblow to our depravity, death, and the devil. "If the Son sets you free, you will be free indeed" (John 8:36).

You may ask, "How can you say we are free? Don't you know that the devil is still moving about like a roaring lion, seeking to devour us?" Let me assure you, the devil cannot devour us; we have overcome him by the blood of the Lamb and by our faith in Christ. The Lord tells us, "Resist the devil, and he will flee from you" (Jas. 4:7). We resist by trusting in the person and work of Christ. The devil is like a big, black, barking dog. But when we look carefully, we see that he is bound with a long iron chain tied to a huge iron stake. He can bark all he wants, but he cannot finally harm us. What freedom!

Martin Luther said, "He who fears death or is not willing to die is not sufficiently Christian. As yet such people lack faith in the resurrection, and love this life more than the life to come."[1] He who does not die willingly should not be called a Christian. We will all surely die. I pray that we will love the Lord so that when he calls, we will go to be with him. He is bringing many sons to glory so that we can dwell with him forever in unspeakable joy. A true believer will agree with Paul, that to be absent from the body is to be present with the Lord (2 Cor. 5:6–8). Death has no sting for a believer. In fact, death is a promotion for a Christian. So Paul says, "For to me, to live is Christ and to die is gain. . . . I desire to depart and be with Christ, which is better by far" (Phil. 1:21, 23).

---

1   Quoted by Philip E. Hughes, *Commentary on Hebrews*, 114.

Help in Temptation

The author concludes this passage: "*Because he himself suffered when he was tempted, he is able to help those who are being tempted*" (Heb. 2:18). There is help for us when we are being tempted. The church of the Hebrews was experiencing such severe trials that they were about to quit their faith in Christ and go back to Judaism. Here the writer says that Christ became incarnate to do away with our sins and to help us when we are tempted. He goes with us through the tunnel of suffering and temptation and brings us out into the glorious sunshine of his presence.

Christ is able to help us because he was tempted like no other human being ever was. His temptation was unique because it was a messianic temptation. Jesus was tempted most powerfully in every respect like us, and he withstood all temptation. As a compassionate high priest, touched with the feeling of our infirmity, he understands us completely.

He is able to help because he himself was tempted. The word for help, *boētheō*, comes from *boē*, to cry, and *theō*, to run. Jesus is able and willing to run to the one who is crying, like parents run to help their child. The same word is used in Matthew 15:25 of the Syro-Phoenician woman whose daughter was demonized. She cried, "Lord, help me!" and Jesus came to her aid.

If you are tempted, I urge you to memorize 1 Corinthians 10:13 and live in the light of it. Paul begins, "No temptation has seized you except what is common to man." Only Jesus has experienced temptation not common to man. We must not exaggerate and say our experience is unique. Then Paul says, "God is faithful." Our God can be relied upon. Every promise he made is fulfilled in Jesus Christ. He is our faithful and merciful high priest. Paul continues, "He will not let you be tempted beyond what you can bear." Our Sovereign God has control over everything, including the devil. Then he concludes, "But when you are tempted, he will also provide a way out so that you can stand up under it." Elsewhere Paul exhorts, "Be strong in the Lord and in his mighty power. Put on the full armor of God so that you can take your stand against the devil's schemes . . . and after you have done everything, to stand" (Eph. 6:10–11, 13). We must not yield to temptation. It takes great resolution to stand up under life's trials and temptations, but with God's help, we can stand. Paul also writes, "I can do all things through Christ who strengthens me" (Phil. 4:13, NKJV). It is in the present tense in the Greek: "who continually infuses into me strength." We receive this strength by faith, so that having done all, we will stand.

6

Consider Jesus

¹Therefore, holy brothers, who share in the heavenly calling, fix your thoughts on Jesus, the apostle and high priest whom we confess. ²He was faithful to the one who appointed him, just as Moses was faithful in all God's house. ³Jesus has been found worthy of greater honor than Moses, just as the builder of a house has greater honor than the house itself. ⁴For every house is built by someone, but God is the builder of everything. ⁵Moses was faithful as a servant in all God's house, testifying to what would be said in the future. ⁶But Christ is faithful as a son over God's house. And we are his house, if we hold on to our courage and the hope of which we boast.

Hebrews 3:1–6

In this passage we are told to consider, or fix our thoughts on, Jesus. "Consider" means to bring one's mind in all its capacity to bear upon something. It is what a young man does when he is dating. He is thinking very seriously about who the woman is. After careful consideration, he may confess that he loves her, and they marry and continue in the married state until death. Today we want to look at what it means to consider Jesus, confess Jesus, and continue in Jesus.

Consider Jesus

First, we read, *"Therefore, holy brothers, who share in the heavenly calling, fix your thoughts on Jesus, the apostle and high priest whom we confess"* (Heb. 3:1). We need to consider Jesus because we can be tempted to forsake Christ when we face troubles. Ironically, we are also tempted to abandon our faith when we experience material prosperity. Remember how the church of Laodicea boasted, "I am rich; I have acquired wealth and do not need a thing" (Rev. 3:17). What a tragic statement!

The church of the Hebrews was facing persecution for its faith in Jesus Christ and was tempted to go back to Judaism to avoid troubles. These people were probably feeling pressure to consider Moses superior to Jesus, as the unbelieving Jews did, who revered Moses because he gave them the law and saw God face to face. But in Hebrews 3:1–6 the author directly appeals to the congregation to persevere in their faith, exhorting them to exercise their minds to know the infinite superiority of Jesus, not only over angels, but also over Moses.

Christianity demands acute mental activity, not hollow enthusiasm. The author begins, *"Therefore, holy brothers . . ."* (Heb. 3:1). "Therefore" means there is a reason. In the preceding chapters, the author told us that Jesus Christ is the Son who brought us the final revelation of God. He is the radiance of God's glory, the Creator, Upholder, and Heir of all things. He is the Redeemer who, after providing purification for our sins, is now seated as the King of kings. He is superior to angels; in fact, angels worship him as God. He is crowned with glory and honor, for he tasted death in our place and regained what Adam lost. He is our elder brother, our kinsman-redeemer, our Boaz, who by his incarnation became our perfect high priest and perfect victim, making atonement for our sins so that we could worship God. By his propitiatory death, this Jesus destroyed the devil and liberated us once for all from the fear of death. This Jesus is also able to help his brothers, who are being tempted daily.

Notice the phrase *"holy brothers."* We are brothers of Jesus and of one another because we belong to the family of God. We are holy because Jesus the Sanctifier consecrates us and now we have access to God in Christ's name. In Hebrews 13:24 we are called "saints" or "holy ones."

Then the writer says that we are those who *"share in the heavenly calling"* (Heb. 3:1). Ours is a calling *from* heaven *to* heaven. God takes the initiative in our salvation, inviting us to eternal fellowship with him. When God calls us to enter heaven through his Son Jesus, we are to turn away from all idols and turn to the true and living God. Paul calls this an "upward calling" (Phil. 3:14). It is a calling to a heavenly city, the new Jerusalem. What a privilege it is to be invited by God himself to his great eschatological feast! Have you shared in this heavenly calling? Have you become a member of his church (his *ekklēsia*), the company of those who are called out from the world?

The author continues, *"Fix your thoughts on Jesus"* (Heb. 3:1). The Greek word *katanoeō* means to "fix one's thoughts on something." We fix our thoughts either on ourselves or on Jesus. Those who are unhappy and complaining are those who refuse to fix their thoughts on Jesus. Instead, they are thinking about themselves and their problems. This word was used by Jesus in Matthew 7 to describe people who are careful to notice the speck in others' eyes but who refuse to consider the beam in their own eyes. Jesus also used this word when he said, "Consider the ravens" and "Consider the lilies" (Luke 12:24, 27). He was encouraging his people to study carefully how God feeds the ravens and clothes the lilies in beauty that transcends all the glory of Solomon.

When we bring all our mental powers to bear upon the Lord Jesus, we will discover him to be all-sufficient. Notice, it is a command. We *must* bring our minds to focus on Jesus intensely to know him fully. That means we must meditate on the Scripture so that we can know the person and work of Christ and love him, treasure him, worship and serve him only, and be completely satisfied with him. Faith comes by hearing the gospel, and faith in Jesus increases by considering Jesus as revealed in the Scripture.

We are commanded to love God with all our heart, soul, strength, and mind. When our minds are renewed, we love Jesus with all our mind. Those who become apostate are mindless people, like the first three soils in the parable of the sower. Mindless Christians are weak and become easy prey for Satan. They will not say, "It is written," and thus defeat Satan.

Consider Jesus! In Hebrews 2:9 the writer says, "But we see Jesus," and in Hebrews 12:2–3 he exhorts, "Let us fix our eyes on Jesus, the author and perfecter of our faith. . . . Consider him who endured such opposition from sinful men." Consider him. Know him. Think about him. Know his person and work. Know that he is our high priest. Know this, so that we will not grow weary and lose heart. The antidote to backsliding is to consider Jesus.

What are you considering? Are you thinking about the world or about the Savior of the world? Consider Jesus, and you will truly be happy. The psalmist speaks of the one whose "delight is in the law of the LORD, and on his law he mediates day and night. . . . Whatever he does prospers" (Ps.1:2–3). The writer of Proverbs says, "My son, pay attention to what I say; listen closely to my words. Do not let them out of your sight, keep them within your heart; for they are life to those who find them and health to man's whole body" (Prov. 4:20–22). We cannot consider Jesus and remain confused, miserable, and depressed.

Confess Jesus

Those who consider Jesus will also confess him: *"Fix your thoughts on Jesus, the apostle and high priest whom we confess"* (Heb. 3:1). Confession has two parts. We can say, "God is our God," but it means nothing unless God also confesses, "You are my people."

Jesus is *"the apostle and high priest"* of our confession. "Apostle" means he is the ambassador from God the Father who comes with authority and a mission. He is the final revelation of God. Christ did not glorify himself, but his Father, by fulfilling God's purpose of accomplishing redemption through Jesus' substitutionary, penal, and propitiatory death on the cross. Isaiah said God's purpose would prosper in his hand (Isa. 53:10). He took away the sin of the world.

As the Apostle of all apostles, he declares the gospel of our eternal salvation. This Apostle is God's Son, the Creator and Upholder of all things. God the Father sent Jesus into the world to declare the gospel because he is the gospel. Having accomplished redemption on the cross, he now commissions others to go into all the world to preach repentance and forgiveness of sins. He said, "Now this is eternal life: that they may know you, the only true God, and Jesus Christ, whom you have sent. I have brought you glory on earth by completing the work you gave me to do. . . . As you sent me into the world, I have sent them into the world" (John 17:3, 4, 18). He also said, "Peace be with you! As the Father has sent me, I am sending you" (John 20:21).

Jesus saves his people from their sins. Have you confessed him as your Savior and Apostle? Do you recognize his person, power, and purpose? In Jesus Christ, God the Father is speaking. To deny

Jesus is to deny the Father and be judged by him on the last day. He who receives Christ receives the One who sent him.

This Jesus is also the sinless God-man, the high priest who offered himself as an acceptable sacrifice for our sin. Have you considered this aspect of his person and his work? Because he dealt with our sin problem once and for all, now in Jesus we can fearlessly approach the throne of grace with a pure conscience cleansed by the sprinkling of the blood of Christ. Now the Father will receive us and give us the heavenly blessings of mercy and grace.

The author tells us to consider Jesus, the apostle and high priest of *our* confession. Do you confess this Jesus as your high priest? Have you trusted in his propitiation to take away your sins forever from the sight of God? Have your sins been covered by the shed blood of Jesus our high priest? Have you confessed him before the church and before the world?

Let us look at this idea of confession. In 1 Timothy 6:12 we read, "Fight the good fight of the faith. Take hold of the eternal life to which you were called when you made your good confession." Romans 10:9 says, "If you confess with your mouth, 'Jesus is Lord,' and believe in your heart that God raised him from the dead, you will be saved." First Corinthians 12:3 tells us that no one that is able to make this confession except by and through the Holy Spirit: "Therefore I tell you that no one who is speaking by the Spirit of God says, 'Jesus be cursed,' and no one can say, 'Jesus is Lord,' except by the Holy Spirit."

We are to confess Christ in the presence of God's people, but we must also confess him before the world: "Whoever acknowledges me before men, I will also acknowledge him before my Father in heaven. But whoever disowns me before men, I will disown him before my Father in heaven" (Matt. 10:32–33). When the apostles were commanded by the Sanhedrin not to confess Jesus and preach in his name, they replied, "We cannot help speaking about what we have seen and heard" (Acts 4:20).

This confession can result in trouble. When Jesus healed the blind man, the man's parents said they did not know who healed him: "His parents said this because they were afraid of the Jews, for already the Jews had decided that anyone who acknowledged that Jesus was the Christ would be put out of the synagogue"

(John 9:22). This tells us why we are very quiet in the world: we are afraid. When the blind man spoke favorably of Jesus, the Pharisees told him, "You were steeped in sin at birth; how dare you lecture us!" and threw him out (v. 34). Notice what happened when the apostles confessed Jesus before the Sanhedrin: "They called the apostles in and had them flogged" (Acts 5:40). But "the apostles left the Sanhedrin, rejoicing because they had been counted worthy of suffering disgrace for the Name" (v. 41).

In Hebrews 10 we read what these people themselves experienced in their earlier days because of their confession: "Remember those earlier days after you had received the light, when you stood your ground in a great contest in the face of suffering. Sometimes you were publicly exposed to insult and persecution; at other times you stood side by side with those who were so treated. You sympathized with those in prison and joyfully accepted the confiscation of your property, because you knew that you yourselves had better and lasting possessions" (vv. 32–34). In Hebrews 11 we read about others who suffered for their confession: "Some faced jeers and flogging, while still others were chained and put in prison. They were stoned; they were sawed in two; they were put to death by the sword. They went about in sheepskins and goatskins, destitute, persecuted and mistreated—the world was not worthy of them. They wandered in deserts and mountains, and in caves and holes in the ground" (vv. 36–38).

If you consider Jesus and his gospel, you will confess him. Most people refuse to confess Christ because they refuse to consider him. They suppress the truth of Jesus and exchange the gospel for a lie. But if you fix your thoughts on Jesus, you will confess him as your apostle and high priest. Paul tells us, "It is because of [God the Father] that you are in Christ Jesus, who has become for us wisdom from God—that is, our righteousness, holiness and redemption" (1 Cor. 1:30). Jesus is wisdom, righteousness, sanctification, and redemption for us; thus, we confess him.

The psalmist was miserable until he went to the temple of the Lord. Then he confessed: "Whom have I in heaven but you? And earth has nothing I desire besides you. My flesh and my heart may fail, but God is the strength of my heart and my portion forever" (Ps. 73:25–26). This man was a realist. He acknowledged the eventual decay and failure of his flesh. But he also believed in the resurrection unto eternal life and a life of celestial felicity with God. He agreed with Paul that to be absent from the body is to be present with Christ.

The prophet Habakkuk was not a fair-weather Christian. He declared, "Though the fig tree does not bud and there are no grapes on the vines, though the olive crop fails and the fields produce no food, though there are no sheep in the pen and no cattle in the stalls, yet I will rejoice in the LORD, I will be joyful in God my Savior" (Hab. 3:17–18). What a terrible thing to teach that prosperity can be gained through Jesus! Such teaching leaves no room for problems and persecutions. Jesus told Martha that only one thing is needful, and Jesus is that one thing (Luke 10:41–42). When we consider him, we will confess him and discover him to be sufficient for all our needs. Can you say Jesus is the apostle and high priest of your confession?

Continue in Jesus

"But Christ is faithful as a son over God's house. And we are his house, if we hold on to our courage and the hope of which we boast" (Heb. 3:6). Finally, we must continue in Jesus. If troubles begin the moment we confess based on our consideration of him, will we continue? This Jesus is the faithful One who is infinitely superior to faithful Moses. We must not stop following Jesus because of persecution. If we stop, we will be proving that we have nothing to do with him and that we are not his people.

The writer to the Hebrews was telling this church, "If you fix your thoughts on Jesus, you will not quit and go back to the shadow of the Mosaic economy of bloody sacrifices and external ceremonies." The Jews adored Moses and rejected Jesus. But this is the wrong way to think of Moses. Moses is not the final revelation of God to man; rather, Moses was pointing to the coming Messiah. Moses pointed to Jesus, and Jesus pointed to himself, saying, "I am that I am," "I am the light of the world," "I am the bread of life," "I am the good shepherd," "I am the resurrection and the life," "You have heard it said. . . . But I say to you." Jesus is the final revelation; therefore, it is utterly foolish to adore Moses and refuse to worship Jesus, who is the Creator, God, and Savior of Moses.

In fact, Moses himself was looking forward to Christ: "He regarded disgrace for the sake of Christ as of greater value than the treasures of Egypt, because he was looking ahead to his reward" (Heb. 11:26). Jesus said, "If you believed Moses, you would believe me, for he wrote about me" (John 5:46). Moses himself insisted, "The LORD your God will raise up for you a prophet like me from among your own brothers. You must listen to him" (Deut. 18:15). This was fulfilled on the Mount of Transfiguration when the Father declared of Christ in the presence of Moses and Elijah, "This is my Son, whom I love; with him I am well pleased. Listen to him!" (Matt. 17:5).

Referring to Jesus, Peter asserted, "All the prophets testify about him that everyone who believes in him receives forgiveness of sins through his name" (Acts 10:43). Peter did not say, "Everyone who believes in Moses receives forgiveness." Like John the Baptist, meek Moses would say, "Do not believe in me; believe in the one coming after me. Let me decrease and let him increase, because he is my God and my Savior. Christ is the one I wrote about and am expecting to come into the world to save sinners."

Hebrews 3:1–6 speaks six times about a house being built. This house is the church, the body of Christ, the people of God. God builds his temple with living stones (1 Pet. 2:4–6). The church is not a place where people come and go independently and autonomously. It is a house of living stones, with each one connected to God and to each other. It is the family of God.

In this house of God, Moses served as a faithful steward for God. Here again the author emphasizes that Jesus is superior to Moses, and so it would be foolish for these Hebrew Christians to go back to Moses and Judaism. The writer says that Moses was faithful as a servant in the house of God, but Jesus was faithful as a Son over the house of God. Jesus was the builder of God's house; Moses was part of the house he built. The author was saying, "Do not be infatuated with Moses and Judaism and its rituals. Do not be tempted to forsake the reality of Jesus for the shadow of Judaism. Jesus Christ is of greater glory than Moses. If you go back to Judaism to avoid persecution, you will prove that you are not heirs of salvation and that your confession is false."

The author exhorts us to think clearly. Moses is part of the house; Christ is the builder of the house. Moses was faithful in the house; Jesus is faithful over the house. Moses was a servant in the house; Jesus was a Son over the house. Moses loved God; Jesus is the God whom he loved. Moses was sinful and in need of salvation; Jesus was sinless and saves sinners. Moses brought his people out from the bondage of Pharaoh; Jesus is bringing his people out from bondage to sin, death, and the devil. Moses was a creature; Jesus is the Creator. Jesus is building the house of his church. He owns it, rules it, and provides for it. Moses was faithful as a servant; Jesus is faithful as a Son.

The author concludes, *"And we are his house, if we hold on to our courage and the hope of which we boast"* (Heb. 3:6). The idea here is that we must be faithful to continue in the confession we made after considering carefully the person and work of Christ.

If we consider Jesus and live out our confession in spite of persecution, then we shall inherit a heavenly city. We must persevere to the end as Jesus did. The writer later exhorts, "Let us fix our eyes on Jesus, the author and perfecter of our faith, who for the joy set before him endured the cross, scorning its shame, and sat down at the right hand of the throne of God. Consider him who endured such opposition from sinful men, so that you will not grow weary and lose heart. In your struggle against sin, you have not yet resisted to the point of shedding your blood" (Heb. 12:2–4). In other words, we may even die for the sake of our faith in Jesus Christ.

Only perseverance can prove the authenticity of one's consideration and confession. F. F. Bruce says, "The doctrine of the final perseverance of the saints has as its corollary the salutary teaching that the saints are the people who persevere to the end."[1] I do not believe in a teaching of eternal security where a person does not persevere. The saints will persevere to the end, enabled by their God.

If a person fails to be faithful to God till death, he never was a part of Christ's house. A true Christian will hold on fearlessly to his confession. Such a person will carefully apply his mind to consider Jesus and will freely boast in the hope of the glory of God. He will defy death for the sake of his confession that Jesus is Lord and will rejoice in tribulations, knowing that "suffering

---

1 Bruce, *Epistle to the Hebrews*, 94.

produces perseverance; perseverance, character; and character, hope" (Rom. 5:3–4)—a hope that does not make us ashamed, a hope in the glorious return of the Lord, when "we shall be like him, for we shall see him as he is" (1 John 3:2).

We must continue in our confession and take warning from those who did not. Remember Lot's wife. Remember Judas. Remember Demas, a fellow minister of Paul, who abandoned the gospel toward the end of his life, having loved this present world (2 Tim. 4:10). Of such people John writes, "They went out from us, but they did not really belong to us. For if they had belonged to us, they would have remained with us; but their going showed that none of them belonged to us" (1 John 2:19). Heed the words of Jesus to the church of Smyrna and all the martyrs of the church: "Be faithful, even to the point of death, and I will give you the crown of life" (Rev. 2:10). Our boast is in Christ and the glory of God. Do not be ashamed or timid: "God did not give us a spirit of timidity, but a spirit of power, of love and of self-discipline" (2 Tim. 1:7). Above all, remember Jesus, who endured the cross, scorning its shame, and died and rose from the dead. See him as the Sovereign Ruler of the universe, crowned with glory and honor. Consider Christ by the full application of your renewed mind, confess Christ before the world by proclamation and by proper conduct, and continue in the faith till death with fearless, death-defying confidence in the sure hope of the glory of God.

7
How to Experience Happiness

³⁻⁷So, as the Holy Spirit says: "Today, if you hear his voice, ⁸do not harden your hearts as you did in the rebellion, during the time of testing in the desert, ⁹where your fathers tested and tried me and for forty years saw what I did. ¹⁰That is why I was angry with that generation, and I said, 'Their hearts are always going astray, and they have not known my ways.' ¹¹So I declared on oath in my anger, 'They shall never enter my rest.'" ¹²See to it, brothers, that none of you has a sinful, unbelieving heart that turns away from the living God. ¹³But encourage one another daily, as long as it is called Today, so that none of you may be hardened by sin's deceitfulness. ¹⁴We have come to share in Christ if we hold firmly till the end the confidence we had at first. ¹⁵As has just been said: "Today, if you hear his voice, do not harden your hearts as you did in the rebellion." ¹⁶Who were they who heard and rebelled? Were they not all those Moses led out of Egypt? ¹⁷And with whom was he angry for forty years? Was it not with those who sinned, whose bodies fell in the desert? ¹⁸And to whom did God swear that they would never enter his rest if not to those who disobeyed? ¹⁹So we see that they were not able to enter, because of their unbelief.

⁴·¹ Therefore, since the promise of entering his rest still stands, let us be careful that none of you be found to have fallen short of it. ²For we also have had the gospel preached to us, just as they did; but the message they heard was of no value to them, because those who heard did not combine it with faith. ³Now we who have believed enter that rest, just as God has said, "So I declared on oath in my anger, 'They shall never enter my rest.'" And yet his work has been finished since the creation of the world. ⁴For somewhere he has spoken about the seventh day in these words: "And on the seventh day God rested from all his work." ⁵And again in the passage above he says, "They shall never enter my rest." ⁶It still remains that some will enter that rest, and those who formerly had the gospel preached

to them did not go in, because of their disobedience. ⁷Therefore God again set a certain day, calling it Today, when a long time later he spoke through David, as was said before: "Today, if you hear his voice, do not harden your hearts." ⁸For if Joshua had given them rest, God would not have spoken later about another day. ⁹There remains, then, a Sabbath-rest for the people of God; ¹⁰for anyone who enters God's rest also rests from his own work, just as God did from his. ¹¹Let us, therefore, make every effort to enter that rest, so that no one will fall by following their example of disobedience.

Hebrews 3:7–4:11

What is true happiness? It is the everlasting

rest of the saints of God. In Hebrews 3:7–4:11, the idea of rest appears eleven times. Rest is the central message of this portion of Scripture.

According to Leon Morris, this rest is "a place of blessing where there is no more striving but only relaxation in the presence of God and in the certainty that there is no cause to fear."[1] In his *Confessions*, St. Augustine also spoke of such rest: "Lord God, grant us peace . . . the peace of rest, the peace of the sabbath, the peace without an evening. All this most beautiful array of things, all so very good, will pass away when all their courses are finished—for in them there is both morning and evening. But the seventh day [of rest] is without an ending, and it has no setting, for thou hast sanctified it with an everlasting duration. . . . [All this thou hast done, that] we may find our rest in thee in the sabbath of life eternal."[2] John Newton wrote in his hymn:

> Safely through another week
> God has brought us on our way;
> let us now a blessing seek,
> waiting in his courts today;
> day of all the week the best,
> emblem of eternal rest.

Rest Revealed in the Gospel

The gospel reveals this rest to us. The bad news is that our sin dooms us to a destiny of everlasting restlessness. But God has

---

1 Morris, "Hebrews," in vol. 12 of *Expositor's Bible Commentary*, 35.
2 Quoted by Philip E. Hughes, *Commentary on Hebrews*, 162.

good news for us, achieved by his Son's sacrificial death on the cross for our sins. Isaiah anticipated this, saying, "How beautiful on the mountains are the feet of those who bring good news, who proclaim peace, who bring good tidings, who proclaim salvation, who say to Zion, 'Your God reigns!' . . . Burst into songs of joy together, you ruins of Jerusalem, for the LORD has comforted his people, he has redeemed Jerusalem" (Isa. 52:7, 9). How did this redemption come about? "The chastisement of our peace was upon him, and with his stripes we are healed" (Isa. 53:5b, KJV). And in the fullness of time, the angel brought this gospel to the despised shepherds of Bethlehem: "Do not be afraid. I bring you good news of great joy that will be for all the people. Today in the town of David a Savior has been born to you; he is Christ the Lord" (Luke 2:10–11).

Jesus calls all sin-weary people to everlasting rest: "Come to me, all you who are weary and burdened, and I will give you rest" (Matt. 11:28). The eternal torment and weariness of sinners can be exchanged for the saints' everlasting comfort. This is what the Bible declares, for the whole Bible is the gospel of our Lord Jesus Christ.

This gospel of eternal joy and peace was also preached to the people of God in the wilderness, as the writer to the Hebrews discloses in this passage: *"For we also have had the gospel preached to us, just as they did. . . . It still remains that some will enter that rest, and those who formerly had the gospel preached to them did not go in, because of their disobedience"* (Heb. 4:2, 6).

How does this gospel come to us? In Hebrews 3:7 he writes, "So, as the Holy Spirit says . . ." Through the Scriptures, through parents, through pastors, and through all believers, the Holy Spirit declares the good news of God's everlasting rest to the restless people of the world. As we are told repeatedly in Revelation 2 and 3, "He who has an ear, let him hear what the Spirit is speaking to the church."

Responding to the Gospel of Rest

Hebrews 3 and 4 tell us that the vast majority of the people in the wilderness responded to the gospel by provoking God, going astray from his ways, and worshiping and serving idols instead of the living God. They hardened their hearts to the message of salvation and exchanged the truth of the gospel for the lie of the devil. They rejected the Lord and his gospel, in spite of experiencing God's goodness in delivering them from Egyptian bondage, bringing them through the Red Sea, providing them with water from the rock and daily manna, protecting them from all their enemies, and guiding them by his own presence.

They also saw God's deeds of judgment. Hebrews 3:17 speaks of carcasses lying in the desert, the bodies of thousands of his unbelieving people killed by the sword, plague, and fire of divine judgment. Yet they continued to revolt against God, thereby discovering in the gracious and saving God an enemy. They deliberately chose eternal restlessness over the everlasting rest of the saints by becoming sinful, unbelieving, and apostate.

The Lord was testing the Israelites in the desert, as he tests all his people, to see whether they will truly walk in his ways. But these people also tested their God. They did not mix the gospel with saving faith. Instead, they mocked the voice of the Holy Spirit and turned a deaf ear to him.

In Hebrews 3:10–11 God gives justification for the righteous anger by which he destroyed these people: *"That is why I was angry with that generation, and I said, 'Their hearts are always going astray and they have not known my ways.' So I declared on oath in my anger, 'They shall never enter into my rest.'"*

The God of the Bible is angry at sin and sinners every day unless they repent, believe, obey, and worship him (Ps. 7:11). Paul writes, "The wrath of God is being revealed from heaven against all the godlessness and wickedness of men" (Rom. 1:18). It is not wickedness that God sends to hell, but wicked people.

God diagnoses the human problem in this passage: *"Their hearts are always going astray and they have not known my ways"* (Heb. 3:10). Our problem of wickedness is not circumstantial, but internal. It is endemic to our nature. *"Their hearts"* means their intellects, their wills, and their affections have become twisted. Jeremiah says the heart is "deceitful above all things, and desperately wicked: who can know it?" (Jer. 17:9, KJV). Psychiatrists and psychologists cannot truly discern a man's heart. The Lord alone knows the nature of our twistedness and reveals it in the Scriptures.

The heart is the problem. Jesus teaches that all evil comes out of the heart (Matt. 15:18–19). Genesis 6:5 says, "Every inclination of the thoughts of [man's] heart [is] only evil all the time." The human heart is so perverted that it refuses to believe the truth. Paul gives a profound revelation of the nature of human depravity: "They perish because they refused to love the truth and so be saved. For this reason God sends them a powerful delusion so that they will believe the lie and so that all will be condemned who have not believed the truth but have delighted in wickedness" (2 Thess. 2:10–12).

Twisted man exchanges truth for lie. Not only does he not will God's will, but he also refuses to do it. He declares, "I am, and my will be done." His affections are devoted to evil; he loves wickedness from the depths of his being. This is the problem not only of atheists but also of "Christians" who claim they can be characterized by disobedience and still be part of the family of God.

Look again at Hebrews 3:10: *"Their hearts are always going astray."* The hearts of the wicked go astray in the morning, at noon, and at night. They go astray when they are young and when they are old. They are always moving away from the straight and narrow way that leads to the living God and the everlasting comfort of the saints. They prefer the broad way of human will and desires. But note God's response: *"So I declared on oath in my anger, 'They shall never enter my rest'"* (Heb. 3:11). God's declaration is authoritative: what he declares shall happen. He declared that his rebellious people would not enter into his rest, and they did not. And as if God's declaration were not enough, he also gave an oath, making it even more certain (Num. 14:21ff.).

We see a similar oath in Luke 14, where a great feast was prepared, but those who were invited refused to come: "I tell you, not one of those men who were invited will get a taste of my banquet" (v. 24). The banquet is the saints' everlasting rest.

God swore that his rebellious people would not enter into his rest, and they did not. God also swears to us about our salvation. He promised to save us, and then made an oath to prove he would keep his promise: "Men swear by someone greater than themselves, and the oath confirms what is said and puts an end to all argument. Because God wanted to make the unchanging nature of his purpose very clear to the heirs of what was promised, he confirmed it with an oath. God did this so that, by two unchangeable things [his promise and his oath] in which it is impossible for God to lie, we who have fled to take hold of the hope offered to us may be greatly encouraged" (Heb. 6:16–18).

If we turn away from God and seek our own will, God promises to judge us, and then adds an oath to prove it will be done. But for those who trust in him, he gives his promise and oath to save them. God himself sees to it that we will enter into everlasting rest.

Look again at the language of Hebrews 3:11: *"They shall never enter my rest."* Never! Man has only two destinies: eternal restlessness or eternal comfort. Jesus spoke about this in the story of the rich unbeliever and the poor believer, Lazarus. After they died, the rich man found himself in hell while Lazarus went to heaven. Abraham told the rich man, "Son, remember that in your lifetime you received your good things, while Lazarus received bad things, but now he is comforted here and you are there in agony" (Luke 16:25). Revelation 22:14 tells us, "Blessed are those who wash their robes, that they may have the right to the tree of life and may go through the gates into the city." The blessed are believers going into the city of God to enjoy eternal life. But notice verse 15: "Outside are the dogs, those who practice magic arts, the sexually immoral, the murderers, the idolaters and everyone who loves and practices falsehood."

All these oaths are spoken against those who have heard the gospel yet refuse to believe. This can include children who are brought up in a church. All who reject the gospel will enter into everlasting restlessness and eternal torment.

The Promise of Rest Still Remains

The good news is that God's promise of eternal rest still stands! The writer is not emphasizing the restlessness of the dead. Rather, he has a positive message for the living—that God's promise of eternal rest still remains for all who believe and obey God: *"Therefore, since the promise of entering his rest still stands . . . Now we who have believed enter that rest. . . . It still remains that some will enter that rest. . . . There remains, then, a Sabbath-rest for the people of God"* (Heb. 4:1, 3, 6, 9). In the creation account, the seventh day is not described as having morning and evening. It represents the endless rest of heaven.

We enter into that rest now by faith in the gospel, and we will experience greater enjoyment of it at the moment of our death. Our earthly lives are mixed with suffering; when we are afflicted, we should pray for healing so that we can labor more for the Lord. But do not become discouraged if you are not healed; God may be ready to call you to himself. Death is a promotion to everlasting rest. I hope we can say, with the help of the Holy Spirit, "To me, to live is Christ and to die is gain," and "To depart [is to] be with Christ" (Phil. 1:21, 23). Revelation 14:13 tells us, "Blessed are the dead who die in the Lord. . . . 'Yes,' says the Spirit, 'they will rest from their labor.'"

We will experience rest in its highest degree when Christ returns in the new heaven and the new earth. John writes,

> Then I saw a new heaven and a new earth, for the first heaven and the first earth had passed away, and there was no longer any sea. I saw the Holy City, the new Jerusalem, coming down out of heaven from God, prepared as a bride beautifully dressed for her husband. And I heard a loud voice from the throne saying, "Now the dwelling of God is with men, and he will live with them. They will be his people, and God himself will be with them and be their God. He will wipe every tear from their eyes. There will be no more death or mourning or crying or pain, for the old order of things has passed away." (Rev. 21:1–4)

Those Israelites who died in unbelief did not enter this rest. Although they experienced God's grace and mercy and saw God's judgment, they refused to believe. They revolted against the true and living God and chose the way of the devil and eternal death instead of God's way of life. God swore they would not enter his rest, and they did not.

Their opportunity is gone forever. But we still have opportunity to hear the gospel, believe it, obey it, and enter into rest. In Hebrews 3:7, 15 and 4:7, we find a phrase from Psalm 95 repeated: *"Today, if you hear his voice, do not harden your hearts."* The Holy Spirit is telling us, "Today, if you hear God's voice, do not behave like those people in the wilderness. Do not harden your heart as in the day of provocation." The emphasis is positive. Rest still remains for the people of God.

"Today, if you hear his voice . . ." We must listen to the preacher of the gospel, for the Holy Spirit speaks through him. When parents speak to children, they are speaking by the Spirit of God. When our fellow believers speak to us, it is the voice of the Holy Spirit.

Today is our day of opportunity. Today the gospel still comes to us with comfort, salvation, peace, hope, and joy. Today the Holy Spirit is still speaking to our hearts. Today we can still assemble to hear the gospel clearly proclaimed. This Today will continue until Christ comes again, though our own Today ends with our death.

For many people, their Today has already ended, though they are still alive, because the Holy Spirit has stopped speaking to them. Such people experience only the Spirit's silence. Saul longed to hear the voice of Samuel, but he could not. Someday you also may long to hear the voice of a preacher, or the voice of your mother or father, but there will only be silence, because your Today is over.

Thank God, the Holy Spirit is still speaking to us now! Therefore, do not harden your heart or be deceived by sin or the riches of this world. Ask God to give you a soft heart, a heart of flesh. Cry out for the gifts of godly repentance and obedient faith. Come to Jesus, who by his death and resurrection accomplished redemption for all who come to him. As the Holy Spirit applies salvation to you, you shall enter into God's endless rest—the rest of forgiveness of all our sins; the rest of justification, that God declares us righteous and not subject to being consumed by his anger; the rest of adoption, that we can call him "Abba, Father," and he will hear our prayers; the rest of glorification, that the presence of sin itself will be removed, and we will be given glorious bodies like unto his own and dwell with him forever; and the rest of eternal fellowship with God.

The pleasure of sin lasts only for a season, but the pleasure of salvation from sin is eternal. Unbelief in the gospel is the greatest sin we can commit. Whether young or old, educated or not, all unbelievers are by definition mocking the living God, calling him a liar.

May we be like the Philippian jailer, who cried out in utter panic in the middle of the night, "What must I do to be saved?"

The Holy Spirit replied through Paul: "Believe on the Lord Jesus, and you will be saved" (Acts 16:30–31). Believe on him who died for your sins and was raised for your justification. Trust him and be saved, both now and forever.

Divine Demands Leading to Eternal Happiness

Do you want to be eternally happy, with a happiness that infinitely transcends all the happiness we can imagine? We are created to enjoy such happiness. God himself came in the cool of the day to fellowship with Adam and Eve. That is true happiness. Such happiness endures in the face of death itself.

How do we obtain this happiness? There are several imperatives in this passage directed to us. They are not suggestions, but divine demands. As believers, we must pay attention.

1. *Harden not your hearts* (Heb. 3:7, 15; 4:7). We find this imperative repeated three times in this passage. Whenever someone preaches the gospel to us, the Holy Spirit is speaking. We must not harden our hearts, but believe. How do we keep our hearts soft? Through repentance, prayer, reading of the word, fellowship with God's people, and worship.

2. *See to it* (Heb. 3:12). In the Greek it is, "Be watchful." We must not live carelessly. And it is not enough to watch ourselves; we are our brother's keepers. We must observe whether or not others are walking with us in the straight and narrow path to everlasting rest. We must do our best to see that not a single member of our family, our small group, or our church becomes apostate and perishes because of a sinful and unbelieving heart.

3. *Encourage* (Heb. 3:13). The Greek word means to put strength into a weak person so that he becomes able to walk. Each one is to do this. Thus, we must speak to others in the church and know their situations, just as we do in our own families. The antidote to falling away is being encouraged by others. The Greek text says, "Encourage yourselves," not "Encourage one another," because the church is seen as a unity, as a family. We are to encourage, exhort, and admonish our fellow believers, not through psychology or politics, but by the word of God. Nothing else will help. The word of God alone can truly encourage people (cf. Rom. 15:1–6; 1 Cor. 10:11; Col. 3:16; 2 Tim. 3:16). Jesus himself said, "My word

is spirit and my word is life" (John 6:63, author's translation). Whenever the word is preached it encourages the hearers. The weak are made strong.

It is the responsibility of every believer to encourage others, and we are to do so daily. We must be connected with other believers. Call a brother or sister on the phone, or send an email to encourage that person. Encourage each other when you are dating. If you are married, encourage your spouse and children, especially during family devotions. Encourage each other in your small groups and in the church whenever you come together. Encourage each other, so that no one will fall away, but that everyone will enter into this everlasting rest. And if you are not a member of a church, join one to ensure your daily progress to the heavenly city. F. F. Bruce comments: "In a fellowship which exercised a watchful and unremitting care for its members, the temptation to prefer the easy course to the right one would be greatly weakened and the united resolution to stand firm would be correspondingly strengthened."[3] We must encourage others as long as we live.

4. *Be careful* (Heb. 4:1). The Greek text reads, "Let us fear." John Newton wrote,

> 'Twas grace that taught my heart to fear,
> and grace my fears relieved.

If we are touched by grace, we will fear God and be careful to do his will. Let us fear not people nor death but God, by eagerly doing his will. The fear of God is godliness. The fear of God keeps us from sinning (cf. Heb. 10:26–27, 31; 12:21, 29).

5. *Make every effort* (Heb. 4:11). The Greek word means to strive, to make haste, to spare no effort, to labor, to run, to be in earnest, to concentrate all of one's energies on achieving this goal of eternal rest. Paul speaks of such striving: "Brothers, I do not consider myself yet to have taken hold of it. But one thing I do: Forgetting what is behind and straining toward what is ahead, I press on toward the goal to win the prize for which God has called me heavenward in Christ Jesus" (Phil. 3:13–14). This is

---

3   Bruce, *Epistle to the Hebrews*, 101.

not giving superficial attention to religious matters. When Mary heard the gospel from the mouth of the angel, she left right away to see Elizabeth. When the shepherds heard the gospel, they went in haste to see this baby, Christ the Lord. It is the same word.

Conclusion

What is the purpose of all this striving, encouraging and carefulness? That none fall away, but that all persevere to the end and arrive at rest. Hebrews 3:14 says, "*We have come to share in Christ if we hold firmly till the end the confidence we had at first.*" And in Hebrews 3:6 we read, "But Christ is faithful as a son over God's house. And we are his house, if we hold on to our courage and the hope of which we boast." Those who persevere to the very end will enjoy security. They will not fall away, as did Lot's wife, Judas, and Demas.

How can we persevere to the very end? God himself will help us. In Hebrews 13:20–21 we read, "May the God of peace, who through the blood of the eternal covenant brought back from the dead our Lord Jesus, that great Shepherd of the sheep, equip you with everything good for doing his will, and may he work in us what is pleasing to him, though Jesus Christ, to whom be glory for ever and ever. Amen." If you are born of God, you will persevere to the very end. As Paul exhorted the Philippians, "Work out your salvation with fear and trembling, for it is God who works in you to will and to act according to his good purpose" (Phil. 2:12–13).

The promise of rest still remains for those who believe the gospel. May God help us to strive to enter God's rest while it is still Today, that we may join the throng of God's saints even now marching to Zion to their everlasting comfort and rest.

8
Nowhere to Hide

¹²For the word of God is living and active. Sharper than any double-edged sword, it penetrates even to dividing soul and spirit, joints and marrow; it judges the thoughts and attitudes of the heart. ¹³Nothing in all creation is hidden from God's sight. Everything is uncovered and laid bare before the eyes of him to whom we must give account.

Hebrews 4:12–13

There is nowhere to hide from God and his

word. When Adam and Eve sinned against the Lord, they thought that they could hide from God and escape judgment. They made for themselves fig-leaf garments and hid themselves among the trees of the garden. But the Lord found them and drove them out of the garden (Gen. 3). Achan thought that he could hide from God, but he and his family were found out and destroyed (Josh. 7). Ananias and Sapphira thought that they could hide from God, but they were discovered and destroyed (Acts 5). The psalmist said, "Where can I go from your Spirit? Where can I flee from your presence? . . . If I say, 'Surely the darkness will hide me' . . . even the darkness will not be dark to you; the night will shine like the day, for darkness is as light to you" (Ps. 139:7, 11–12).

In our previous study we noted that the eternal judgment of God is coming, when some shall enter into the saints' everlasting rest, while others go to the sinners' everlasting torment. There is nowhere we can hide from this judgment of God, whom Abraham called "the Judge of all the earth" (Gen. 18:25). But there is an everlasting rest remaining for the people of God, and the writer to the Hebrews encourages us to strive to enter that rest (Heb. 4:11).

God's supreme desire is for all of us to enter that eternal happiness which the gospel clearly proclaims. If anyone goes to hell, it is because he hates God. Such a person does not believe he really will go to hell; he thinks he can hide from God and his judgment. But there is no place to hide. God is called *Lahai Roi*, "the Living One who sees me" (Gen. 16:14).

This passage reminds us that God sees all of us at all times and knows our thoughts before we think them: *"Nothing in all creation is hidden from God's sight. Everything is uncovered and laid bare before the eyes of him to whom we must give account"* (Heb. 4:13). Naked we came into this world, naked we shall go out, and naked we shall stand in the great judgment, utterly defenseless and totally vulnerable.

After exhorting us to strive to enter heaven's rest by believing the gospel, the Hebrews writer now issues a warning to those who think they can reject the gospel without dire consequences. The Bible is God's word and so possesses the nature and qualities of God himself; thus, it is utter folly not to believe it. The Bible is not a dead book dealing with mere history, nor is it the word of man. In it, God himself is speaking, Christ is speaking, the Holy Spirit is speaking, the apostles are speaking, and the ministers of the gospel are speaking (cf. Heb. 1:1–2; 13:7). Hebrews 2:2–3 warns, "For if the message spoken by angels was binding, and every violation and disobedience received its just punishment, how shall we escape if we ignore such a great salvation?" The word of God is the gospel, which proclaims great salvation from God's own just wrath against our sins.

Friends, there is no escape. No one can hide, whether in the mountains of the world or in the mountains of books written to refute the word of God. Every knee shall bow before the Lord, and every tongue shall confess that Jesus Christ is Lord, to the glory of God the Father. In Hebrews 4:12–13 the writer outlines five qualities of the word of God as a warning to those who refuse to believe.

1. *The Word of God Is Living*

"*Living is the word of God,*" says the Greek text (Heb. 4:12). Note the emphasis on "living." The word of God is not myth or legend.

It is not the primitive notions of primitive people about God and the universe. Deuteronomy 32:45–47 says, "When Moses finished reciting all these words to all Israel, he said to them, 'Take to heart all the words I have solemnly declared to you this day, so that you may command your children to obey carefully all the words of this law. They are not just idle words for you—they are your life. By them you will live long in the land you are crossing the Jordan to possess.'" God's words are not dead commands, void of meaning. By them we live and die.

The whole Bible pulsates with life. Peter writes, "For you have been born again, not of perishable seed, but of imperishable, through the *living and enduring* word of God" (1 Pet. 1:23, italics added). The word of God has power to save and destroy, bless and curse.

The word of God is living because its source is living: "See to it, brothers, that none of you has a sinful, unbelieving heart that turns away from the *living* God. . . . How much more, then, will the blood of Christ, who through the eternal Spirit offered himself unblemished to God, cleanse our consciences from acts that lead to death, so that we may serve the *living* God! . . . But you have come to Mount Zion, to the heavenly Jerusalem, the city of the *living* God" (Heb. 3:12; 9:14; 12:22, italics added).

The living nature of God's word is described throughout the Scripture. In Isaiah 40:8 we read, "The grass withers and the flowers fall, but the word of our God stands forever." Jesus declared to his disciples, "The Spirit gives life; the flesh counts for nothing. The words I have spoken to you are spirit and they are life" (John 6:63). Then Peter asked him, "Lord, to whom shall we go? You have the words of eternal life" (John 6:68). Paul proclaims, "All Scripture is God-breathed and is useful for teaching, rebuking, correcting and training in righteousness, so that the man of God may be thoroughly equipped for every good work" (2 Tim. 3:16–17).

If you are tempted to reject the word of God, remember that you must give an account to God for doing so. Hebrews 10:30–31 warns, "For we know him who said, 'It is mine to avenge; I will repay,' and again, 'The Lord will judge his people.' It is a dreadful thing to fall into the hands of the living God." Again, the Hebrews writer says, "See to it that you do not refuse him who speaks. If they did not escape when they refused him who warned them on earth, how much less will we, if we turn away from him who warns us from heaven? . . . Our 'God is a consuming fire'" (Heb. 12:25, 29).

Do you understand the extreme gravity of what it means to hear the word of God? When people speak God's word to you, it is a living word that will either save or condemn you.

2. The Word of God Is Active

Not only is the word of God living, but it is also active: *"For the word of God is living and active"* (Heb. 4:12). The Greek word is *energēs*, from which we get "energy." Work is a function of energy. When the writer says God's word is active, he means it works, fulfilling its promises as well as its threatenings.

The word of God powerfully performs the works of God. Look at the language of the psalmist:

> The voice of the LORD is powerful; the voice of the LORD is majestic. The voice of the LORD breaks the cedars; the LORD breaks in pieces the cedars of Lebanon. He makes Lebanon skip like a calf, Sirion like a young wild ox. The voice of the LORD strikes with flashes of lightning. The voice of the LORD shakes the desert; the LORD shakes the Desert of Kadesh. The voice of the LORD twists the oaks and strips the forests bare. And in his temple all cry, "Glory!" (Ps. 29:4–9)

In Isaiah 55:11 God says, "My word that goes out from my mouth . . . will not return to me empty, but will accomplish what I desire and achieve the purpose for which I sent it."

God's powerful word always accomplishes either salvation or judgment. Paul writes, "For the message of the cross is foolishness to those who are perishing, but to us who are being saved it is the power of God" (1 Cor. 1:18). Elsewhere he declares, "I am not ashamed of the gospel, because it is the power of God for the salvation of everyone who believes: first for the Jew, then for the Gentile" (Rom. 1:16).

God's word is also the creating word. God spoke, and the universe came into existence: "By faith we understand that the universe was formed at God's command, so that what is seen was not made out of what was visible" (Heb. 11:3). It is also the sustaining word: "The Son is the radiance of God's glory and the exact representation of his being, sustaining all things by his powerful word" (Heb. 1:3). It is the regenerating word, raising up those who are dead in trespasses and sins, making new creations out of them, and seating them with Christ in the heavenly places (Eph. 2:1–10). It is also the healing word: "[God] sent forth his word and healed them" (Ps. 107:20).

Finally, it is the word that either saves or condemns. Never think that the word of God is ineffectual, even if people walk away after hearing the preacher as though nothing happened. Every time the word of God is proclaimed, it operates powerfully by either saving or condemning. Paul says, "For we are to God [in our function as preachers] the aroma of Christ among those who are being saved and those who are perishing. To the one we are the smell of death; to the other, the fragrance of life" (2 Cor. 2:15–16). Two activities are taking place by the same word. To some, the gospel proclamation becomes the sentence of death, while others are saved and made alive. Then Paul asks, "Who is equal to such a task?" (v. 16). Preaching the gospel is life or death business. Who is competent to do this? Only God, who makes his ministers competent.

F. F. Bruce says that the word of God is self-fulfilling in that it "speeds to fulfill the purpose for which it has been uttered" by God.[1] How many children understand that when their parents speak the word of God to them, it is a self-fulfilling word? Blessing will result from their obedience and curse from disobedience. The word of God is not idle. Do you trust and obey God's energetic, performative word?

3. The Word of God Is Cutting

Next, we are told that God's word is cutting, like the sharpest sword: *"Sharper than any double-edged sword . . ."* (Heb. 4:12). The word of God has no blunt side to it. In spite of any lack of eloquence of the preacher, the word of God is always effectual.

In the ancient world, a double-edged sword was the sharpest instrument one could have. Judges 3 speaks about a judge named Ehud who made an eighteen-inch-long double-edged sword. He

---

[1] Bruce, *Epistle to the Hebrews*, 112.

hid it and then plunged it into the belly of Eglon, the Moabite king. Isaiah 49:2 says that God made the mouth of Jesus Christ "like a sharpened sword." Revelation 1:16 also refers to this aspect of the resurrected Christ: "Out of his mouth came a sharp double-edged sword."

The word of God cuts to the heart, the center of human personality: the will, affections, and intellect. It cuts either to save or to destroy. In Acts 2:37–38 we see one reaction to the gospel message: "When the people heard this, they were cut to the heart and said to Peter and the other apostles, 'Brothers, what shall we do?' Peter replied, 'Repent and be baptized, every one of you, in the name of Jesus Christ for the forgiveness of your sins.'" These people were saved. Later, however, when the apostles spoke the same gospel to the Sanhedrin, their reaction was different: "When they heard this, they were furious" (Acts 5:33). The word of God also cut them to their very core, but instead of saving them, it condemned them. We find the same reaction in response to the gospel preached by Stephen: "When [the Sanhedrin] heard this, they were furious and gnashed their teeth at him" (Acts 7:54). The word of God cut to destroy them.

God has ultimate power over all his creatures. No one, therefore, should ignore his word. It will either save or destroy us, for the word of God is always effectual. We may think nothing is happening when we hear the word of God, but if we are not saved by it, we are being condemned.

4. The Word of God Is Piercing

The word of God is piercing: "*It penetrates even to dividing soul and spirit, joints and marrow*" (Heb. 4:12). The Greek implies continuous action. The word of God continually pierces and probes the innermost parts of the otherwise inaccessible citadels of our hearts. We can hide secrets from our neighbors or spouses, but not from God. God's word penetrates to the very core of our being and detects any unbelief toward God and his word.

We see this idea of piercing throughout the Scriptures:

1. "The Lord saw how great man's wickedness on the earth had become, and that every inclination of the thoughts of his

heart was only evil all the time" (Gen. 6:5);
2. "Serve [God] with wholehearted devotion and with a willing mind, for the LORD searches every heart and understands every motive behind the thoughts" (1 Chron. 28:9);
3. "The heart is deceitful above all things and beyond cure. Who can understand it? 'I the LORD search the heart and examine the mind.'" (Jer. 17:9–10);
4. "O LORD, you have searched me and you know me. You know when I sit and when I rise; you perceive my thoughts from afar. You discern my going out and my lying down; you are familiar with all my ways. Before a word is on my tongue you know it completely, O LORD. . . . Search me, O God, and know my heart; test me and know my anxious thoughts. See if there is any offensive way in me, and lead me in the way everlasting" (Ps. 139:1–4, 23–24).

In 1 Samuel 16:7 we are told, "Man looks at the outward appearance, but the LORD looks at the heart." Jesus did not trust any person because "he knew what was in a man" (John 2:25). We can fool other people, but we can never fool God. Paul exhorts, "Therefore judge nothing before the appointed time; wait till the Lord comes. He will bring to light what is hidden in darkness and will expose the motives of men's hearts" (1 Cor. 4:5).

God's word enters into the dark recesses of our hearts, disclosing every intention, motivation, and thought. It investigates thoroughly and discovers every bit of unbelief. Such knowledge renders us speechless and defenseless before him. There is nowhere we can hide from the living God. Thus, Proverbs 28:13 counsels us, "He who conceals his sins does not prosper, but whoever confesses and renounces them finds mercy."

5. The Word of God Judges

Finally, the word of God judges: *"It judges the thoughts and attitudes of the heart"* (Heb. 4:12). *Kritikos* is the Greek word, from which we have "critic" and "criticize." Not only does the word of God probe our hearts, discerning our feelings, thoughts, and motivations, but it also criticizes and judges us with a judgment that is always true and final.

As creatures, we are to hear and do God's perfect will. But because we are fallen, we sit in judgment of God and his everlasting word.

Man has long been in the business of judging the word of God and rejecting it as foolishness. But man's judgment of God and his word cannot stand. God's judgment of man shall prevail: "For it is written: 'I will destroy the wisdom of the wise; the intelligence of the intelligent I will frustrate.' Where is the wise man? Where is the scholar? Where is the philosopher of this age? Has not God made foolish the wisdom of the world?" (1 Cor. 1:19–20).

God's word is our judge. Jesus says, "There is a judge for the one who rejects me and does not accept my words; that very word which I spoke will condemn him at the last day" (John 12:48). Every word God has spoken to us, whether from the pulpit or from the written word, will judge us on the last day.

Nothing is more inaccessible than the emotions, notions, intentions, and motives concealed in the depths of man's depraved heart. We all have an innate tendency to circumvent truth when confronted with our sin. But God's word exposes and judges our hearts, just as the prophet Samuel exposed the wicked heart of Saul (1 Sam. 15) and the prophet Nathan uncovered the wickedness of David (2 Sam. 12). A sinner hates this truth, choosing instead to believe that he will not face God in judgment. He does so because the idea of facing God as Judge damages his self-esteem. He wants to sit in his Jericho, protected by high walls and locked gates. But in a flash, by the power of God, his protection shall disappear.

The word of God judges us for our benefit, so we must pay attention to it. May we be instructed, rebuked, corrected, and trained by it. May we stand under it and be saved, for all who stand over it shall be destroyed.

Nowhere to Hide

"Nothing in all creation is hidden from God's sight. Everything is uncovered and laid bare before the eyes of him to whom we must give account" (Heb. 4:13). There is nowhere we can hide from God. Adam and Eve found that out, as did Achan, Ananias and Sapphira, Saul, and David. Jesus declares, "There is nothing concealed that will not be disclosed, or hidden that will not be made known" (Luke 12:2). Paul tells us, "For we must all appear before the judgment seat of Christ, that each one may receive

what is due him for the things done while in the body, whether good or bad" (2 Cor. 5:10).

We cannot hide from God. "'Can anyone hide in secret places so that I cannot see him?' declares the Lord" (Jer. 23:24). In Revelation 6:15–17 we read, "Then the kings of the earth, the princes, the generals, the rich, the mighty, and every slave and every free man hid in caves and among the rocks of the mountains. They called to the mountains and the rocks, 'Fall on us and hide us from the face of him who sits on the throne and from the wrath of the Lamb! For the great day of their wrath has come, and who can stand?'" The mountains will not obey these people; they must obey their Creator.

John writes,

> Then I saw a great white throne and him who was seated on it. Earth and sky fled from his presence, and there was no place for them. And I saw the dead, great and small, standing before the throne, and books were opened. Another book was opened, which is the book of life. The dead were judged according to what they had done as recorded in the books. The sea gave up the dead that were in it, and death and Hades gave up the dead that were in them, and each person was judged according to what he had done. Then death and Hades were thrown into the lake of fire. The lake of fire is the second death. If anyone's name was not found written in the book of life, he was thrown into the lake of fire. (Rev. 20:11–15)

No creature can hide from God; all must stand before him naked. The fig-leaf garment of human philosophy will fail. Every creature must give an account to God on the last day, when he asks, "Did you worship and serve me only, or did you worship and serve yourself?"

Strive to enter the saints' everlasting rest by believing the word preached to you. When you sin, do not try to conceal your sins, but confess them and find mercy. Let the living word of God cut you, probe you, expose you, and judge you. Agree with the judgment of God's word and submit to it. Today, if you hear his voice, harden not your heart, but repent, believe, and call upon the name of the Lord. "Everyone who calls on the name of the Lord will be saved" (Rom. 10:13). Do not try to hide or run away from God; rather, run to him, hide in him and be safe.

There is only one place where we can hide from the wrath of God—in Christ and his shed blood for our sins. Let us, therefore, pray this prayer of an ancient saint: "O thou elect blade and sharpest sword, . . . pierce, I beseech thee, this most obdurate mind."[2] Let us consider the words of John Wesley:

> I am a creature of a day, passing through life as an arrow through the air. I am a spirit come from God and returning to God; just hovering over the great gulf, till a few moments hence I am no more seen—I drop into an unchangeable eternity! I want to know one thing, the way to heaven—how to land safe on that happy shore. God himself has condescended to teach the way: for this very end he came from heaven. He hath written it down in a book. O give me that book! At any price give me the Book of God! I have it. Here is knowledge enough for me. Let me be *homo unius libri* [a man of one book]. Here then I am, far from the busy ways of men. I sit down alone: only God is here. In his presence I open, I read his Book; for this end, to find the way to heaven. [3]

Praise God for his Book of life! The word of God is living, performing, cutting, piercing, and judging. May God help us to find through this Book that place to hide in Jesus Christ and be saved.

---

2 Quoted by Philip E. Hughes, *Commentary on Hebrews*, 166.
3 John Wesley, "Preface to 'Sermons on Several Occasions'" in *The Works of John Wesley*, vol. 5 (Peabody, MA: Hendrickson, reprinted 1986), 3.

9

Grace for Living

> [14]Therefore, since we have a great high priest who has gone through the heavens, Jesus the Son of God, let us hold firmly to the faith we profess. [15]For we do not have a high priest who is unable to sympathize with our weaknesses, but we have one who has been tempted in every way, just as we are—yet was without sin. [16]Let us then approach the throne of grace with confidence, so that we may receive mercy and find grace to help us in our time of need.
>
> Hebrews 4:14–16

As Christians, we have many weaknesses, temptations, and troubles. Though justified, we are still sinners living in a fallen world. Our bodies grow sick and frail, and eventually we will die. We also constantly face strong enemies, like the devil and his demons. We are hated by the world, which also opposes Jesus Christ and his gospel.

Jesus warned about such troubles: "Then you will be handed over to be persecuted and put to death, and you will be hated by all nations because of me. At that time many will turn away from the faith and will betray and hate each other" (Matt. 24:9–10). Paul said that we wrestle not against flesh and blood, but against principalities and powers arrayed against us (Eph. 6:12).

Because of our many weaknesses, we need the superior, supernatural help of the almighty Sovereign Lord of the universe. We need God's grace! Hebrews 4:14–16 gives us the good news that God has made provision to give us grace through his Son, who is superior to the prophets, to angels, to Moses, and to Aaron and his priesthood. By his incarnation and death on the cross, this superior One earned for us eternal rest, which every believer enters into even now.

When we are facing difficulties, the most foolish thing we can do is to turn away from Christ, yet that is what the Hebrews were tempted to do. We must hold fast to our confession! Later in this epistle the writer exhorts, "Do not throw away your confidence; it will be richly rewarded. You need to persevere so that when you have done the will of God, you will receive what he has promised. For in a just a very little while, 'He who is coming will come and will not delay. But my righteous one will live by faith. If he shrinks back, I will not be pleased with him'" (Heb. 10:35–38).

Because the unbelieving people of Israel in the wilderness did not persevere, they failed to enter into God's everlasting rest for the saints. Like them, we face many troubles and have many needs. But God has given us a solution in this section of Scripture: We must draw near to him and enjoy divine help for living our Christian lives here and now. This passage gives us three reasons for doing so: we have a great high priest, a sympathizing high priest, and a welcoming high priest.

Our Great High Priest

"*Therefore, since we have a great high priest who has gone through the heavens, Jesus the Son of God, let us hold firmly to the faith we profess*" (Heb. 4:14). Throughout this epistle the writer speaks about the work of Jesus Christ, our great high priest, who has solved our problem of sin once and for all: "After he had provided purification for sins, he sat down at the right hand of the Majesty in heaven" (Heb. 1:3). He is the author of our salvation, made perfect through suffering (Heb. 2:10). Through his perfect obedience to God's will, he became the source of our eternal salvation (Heb. 5:9). This Son learned obedience through suffering, becoming man so that he could pay our debt by his death on the cross. Jesus is our elder brother who is interested in helping his weak younger brothers.

Hebrews 2 told us that Jesus is our propitiation, having made atonement for our sins and turning the wrath of God away from us. Though he was tempted in all things, he never yielded to temptation. As we said before, he knew the power of temptation to the fullest degree, for only the one who does not yield knows the full power of temptation. And because he was victorious over all temptations, he is all-powerful to help us. He knows we are weak and he understands our temptations. Do not worry: he is able to help us in every trial we face.

The priesthood of Christ is superior to that of Aaron in every way. The Aaronic high priests could enter the Holy of Holies only on the Day of Atonement. Because they were sinners, they needed to atone for their own sins before they could sacrifice for the sins of the people. So once a year, for a very short time, they would enter the Most Holy Place with the sacrificial blood of an animal and sprinkle the blood on the mercy seat. These Levitical priests could not sit down, for their work was never complete. Additionally, Hebrews 7:23 tells us that there has been a continuous succession of many such high priests, "since death prevented them from continuing in office."

Because of the limitations of these Levitical priests, their sacrifices could not save anyone. Man needed a sinless high priest who could enter into the heavenly sanctuary and finish his work once for all, that he may be seated there forever. Jesus is that great high priest. Having died, risen, and ascended, he has gone through the heavens into the very presence of God. In Christ, then, we have a great high priest who makes intercession for us in the presence of God on the basis of his atonement. He is also called our elder brother, whose atonement was designed to bring many sons to glory.

Christ's atonement is infinitely worthy to deal with our every sin because he is God-man. The Levitical priests could not save anyone, for they themselves were weak and imperfect, and the blood of their animal victims could not atone for sin. The Old Testament sacrificial system pointed to the need of a perfect priest and perfect victim; this need was met in Jesus Christ. As one person in two natures, he alone can sympathize with our weaknesses, yet is almighty to help us.

Our Sympathizing High Priest

Not only do we have a great high priest, but we also have a sympathizing high priest: "*We do not have a high priest who is unable to sympathize with our weaknesses, but we have one who has been tempted in every way, just as we are—yet was without sin"* (Heb. 4:15). The author is using a literary device called litotes—a double negative expressing a positive idea—just as Paul did when he said, "I am not ashamed of the gospel," to mean, "I am proud of the gospel" (Rom. 1:16).

Our great high priest is able to sympathize with *all* our weaknesses. Why should we groan and weep about all our troubles? Why not look up to him who is able to do something about our problems? Jesus is our able high priest (Heb. 2:18). As God-man, he was tempted by the devil in the wilderness, through Peter at Caesarea Philippi, and in the garden of Gethsemane. He endured desertions, denials, defamations, mockings, scourgings, and injustices of every kind. He alone experienced the full range of human infirmities and temptations, yet he was without sin. His sinlessness was demonstrated by his complete conquest of all temptations. Jesus declared, "The prince of this world . . . has no hold on me" (John 14:30).

Hebrews 7:26–27 tells us, "Such a high priest meets our need—one who is holy, blameless, pure, set apart from sinners, exalted above the heavens. Unlike the other high priests, he does not need to offer sacrifices day after day, first for his own sins, and then for the sins of the people." If Jesus were a sinner, he could not meet our need; he himself would need atonement for his sins. But he was not, so we read: "How much more, then, will the blood of Christ, who through the eternal Spirit offered himself unblemished to God, cleanse our consciences from acts that lead to death, so that we may serve the living God!" (Heb. 9:14). Christ's atonement qualifies us to come into God's presence. Paul tells us, "God made him who had no sin to be sin for us, so that in him we might become the righteousness of God" (2 Cor. 5:21).

We do not worship an apathetic Greek god who is unfeeling and therefore cannot identify with us in our weaknesses, problems, and troubles. We have a sympathizing high priest who has been made perfect through suffering.

Jesus sympathizes with us actively. He is not like modern politicians who claim that they feel our pain. To sympathize with us actively means to help us in our time of need. The same word is used to speak of the sympathy the believers showed to their suffering brothers and sisters: "You sympathized with those in prison" (Heb. 10:34). They showed their sympathy by actively helping them—visiting them, giving them food, praying with them, and having fellowship with them.

Paul speaks of actively sympathizing with others through sharing money: "Because of the service by which you have proved yourself, men will praise God for the obedience that accompanies your confession of the gospel of Christ, and for your generosity in sharing with them and with everyone else" (2 Cor. 9:13). Jesus himself told his disciples: "For I was hungry and you gave me something to eat, I was thirsty and you gave me something to drink, I was a stranger and you invited me in, I needed clothes and you clothed me, I was sick and you looked after me, I was in prison and you came to visit me" (Matt. 25:35–36). When they asked how they did these things for him, Jesus answered, "I tell you the truth, whatever you did for one of the least of these brothers of mine, you did for me" (Matt. 25:40). This is the active sympathy that Christ demands we have for our brothers and that he continuously has for us.

Our great high priest not only understands our weaknesses, but he also makes them his own. Isaiah 53:4 (quoted in Matthew 8:17) says, "He took up our infirmities and carried our sorrows." This priest is not a stranger; he is our elder brother. He became incarnate, suffered, died, and made atonement for our sins, not his. He made our problem his problem.

Jesus also sends the Holy Spirit to help us in our weaknesses. Do you need help? The triune God is ready to come to your aid. "In the same way, the Spirit helps us in our weakness" (Rom. 8:26). The Holy Spirit himself prays through us, with groanings that cannot be uttered, and his prayer is always heard.

John MacArthur quotes a story about an evangelist named Booth Tucker:

> [Tucker] was conducting evangelistic meetings in the great Salvation Army Citadel in Chicago. One night after he had preached on the sympathy of Jesus, a man came forward and asked Mr. Tucker how he could talk about a loving, understanding, sympathetic God. "If your wife had just died, like mine had . . . and your babies were crying for their mother who would never come back, you wouldn't be saying what you're saying."

A few days later Mr. Tucker's wife was killed in a train wreck. Her body was brought to Chicago and carried to the Citadel for the funeral. After the service the bereaved preacher looked down into the silent face of his wife and then turned to those who were attending. "The other day when I was here . . . a man told me that if my wife had just died and my children were crying for their mother, I would not be able to say that Christ was understanding and sympathetic, or that he was sufficient for every need. If that man is here, I want to tell him that Christ is sufficient. My heart is broken, it is crushed, but it has a song, and Christ put it there. I want to tell that man that Jesus Christ speaks comfort to me today." The man was there, and he came and knelt beside the casket while Booth Tucker introduced him to Jesus Christ.[1]

Never say that Jesus does not understand. He is our sympathizing high priest, and the object of his sympathy is our weakness.

Our Welcoming High Priest

We also have a welcoming high priest: *"Let us then approach the throne of grace with confidence, so that we may receive mercy and find grace to help us in our time of need"* (Heb. 4:16). Whenever my grandson knocks at the door, I tell him to come in. He has access to my presence, and I gladly welcome him. In the same way, God welcomes us to come to him, especially in our time of need.

These Hebrews were in danger of forsaking their faith in Christ because of false teaching and severe persecution. They wanted to enjoy a trouble-free life of peace and affluence. Knowing they were about to commit the most foolish thing they could do by turning away from the living God, the author exhorts them to do two things that would encourage them: hold firmly to the faith and draw near to God.

Hold Firmly to the Faith

First he exhorts, *"Let us hold firmly to the faith we profess"* (Heb. 4:14). It is in the present tense, meaning, "Let us continuously confess

---

1   MacArthur, *Hebrews*, 114.

and hold on to our faith." To these people who were tempted to turn away to false teaching the writer is saying, "Let us hold fast to our faith that Jesus Christ is our high priest, the Son of God who made purification for our sins. He is the perfect high priest and perfect victim. He was without sin, yet he was crucified for our sins. He died and rose from the dead on the third day according to the Scriptures, was seen by many, and ascended into the heavens to the presence of God, where he is seated at the right hand of God, making intercession for our sins. To him all things are subject; he is made the head of the church, the fullness of him that fills all in all, and he is coming again to judge the living and the dead."

What we believe in our hearts we must publicly proclaim with our mouths. Why do we not declare the gospel? Because we do not believe. In reference to preaching the gospel, Paul quotes Psalm 116:10: "I believed; therefore I have spoken" (2 Cor. 4:13). Jesus himself teaches, "Out of the overflow of the heart the mouth speaks" (Matt. 12:34). What we are convinced of, we will speak.

It is time to be convinced about this great, sympathizing high priest who welcomes us into his heaven. If we really believe the gospel of Christ, we will not hide it: "Let your light shine before men, that they may see your good deeds and praise your Father in heaven" (Matt. 5:16). Throughout the book of Acts, the disciples were constantly witnessing about their faith in Christ. If we are Spirit-filled Christians who believe and hold fast to this confession, then we will also proclaim the gospel without fear. Witnessing faith is the victory that overcomes the world. We must advertise what we believe; if we do not, we must question whether we believe it at all. May God help us to believe and may God forgive us our sin of silence. Do not shrink back! We are to hold fast to our confession even if it means dying for the faith.

Hebrews 12:3–4 exhorts, "Consider him who endured such opposition from sinful men, so that you will not grow weary and lose heart. In your struggle against sin, you have not yet resisted to the point of shedding your blood." To cling to our faith is to be willing to die for it. Christianity is the only faith worth dying for. In Hebrews 13:12–13 we read, "And so Jesus also suffered outside the city gate to make the people holy through his own blood. Let us, then, go to him outside the camp, bearing the disgrace he bore." That is exactly what these people did not want to do. They wanted to have a comfortable life without persecution, shame, and trouble. But there is no such life for a true Christian.

Jesus says, "Whoever acknowledges me before men, I will also acknowledge him before my Father in heaven. But whoever disowns me before men, I will disown him before my Father in heaven" (Matt. 10:32–33). Therefore, let us hold fast and cling to our confession. May we believe it in our heart and prove that we believe by declaring it before men.

Draw Near to God

The second exhortation is *"Let us then approach the throne of grace with confidence"* (Heb. 4:16). We must draw near to God with boldness—not draw back or fall away. Why do people backslide? Because they want to sin. There is no other reason to move away from the true and living God. Such people do not want to be light of the world.

Draw near to God! We have weaknesses and problems, and we need help. The poor widow came to Elisha with a problem, and he solved it (2 Kings 4). When Jesus was on earth, people were constantly bringing problems to him: "My son is full of demons"; "My servant is dying"; "My daughter is dead." Their common cry was that Jesus alone was able to solve their problem.

Thank God, we do not have to go to Jerusalem, or make a hole in the roof of a house to bring our concerns before Jesus. Jesus has made it easy for us to draw near to him. Let us, therefore, draw near to our able, sympathizing, helping high priest.

The Old Testament uses the term "draw near" to describe the service of the priests in the temple. But we need no human priest. Everyone who believes in Jesus is a priest and has the right to draw near to the throne of grace. Whether young or old, weak or strong, every believer is invited to approach God in Jesus Christ. Jesus himself says, "Come to me, all you who are weary and burdened, and I will give you rest" (Matt. 11:28). And in Revelation 22:17 we read, "The Spirit and the bride say, 'Come!' And let him who hears say, 'Come!' Whoever is thirsty, let him come; and whoever wishes, let him take the free gift of the water of life."

When we come to Jesus with all our weaknesses and sins, he will give us rest. He will remove our confusion and give us understanding. He will solve our problems and show us the way to go. He will open a way where there is none, drying up our Red Sea and overflowing Jordan River.

As we come to Christ in repentance and faith, he will receive us, for he promises to never cast us out of his presence. The cross opened what our sin closed; he has prepared heaven for us. The veil is torn from top to bottom. The cross has transformed the throne of judgment to the throne of grace. We must come to that throne. The blood of Christ was sprinkled on the throne, so mercy and grace are now there for us. There is a new and living way made for us by Jesus Christ. Philip Hughes says, "The Son of God came to our aid in the incarnation in order that as our fellow man he might take our place on the cross and then by his resurrection, ascension, and glorification, open the way for us into the presence of God himself."[2]

Draw near! If we are believers, we are priests. Peter tells us, "As you come to him, the living Stone—rejected by men but chosen by God and precious to him—you also, like living stones, are being built into a spiritual house to be a holy priesthood, offering spiritual sacrifices acceptable to God through Jesus Christ" (1 Pet. 2:4–5). We do not need a priest; we have one in the Lord Jesus Christ, and he makes us kings and priests in him: "But you are a chosen people, a royal priesthood, a holy nation, a people belonging to God, that you may declare the praises of him who called you out of darkness into his wonderful light" (1 Pet. 2:9). And not only are we priests, but we are also sons of glory, possessing the full rights of sons. Because we are sons, God our Father welcomes us. We can come to him any and every time, with all our weaknesses, and he will hear our prayers.

We must come to him in boldness. The disciples in the book of Acts were all bold people. Timidity and shame are a result of sin. When we are clothed with salvation and the Spirit of the living God, we will be confident and fearless.

When Christ died for our sins, the barrier of sin was removed, our sins were forgiven and we were justified and adopted into

---

2 Philip E. Hughes, *Commentary on Hebrews*, 170.

God's family. As sons and daughters of God, we may come to the Father, the Son, and the Holy Spirit. We are citizens of the kingdom of God, heirs of God and joint heirs with Christ. We are kings and priests in Christ.

Come, therefore, with confidence; our sin problem has been solved! Draw near in private prayer, family devotions, and Sabbath worship. The writer instructs us: "And let us consider how we may spur one another on toward love and good deeds. Let us not give up meeting together, as some are in the habit of doing, but let us encourage one another—and all the more as you see the Day approaching" (Heb. 10:24–25).

When can we draw near? There is no specific time or place. We can drive and draw near. We can wash the dishes and draw near. Our Father's door is always open. We can come now with all our problems and fears to our welcoming high priest.

We are told to "*approach the throne of grace . . . so that we may receive mercy and find grace*" (Heb. 4:16). We need God's mercy for our failures and his forgiveness for our many sins, both of commission and omission. We receive mercy from the One who is seated on the mercy seat. From there mercy flows to us because of Jesus. Yes, he knows our sins and failures, but he still bids us come to him to receive mercy. Our sins will be forgiven because Jesus Christ is always interceding in behalf of us, and his intercession is always effectual. And not only do we need mercy, but we also need grace to live a Christian life in this world of trouble. We need grace to deal with diseases and chronic conditions. We need grace to live a married life and grace to live a single life. We need grace to get pregnant and give birth and raise those children in godly fear. We need grace to go to school and study under unbelieving teachers. We need grace to witness for Jesus Christ and grace to be longsuffering toward our Christian brothers. We need grace when we face marital troubles. We need grace to resist the devil and overcome daily temptation. We need grace to pray effectually, to help those in need, and to die a good death.

Finally, we are told to draw near to find grace "*to help us in our time of need*" (Heb. 4:16). When we cry out to God in the name of Jesus, our heavenly older brother runs to help us in the nick of time. The sinking Peter cried out, "Lord, save me!" and Jesus reached out and drew him into the boat (Matt. 14:22–33).

Our Christ is not hard-hearted. He is a sympathizing high priest, tender and sensitive to our needs. He gives us timely help.

Paul encourages us: "And God is able to make all grace abound to you, so that in all things at all times, having all that you need, you will abound in every good work" (2 Cor. 9:8). He also wrote about the troubles he faced: "Three times I pleaded with the Lord to take it away from me. But he said to me, 'My grace is sufficient for you, for my power is made perfect in weakness.' Therefore I will boast all the more gladly about my weaknesses, so that Christ's power may rest on me. . . . For when I am weak, then I am strong" (2 Cor. 12:8–10).

We can think all we want about our weaknesses and problems. But after doing so, may we go to our welcoming high priest, who will put his strength into us to deal with those problems. Paul declares, "I can do all things through Christ who strengthens me" (Phil. 4:13, NKJV). Our God does not come late to help us; he comes when we need him.

Let Us Draw Near to God!

Are we afraid, murmuring, and defeated? If so, we are not holding fast to our confession. When we do not draw near to our great high priest and tell him our problems, we forfeit the grace and mercy we could have received. We are trying to be self-sufficient, thinking we can solve our problems without God by leaning onto our own understanding, only to learn that we really cannot solve them.

How do we draw near to God? Let me give an illustration from Luke 11:5–8. A man visited a friend at midnight. This host did not have any bread, so he went to another friend in the middle of the night and asked for bread. The third man said, "I am not going to get up to give you anything. I am tired, I am lying down, and my children are with me." But the man looking for bread did not go away. He kept knocking, and finally his friend got out of bed and gave him all the bread he needed.

That is what God is asking us to do. We have a friend, an older brother, our Lord and Savior Jesus Christ. He is seated in heaven and the door is open. We may come to him any time. "Draw near" is in the present tense, meaning we are to continually draw near because of our continuous need. He is our constant, permanent, and present help. "God is our refuge and strength, an ever-present help in trouble" (Ps. 46:1).

Are you tempted? Are you troubled? Do you have problems? Go to God. Consider this encouraging word from the apostle Paul: "No temptation has overtaken you but such as is common to man; and God is faithful, who will not allow you to be tempted beyond what you are able; but with the temptation will provide the way of escape also, that you may be able to endure it" (1 Cor. 10:13, NASB). This is grace. Our great, sympathizing, welcoming high priest is waiting, in spite of our sins, to welcome us to him. "Come," he says, to the heavenly Zion, to our great God through Jesus Christ. May God help us to heed these exhortations to hold fast to our confession and draw near to him with confidence that we may receive grace in our time of need.

10

Jesus, Our Perfect High Priest

¹*Every high priest is selected from among men and is appointed to represent them in matters related to God, to offer gifts and sacrifices for sins.* ²*He is able to deal gently with those who are ignorant and are going astray, since he himself is subject to weakness.* ³*This is why he has to offer sacrifices for his own sins, as well as for the sins of the people.* ⁴*No one takes this honor upon himself; he must be called by God, just as Aaron was.* ⁵*So Christ also did not take upon himself the glory of becoming a high priest. But God said to him, "You are my Son; today I have become your Father."* ⁶*And he says in another place, "You are a priest forever, in the order of Melchizedek."* ⁷*During the days of Jesus' life on earth, he offered up prayers and petitions with loud cries and tears to the one who could save him from death, and he was heard because of his reverent submission.* ⁸*Although he was a son, he learned obedience from what he suffered* ⁹*and, once made perfect, he became the source of eternal salvation for all who obey him* ¹⁰*and was designated by God to be high priest in the order of Melchizedek.*

Hebrews 5:1–10

Hebrews 5:1–10 speaks about Jesus, our perfect high priest, and his ability to deal with all our problems of sin, ignorance, and wandering away from God. As weak sinners, we need a perfect high priest as well as a perfect victim to be our substitute. We need a perfect mediator who is both perfect God and perfect man to reconcile weak and sinful people to a holy God.

We have such a perfect high priest in Jesus Christ, in whom we have eternal salvation. All our weaknesses are due to our sin.

Through Adam we all became sinners who practice sin daily. For this reason, God must pour out his wrath upon us. Only our perfect high priest can save hell-bound sinners from the wrath to come.

We cannot save ourselves; by God's grace alone are we saved. God instituted a sacrificial system and the Aaronic priesthood for sinners in the Old Testament, all of which pointed to Christ. He is a priest after the order of Melchizedek, a universal and eternal priesthood. Let us, then, examine the characteristics of our great high priest.

1. A Human High Priest

First, we are told that Christ is a human priest: *"Every high priest is selected from among men and is appointed to represent them in matters related to God"* (Heb. 5:1). As humans, we need a human priest, not an angel, to redeem us. Additionally, there is no plan of salvation for fallen angels: "Surely it is not angels he helps, but Abraham's descendants" (Heb. 2:16). Jesus our human high priest is able to sympathize with ignorant and wandering sinners.

2. A Sympathizing High Priest

As we learned in our previous study, Jesus is a sympathizing high priest. In this passage we read, *"He is able to deal gently with those who are ignorant and are going astray, since he himself is subject to weakness"* (Heb. 5:2). "Beset with weakness" is a better translation. Every Aaronic high priest was himself a sinner. Exodus 32:21 speaks about the sin of Aaron, and Zechariah 3:1–5 describes how God removed the sin of the high priest Joshua.

Concerning the high priests of New Testament times, Leon Morris writes:

> In the first century, as [the high priest] laid his hands on the head of the animal, he would say, "O God, I have committed iniquity and transgressed and sinned before thee, I and my house and the children of Aaron, thy holy people. O God, forgive, I pray, the iniquities and transgressions and sins which I have committed and transgressed and sinned before thee, I and my house." Only then was he able to minister on behalf of the people.[1]

Once a year, on the Day of Atonement, the high priest would first offer a bullock for his own sins and then sacrifice a goat for

---

1   Morris, "Hebrews," in vol. 12 of *Expositor's Bible Commentary*, 47.

the sins of the people (Lev. 16). The high priest would have to enter the Holy of Holies twice to sprinkle the blood of these sin offerings upon the mercy seat. Because he himself was a sinner, he was able to deal gently with those who were ignorant and erring from the way of the Lord.

These sinful priests had to make atonement for themselves before they could sacrifice for others. They could not save anyone, for they themselves needed a savior. We, like they, need a perfect, sinless high priest, and we have one in Jesus Christ: "For we do not have a high priest who is unable to sympathize with our weaknesses, but we have one who has been tempted in every way, just as we are—yet was without sin. . . . Such a high priest meets our need—one who is holy, blameless, pure, set apart from sinners, exalted above the heavens. Unlike the other high priests, he does not need to offer sacrifices day after day, first for his own sins, and then for the sins of the people. He sacrificed for their sins once for all when he offered himself" (Heb. 4:15; 7:26–27).

Jesus Christ became a human high priest so that he could help weak, sinful humans like us: "Since the children have flesh and blood, he too shared in their humanity so that by his death he might destroy him who holds the power of death—that is, the devil"—and free us from the devil and from death (Heb. 2:14). And he is able to sympathize with us in our weaknesses and help us in our time of temptation. When we are tempted, he will always make a way out for us.

We need a mediator who is both God and man, one person in two natures, to reconcile us to God and to represent us. This mediator has to be God so that his atonement will have infinite efficacy. Additionally, since the blood of bulls and goats cannot save anyone (Heb. 10:4), we need a perfect victim to be sacrificed as our substitute. We have this perfect high priest, this perfect mediator, this perfect victim in Jesus, the God-man. He did not offer an animal; he offered himself in our place.

3. A High Priest Ordained by God

The high priest was chosen by God himself: "*No one takes this honor upon himself; he must be called by God*" (Heb. 5:4). It was a great honor to be a high priest of Israel and mediate between God and man. A high priest was ordained to his office by God.

Some people wanted to be priests and high priests even though God did not ordain them. God's response was to put such upstarts to death. Korah and his followers rebelled against Moses and Aaron and challenged Aaron's priesthood (Num. 16). After killing these rebels, God declared, "I am going to put an end to this strife. Bring twelve staffs, and the staff that buds and blossoms and bears fruit will be that of the man I have chosen," and Aaron's staff sprouted and bore fruit (Num. 17). Later, when King Uzziah wanted to become a priest to offer sacrifices in the temple, God struck him with leprosy (2 Chron. 26:16–21).

God will not put up with those who take the honor of ministry upon themselves. Pastor T. K. Thomas of India said there are three types of preachers: those who call themselves, those who are called by others, and those who are called by God. I say that ten percent of ministers are called by others, eighty percent are called by themselves, and ten percent are called by God. A number of years ago the president of a seminary told his freshman class: "Unless the Lord has called you to study for the ministry, we do not want you to be here."[2]

Jesus did not take this honor upon himself, but was ordained and appointed by God: "*No one takes this honor upon himself; he must be called by God, just as Aaron was. So Christ also did not take upon himself the glory of becoming a high priest*" (Heb. 5:4–5). To make this point, the author quotes Psalm 2:7: "*You are my Son; today I have become your Father*" and Psalm 110:4: "*You are a priest forever, in the order of Melchizedek*" (Heb. 5:5–6). God the Father chose his eternal Son to be our eternal high priest. We already read that the Son is the eternal king, a descendant of David (Heb. 1:13). The Hebrews author is the only person in the New Testament to bring out this idea that Christ is not only the king eternal, but also the high priest eternal.

In the history of Israel, priesthood and kingship were never combined in one person. In fact, the Qumran community of New Testament times expected two messiahs—a royal messiah of the

---

2   Hendriksen and Kistemaker, *Thessalonians, The Pastorals, and Hebrews*, 134.

Davidic line and a priestly messiah from the line of Aaron. They failed to realize that these two offices were united in Jesus Christ, who is eternal king and eternal high priest after the order of Melchizedek, which is an eternal and universal priesthood. Aaron only represented the Jewish people, but Jesus Christ represents all peoples, both Jew and Gentile.

The writer to the Hebrews tells us: "In the past God spoke to our forefathers through the prophets at many times and in various ways, but in these last days he has spoken to us by his Son, whom he appointed heir of all things, and through whom he made the universe. The Son is the radiance of God's glory and the exact representation of his being, sustaining all things by his powerful word. After he had provided purification for sins, he sat down at the right hand of the Majesty in heaven" (Heb. 1:1-3). Here we see one person fulfilling not only two but, in fact, three offices—prophet, priest and king.

Psalm 110 also declares that the Messiah will be both king and priest, as does the prophet Zechariah:

> Take the silver and gold and make a crown, and set it on the head of the high priest, Joshua son of Jehozadak. Tell him this is what the LORD Almighty says: "Here is the man whose name is the Branch and he will branch out from his place and build the temple of the LORD. It is he who will build the temple of the LORD, and he will be clothed with majesty and will sit and rule on his throne. And he will be a priest on his throne. And there will be harmony between the two." (Zech. 6:11-13)

4. A Suffering High Priest

Next, we learn that Jesus is a suffering high priest who suffered in obedience to God's will: *"During the days of Jesus' life on earth, he offered up prayers and petitions with loud cries and tears to the one who could save him from death, and he was heard because of his reverent submission. Although he was a son, he learned obedience from what he suffered"* (Heb. 5:7-8a). The purpose of the Son's incarnation was to do what Adam failed to do as our representative head. Psalm 40:6-8 (quoted in Heb. 10:5-7) discloses this purpose: "Sacrifice and offering you did not desire, but a body you prepared for me; with burnt offerings and sin offerings you were not pleased. Then I said, 'Here I am—it is written about me in the scroll—*I have come to do your will, O God*'" (italics added).

Christ came to do the will of God perfectly. Isaiah prophesied that "the will of the LORD will prosper in his hand" (Isa. 53:10). This purpose was accomplished specifically through the suffering and death of Jesus for our sins. He came to John the Baptist to be baptized without confessing sins, for he had nothing to confess, but was baptized to fulfill all righteousness. He began his public life with baptism in water and finished it by the baptism of the death of the cross. Jesus walked the way of the will of God—the narrow way of righteousness, the way of the cross—without yielding to temptation.

Isaiah speaks about the Son's obedience in suffering:

> The Sovereign LORD has opened my ears, and I have not been rebellious; I have not drawn back. I offered my back to those who beat me, my cheeks to those who pulled out my beard; I did not hide my face from mocking and spitting. Because the Sovereign LORD helps me, I will not be disgraced. Therefore have I set my face like flint, and I know I will not be put to shame. (Isa. 50:5–7)

I hope we will reject the theology that a Christian should never suffer but always enjoy prosperity and health. Such teaching is the damnable doctrine of demons. Suffering is part of doing the will of God.

Jesus learned obedience in the school of suffering. In fact, he chose the way of suffering, learning what it was to obey when obedience meant suffering. With all his frailties in this fallen world, Christ fully obeyed the will of his Father. Therefore his Father was pleased with him and said, "This is my Son, whom I love; with him I am well pleased. Listen to him!" (Matt. 17:5). Living a life of dependence and prayer, Christ taught his disciples to pray that they may not enter into temptation. He taught them to deny themselves daily, take up the cross, and follow him to death.

"*He offered up prayers and petitions with loud cries and tears*" (Heb. 5:7). The specific reference is likely to Gethsemane, where Christ experienced the intense agony of hell even to the point of sweating blood (cf. Mark 14:34; Luke 22:44). Jesus was not asking God to save him from physical death; many people had experienced the physical death of crucifixion. But he was greatly troubled because of the eternal death he was about to die for the sin of the world. He who knew no sin became the worst sinner as the sins of the world were put on him. He was about to suffer what the book of Revelation calls the second death, to be forsaken by his Father and cut off from his cherished communion with him. He was about to go to hell, so he prayed with loud cries and tears.

B. F. Westcott speaks about three kinds of prayer: silent prayer, crying with raised voice, and prayer with tears. He notes, "There is no door through which tears do not pass." [3] The prayer of tears overcomes all obstacles and goes directly to the throne of God.

We are told the Father heard the prayer of Jesus because of his *eulabeia*—his life surrendered to the will of God. I would translate it as "his obedience," for God does not hear the prayers of rebels. *Eulabeia* is also used in Hebrews 12:28–29: "Therefore, since we are receiving a kingdom that cannot be shaken, let us be thankful, and so worship God acceptably *with reverence and awe*, for our 'God is a consuming fire'" (italics added). Contrast this with much of today's "worship," which is, in reality, pure entertainment with no consciousness of a holy God in the midst of the people.

As Jesus cried out with loud shouts and tears, the Lord heard him and sent an angel to strengthen him. We know his prayer was heard because God raised him from the dead on the third day. Jesus fulfilled God's will actively by obeying his Father in life and passively by his death on the cross. By his obedience, he accomplished redemption for us.

5. A Perfect High Priest

We then learn that Jesus is a perfect high priest after the order of Melchizedek: *"Son though he was, he learned obedience through suffering, and was made perfect"* (Heb. 5:8–9a, author's translation). When Adam sinned, he plunged the whole world into sin. Thus, even the Aaronic priesthood was imperfect because of the sin of

---

3   Westcott, *Epistle to the Hebrews*, 126.

the high priests. We needed a high priest who was perfect and would perfectly obey the Father.

Jesus said always, "Not my will but thine be done," despite any suffering he would experience. Through his perfect obedience, he became both perfect mediator and perfect victim on our behalf. So he alone is completely qualified to be our high priest. Hebrews 2:10 says, "In bringing many sons to glory, it was fitting that God, for whom and through whom everything exists, should make the author of their salvation perfect through suffering." There was no other way.

Unlike us, Jesus Christ did not move from disobedience to obedience; instead, he moved from untested to tested and proven obedience. He did not go from imperfection to perfection, but from perfection to tested and proven perfection. He is our perfect high priest.

6. *The Source of Eternal Salvation*

"Once made perfect, [Christ] became the source of eternal salvation for all who obey him" (Heb. 5:9). From the eternal Son comes eternal salvation. There is no other high priest, no other mediator between God and man, no other Savior. Jesus alone is the well of salvation to which all must come and drink: "Come unto me and drink . . . and out of your innermost being shall flow rivers of living water" (John 7:37–38, author's translation). He gave living water to the sinful Samaritan woman (John 4). He alone is our propitiation, the source of our eternal salvation. Paul writes, "It is because of him that you are in Christ Jesus, who has become for us wisdom from God—that is, our righteousness, holiness and redemption" (1 Cor. 1:30).

When Jesus saves a sinner, he does so, not for a day, but for eternity; he is the source of *eternal* salvation. This is an Old Testament idea: "But Israel will be saved by the Lord with an everlasting salvation" (Isa. 45:17), which we find repeated in Hebrews 9: "He did not enter by means of the blood of goats and calves; but he entered the Most Holy Place once for all by his own blood, having obtained eternal redemption. . . . For this reason Christ is the mediator of a new covenant, that those who are called may receive the promised eternal inheritance" (vv. 12, 15).

Hebrews 13:20 also speaks about this eternal covenant. Jesus Christ has no successor as high priest because his once-for-all sacrifice accomplished our eternal redemption. The eternal Son gives us eternal salvation in which we can be secure forever.

7. The Savior of All Who Obey Him

If Jesus has saved us by grace, we will obey him throughout our lives: *"And once made perfect, he became the source of eternal salvation for all who obey him"* (Heb. 5:9). "Obey" is in the present tense, meaning our obedience is ongoing. To say we believe in Jesus and disobey him at the same time is anti-Christian. Yet we see this phenomenon often, especially in countries with great material prosperity and political peace. If a person habitually disobeys Jesus, we must conclude that Jesus did not save that person and that person's claim to be a Christian is false. All antinomians are antichrists.

The apostles would not have agreed with the modern teaching that one can reject God's law and yet be a Christian. In his first epistle, John wrote, "If we claim to have fellowship with him yet walk in the darkness, we lie and do not live by the truth. . . . The man who says, 'I know him,' but does not do what he commands is a liar, and the truth is not in him" (1 John 1:6; 2:4). In the beginning of Romans, Paul speaks about the commission he received from God: "Through him and for his name's sake, we received grace and apostleship to call people from among all the Gentiles *to the obedience that comes from faith*" (Rom. 1:5, italics added). At the end of the same epistle, he declares the hope that "all nations might believe and obey him" (Rom. 16:26). Elsewhere Paul writes, "For we are God's workmanship, created in Christ Jesus to do good works, which God has foreordained that we should walk in them" (Eph. 2:10, author's translation). And Peter says: "We are witnesses of these things, and so is the Holy Spirit, whom God has given to those who obey him" (Acts 5:32).

Finally, look at the words of Jesus: "Not everyone who says to me, 'Lord, Lord,' will enter the kingdom of heaven, but only he who does the will of my Father who is in heaven. Many will say to me on that day, 'Lord, Lord, did we not prophesy in your name, and in your name drive out demons and perform many miracles?'

Then I will tell them plainly, 'I never knew you. Away from me, you evildoers!" (Matt. 7:21–23). A good tree will produce good fruit, while a bad tree produces bad fruit. It is that simple. Philip Hughes says, "The eternal salvation of which he is the source is a reality in the experience of those *who obey him.*" Then Hughes quotes B. F. Westcott: "Continuous active obedience is the sign of real faith."[4]

Examine yourselves. If Jesus saved you by grace, you will live an obedient life by grace. What God has united, no one shall put asunder. Jesus is both Lord and Savior. Even now he is saving all who obey him, whether Jew and Gentile, because his priesthood is the universal priesthood of the order of Melchizedek. He is not saving those who disobey him. We are to confess with our mouths, "Jesus is Lord," as an acknowledgment that we are his subjects and servants. Jesus saves such people with eternal salvation. If Jesus learned obedience by the things he suffered, we are not exempt. Jesus said we are to deny ourselves daily, take up the cross, and follow him to death. But we do not worry about death. We can say with Paul, "To me to live is Christ and to die is gain" (Phil. 1:21).

Is Jesus Your High Priest?

Are you a sinner? If so, you have a perfect high priest and perfect victim whose sacrifice has been accepted by the Father. Jesus Christ alone accomplished eternal salvation. Surrender to him today and be saved forever.

Are you a saint, saved by Christ? If so, know that he is not only your high priest, but he is also your eternal king. Therefore, ask yourself: Do I obey him gladly? If not, your profession is false. But if you are an obedient Christian, rejoice and proclaim this eternal salvation.

We were ignorant and erring hell-bound people of weakness and sin. But "God so loved the world that he gave his one and only Son, that whoever believes in him shall not perish but have eternal life" (John 3:16). It is pure grace that saves us and enables us to love God and walk in the straight and narrow way to the

---

4   Philip E. Hughes, *Commentary on Hebrews*, 188.

end. May God save his people today that they may rejoice in their eternal salvation.

11
Muscular Christianity

[11]We have much to say about this, but it is hard to explain because you are slow to learn. [12]In fact, though by this time you ought to be teachers, you need someone to teach you the elementary truths of God's word all over again. You need milk, not solid food! [13]Anyone who lives on milk, being still an infant, is not acquainted with the teaching about righteousness. [14]But solid food is for the mature, who by constant use have trained themselves to distinguish good from evil.

Hebrews 5:11–14

The writer begins this section, "*We have much to say about this, but it is hard to explain because you are slow to learn*" (Heb. 5:11). The recurring theme of the book of Hebrews is the high priesthood of Jesus Christ after the order of Melchizedek. But the church of the Hebrews, now about thirty years old, was not mentally equipped to understand this doctrine and live out its vital implications. This doctrine demands muscular, not mushy, Christians. It requires adult Christians, not ones who desire to regress to infancy.

Hindrances to Muscular Christianity

The Hebrews were not growing intellectually because mature knowledge of Christianity demanded that they forsake Judaism with its laws, covenant, and high priesthood, and follow Jesus Christ as the perfect high priest. It demanded continued suffering for the gospel, and these people had grown tired of being persecuted. They said, "No more of this denying ourselves, taking up the cross, and following Jesus to death." They wanted a religion that entertained them, a religion of escape and mental inactivity. They were not ready to go to heaven; they wanted to enjoy life in the here and now.

These people were in danger of abandoning the true gospel that includes suffering and high spiritual discipline in order to embrace a trouble-free gospel of peace, health, and affluence at all costs. They wanted a second childhood in which they would be taken care of and not have to assume any responsibility, especially the responsibility of evangelizing. They did not want the solid food of Christian thought. Like children, they just wanted a little colored sugar water.

This is true of many churches today. People want to enjoy life, not to suffer for Christ. It is as if people are declaring, "Don't teach us doctrines. Don't even speak about basic Christianity! We will fill the church, but only if you stop preaching the truth of God's word and start speaking pleasant things to amuse us."

The author is warning these Hebrews about their spiritual inertia, mental laziness, and regression into childhood. He has already warned them several times: "We must pay more careful attention. . . . Therefore, holy brothers, fix your thoughts on Jesus. . . . Do not harden your hearts. . . . See to it, brothers, that none of you has a sinful and unbelieving heart that turns away from the living God. . . . Therefore, since the promise of entering his rest still stands, let us be careful that none of you be found to have fallen short of it. . . . Therefore, since we have a great high priest who has gone through the heavens, Jesus the Son of God, let us hold fast to our confession" (Heb. 2:1; 3:1, 8, 12; 4:1, 14). Now he gives another warning in this passage—a warning against the enemies of muscular Christianity. Who are these enemies?

Delighting in Laziness

The first enemy of muscular Christianity is a delight in laziness. The author wants to discuss the gloriously liberating doctrine of the Melchizedekian high priesthood of Christ. But he finds it difficult to do so, not because he is incapable of expressing it clearly or because the doctrine is shrouded in mystery, but because the people he is addressing have become mentally lazy. It was not the writer's problem nor the problem of the doctrine; it was the people's problem. This author uses the word *nōthros*, "not pushing," translated here as "slow to learn," meaning his listeners were not putting forth much intellectual effort. This word is used again in Hebrews 6:12. These people were not working hard to understand the gospel they were hearing. It is also used in the Septuagint version of Proverbs to mean "sluggard" when addressing those who refused to do hard work.

The church of the Hebrews was filled with spiritual sluggards. This was a strong rebuke from their pastor. Theirs was not a natural intellectual deficiency but an acquired one. These people willfully refused to understand the gospel with its liberating implications, and then refused to believe what they did understand. They had become like the soils that did not produce any fruit, for without the root of understanding, they could not produce any fruit of obedience. About such people Jesus teaches, "When anyone hears the message about the kingdom and does not understand it, the evil one comes and snatches away what was sown in his heart" (Matt. 13:19). They stand in stark contrast to the good soil: "But the one who received the seed that fell on good soil is the man who hears the word and understands it. He produces a crop, yielding a hundred, sixty or thirty times what was sown" (v. 23).

We cannot stand still in the Christian life: we are either advancing or backsliding. The Hebrews seemed to be working hard to go backward, like someone going the wrong way on an escalator. Theirs was a revolt against spiritual maturity.

This type of rebellion is found throughout the Bible. The Lord told Ezekiel, "Son of man, you are living among a rebellious people. They have eyes to see but do not see and ears to hear but they do not hear, for they are a rebellious people" (Ezek. 12:2). Jeremiah asked, "To whom can I speak and give warning? Who will listen to me? Their ears are closed so they cannot hear. The word of the LORD is offensive to them; they find no pleasure in it" (Jer. 6:10). The word of God is designed to give us unending joy. Yet these people found it offensive and rejected it.

Quoting Isaiah, Jesus says, "This is why I speak to them in parables: 'Though seeing, they do not see; though hearing, they do not hear or understand.' In them is fulfilled the prophecy of

Isaiah: 'You will be ever hearing but never understanding; you will be ever seeing but never perceiving. For this people's heart has become calloused; they hardly hear with their ears, and they have closed their eyes. Otherwise they might see with their eyes, hear with their ears, understand with their hearts and turn, and I would heal them'" (Matt. 13:13–15). Elsewhere he warns, "Therefore consider carefully how you listen" (Luke 8:18). Faith comes by hearing. If we fail to understand, how can we believe and enter the saints' everlasting rest?

The Hebrews failed to put forth effort and exercise their mental faculties. They became passive, desiring only to be entertained. But such passivity produces perpetual babies. God's revelation is always coming to us through our parents, teachers, and pastors. But after some time, it becomes mere background noise instead of clear propositional revelation—not because their words have ceased to be revelational, but because we have become so accustomed to them that we have ceased to pay attention.

What are we hearing when the word of God is preached? Is it just static, mere noise? If so, may God take the wax out of our spiritual ears. "He who has an ear, let him hear what the Spirit says to the churches" (see Rev. 2 and 3).

Delighting in Second Childhood

The second hindrance to muscular Christianity is taking delight in a second childhood. These people had enough time to learn God's word, graduate, and become teachers. They had enough time to become the parents of spiritual children by evangelizing and discipling others. But these Hebrews refused to father spiritual children and teach them, like many people today who abort children so that they can have a good life for themselves. They refused to produce the fruit that comes from abiding in Christ and his teachings.

Paul understood this problem of immaturity: "Brothers, I could not address you as spiritual but as worldly—mere infants in Christ. I gave you milk, not solid food, for you were not yet ready for it. Indeed, you are still not ready" (1 Cor. 3:1–2). Peter describes what mature believers are expected to do: "But in your hearts set apart Christ as Lord. Always be prepared to give an

Muscular Christianity

answer to everyone who asks you to give the reason for the hope that you have" (1 Pet. 3:15). Muscular Christianity evangelizes, teaches, and produces mature adults.

The text tells us that these people had an obligation to teach others, but they refused to fulfill it because they were self-centered. Not wanting to grow up, they became like the fig tree that produced no fruit for the master. So the master came and demanded, "Cut it down! Why should it use up the soil?" (Luke 13:7). They wanted to regress into the comfort zone of a second childhood, as if they were college seniors blissfully going back to kindergarten. They needed to be re-taught the elementary and foundational teachings, the ABCs of divine revelation, which are listed in Hebrews 6:1-2.

The writer was saying, "You still need milk, not the solid food of this great teaching of Christ's high priesthood." Parents want their children to eat solid food so that they can grow up, be responsible, and have families of their own. But to eat solid food, we need teeth and the ability to digest such food. Many modern evangelicals are undergoing a second childhood experience like that of the Hebrews. In fact, some do not even want to drink the milk of the basic gospel; they prefer colored sugar water that lacks any spiritual nutrition. Such a diet can never produce the muscular, death-defying, cross-bearing Christianity that Paul speaks about: "Not that I have already obtained all this, or have already been made perfect, but I press on to take hold of that for which Christ Jesus took hold of me. Brothers, I do not consider myself yet to have taken hold of it. But one thing I do: Forgetting what is behind and straining toward what is ahead, I press on toward the goal to win the prize for which God has called me heavenward in Christ Jesus" (Phil. 3:12-14).

The Hebrew Christians wanted to go back to childhood because children do not have to be responsible for themselves, suffer, or produce more children. It is the duty of others to feed, carry, clean, and entertain them. Whenever they cry, someone comes. They can make a mess and someone else will take care of it. Childhood is a beautiful stage of life, but a second childhood is a monstrosity. Every normal child wants to grow up as quickly as possible. But the Hebrews refused to become responsible adults.

The writer says those who drink milk are inexperienced and

unskilled in the "word of righteousness" (Heb. 5:13, KJV). They do not want to learn or teach others about being right with God through Christ's righteousness. They are mentally lazy. Instead of hungering and thirsting after righteousness, they have a blank look and sometimes even fall asleep when serious doctrines are taught. Thus, they remain immature and weak. They are not interested in learning how to live a holy life; they want to live the way they please. They will confess Jesus as Savior but never as Lord. They want to be babies forever.

These Hebrews were enjoying their second childhood and glorying in being lazy and infantile. But arrested development is not normal for Christians. Paul exhorts us to stretch our minds: "Brothers, stop thinking like children. In regard to evil be infants, but in your thinking be adults" (1 Cor. 14:20). Elsewhere, in writing about God's goal for his people, he explains:

> It was [Christ] who gave some to be apostles, some to be prophets, some to be evangelists, some to be pastors and teachers, to prepare God's people for works of service, so that the body of Christ may be built up until we all reach unity in the faith and in the knowledge of the Son of God and become mature, attaining to the whole measure of the fullness of Christ. Then we will no longer be infants, tossed back and forth by the waves, and blown here and there by every wind of teaching and by the cunning and craftiness of men in their deceitful scheming. Instead, speaking the truth in love, we will in all things grow up into him who is the Head, that is, Christ. (Eph. 4:11–15)

Again, Paul says, "When I was a child, I talked like a child, I thought like a child, I reasoned like a child. When I became a man, I put childish ways behind me" (1 Cor. 13:11).

Hating Discipline

The third hindrance to muscular Christianity is a hatred of discipline. This leads to an incapacity to discern correctly. As lazy infants who prefer the baby food of stories and entertainment, such people cannot eat the meat of the gospel because they have no spiritual teeth. They have no experience with the word of righteousness. They sleep through family devotions and worship

Muscular Christianity

services, especially when the gospel is being preached with all power and unction. They have no delight in regular, methodical, and painstaking Bible study. Therefore, they lack the ability to discern and make decisions correctly. They are like Esau, who married pagan women, though he was a member of the covenant and circumcised by his godly father, Isaac. They are like Judah, who chose to have sexual relations with a presumed temple prostitute, though he was a covenant son of Jacob.

Because these people refuse to acquaint themselves with God's standard of life revealed in the Bible, they lack wisdom and cannot discriminate between good and evil. This is the nature of perpetual babyhood. Children are known for their lack of judgment. Unattended, they may even eat mud, poison, or whatever else their little hands find.

Spiritual babies are cultural conformists and spiritual chameleons. They will say that premarital sex, pornography, abortion, homosexuality, divorce, lying, and other sins are acceptable. They have no problem asking their parents to take care of them, even when they themselves are in their thirties, forties, or fifties. They reason, "Don't most people work too much and try too hard to succeed? I think it is better to relax and not be very serious about studying. Not only that, why should I evangelize anyone? Don't all religions teach the same thing?"

Such people lack judgment because they refuse to discipline their mental faculties in the word of righteousness. Christians are to hear and do the word of God until obedience becomes their second nature. Jesus himself said we are to hear and do these things. Such people, however, refuse to become athletic Christians of great discernment and judgment, competent to make correct decisions and give wise counsel in every life situation.

Mature muscular Christians are those who have disciplined themselves in acquiring the wisdom of the word (see Psalms 1, 19, and 119). When we love discipline, we will be spiritual people who can make judgments about all things, yet are not subject to any man's judgment (1 Cor. 2:15). We will be like young Joseph, who lived a life of godly discipline even when he was in Egypt. When Potiphar's wife approached him to sleep with him, he said, "How then could I do such a wicked thing and sin against God?" (Gen. 39:9). It is not that he just came up with this idea; he spoke that way because he had a habit of godly living and knew that adultery is against God's word. We will be like Daniel, who refused to defile himself by eating food not permitted by the word of God. We will be like the three young Hebrew men who, because they had lived in godliness all their lives, decided to suffer death rather than to worship the image of gold (Dan. 3).

Discipline gives us the *habit* and *power* to make right decisions and stick with them. Muscular Christians are strong in spirit to always choose what is in accord with God's word. They have the power of the habit of godliness, which then manifests itself in successful lives. The enemy of muscular Christianity is a detestation of discipline—spiritual, regular exercise in godliness. Those who detest spiritual discipline are weak and self-indulgent. They are incapable of resisting even the weakest form of temptation.

Donald Guthrie said that muscular Christianity "comes neither from isolated events nor from a great spiritual burst. It comes from a steady application of spiritual discipline."[1] Isaiah 40 speaks about such spiritual power: "[God] gives strength to the weary and increases the power of the weak. Even youths grow tired and weary, and young men stumble and fall; but those who hope in the LORD will renew their strength. They will soar on wings like eagles; they will run and not grow weary, they will walk and not be faint" (vv. 29–31). Paul, a great spiritual athlete and muscular Christian, tells us, "Have nothing to do with godless myths and old wives' tales; rather, train yourself to be godly. For physical training is of some value, but godliness has value for all things, holding promise for both the present life and the life to come" (1 Tim. 4:7–8). In 1 Corinthians 9:24–27 Paul tells us how he disciplined himself to become a muscular Christian.

Due to his habit of exercising his mental faculties in God's word, a muscular Christian is able to judge what is right before God and what is evil, and to embrace the good while rejecting the evil. Like Jesus, he would say, "It is written, so I decide to do this and not that." A baby Christian has no such capacity and tends to choose evil rather than good.

A muscular Christian will walk in the way outlined for him

---

[1] Guthrie, *Letter to the Hebrews*, 136.

in the word: "For we are God's workmanship, created in Christ Jesus to do good works, which God prepared in advance for us to do" (Eph. 2:10). Led by the Spirit and the Scripture, he makes steady progress forward to attain the maturity of knowing Christ. Walking in the narrow way and avoiding the broad way, he loves righteousness and hates wickedness. As a spiritual adult, he is always advancing in his knowledge of God. From glory to glory, he is being changed. Such a person is a wise man. What a blessing it is to listen to such a wise Christian adult!

We must refuse to conform to the regression and retardation of the evangelical and charismatic world. We must refuse the colored sugar water of modern evangelists; instead, we must teach the word of God. Our goal is to present everyone mature in Christ. Let us, therefore, determine to stop being undiscerning, lazy, culturally conforming babies, and begin to work hard to become muscular, athletic Christians. May we be soldiers of Christ, faithfully exercising ourselves in godliness. May we hear and do God's word until it becomes a habit in our lives to know the will of God and delightfully do it, that we may be changed from glory to glory until we attain to the whole measure of the fullness of Christ (Eph. 4:11–15). May we glory in godliness and, as mature people, produce and train spiritual children, that they too may grow up in the knowledge of God.

12
Eternal Security and Eternal Insecurity

¹*Therefore let us leave the elementary teachings about Christ and go on to maturity, not laying again the foundation of repentance from acts that lead to death, and of faith in God,* ²*instruction about baptisms, the laying on of hands, the resurrection of the dead, and eternal judgment.* ³*And God permitting, we will do so.* ⁴*It is impossible for those who have once been enlightened, who have tasted the heavenly gift, who have shared in the Holy Spirit,* ⁵*who have tasted the goodness of the word of God and the powers of the coming age,* ⁶*if they fall away, to be brought back to repentance, because to their loss they are crucifying the Son of God all over again and subjecting him to public disgrace.* ⁷*Land that drinks in the rain often falling on it and that produces a crop useful to those for whom it is farmed receives the blessing of God.* ⁸*But land that produces thorns and thistles is worthless and is in danger of being cursed. In the end it will be burned.* ⁹*Even though we speak like this, dear friends, we are confident of better things in your case—things that accompany salvation.* ¹⁰*God is not unjust; he will not forget your work and the love you have shown him as you have helped his people and continue to help them.* ¹¹*We want each of you to show this same diligence to the very end, in order to make your hope sure.* ¹²*We do not want you to become lazy, but to imitate those who through faith and patience inherit what has been promised.*

Hebrews 6:1-12

This passage deals with apostasy and the saints' eternal security. Let me begin with a few questions. Can professing Christians become apostate? Surprisingly, the answer is both yes and no. Do all professing Christians go to heaven? The answer is no. Do regenerate Christians become apostate? Again, the answer is no. If the Holy Spirit has granted a person spiritual resurrection, he shall persevere to the end. It is impossible for such a person to become apostate. He cannot lose his salvation because he has been made a good tree by the Spirit of the living God. Jesus said a good tree always produces good fruit, and a bad tree always produces bad fruit; a good tree cannot produce bad fruit, nor can a bad tree produce good fruit. What we need is a miraculous transformation, a new creation in the center of our being.

Many professing Christians are not regenerate; therefore, they cannot enter heaven, but will go to hell to experience eternal punishment. F.F. Bruce declares, "People are frequently immunized against a disease by being inoculated with a mild form of it, or with a related, milder disease."[1] Scores of professing Christians have been immunized against the real Christianity that teaches that we must deny ourselves daily, take up the cross, and follow Jesus Christ to the end of our lives. In reality, many professing Christians are only baptized pagans. Such people are without God and without hope in the world. They confess Jesus as Lord but do not obey him. On the day of judgment, the Lord shall say to them, "Depart from me. I never knew you!"

Every gospel-preaching Christian church can be represented by two concentric circles. There is an inner circle of regenerate Christians, whom the Bible calls wheat, and an outer circle of unregenerate Christians, or weeds. On the day of judgment, when Jesus Christ comes again, he will separate the wheat from the tares.

Let us, then, examine this passage that speaks about eternal security and insecurity, and then look at ourselves to see whether we are truly in the faith.

Desire Maturity

"Let us leave the elementary teachings about Christ and go on to maturity" (Heb. 6:1). The first point is that true believers have a desire to move from the foundational doctrines toward maturity.

---

1   Bruce, *Epistle to the Hebrews*, 144.

Like milk to newborn infants, our foundation in the faith is very important. Without a foundation, no building is possible. Paul says, "By the grace God has given me, I laid a foundation as an expert builder, and someone else is building on it" (1 Cor. 3:10). He says elsewhere that the church is "built on the foundation of the apostles and prophets, with Christ Jesus himself as the chief cornerstone" (Eph. 2:20). The world is filled with churches without biblical foundations. They are not churches of Jesus Christ; they are synagogues of Satan.

Some people resist growing up because they do not want to assume responsibilities. But we are not to remain infants. We must grow, lest we regress and die. So the author urges us to go on to maturity as God permits. The Greek word behind "to go on" is *pherōmetha*, which means to be carried along to maturity. The emphasis here may not be on human effort as much as on God's work in this process. In other words, the Holy Spirit will carry us along as we trust him and yield to his guidance: "Those who are being led by the Spirit of God—they are the sons of God" (Rom. 8:14, author's translation). We are to surrender ourselves fully to the Spirit's leading and teaching.

This word is also used by Peter when he speaks of the human authorship of the Scriptures: "For prophecy never had its origin in the will of man, but men spoke from God as they were carried along by the Holy Spirit" (2 Pet. 1:21). Are you yielded to the Holy Spirit to be taught by him?

Leave Infancy

"Let us . . . go on to maturity; not laying again the foundation of repentance from acts that lead to death, and of faith in God, instruction about baptisms, the laying on of hands, the resurrection of the dead, and eternal judgment" (Heb. 6:1–2). The second point is that we must leave infancy. The author is speaking here of foundational doctrines. A foundation, once laid, should not need to be laid again. What we ought to be doing is building on that foundation as we exercise faith in God's truth and progress to maturity. The author gives a list of these foundational doctrines, which are as vital to the foundation of our Christian lives as milk is to newborn babies.

1. Repentance from Dead Works

The first doctrine is *"repentance from dead works"* (Heb. 6:1). Repentance (*metanoia*) is a change of mind and attitude. It is a whole change of one's worldview, a new *Weltanschauung*, a way of looking at reality that is the exact opposite of what one was accustomed to. It is a change of direction in one's life's journey, a turning around and going in the opposite direction. A repenting person will hate all the wicked works he did while he was living in sin.

This happened to the prodigal son. His repentance was authentic and godly. He "came to his senses" and began to think correctly (Luke 15:17). A non-Christian's thoughts always revolve around himself, not God. "The fool says in his heart, 'There is no God'" (Ps. 14:1). But when we repent, we realize that God is the center of everything.

God commands all people everywhere to repent (Acts 17:30). Jesus proclaims, "Repent or perish!" (cf. Luke 13:1–5). "Perish" means eternal damnation; an unrepentant person cannot go to heaven. John the Baptist and the apostles told people to repent, and today godly preachers, parents, and others also tell us to repent. Tomorrow we may die, but today we have the opportunity to repent.

Repentance is a gift from God. If anyone truly repents, it is because God granted him repentance. Peter declared, "God exalted [Jesus] to his own right hand as Prince and Savior that he might give repentance and forgiveness of sins to Israel" (Acts 5:31). God sent his eternal Son to take upon himself human nature, suffer, and die to make atonement for our sins. This Jesus, who was raised up and ascended into heaven as the Sovereign Lord of the universe, gives this gift of repentance. Receive it from him.

2. Faith in God

Second, the author speaks about *"faith in God"* (Heb. 6:1), or, more literally, "faith upon (*epi*) God." Not only must we turn from wickedness and dead works, but we must also turn to God by trusting in Jesus Christ alone for salvation. There is a turning *from* and a turning *to*. Faith is resting upon Jesus Christ.

Paul speaks often of such faith: "I have declared to both Jews and Greeks that they must turn to God in repentance and have faith in our Lord Jesus" (Acts 20:21). When the Philippian jailer asked, "What must I do to be saved?" Paul answered, "Believe in the Lord Jesus, and you will be saved—you and your household" (Acts 16:31). Elsewhere he describes how the pagans "turned to God from idols to serve the living and true God" (1 Thess. 1:9). If we do not worship Jesus Christ, we are worshipers of idols. We can deny it all we want, but we are worshiping creation rather than the Creator.

Saving faith is not merely agreeing that certain facts of the Bible are true. Such agreement is called *assensus*. True saving faith goes beyond agreeing with information. It is trusting (*fiducia*) in God, resting upon God. Such a person's foundation is the almighty God, not one's self. Saving faith is trusting in this God and his Son and living in obedience to him till death.

3. Teaching about Baptisms

The third foundational doctrine is *"instruction about baptisms"* (Heb. 6:2). Hebrews 9:10 speaks about various ritual washings the people of Israel experienced. There was the proselyte baptism, when a pagan wanted to become a believing Jew, and John's baptism, which was baptism unto repentance. Then, of course, there is Christian baptism, which is the only baptism that matters now. Christian baptism is an external act dramatizing the internal reality of one's identification with Jesus in his death, burial, and resurrection. A person who is baptized in the name of the triune God should live in obedience to God all his life. One who is born of God will find such a life delightful. He enjoys the life of God in his soul. Thus, those who find obedience to God burdensome must examine very seriously their profession of faith in Christ.

4. Laying on of Hands

Fourth, we read about *"laying on of hands"* (Heb. 6:2). The Bible describes several purposes for the laying on of hands. Jesus laid hands on children to bless them and on sick people to heal them (Mark 10:16; Luke 4:40). The New Testament speaks of laying on of hands to ordain and set people apart to work for the Lord (Acts 6:6; 13:3; 1 Tim. 5:22). In Acts we also read of laying on of hands as a way for people to receive the Holy Spirit (Acts 8:17; 19:6).

5. Resurrection of the Dead

Next, the author speaks of *"the resurrection of the dead"* (Heb. 6:2). All who have died throughout the history of the world will be raised up on the last day at God's command: "Do not be amazed at this, for a time is coming when all who are in their graves will hear his voice and come out—those who have done good will rise to live, and those who have done evil will rise to be condemned" (John 5:28-29; cf. Dan. 12:2; Rev. 20:13).

6. Eternal Judgment

The final doctrine is *"eternal judgment"* (Heb. 6:2). Elsewhere, the author writes, "Man is destined to die once, and after that to face judgment" (Heb. 9:27). God the Father has given his Son authority to judge all people (John 5:27). Jesus himself says, "By myself I can do nothing; I judge only as I hear, and my judgment is just" (John 5:30).

Who do you say Jesus is? This is a very important question. Have you confessed him as God's Son, the only Savior, sinless man who was crucified for our sins, buried, and raised from the dead? Do you confess that he is the Sovereign Lord of the universe, the one who sustains you even at this moment, the one who will judge all men? "When the Son of Man comes in his glory, and all the angels with him, he will sit on his throne in heavenly glory" (Matt. 25:31). When he summons, all will come out of their graves and assemble before him, and he will separate the goats from the sheep: "Then they will go away to eternal punishment, but the righteous to eternal life" (Matt. 25:46).

What we think about Jesus matters because if our thinking is wrong, we can be guilty of eternal sin. Jesus tells us, "Whoever blasphemes against the Holy Spirit will never be forgiven; he is guilty of an eternal sin" (Mark 3:29). Eternal sin is rejecting the Holy Spirit's testimony concerning Jesus—that he is the Son of God; that he is the sinless one; that he died on the cross for our salvation; that he was crucified and went to hell; that he was buried and was raised on the third day according to the Scriptures; that he ascended into the heavens and is seated on the right hand of God the Father; that all things are subject to him; that he is the Creator and Sustainer of the universe. This testimony is found in the Scriptures. The Bible is the book of the Holy Spirit, in which God, who cannot lie, testifies concerning his Son. Jesus himself teaches that the Law, the Prophets, and the Writings all speak of him (Luke 24:27, 44).

Eternal sin is rejection of this testimony concerning Christ. Such people will receive eternal judgment, meaning they will remain in hell forever; there is no way out. All who ever lived are going to hell unless they repent and believe in Jesus Christ.

Warning of Apostasy

Next, the author warns his readers about the danger of apostasy:

> It is impossible for those who have once been enlightened, who have tasted the heavenly gift, who have shared in the Holy Spirit, who have tasted the goodness of the word of God and the powers of the coming age, if they fall away, to be brought back to repentance, because to their loss they are crucifying the Son of God all over again and subjecting him to public disgrace. Land that drinks in the rain often falling on it and that produces a crop useful to those for whom it is farmed receives the blessing of God. But land that produces thorns and thistles is worthless and is in danger of being cursed. In the end it will be burned. (Heb. 6:4–8)

This is one of the most serious warnings in the entire Bible; therefore, we must pay careful attention to it. Hebrews 6:4–8 declares that if professing Christians become apostate and fall away, it is impossible to bring them back to repentance. Such apostasy is irremediable and irreversible.

This warning calls for serious examination. The author has given such a warning several times before and will do so again. In Hebrews 2:1 he spoke against drifting, and in Hebrews 3:16–19 he described the unbelief and disobedience of the Israelites in the wilderness, noting that all but two of these people, who had experienced tremendous benefits from God, died in the wilderness and did not enter into the rest of Canaan: "Who were they who heard and rebelled? Were they not all those Moses led out of Egypt? And with whom was he angry for forty years? Was it not with those who sinned, whose bodies fell in the desert?

And to whom did God swear that they would never enter his rest if not to those who disobeyed? So we see that they were not able to enter, because of their unbelief."

I do not believe in "once saved, always saved," but I do believe in "once regenerated, always regenerated." Mere profession does not make us a new creation. But if we are new creations by the miracle of God, we will not become apostate.

The author warns each individual to be careful. Because this man is a pastor, he does not want even one person to fall away. Be careful! he says. Pay attention! Do not drift! Do not be like the vast majority of people whose bodies were strewn in the desert because of their unbelief. They became apostates. All who turn away after professing Christ will be irremediably lost. It is absolutely impossible to restore such people to repentance.

We find this idea of falling away elsewhere: "You who are trying to be justified by law have been alienated from Christ; you have *fallen away from grace*" (Gal. 5:4, italics added); "See to it, brothers, that none of you has a sinful, unbelieving heart that *turns away from the living God*" (Heb. 3:12, italics added).

Some people come to church all their lives but never really embrace what the minister is preaching. Such people are committing "a sin that leads to death" (1 John 5:16). John tells us not to pray for such people. They eventually become enemies of Jesus, though once they experienced salvation in some sense.

Aspects of Salvation Shared by Apostates

"It is impossible for those who have once been enlightened, who have tasted the heavenly gift, who have shared in the Holy Spirit, who have tasted the goodness of the word of God and the powers of the coming age, if they fall away, to be brought back to repentance." (Heb. 6:4–6). In these verses the author describes five aspects of salvation that apostates experience.

1. *They have been enlightened* (Heb. 6:4). The Greek text indicates this is a past, once-for-all inner illumination of the Spirit into the gospel. Hebrews 10:26 concurs: "If we deliberately keep on sinning *after we have received the knowledge of the truth*, no sacrifice for sins is left."

2. *They have tasted the heavenly gift* (Heb. 6:4). The psalmist says, "Taste and see that the Lord is good" (Ps. 34:8). These people have somehow experienced the gift from heaven, which is Jesus Christ (John 4:10). They are like the Israelites, who experienced God's protection in Egypt, whose firstborn sons were not killed, who crossed the Red Sea on dry land, who drank water from the rock and tasted manna daily, who enjoyed the presence of God in the pillars of fire and cloud, who were protected from their enemies, who ate the meat that God provided for them, and who heard the word of God himself from Mount Sinai. Yet all but two of the people who experienced these things died in the wilderness and did not enter the Promised Land. They all experienced God in some beneficial way, but they became apostate.

3. *They have partaken of the Holy Spirit* (Heb. 6:4). In some sense, these people have also shared in the gift of the Holy Spirit.

4. *They have tasted the good word of God* (Heb. 6:5). They once enjoyed the preaching of the gospel so much that they would say, "Preach it, Pastor. We want to hear more." Like the second soil, they were highly emotional and received the word with joy; but they fell away. Emotion will never take anyone to heaven. It is like the caboose of a train. But what matters is the engine and our connection to it.

5. *They have tasted the powers of the coming age* (Heb. 6:5). This is speaking about the miracles, wonders, healings, and gifts of the Holy Spirit. These are powers of the coming age, but they also intrude into this present age (see 1 Cor. 12; Gal. 3:5; Heb. 2:4). Apostates have experienced these things in some sense.

The author is warning that it is impossible for those who have experienced such things and yet have turned against the living God to be renewed to repentance and brought back to the path of light. Such people are apostates.

This passage is not referring to believers who sin, like Peter or David. We understand that believers do sin, but it is not the sin unto death: "If we claim to be without sin, we deceive ourselves and the truth is not in us. If we confess our sins, he is faithful and just and will forgive us our sins. . . . My dear children, I write this to you so that you will not sin. But if anybody does sin, we have one who speaks to the Father in our defense—Jesus Christ, the Righteous One" (1 John 1:8–9; 2:1). Having sinned terribly, David repented and cried out to God: "Against you, you only, have I sinned" (Ps. 51:4). He received mercy, we are told. The man who was living with his father's wife was put out of the Corinthian church, yet it appears that he also repented and was restored (1 Cor. 5; 2 Cor. 2).

We daily commit sins of omission and commission, but these are not sins unto death. If we truly repent of our sins by the aid of the Spirit, God promises to forgive our sins. The warning in Hebrews 6 has to do with the sin unto death, as also mentioned in Hebrews 10:26–29:

> If we deliberately keep on sinning after we have received the knowledge of the truth, no sacrifice for sins is left, but only a fearful expectation of judgment and of raging fire that will consume the enemies of God. Anyone who rejected the law of Moses died without mercy on the testimony of two or three witnesses. How much more severely do you think a man deserves to be punished who has trampled the Son of God under foot, who has treated as an unholy thing the blood of the covenant that sanctified him, and who has insulted the Spirit of grace?

Such people reject the only effectual sacrifice for sin. By rejecting the only Savior and his atonement, they are dooming themselves to destruction. In some sense these people experienced salvation, only to reject Jesus. These covenant breakers are likened to a field that receives the abundant rain of God, yet produces only thorns and thistles, which are useless to the farmer and are burned. They are the opposite of covenant keepers, who, like a good field, produce good fruit for the farmer.

We are the soil on which the rain of God's word comes, and we must produce fruit. The Lord tells us, "As the rain and the snow come down from heaven, and do not return to it without watering the earth and making it bud and flourish, so that it yields seed for the sower and bread for the eater, so is my word that goes out from my mouth: It will not return to me empty, but will accomplish what I desire and achieve the purpose for which I sent it" (Isa. 55:10–11). Elsewhere he says, "For I will pour water on the thirsty land, and streams on the dry ground; I will pour out my Spirit on your offspring, and my blessing on your descendants. They will spring up like grass in a meadow, like poplar trees by flowing streams" (Isa. 44:3–4). The rain of the word of God and the Spirit of God has come upon us many times. Are we producing fruit for God or thorns and thistles?

Like the good field that produces good vegetation for the farmer, covenant keepers receive the blessing of God and bring forth good fruit, while covenant breakers bring forth only thorns and thistles, like the vineyard of Isaiah 5:1–7. God planted a choice vine and took good care of it, but it produced only bitter fruit. Finally, God declared he would destroy it.

It is impossible to bring such people to repentance. When asked, "Who do you say Jesus is?" they now declare, "He is the cursed one, a blasphemer, a demon-possessed person, a Samaritan, a drunkard, and a glutton. He is a liar; he is neither the Son of God nor the sovereign Creator of the universe. He is a pretender." They deliberately join with the enemies of Jesus who cried out, "Crucify him! Crucify him! Give us the murderer Barabbas, but crucify Jesus, and let his blood be upon us and our children." Such people glory in putting Jesus to public shame and mocking him.

What about you? Who do you say Jesus is, and who do you say that you are? If you are embracing the rain of the word and the Spirit, you will say, "I am a lost sinner under the wrath of God, but Jesus is the Son of God, the Creator. Jesus is God and the only Savior, the one of whom it is said, 'His name is Jesus, for he shall save his people from their sins.'"

But if you profess to be a Christian and yet are not obeying Christ, you need to examine yourself to see whether you are an apostate. Fruit is the evidence of whether or not we are new creations who have been regenerated by the mighty operation of the Spirit of God upon our souls.

Examples of Apostates

As a warning to us, the Bible gives several examples of people who became apostates.

1. *The people of Israel.* Hebrews 3:16–19 says that the vast majority of people who came out of Egypt became reprobates and apostates. This is one of the greatest tragedies in the Bible.

2. *Achan* (Josh. 7). When this man arrived in Canaan, he proved to be a covenant-breaking apostate and an idolater who loved gold and silver rather than the God of the covenant.

3. *Saul.* The first king of Israel, Saul is an example of the mystery we are talking about—that one can exhibit certain signs of salvation and yet end up becoming an apostate. The Holy Spirit came upon this covenant man from the tribe of Benjamin and he prophesied (1 Sam. 10:9–10). Yet we are also told that the Holy Spirit left him and an evil spirit came upon him and tormented him (1 Sam. 16:14). Eventually he committed suicide.

We do not understand everything about these matters, but the example of Saul demonstrates how serious the risk of apostasy is. One can be enlightened, taste the heavenly gifts, share the Holy Spirit, taste the good word of God, experience of the powers of the age to come, and preach the gospel, yet prove to be an apostate.

4. *Judas* was an apostle chosen by Christ himself after a night of prayer. Along with the other apostles, he was given authority to preach the kingdom of God, heal the sick, cleanse lepers, and cast out demons. After doing these things, the disciples came back saying, "Even the demons are subject to us!" (Luke 10:17). Like the rest of the disciples, Judas prophesied and performed miracles. Living with Jesus, he received many blessings from him. Yet he proved to be a child of the devil; Jesus himself called him "son of perdition" (John 17:12, KJV). The devil first prompted him and then possessed him (John 13:2, 27). Finally, Judas betrayed Christ and then went and hanged himself. He did not find true repentance and went to hell.

5. *Demas* was a fellow worker, a minister of the gospel, with Paul for many years. Reading what Paul wrote to various churches about him, we can infer that he was a student of Scripture and filled with the Holy Spirit. He probably healed the sick and cast out demons, for these were normal occurrences in New Testament churches. But then Paul wrote in his last letter that Demas had become an apostate. He had turned away from the living God in utter unbelief. Paul wrote to Timothy: "Do your best to come to me quickly, for Demas, because he loved this world, has deserted me and has gone to Thessalonica" (2 Tim. 4:9–10).

Demas had worked as a minister for many years. But now troubles and persecutions had come. The apostles were being imprisoned in cold dungeons, with their feet put in stocks. Demas fell in love with this crooked and perverse generation.

Notice, he was not an average believer; he was a minister who had worked with Paul. Yet he fell away. That is why we must examine ourselves to see whether we are true Christians. We can never rest our confidence on having come to church for many years, or having been baptized, or having contributed money. What matters is our present faith and obedience.

Demas became an idolater. Jesus himself said we cannot serve two masters: we will either serve the living and true God, or money and what it can provide (Matt. 6:24). When the devil showed Jesus all the glories of this world and told him he would give it all to him if he worshiped him, Jesus refused. All true believers will do the same.

6. *Hymenaeus and Alexander.* Paul wrote, "Timothy, my son, I give you this instruction in keeping with the prophecies once made about you, so that by following them you may fight the good fight, holding on to faith and a good conscience." A good conscience comes from holding on to the gospel and living the gospel life. "Some have rejected these and so have shipwrecked their faith. Among them are Hymenaeus and Alexander, whom I have handed over to Satan to be taught not to blaspheme" (1 Tim. 1:18–20).

Hymenaeus and Alexander were disciples who heard the gospel and may have even been preachers. They were enlightened, became partakers of the Holy Spirit in some sense, and were excited about the word of God. Yet they abandoned it all, making a shipwreck of their faith, and became blasphemers and enemies of the gospel. Apostasy occurs gradually—a little unbelief, then a little more, until finally a person experiences the fullness of unbelief, and he turns away from the living God to worship idols and demons. Note, however, this severe judgment: Paul handed them over to Satan.

7. *Hymenaeus and Philetus.* Paul instructed Timothy, "Avoid godless chatter, because those who indulge in it will become more and more ungodly. Their teaching will spread like gangrene. Among them are Hymenaeus and Philetus, who have wandered away from the truth" (2 Tim. 2:16–19). This may have been the same Hymenaeus mentioned in Paul's first epistle to Timothy. These men were probably ordained ministers of the gospel, but they rejected the gospel, preferring darkness to light. "They say

that the resurrection has already taken place, and they destroy the faith of some. Nevertheless, God's solid foundation stands firm, sealed with this inscription: 'The Lord knows those who are his'" (2 Tim. 2:19).

8. *Apostates in the New Testament church.* John writes, "Dear children, this is the last hour; and as you have heard that the antichrist is coming, even now many antichrists have come. This is how we know it is the last hour. They went out from us, but they did not really belong to us." These people were enlightened, yet they went out of the church, for the light was too revealing; they preferred darkness. Then John gives the reason: "For if they had belonged to us, they would have remained with us; but their going showed that none of them belonged to us" (1 John 2:18–19).

There is no perfect church in which every member is a true Christian who will persevere to the end. Pastors and elders do not know in every case whether or not a person is a Christian. They must receive members on the basis of their credible profession, but they have no way of knowing what goes on in the human heart.

Peter also spoke of apostates. The early church was known as the Way, because it followed the straight way, the narrow way, the way of the cross, the way of the gospel. Like Hymenaeus, Alexander, Philetus, and others, these people "left the straight way and wandered off to follow the way of Balaam son of Beor, who loved the wages of wickedness" (2 Pet. 2:15).

9. *False teachers in the church.* Paul writes about ministers, leaders, and teachers who acted as tools of Satan while they purported to be teachers of truth: "For such men are false apostles, deceitful workmen, masquerading as apostles of Christ. And no wonder, for Satan himself masquerades as an angel of light. It is not surprising, then, if his servants masquerade as servants of righteousness" Note, however, Paul's conclusion: "Their end will be what their actions deserve" (2 Cor. 11:13–15).

Eternal Security of the Believer

We believe in the eternal security of the believer, but we must clarify that this pertains only to truly regenerate believers who have experienced the divine miracle of becoming new creations, who have experienced the resurrection from the dead in their souls. Only such people will persevere to the very end in obedient faith and fruit-bearing.

The test is, do we believe the deposit of sound doctrine and put it into practice? The best that most people can say today is that they believe the doctrine, and, indeed, that should be first. But we must also ask the second question: Do you *live* the doctrine? Do you *do* the truth?

After promising them trouble, Jesus Christ said to the church of Smyrna, "Be faithful, even to the point of death, and I will give you the crown of life" (Rev. 2:10). Every true believer will persevere till death. In spite of all storms, persecutions, and even the prospect of martyrdom, true Christians will stay faithful to sound doctrine and live a holy life.

We find this idea of persevering in obedient faith throughout the book of Hebrews:

1. "But Christ is faithful as a son over God's house. And we are his house, if we hold on to our courage and the hope of which we boast" (Heb. 3:6). Notice the "if." Our obedience never makes us God's house; God does that by his divine action. But *if* we are God's house, we will continue in obedient faith till the end.
2. "We have come to share in Christ if we hold firmly till the end the confidence we had at first" (Heb. 3:14). Our obedience and perseverance do not make us Christians, but if we are Christians, we will persevere to the end. If we are people of God, we will obey Jesus Christ, who died in our place and went to hell to bring us out of hell. We will be impelled by love to do his will, both for his glory and our everlasting joy.
3. "Once made perfect, [Jesus] became the source of eternal salvation for all who obey him" (Heb. 5:9). This verse is speaking of those who obey him *all their lives*. The salvation God gives is not temporary. He did not accomplish salvation for a day. He is the author of *eternal* salvation, and those who are given that eternal salvation will obey him to the end.
4. "Because by one sacrifice he has made perfect forever those who are being made holy" (Heb. 10:14). In the Greek, the phrase "he has made perfect" is in the perfect tense, designating an action that took place in the past with the effect continuing to the present. The same Lord Jesus who justifies us also sanctifies us. A person who says he is justified yet lives like a devil is confusing biblical doctrine, because we can never separate justification from God's ongoing work of sanctifying us and bringing us into conformity with his Son.

5. "Therefore he is able to save completely those who come to God through him, because he always lives to intercede for them" (Heb. 7:25). Jesus Christ saves completely.
   6. "May the God of peace, who through the blood of the eternal covenant brought back from the dead our Lord Jesus, the great Shepherd of the sheep, equip you with everything good for doing his will, and may he work in us what is pleasing to him, through Jesus Christ, to whom be glory for ever and ever. Amen" (Heb. 13:20–21). He who justified us also works in us to will and to do his good pleasure (cf. Phil. 2:13).

God commanded the Hebrews to persevere, obey, and continue, but it was he who enabled them to do so. In the same way, if he saved us, he will also work in us and give us the willingness and ability to love God and follow Christ. If we do not have these qualities, we must cry out, "O God, have mercy on us!" He who began a good work in us is faithful to complete it (Phil. 1:6). God is not man; if he begins something, he will finish it. If he justified us, he will sanctify us. He will work in us, equip us, enable us, and cause us to will and to do his good pleasure so that we can work out our salvation with fear and trembling.

Paul reminded Timothy that though some would wander from the truth, "the Lord knows those who are his" (2 Tim. 2:19). The Lord knows his church, the people he chose from before the foundation of the world and whom he saved in time. They will persevere to the very end. In the life of a church, people may come and go, but God's people will thrive and flourish in the gospel and in the Christian life. Jesus promises, "I give them eternal life, and they shall never perish" (John 10:28). We are held by Christ and the Father. No one can snatch us from God's possession. This is eternal security!

One day God will say to many professing Christians, "I never knew you." But Paul says true Christians are those whom God foreknew, which means foreloved. This is not mere intellectual knowledge, for God knows all things; it is knowledge in the same intimate sense whereby Adam knew his wife. Paul writes, "For those God foreknew he also predestined to be conformed to the likeness of his Son, that he might be the firstborn among many brothers. And those he predestined, he also called; those he called, he also justified; those he justified, he also glorified" (Rom. 8:29–30). Then he speaks of the eternal security of every believer who is born of God: "Neither death nor life . . . nor anything else in all creation, will be able to separate us from the love of God that is in Christ Jesus" (Rom. 8:38–39).

Do you have eternal life? If leaders like Demas could become apostates, how much more diligently must we examine ourselves! Peter exhorts, "Be all the more eager to make your calling and election sure" (2 Pet. 1:10). Paul admonishes, "Examine yourselves to see whether you are in the faith" (2 Cor. 13:5). How do we make our calling and election sure? By producing the fruit of obedience to God. Do we obey God and delight in him? Do we do the will of God because it is his will? Do we work out our salvation with fear and trembling? If we are saved by Jesus Christ, we will do these things and "will receive a rich welcome into the eternal kingdom of our Lord and Savior Jesus Christ" (2 Pet. 1:11).

13
Cure for Spiritual Laziness

> ⁹Even though we speak like this, dear friends, we are confident of better things in your case—things that accompany salvation. ¹⁰God is not unjust; he will not forget your work and the love you have shown him as you have helped his people and continue to help them. ¹¹We want each of you to show this same diligence to the very end, in order to make your hope sure. ¹²We do not want you to become lazy, but to imitate those who through faith and patience inherit what has been promised.
>
> Hebrews 6:9–12

Hebrews 6:9–12 gives us a pastor's prescription for spiritual laziness. The church of the Hebrews had serious problems, including spiritual sluggishness, a desire to return again to childhood, and an aversion to persecution for the sake of Christ.

The Lord of the church is well aware of the condition of his people. Remember how he told the church of Ephesus: "Yet I hold this against you: You have forsaken your first love. Remember the height from which you have fallen! Repent and do the things you did at first" (Rev. 2:4–5).

This was exactly the situation of the Hebrew church. The good news, however, is that there is a cure for this condition. We want to examine, first, the pastor's confidence in the members of his church; second, the cause for the pastor's confidence; and, third, the pastor's counsel.

A Pastor's Confidence

Though the Hebrews had many problems, they had not yet become apostates. Some were in danger of falling away unless they heeded counsel, others had grown cold toward God, but many were still following Jesus faithfully. So the pastor-author speaks with great confidence about the people of this church. He is convinced they will not become apostate, though he has already severely warned them of that grave possibility.

The writer first emphasizes his personal confidence in them by using the word *pepeismetha*, meaning to come to a state of persuasion and conviction based on reasons. We can translate Hebrews 6:9: "*Convinced are we* concerning you, beloved, of better things—things that accompany salvation, even though we are speaking in this severe manner."

This pastor is fully convinced that the Hebrews will be finally saved, and he has reasons for his conviction. He uses the word *agapētoi*, "beloved." It is the same word God the Father uses in reference to Jesus Christ: "You are my beloved Son" (Matt. 17:5; Luke 3:22). A word of great intimacy and affection, it is used only once in this epistle. The pastor is saying that all believers in his church are beloved to him because they are beloved to God. They are accepted by the Father in his beloved Son on the basis of Christ's suffering and death for them.

Being thus assured of their eternal security, the pastor writes that he is convinced concerning these people "*of better things in [their] case—things that accompany salvation*" (Heb. 6:9). Better things! That word, *kreissona*, appears in this letter thirteen times. In other words, these people are not the land that produces thorns and thistles, the land soon to be cursed and burned (Heb. 6:7–8). The pastor is sure of better things in their case, things that issue in eternal salvation.

Causes for Confidence

1. God Is Just

What are the reasons for this pastor's confidence? First, the very nature of God: "*God is not unjust*" (v. 10). God is righteousness. He is not light and darkness; he is light, truth, and justice. Titus 1:2 speaks of "God who cannot lie." Malachi 3:6 describes him as "God who cannot change." Our God cannot become unrighteous or unreliable.

God is just; therefore, he cannot forgive our sins without reason. He justifies sinners while upholding his law because he sent his sinless Son to hell on the cross in our place: "God made him who had no sin to be sin for us, so that in him we might become the righteousness of God" (2 Cor. 5:21). The cross supremely reveals the nature of God. God the Father sent Jesus to the cross to demonstrate his justice, "so as to be just and the one who justifies those who have faith in Jesus" (Rom. 3:26). That is why Paul could declare to the church at Philippi, "[I am] confident of this, that he who began a good work in you will carry it on to completion until the day of Christ Jesus" (Phil. 1:6).

This God who has justified us will also equip us and work in us through sanctification. The Hebrews pastor concludes his epistle: "May the God of peace, who through the blood of the eternal covenant brought back from the dead our Lord Jesus, that great Shepherd of the sheep, equip you with everything good for doing his will, and may he work in us what is pleasing to him, through Jesus Christ, to whom be glory for ever and ever. Amen" (Heb. 13:20–21). Elsewhere Paul exhorts, "Work out your salvation with fear and trembling, for it is God who works in you to will and to act according to his good purpose" (Phil. 2:12–13). And John tells us, "If we confess our sins, [God] is faithful and just and will forgive us our sins and purify us from all unrighteousness" (1 John 1:9). God says that if we repent and believe, we shall be saved. If we meet his conditions, God will forgive and cleanse us. The just nature of God and his faithfulness to do what he promises is the first reason for the pastor's confidence.

2. GOD REMEMBERS HIS PEOPLE

"*God is not unjust; he will not forget your work and the love you have shown him as you have helped his people and continue to help them*" (Heb. 6:10). The second reason for the pastor's confidence is that God does not forget his people. There is one thing that God does deliberately forgive and forget—our sins. Isaiah declares, "Surely it was for my benefit that I suffered such anguish. In your love you kept me from the pit of destruction; you have put all my sins behind your back" (Isa. 38:17). The Lord says, "I, even I, am he who blots out your transgressions, for my own sake, and remembers your sins no more" (Isa. 43:25). Micah declares, "You will tread our sins underfoot and hurl all our iniquities into the depths of the sea" (Mic. 7:19).

Thank God, he forgets our sins! In Hebrews 11 we find a list of the heroes of faith, but not even one of their sins is recorded there. Elsewhere we read that Abraham sinned several times, but his sins are not mentioned in this chapter; they are forgotten by God. Thank God for his deliberate, divine amnesia! But we also thank God that he remembers his children and what we do for him out of love, as evidence of our salvation.

How many times have we complained that God has forgotten us! "Why do you say, O Jacob, and complain, O Israel, 'My way is hidden from the LORD; my cause is disregarded by my God?'" (Isa. 40:27). In Isaiah 49 Zion says, "The LORD has forsaken me, the LORD has forgotten me" (v. 14). But note God's response: "Can a mother forget the baby at her breast and have no compassion on the child she has borne? Though she may forget, I will not forget you! See, I have engraved you on the palms of my hands; your walls are ever before me" (vv. 15–16). Jesus asks, "Are not five sparrows sold for two pennies? Yet not one of them is forgotten by God. Indeed, the very hairs of your head are all numbered. Don't be afraid; you are worth more than many sparrows" (Luke 12:6–7). God is just and is committed to our full and complete salvation. He will neither forget nor forsake his people.

3. GOD CONSIDERS OUR LOVE AND WORK

"God . . . will not forget your work and the love you have shown him as you have helped his people and continue to help them" (Heb. 6:10). The third reason for the pastor's confidence in the eternal salvation of his people was their history of loving service. God does not forget our work and the love we do in his name: "If anyone gives even a cup of cold water to one of these little ones, I tell you the truth, he will certainly not lose his reward" (Matt. 10:42). Because we love God, we love our brothers and sisters and minister to their needs. God is aware of what we do in his name and he rewards us.

Cure for Spiritual Laziness

God does not want us to be solo Christians, wandering from church to church. We are not to be like rolling stones, detached from all relationships to God's people. The church is likened to a body, a building, and a vine—many members but one body, many living stones built into one building, many branches vitally united to one vine, the Lord Jesus Christ.

We demonstrate our love for God by loving and helping his beloved children, our fellow believers in Christ. The church of the Hebrews had regularly performed such ministry to the saints in the past: "Remember those earlier days after you had received the light, when you stood your ground in a great contest in the face of suffering. Sometimes you were publicly exposed to insult and persecution; at other times you stood side by side with those who were so treated. You sympathized with those in prison and joyfully accepted the confiscation of your property, because you knew that you yourselves had better and lasting possessions" (Heb. 10:32-34).

Despite their present troubles, these people had a history of good works. They had experienced severe persecution because of their faith, suffered public abuse and slander, and endured the loss of their properties. Yet they did not fall away but kept on believing in Jesus Christ, standing with those who were being persecuted and helping those in prison by visiting them and ministering to their needs. All of these loving deeds proved that these people were truly born of God.

Not only did these people love God and serve his people in the past, but they also were still doing it. In the Greek, it says they were functioning as deacons as they helped their fellow believers. It is true that not all were doing these things, but many were. In spite of their troubles, they loved God and his people, and they worked hard serving their brothers in their serious need. Their present obedience and love convinced their pastor that they were truly born of God and would persevere to the very end.

Our good works done in the name of the Lord to the people of God are evidence that we have the life of God in us. James asks, "What good is it, my brothers, if a man claims to have faith but has no deeds? Can such faith save him? Suppose a brother or sister is without clothes and daily food. If one of you says to him, 'Go, I wish you well; keep warm and well fed,' but does nothing about his physical needs, what good is it?" (Jas. 2:14-16). Such a man is a false Christian, an apostate, whose faith is dead. John speaks of the same idea:

> This is how we know what love is: Jesus Christ laid down his life for us. And we ought to lay down our lives for our brothers. If anyone has material possessions and sees his brother in need but has no pity on him, how can the love of God be in him? Dear children, let us not love with words or tongue but with actions and in truth. This then is how we know that we belong to the truth, and how we set our hearts at rest in his presence....We love because he first loved us. If anyone says, 'I love God,' yet hates his brother, he is a liar. For anyone who does not love his brother, whom he has seen, cannot love God, whom he has not seen. And he has given us this command: Whoever loves God must also love his brother. (1 John 3:16-19; 4:19-21)

Jesus also emphasized the importance of loving with actions: "Then the King will say to those on his right, 'Come, you who are blessed by my Father; take your inheritance, the kingdom prepared for you since the creation of the world. For I was hungry and you gave me something to eat . . .' Then the righteous will answer him, 'Lord, when did we see you hungry and feed you, or thirsty and give you something to drink? . . .' 'I tell you the truth, whatever you did for one of the least of these brothers of mine, you did for me'" (Matt. 25:34-35, 37, 40).

When Paul was imprisoned in Rome, many of his former associates abandoned him. But about one who remained faithful Paul wrote, "May the Lord show mercy to the household of Onesiphorus, because he often refreshed me and was not ashamed of my chains. On the contrary, when he was in Rome, he searched hard for me until he found me. May the Lord grant that he will find mercy from the Lord on that day! You know very well in how many ways he helped me in Ephesus" (2 Tim. 1:16-18). God does not forget the work and love we show in his name to his people. Paul says, "For we must all appear before the judgment seat of Christ, that each one may receive what is due him for the things done while in the body, whether good or bad" (2 Cor. 5:10). God will reward us for everything we do, even our giving a cup of cold water in his name to others.

How, then, do we know that we are truly saved? We love God and act on behalf of his people. If we love God, we will love his people and serve them sacrificially. That is how the early church lived: "All the believers were together and had everything in common. Selling their possessions and goods, they gave to anyone as he had need. . . . All the believers were one in heart and mind. No one claimed that any of his possessions was his own, but they shared everything they had. . . . There were no needy persons among them. For from time to time those who owned lands or houses sold them, brought the money from the sales and put it at the apostles' feet, and it was distributed to anyone as he had need" (Acts 2:44–45; 4:32, 34–35). We need not depend on government help. What we need is the church to do the work it is called to do.

A Pastor's Counsel

The Hebrews' pastor was convinced that his congregation was not apostate, based on solid reasons. But now he wants to counsel them about their spiritual sluggishness and retardation. He shakes them up so they may shake off their laziness.

Not all of these people were expressing their love for God by helping their fellow saints. Some had fallen into the habit of neglecting the assembling together with their fellow saints. Others had grown cold toward God and his church. They were tired of being persecuted and slandered, having their properties confiscated, and being imprisoned for the gospel.

Some of these people were even considering forsaking Christ. But this pastor cared about each saint. Everyone was dear to him; he could not be satisfied with only some loving God. Therefore, he exhorts: "*We want each of you to show the same diligence to the very end, in order to make your hope sure*" (Heb. 6:11). Each one! If you have five children, do you love each one, or just two or three? This pastor is saying, in effect, "We earnestly yearn for each one of you to show the same diligence. We want each one of you, inspired by the love of God, to work hard in helping the saints. We want each one of you to burn with intense love and work with great industry to demonstrate that you are on your way to heaven and will persevere to the very end."

These people had fallen from their first love; they had to return to that first love, zeal, and vigorous activity. Paul says that Christ's love compels, impels, and motivates him to do everything he does (2 Cor. 5:14). Where there is love, there is labor; where there is faith, there is work; where there is hope, there is patient endurance (1 Thess. 1:3). This is the triad of virtue. Faith, love, and hope result in intense spiritual and sacrificial activity in God's church, proving that we are truly born of God and will persevere to the very end.

So the pastor's counsel is: "Each one of you, shake off your sluggishness and selfishness! Show the same diligence that you showed when you first loved God. Come back to your first love! Make every effort to stir it up! Move out of the danger zone of apostasy! Wake up, O sleeper, rise from the dead! Be set ablaze by the love of God and the cross of Christ. Fight the good fight of faith, each one of you!" As Peter would say, "Make your calling and election sure by adding goodness to faith, knowledge to goodness, self-control to knowledge, perseverance to self-control, godliness to perseverance, brotherly kindness to godliness, and love to brotherly kindness" (See 2 Pet. 1:5–11).

These Hebrews had demonstrated these things before. Now their pastor was exhorting them to rouse themselves and produce actions demonstrating their love: "Remember those earlier days after you had been enlightened" (Heb. 10:32). This was their history, but it was, in a measure, now past and they somehow had become sluggish. So he exhorts, "See to it, brothers, that no one of you has a sinful and unbelieving heart. . . . Therefore, since the promise of entering his rest still stands, let us be careful that no one of you be found to have fallen short of it" (Heb. 3:12; 4:1).

This pastor is also concerned that these people arrive at full assurance of salvation. If we are not obedient, we cannot enjoy such assurance. He says, in effect, "I intensely desire that each one of you demonstrates the same diligence you showed at first when you suffered persecution and loss of property, when you stood with the persecuted and helped those in prison, when you came together to worship God and have fellowship with God's people, when you eagerly witnessed to Christ and lived a holy life." He is counseling each *"Make your hope sure"* (Heb. 6:11). When we obey God by doing his will, we will experience full assurance of salvation. We will be filled to overflowing with the hope of the glory of God as we look forward to the coming of Christ.

Those who do not live an obedient life are hoping only in this world. Led astray by the deceitfulness of riches and the pleasures of this life, such people will have no assurance of the blessed life awaiting them in the glory land. But they are in danger of becoming truly hopeless. So this pastor counsels each one to wake up, shake off spiritual slumber, and begin laboring for God fearlessly so that each one would be filled with the fullness of hope. The idea was that now they lacked this assurance, but by loving God and doing his work, they could experience this great hope, this full assurance, until Christ comes again. They could say with Paul, "To me, to live is Christ and to die is gain. . . . To me, to depart from this life is to be present with Christ" (Phil. 1:21, 23).

Every obedient Christian enjoys assurance of eternal salvation. When we are filled with such assurance and the hope of the coming of our Lord Jesus Christ, we will purify our lives. This hope will keep us from putting down roots in this world as we understand that we are sojourners, like Abraham. When we are filled with such hope and assurance, we will rejoice in suffering and fight the good fight as we eagerly await the crown of life.

The Lord is our hope. Paul writes, "May the God of hope fill you with all joy and peace as you trust in him, that you may overflow with hope by the power of the Holy Spirit" (Rom. 15:13). An unbeliever is without God and without hope in the world (Eph. 2:12). But a Christian is filled to overflowing with hope. Our blessed hope is not in political leaders, nor in our country, nor in amassing wealth and possessions. Our hope is in the coming of our Lord Jesus Christ and being caught up together with him to live with him forever.

The final counsel the pastor gave to cure the people's disease of laziness was to imitate those *"who through faith and patience inherit what has been promised"* (Heb. 6:12). We need heroes to imitate, and we do not have many today. But we have heroes in the Bible, and a list of them is given in Hebrews 11. There is Abraham, who believed God and persevered through all his troubles until he arrived at the city of God. There are Moses, Elijah, Elisha, and so many others. Above all, we have the Lord Jesus Christ: "Be imitators of God, therefore, as dearly loved children" (Eph. 5:1).

I encourage you to find some living heroes, such as pastors, teachers, and parents who stand for truth: "Remember your leaders, who spoke the word of God to you. Consider the outcome of their way of life and imitate their faith" (Heb. 13:7). We need to imitate such people so that we also may experience the promises of God. Do not think we must wait until we get to heaven. Even now those who persevere in obedient love for God can experience joy unspeakable and full of glory.

14

Jesus, Our Anchor of Hope

¹³*When God made his promise to Abraham, since there was no one greater for him to swear by, he swore by himself,* ¹⁴*saying, "I will surely bless you and give you many descendants."* ¹⁵*And so after waiting patiently, Abraham received what was promised.* ¹⁶*Men swear by someone greater than themselves, and the oath confirms what is said and puts an end to all argument.* ¹⁷*Because God wanted to make the unchanging nature of his purpose very clear to the heirs of what was promised, he confirmed it with an oath.* ¹⁸*God did this so that, by two unchangeable things in which it is impossible for God to lie, we who have fled to take hold of the hope offered to us may be greatly encouraged.* ¹⁹*We have this hope as an anchor for the soul, firm and secure. It enters the inner sanctuary behind the curtain,* ²⁰*where Jesus, who went before us, has entered on our behalf. He has become a high priest forever, in the order of Melchizedek.*

Hebrews 6:13–20

The psalmist asks, "When the foundations are being destroyed, what can the righteous do?" (Ps. 11:3). What would you do when your foundations are shaken by unexpected economic reversals, severe sickness, unjust treatment by authorities, a child's rebellion, the death of a parent, or divorce? What would you do if you were tried like Job? When severe storms beat against the ship of your life, do you have an anchor that steadies your soul?

Our text tells us of such an anchor, even Jesus Christ, who provided purification for sins by his atonement and then, after rising from the dead, ascended into heaven. As our anchor of hope, he is linked to us and to God, at whose right hand he is seated in the Holy of Holies in the heavenly sanctuary.

The pastor-author has previously exhorted the Hebrews to be diligent in obedient service to Christ so that they might be filled with assurance of hope and imitate those who by patient faith received God's promises. Now he encourages them by examining the patient faith of Abraham, the father of all believers.

God's Promise to Abraham

First, the author speaks about God's promise to Abraham: "*When God made his promise to Abraham . . .*" (Heb. 6:13). God graciously chose to reveal himself as Savior to the idol-worshiping Abraham in Mesopotamia, saying, "Leave your country, your people and your father's household and go to the land I will show you. I will make you into a great nation and I will bless you; I will make your name great, and you will be a blessing. I will bless those who bless you, and whoever curses you I will curse; and all peoples on earth will be blessed through you" (Gen. 12:1–3). God repeated this promise to Abraham a number of times (Gen. 13:14–16; 15:4–5; 17:4–8, 15–19). Later on, God confirmed it with Isaac (Gen. 26) and Jacob (Gen. 28:13). In sheer mercy, the Lord promised salvation to Abraham and his descendants.

When God makes a promise, he will fulfill it. Thus, we must trust this God who cannot lie (cf. Num. 23:19; Tit. 1:2). Jesus himself said, "Your word is truth" (John 17:17); "Heaven and earth will pass away, but my words will never pass away" (Mark 13:31).

Abraham faced one seemingly insurmountable problem: he had no descendants. How, then, could God's promise to him be fulfilled? Twenty-five years passed, until Abraham was about one hundred years old. The Scriptures tell us that his body was as good as dead, as was Sarah's at almost ninety years of age (Gen. 17:17; Rom. 4:19). Yet Paul tells us, "Abraham believed God, and it was credited to him as righteousness. . . . Against all hope, Abraham in hope believed and so became the father of many nations" (Rom. 4:3, 18). He was fully persuaded that this God who "calls things that are not as though they were . . . had power to do what he had promised" (Rom. 4:17, 21). And after twenty-five years of patient endurance, Abraham received the promised son, Isaac.

After Isaac grew up, Abraham was faced with yet one more test of his faith in God's promise. No one else has experienced such severe testing, which was not from the devil, but from God himself. God commanded Abraham to sacrifice Isaac as a burnt offering, although Isaac was the son whom he loved and through whom God had promised that salvation would come to the whole world (Gen. 22:18). Abraham immediately obeyed and journeyed in faith to Mount Moriah, having reasoned that the God of glory could raise the dead. We are told that "figuratively speaking, he did receive Isaac back from death" (Heb. 11:19).

God's Oath to Abraham

"*When God made his promise to Abraham, since there was no one greater for him to swear by, he swore by himself, saying, 'I will surely bless you and give you many descendants'*" (Heb. 6:13–14). God's promises are inviolable, irrevocable, and immutable. In God there is no shadow of turning; his word can be fully trusted. Yet in response to Abraham's obedient faith, God then gave an oath in addition to his promise, for the greater comfort and assurance of Abraham and all the heirs of promise.

In this fallen world, sinful men make many promises and covenants. Yet men are unreliable, so they sometimes strengthen their promises by taking oaths, particularly in the name of the Lord. Deuteronomy 6:13 instructs, "Fear the LORD your God, serve him only and take your oaths in his name." Such an oath is the highest affirmation of one's trustworthiness. It is designed to stop all disputes and guarantee one's promise. If a man lies under such an oath, he violates the third commandment: "You shall not misuse the name of the LORD your God, for the LORD will not hold anyone guiltless who misuses his name" (Exod. 20:7). Abraham himself made such an oath before the king of Sodom (Gen. 14:22).

God has no need to take an oath, but he did so to encourage Abraham and all the heirs of God's promise: "I swear by myself . . . that because you have done this and have not withheld your son, your only son, I will surely bless you and make your descendants as numerous as the stars in the sky and as the sand on the seashore. Your descendants will take possession of the cities of their enemies, and through your offspring all nations on earth will be blessed, because you have obeyed me" (Gen. 22:16–18).

Abraham received partial fulfillment of this promise during his lifetime. Certainly, he received much wealth, and after a twenty-five year wait, he received Isaac. After another fifteen years, he received his son back from destruction. Then he lived long enough to see Jacob, Isaac's covenant son, who was fifteen years old when Abraham died. Abraham believed that salvation was to come through his son Isaac, and in some sense, he saw the day of the Savior, as Jesus himself said: "Your father Abraham rejoiced at the thought of seeing my day; he saw it and was glad" (John 8:56). Hebrews 11:10 says that Abraham was not merely looking forward to Canaan, but to a heavenly city, whose builder and maker is God. By faith he was looking forward to the day of Jesus Christ for his salvation. But Abraham received only the first installment of the promise. The Hebrews writer says of Abraham and others who came after him: "All these people were still living by faith when they died. They did not receive the things promised; they only saw them and welcomed them from a distance. . . . These were all commended for their faith, yet none of them received [in its fullness] what had been promised" (Heb. 11:13, 39).

None of the Old Testament prophets saw the complete fulfillment of God's promise regarding the Seed of Abraham, through whom the blessing of salvation was to come to all the world:

> Concerning this salvation, the prophets, who spoke of the grace that was to come to you, searched intently and with the greatest care, trying to find out the time and circumstances to which the Spirit of Christ in them was pointing when he predicted the sufferings of Christ and the glories that would follow. It was revealed to them that they were not serving themselves but you, when they spoke of the things that have now been told you by those who have preached the gospel to you by the Holy Spirit sent from heaven. Even angels long to look into these things. (1 Pet. 1:10–12)

God's Purpose

"Because God wanted to make the unchanging nature of his purpose very clear to the heirs of what was promised, he confirmed it with an oath. God did this so that, by two unchangeable things in which it is impossible for God to lie, we who have fled to take hold of the hope

offered to us may be greatly encouraged" (Heb. 6:17-18). God wants his people to enjoy great assurance. What was God's purpose in giving this promise and oath? He did so to demonstrate more convincingly to the heirs of the promise the immutability of his decree to save a people for himself and to encourage them in their faith.

God does not want us to have a weak and nebulous encouragement. He wants his people to be filled to overflowing with full assurance of hope and to have a powerful conviction and comfort when all other foundations fail. He wants us to be able to say with Job, "Though he slay me, yet will I hope in him" (Job 13:15), and with Paul, "Neither death nor life . . . nor anything else in all creation, will be able to separate us from the love of God that is in Christ Jesus" (Rom. 8:38-39). Both Peter and Paul experienced such mighty encouragement when they were martyred for their faith. For them, to depart from this life was to be present with the Lord.

Has God fulfilled his promise to save a people for himself and for his great glory? The answer is yes! Paul writes, "For no matter how many promises God has made, they are 'Yes' in Christ" (2 Cor. 1:20). In Jesus, the Seed of Abraham, all the promises of God are fulfilled. Paul says, "But when the time had fully come, God sent his Son, born of a woman, born under the law, to redeem those under law, that we might receive the full rights of sons" (Gal. 4:4-5).

Heirs of God

"Because God wanted to make the unchanging nature of his purpose very clear to the heirs of what was promised, he confirmed it with an oath" (Heb. 6:17). Who are God's heirs? Are they just the Jewish people, or are Gentiles also included? The truth is, all who trust in Jesus for their eternal salvation are God's heirs, whether Jew or Gentile. God has only one people, without any distinction or difference.

Paul writes, "Consider Abraham: 'He believed God, and it was credited to him as righteousness.' Understand, then, that those who believe are children of Abraham. The Scripture foresaw that God would justify the Gentiles by faith, and announced the gospel in advance to Abraham: 'All nations will be blessed through you.' So those who have faith are blessed along with Abraham, the man of faith. . . . If you belong to Christ, then you are Abraham's seed, and heirs according to the promise" (Gal. 3:6–9, 29). Elsewhere he says, "Therefore, the promise comes by faith, so that it may be by grace and may be guaranteed to all Abraham's offspring—not only to those who are of the law but also to those who are of the faith of Abraham. He is the father of us all" (Rom. 4:16).

Hebrews 2:16 tells us, "For surely it is not angels [Jesus] helps, but Abraham's descendants." We are Abraham's descendants if we trust in God's Son for our eternal salvation. All other foundations will fail, but we can stand on the sure foundation of God—on his promise confirmed by his oath.

What do the heirs of God's promise do? Hebrews 6:18 says that we have fled "to take hold of the hope offered to us." As Noah and his family fled to the ark of salvation to escape the flood of God's wrath, so we have fled from the wrath of God to Jesus Christ for refuge and salvation. As Lot fled from the fire of God's wrath, so we have fled to Jesus from the allurements of the world and its pleasures of sin for a season. In Israel, those who killed someone unintentionally could flee to a city of refuge and be safe. Likewise, we who have sinned against God, both intentionally and unintentionally, have fled by his grace from the avenger of blood to Jesus our Savior.

As heirs of God's promise, we have turned from sin to serve the risen Lord. Having truly repented of our sins, now we hate wickedness and love righteousness. We have fled for refuge to lay hold of the promise of hope set before us.

Christian hope is objective—our hope is in the Son of God who became man, who died in our place for our sins, was buried, and was raised for our justification, who went through the heavens and is seated on the right hand of God the Father, and who is coming again. Our hope is based on this objective reality, which leads to a subjective confidence and conviction. So Paul speaks of "Jesus our hope" (1 Tim. 1:1).

The Hebrews writer says we have taken hold of Jesus our hope, and the Greek text implies that we continue to hold on to him. Moment by moment we are grasping him tightly and we will not let him go. Every heir of salvation will do that, for we have no other hope and no other savior. It is only through Jesus that salvation comes to the world. He is the perfect high priest, the perfect victim, the perfect altar, and the perfect atonement. He alone can say, "I give them eternal life, and they shall never perish; no one can snatch them out of my hand" (John 10:28). Not only do we grasp him, but he also grasps us, and nothing can separate us from his grip. Because he grasped us, we grasped him and are eternally saved.

The writer says that God gives his oath and promise that we may have mighty encouragement. It is in the present tense, meaning we are continually encouraged, but not by the security of health, relationships, power, beauty, or wisdom of this world. Our security rests on God's Son, the mighty security of God's unfailing promise and oath to save us. He has saved us, he is saving us, and he will save us.

We experience this encouragement continually. Not only have we experienced it once, but we can also have it every day, especially as we face severe trials. We are people of hope. The author exhorts us to look before us and find our hope in Jesus. When we lay hold of him by reading and believing God's word, we shall enjoy great comfort, hope, and mighty encouragement. What is this hope we are grasping? It is not money or things or a country. Hebrews 11 says we are looking forward to a heavenly city and a heavenly country.

Jesus Is Our Anchor of Hope

"*We have this hope as an anchor for the soul, firm and secure*" (Heb. 6:19). Our anchor of hope is Jesus himself, who died for our sins and was raised for our justification. The author says, "*We have* this hope"; the verb is in the present tense, meaning we have it now, continuously. When we face our university examinations, we have it; when our spouse is sick or when our child dies, we have it; when we go to the doctor and hear our disease is terminal, we have it; at the hour of our death, we have it.

Jesus, our hope, is the anchor for our souls. This does not mean he is the anchor only for the immaterial part of our being; it means Christ is the anchor of our entire life, both body and soul.

Our life's ship will face severe winds, rain, and mighty storms. But we are securely fastened, or moored, to Jesus, who is moored to God, who dwells in the heavenly Holy of Holies.

Sailors do not see the anchor that grips the bottom of the harbor, yet they are certain of their safety because of it. Likewise, Jesus our anchor, though invisible to us but visible to faith and hope, is in us as the hope of glory (Col. 1:27). But he is also with God. Two chains are linked together: one is promise, the other is oath. In Jesus our hope is linked to us and to God. Christ is in us and he is also with God, for he has entered the heavens and is seated on the right hand of God as high priest forever to intercede for us.

We are told that this anchor is sure. The Greek word means it does not slip. Jesus will not fall asleep and lose his grip on us. He will not change his mind. Even when we slip into sin, our anchor still holds and grips the solid rock. Our anchor is steadfast and dependable forever. In the hour of sickness, persecution, and death, when all other anchors fail, Jesus will hold us fast.

> Heaven and earth may pass away,
> but Jesus never fails.

When a storm arose and filled their boat with water, the disciples were afraid and cried out, "We are perishing. Save us, O Lord!" Jesus saved them by calming the storm. Even so, Jesus calms all of our great storms. In Christ, the peace of God that passes all human understanding will grip and guard our hearts and minds (Phil. 4:7).

He tells us not to be afraid, for he is with us in all of life's ebbs and flows. Our anchor of hope has died, risen, and entered the heavenly Holy of Holies as our forerunner and scout. He has entered God's presence on our behalf, that he may bring every one of us to God's presence, and he will not fail in this mission. By his sacrifice, he made the way for us to come to God. He is our shepherd, who guides us to the Celestial City and brings us into the Holy of Holies, behind the veil, and into God's presence.

The mission of Christ is to bring many sons to glory (Heb. 2:10) and he has done it. He is there already, and we will arrive there soon, one by one. In fact, in one sense we are already seated with

Christ (Eph. 2:6), for as branches are united to the vine, so we are vitally united with him.

Therefore, fear not! Fear not the fiery trials of life nor your own death. To us, to live is Christ and to die is gain, and to depart is to be present with Christ (Phil. 1:21–23). By faith and hope, fix your eyes not on the storms of life but on Jesus, our hope and sure anchor.

How do we fix our eyes on him? We see him in the Scriptures. Paul tells us that the Scriptures are written for our hope and encouragement (Rom. 15:4). Those who read and believe the Bible will overflow with encouragement, comfort, and hope. We must see Christ as Stephen did while he was being stoned to death: "But Stephen, full of the Holy Spirit, looked up to heaven and saw the glory of God, and Jesus standing at the right hand of God. 'Look,' he said, 'I see heaven open and the Son of Man standing at the right hand of God'" (Acts 7:55–56). Christ was standing, ready to usher Stephen into the very presence of God. Then Stephen prayed: "Lord Jesus, receive my spirit" (v. 59). Just as Stephen was welcomed by Jesus into heaven, so Christ will welcome every child of God into the presence of the Father.

Conclusion

Have you fled from the world of sin to Jesus for your safety and salvation? Have you believed in his oath-backed promise to save you? Is your soul moored to Jesus, who is moored to God the Father, that you may enjoy the peace of God when all other foundations give way? Have you laid hold of the hope that is laid before you in the gospel? Jesus said that the Law, the Prophets, and the Psalms all spoke of him, that Christ must die and be raised from the dead, that repentance and forgiveness of sins might be proclaimed to all nations (Luke 24:44–47).

What is the foundation of your life? Consider the words of Jesus: "Therefore everyone who hears these words of mine and puts them into practice is like a wise man who built his house on the rock. The rain came down, streams rose, and the winds blew and beat against that house; yet it did not fall, because it had its foundation on the rock" (Matt. 7:24–25). All earthly foundations will fail. Hebrews 12:26–27 says that God is going to shake everything one more time, and only the unshakable kingdom of God will stand.

Consider the hope of John and Betty Stam, a young missionary couple. In their late twenties, they were serving in the Anhwei province of China when they were captured by Communists in 1934. As their captors led them away to execute them for their faith in Christ, someone asked, "Where are you going?" John Stam answered, "I do not know where they are going, but we are going to heaven."

At the hour of your certain death, will you be able to say, "I am going to heaven, where Jesus my anchor of hope is waiting for me"? May God help all of us to trust in Jesus Christ alone and be saved, that we might experience this great and mighty encouragement that Jesus is the anchor of our souls. When we are buffeted by all the storms of life, may we know and be steadied by the peace of God that passes all human understanding.

15
Jesus, Our Eternal Savior

¹This Melchizedek was king of Salem and priest of God Most High. He met Abraham returning from the defeat of the kings and blessed him, ²and Abraham gave him a tenth of everything. First, his name means "king of righteousness"; then also, "king of Salem" means "king of peace." ³Without father or mother, without genealogy, without beginning of days or end of life, like the Son of God he remains a priest forever.

⁴Just think how great he was: Even the patriarch Abraham gave him a tenth of the plunder! ⁵Now the law requires the descendants of Levi who become priests to collect a tenth from the people—that is, their brothers—even though their brothers are descended from Abraham. ⁶This man, however, did not trace his descent from Levi, yet he collected a tenth from Abraham and blessed him who had the promises. ⁷And without doubt the lesser person is blessed by the greater. ⁸In the one case, the tenth is collected by men who die; but in the other case, by him who is declared to be living. ⁹One might even say that Levi, who collects the tenth, paid the tenth through Abraham, ¹⁰because when Melchizedek met Abraham, Levi was still in the body of his ancestor.

¹¹If perfection could have been attained through the Levitical priesthood (for on the basis of it the law was given to the people), why was there still need for another priest to come—one in the order of Melchizedek, not in the order of Aaron? ¹²For when there is a change of the priesthood, there must also be a change of the law. ¹³He of whom these things are said belonged to a different tribe, and no one from that tribe has ever served at the altar. ¹⁴For it is clear that our Lord descended from Judah, and in regard to that tribe Moses said nothing about priests. ¹⁵And what we have said is even more clear if another priest like Melchizedek appears, ¹⁶one who has become a priest not on the basis of a regulation as to his ancestry but on the basis of the power of an indestructible life. ¹⁷For it is declared: "You are a priest forever, in the order of Melchizedek."

¹⁸*The former regulation is set aside because it was weak and useless* ¹⁹*(for the law made nothing perfect), and a better hope is introduced, by which we draw near to God.*

²⁰*And it was not without an oath! Others became priests without any oath,* ²¹*but he became a priest with an oath when God said to him: "The Lord has sworn and will not change his mind: 'You are a priest forever.'"* ²²*Because of this oath, Jesus has become the guarantee of a better covenant.*

²³*Now there have been many of those priests, since death prevented them from continuing in office;* ²⁴*but because Jesus lives forever, he has a permanent priesthood.* ²⁵*Therefore he is able to save completely those who come to God through him, because he always lives to intercede for them.*

²⁶*Such a high priest meets our need—one who is holy, blameless, pure, set apart from sinners, exalted above the heavens.* ²⁷*Unlike the other high priests, he does not need to offer sacrifices day after day, first for his own sins, and then for the sins of the people. He sacrificed for their sins once for all when he offered himself.* ²⁸*For the law appoints as high priests men who are weak; but the oath, which came after the law, appointed the Son, who has been made perfect forever.*

Hebrews 7:1–28

Because Jesus is our eternal high priest, he is

also our eternal savior. The church of the Hebrews was tempted to return to Judaism's Aaronic priesthood, law, and sacrificial system, probably to avoid persecution and suffering. The author tells them that to do so would be to go back to the shadow after having seen the reality of Jesus Christ. They needed to consider the reality of the priesthood of Christ, which made the old sacrificial system and law obsolete.

Having already demonstrated that Jesus is superior to angels and Moses (Heb. 1–3), the author now presents Jesus as superior to Aaron and the Aaronic priesthood. He acknowledges that this teaching, which is meat for spiritual adults, may be difficult to understand because these people had become slow of learning.

The author had already touched on this subject of the priesthood of Christ: "For this reason, he had to be made like his brothers in every way in order that he might become a merciful and faithful high priest in service to God. . . . Therefore, holy brothers, who share in the heavenly calling, fix your thoughts on Jesus, the apostle and high priest whom we confess" (Heb. 2:17; 3:1; see also Heb. 4:14-15; 5:5, 10; 6:20).

To solve their spiritual problem, the author is saying these people must meditate earnestly on the high priesthood of Christ, which he deals with in detail in Hebrews 7:1-10:18. Christ is a high priest forever in the order of Melchizedek. The superiority of the priesthood of Christ to the Aaronic priesthood is the heart of this epistle. This doctrine provides infinite comfort for the people of God and is meant to cure the church's serious problem of backsliding.

The Historical Melchizedek

First, we want to look at the historical Melchizedek, whom we also read about in Genesis 14 and Psalm 110. Melchizedek, whose name means "king of righteousness," was king of Jerusalem (Gen. 14:18; Ps. 76:2). Called the priest of God Most High, he was both king and priest, ruling in righteousness and peace. Both Melchizedek and Abraham served the true God of glory.

This Melchizedek appears suddenly and no background is given for him. Yet this is not a supernatural appearance of the preincarnate Christ, as some suppose. The text says Melchizedek was *"like the Son of God"* (Heb. 7:3). He met Abraham as he returned from defeating the four eastern kings and rescuing Lot. After Melchizedek refreshed Abraham with wine and bread, he blessed Abraham, and Abraham gave him a tenth of all the choicest plunder in the name of the Lord.

The Great Melchizedek

"Just think how great he was: Even the patriarch Abraham gave him a tenth of the plunder!" (Heb. 7:4). This priest of the Most High God was great. The author treats him as a type of Christ whose priesthood is superior to that of Aaron. We are not given any genealogical information about him, even though it was important for the Aaronic priests to have a clear record of their ancestry.

The author sees a divine purpose for this silence and concludes that Melchizedek's priesthood is of a different order than that of Aaron. His priesthood should be likened to that of the eternal Son of God, who is also *"without beginning of days or end of life"* (Heb. 7:3). This does not mean Melchizedek was a biological anomaly. As a historical person, Melchizedek lived and died just like any other human. Yet God presents him in Genesis 14 without genealogical record of his birth or death, that he may function as a type of the Son of God, who truly has no beginning or end. So the priesthood of Jesus is after the order of Melchizedek (Ps. 110:4).

Melchizedek was superior to Abraham. As the patriarch of the Jewish nation and greatly revered in Jewish history, Abraham received promises from God and is called a prince and a friend of God. The Savior of the world was to come through the line of Abraham. Yet Abraham himself recognized Melchizedek as the royal priest of the Most High God and spontaneously paid him the tithe of the plunder (Gen. 14:20). In this act Abraham acknowledged Melchizedek's superiority, because he who receives the tithe is superior to him who gives it. Then Melchizedek blessed Abraham, and we are told the lesser receives blessing from the greater (Heb. 7:7). The greater always blesses the lesser: Isaac blessed Jacob (Gen. 27), the Lord blessed Jacob (Gen. 32), Jacob blessed his twelve children (Gen. 48–49), and Moses blessed the people of Israel (Deut. 33).

The author also says that in some way Levi paid Melchizedek the tithe because Levi was a great-grandson of Abraham: *"One might even say that Levi, who collects the tenth, paid the tenth through Abraham, because when Melchizedek met Abraham, Levi was still in the body of his ancestor"* (Heb. 7:9–10). As the one who was to collect the tithe from his brothers, Levi was considered superior to them. Yet through Abraham, Levi also paid tithes to this superior priest. So the Melchizedekian priesthood is greater than the Aaronic priesthood, because Melchizedek blessed Abraham and Melchizedek received tithes from Abraham and his descendant Levi.

Jesus Christ, Greater than Aaron and Melchizedek

> *"For it is clear that our Lord descended from Judah, and in regard to that tribe Moses said nothing about priests. . . . Because of this*

oath, Jesus has become the guarantee of a better covenant. Now there have been many of those priests, since death prevented them from continuing in office" (Heb. 7:14, 22–23). The author next speaks about the One who is greater than Aaron and Melchizedek—Jesus Christ, our eternal Savior and eternal High Priest. Calling him our Lord, he pictures Jesus as superior not only to Aaron and his priesthood, but also to Melchizedek, as the original is superior to the copy, as the antitype is superior to the type, and as reality is superior to shadow.

Melchizedek's priesthood without genealogy points to the eternal priesthood of the eternal Son. The incarnate Christ did have an earthly genealogy (Matt. 1; Luke 3), but the author is here speaking about the eternal Son, who is without beginning or end. Melchizedek's priesthood is a forever-living priesthood (Heb. 7:3, 8). Because there is no description of when he was born or when he died, for all practical purposes the author sees Melchizedek as practicing a living priesthood.

The Melchizedekian priesthood stands in contrast to the Levitical priesthood, which was a dying priesthood. History says that more than eighty high priests served in the sanctuary from the time of Aaron to the destruction of the temple. Because they were weak and sinful, they died. The Aaronic priesthood was temporary, partial, preparatory, and provisional, to be made obsolete in due time. God's eternal decree was that a superior priesthood would eventually replace the Aaronic priesthood, as he revealed even while the Aaronic priesthood was functioning (Ps. 110:4). The Hebrews author refers to this decree at least five times, quoting from Psalm 110. For instance, in Hebrews 7:21 he writes that God said to his Son in eternity, "*The Lord has sworn and will not change his mind: 'You are a priest forever.'*" God's eternal purpose was to save his people through the ministry of his Son's eternal priesthood.

As God promised Abraham salvation and established the promise with an oath for his greater encouragement, he also made an oath to his Son that he would be a priest forever for our eternal comfort. He promised on oath that the Son would fulfill the eternal covenant (Heb. 13:20) by means of his eternal priesthood. We were chosen in Jesus Christ "before the creation of the world" (Eph. 1:4). Likewise, "In him we were also chosen, having been predestined according to the plan of him who works out everything in conformity with the purpose of his will" (Eph. 1:11). God's eternal covenant is fulfilled through an eternal priesthood.

What was the priesthood of Christ to accomplish? The eternal priest would become incarnate and live a perfectly obedient life, offer himself to God in behalf of our sins, be raised from the dead, ascend into the presence of God, and continuously make intercession for all those who draw near to God through Jesus. The Father made this oath from eternity, that he might be just and the justifier of all who come to him through the priesthood of Christ.

The Aaronic priesthood had to be annulled and replaced by the priesthood of Christ because it was a shadow, not reality: "[The Aaronic priests] serve at a sanctuary that is a copy and shadow of what is in heaven. . . . The law is only a shadow of the good things that are coming—not the realities themselves" (Heb. 8:5; 10:1). The law and the Aaronic priesthood could never make anyone acceptable enough to approach God in worship. They never brought forgiveness of sins nor could they justify anyone before God. They could not cleanse the human conscience or make purification for sins. They prevented people from coming to God's presence in the Holy of Holies beyond the veil, requiring them instead to worship God from a distance (Exod. 24:1). So the author tells us, *"If perfection could have been obtained through the Levitical priesthood . . . why was there still need for another priest to come? . . . The former regulation is set aside because it was weak and useless (for the law made nothing perfect), and a better hope is introduced, by which we draw near to God"* (Heb. 7:11, 18–19).

That better hope is Christ and the better covenant and promises that he brings. When Christ sacrificed himself on the cross and rose from the dead, the Aaronic priesthood was superseded. It disappeared completely with the destruction of the temple in AD 70.

The shadow is replaced by the reality of salvation based on the sacrifice of Jesus Christ. But what about those who lived before Jesus? Were their sins forgiven? Undoubtedly! Consider Abraham, David, and all the people in Hebrews 11. God regenerated them by the Holy Spirit and granted them faith to believe in the coming Messiah, to whom the sacrificial system and law pointed. So their sins were forgiven and they were saved just as we are, for there is no other way of salvation. They trusted in the Messiah who was to come; we trust in the Messiah who has come and died on the cross in our place. Hebrews 11 asserts that all these people of the Old Testament era lived by faith.

If the law and Aaronic priesthood could not save anyone, why did God give them to his people? Paul tells us what the purpose was not: "For if a law had been given that could impart life, then righteousness would certainly have come by the law" (Gal. 3:21). The law was not given to impart life: "For what the law was powerless to do in that it was weakened by the sinful nature, God did by sending his Son, Jesus Christ" (Rom. 8:3). The law is holy, spiritual, and good; the problem is our inability to keep it. Elsewhere Paul writes that the law brought death and condemnation (2 Cor. 3:7, 9). The law gives power to sin, so sinful people sin more when the law is spoken.

Romans 3:20 reveals why the law was given: "Therefore no one will be declared righteous in his sight by observing the law; rather, through the law we become conscious of sin." Our rottenness and the pervasiveness of sin is revealed through God's law. And Romans 4:15 says the "law brings wrath." So it was not meant to impart life, but to bring consciousness of sin and point to the wrath of God. Romans 5:20 adds, "The law was added so that the trespass might increase."

The author tells us, "Day after day every priest stands and performs his religious duties; again and again he offers the same sacrifices, which can never take away sins" (Heb. 10:11). So the law was given, not to save us, but to lead us to Christ: "The law was put in charge to lead us to Christ, that we might be justified by faith" (Gal. 3:24). Galatians 2:15–16 says, "We who are Jews by birth and not 'Gentile sinners' know that a man is not justified by observing the law, but by faith in Jesus Christ. So we, too, have put our faith in Christ Jesus that we may be justified by faith in Christ and not by observing the law, because by observing the law no one will be justified." Romans 10:4 tells us, "Christ is the end of the law so that there may be righteousness for everyone who believes."

Aaron, who himself was sinful and dying, sacrificed animals as substitutes for sinners. But no animal's blood can cleanse us from our sins. We need a priest who is perfect God and perfect man—a priest, not after the order of Aaron, but after the order of Melchizedek. Such a priest came in the fullness of time, "born of a woman, born under law, to redeem those under law, that we might receive the full rights of sons" (Gal. 4:4-5). He was perfect and was made perfect through his sufferings: "Although he was a son, he learned obedience from what he suffered and, once made perfect, he became the source of eternal salvation for all who obey him" (Heb. 5:8-9). Jesus took away our sins once for all by making atonement for them, which was impossible for the Aaronic priesthood to do.

Hebrews 10 tells us that the priesthood of Jesus is absolutely superior because he is our eternal Savior: "It is impossible for the blood of bulls and goats to take away sins. . . . By [God's] will, we have been made holy through the sacrifice of the body of Jesus once for all . . . because by one sacrifice he has made perfect forever those who are being made holy" (vv. 4, 10, 14). Jesus is greater than angels, Moses, Aaron, the Aaronic priesthood, and even Melchizedek, because Jesus alone makes us perfect.

The Superiority of Jesus Christ

Let us now examine seven reasons why the priesthood of Christ is superior to the Aaronic priesthood.

1. An Indestructible Life

He "has become a priest not on the basis of a regulation as to his ancestry but on the basis of the power of an indestructible life" (Heb. 7:16). Jesus Christ is characterized by indestructible life. Aaron was sinful, weak, and mortal. But now we have a high priest, the Son of God, who is sinless, powerful, and eternal.

2. A Divine Oath

"And it was not without an oath! Others became priests without any oath, but he became a priest with an oath when God said to him: 'The Lord has sworn and will not change his mind: You are a priest forever'" (Heb. 7:20-21). Jesus is high priest through a divine oath. The priesthood of Aaron was based on an ordinance, not an oath.

The priesthood of Jesus Christ was not provisional but eternal, given by divine oath.

3. A Perfect High Priest
"For the law appoints as high priests men who are weak; but the oath, which came after the law, appointed the Son, who has been made perfect forever" (Heb. 7:28). The Aaronic priests were weak and died because of sin. We now have a high priest, the Father-appointed Son of God, who is perfect and able to perfect us.

4. A Guarantee for Eternal Salvation
"Because of this oath, Jesus has become the guarantee of a better covenant" (Heb. 7:22). This high priest is our guarantee for eternal salvation. Another word for guarantor is mediator: "But the ministry Jesus has received is as superior to theirs as the covenant of which he is mediator is superior to the old one. . . . For this reason Christ is the mediator of a new covenant, that those who are called may receive the promised eternal inheritance" (Heb. 8:6; 9:15). Jesus Christ is our guarantor; therefore, we receive an eternal inheritance.

There was no guarantee with the priesthood of Aaron. But Jesus, who fulfilled the law perfectly in our behalf, is the mediator between God and us. As man, he represents us to God; as God, he represents God to us. Thus, he alone can and does guarantee our full and final salvation.

5. A Permanent Priesthood
"Now there have been many of those priests, since death prevented them from continuing in office; but because Jesus lives forever, he has a permanent priesthood" (Heb. 7:23–24). The priesthood of Christ is not transferable. Because of human frailty, the Aaronic priesthood was transferred to more than eighty high priests as each man grew old and died. But the Melchizedekian priesthood of Jesus needs no transfer because Christ the Living One never dies (Rev. 1:18). Therefore, his priesthood is permanent.

6. An Able High Priest
"Therefore he is able to save completely those who come to God through him, because he always lives to intercede for them" (Heb. 7:25).

This key verse summarizes the argument of this chapter. In the Greek, the word for "able" is *dunatai*, mighty. It can be contrasted with *adunaton*, "not capable" or "impossible," which is used in Hebrews 10:4 to refer to the inability of the sacrifices offered by the Aaronic priesthood to remove sin. Let us look at the following truths we can learn from this verse.

a. He is able to save

The Aaronic priesthood and its sacrifices did not have the power to save anyone. But verse 25 tells us that our Lord Jesus Christ is mighty, and the first thing our Lord is mighty to do is to save us. From what are we being saved? The author is not speaking about salvation from marriage troubles or work troubles. No, fundamentally, we need to be saved from God himself, especially from his wrath: "The wrath of God is being revealed from heaven against all the godlessness and wickedness of men" (Rom. 1:18). God's wrath is against us because of our sin; only Christ can save us from that wrath.

b. He saves us completely

This high priest saves us totally. The Greek phrase means he saves us completely and forever. What eternal security! He is mighty to save both body and soul forever. Not only does he save us now, but also at death we will go to him. Then, at his second coming, we shall come with him to be clothed with a physical, spiritual body like unto the glorious body of Christ.

This high priest saves us from God's wrath that we may fellowship with God forevermore. He not only justifies and sanctifies us, but he also helps us in all life's problems. This is comprehensive salvation of spirit and body. The Hebrews writer here uses the word "save" in the present tense. Elsewhere, the Bible speaks about salvation in three tenses: He saved us (Tit. 3:5), he is saving us (1 Cor. 1:18), and he will save us (Acts 15:11). This all-encompassing salvation depends on our great high priest after the order of Melchizedek.

c. He saves all who draw near

Next, we are told that this high priest saves every person who draws near to God. Throughout this book we are encouraged to draw near to God (Heb. 4:16; 10:22). How often do we draw near to everything and everyone else but God! We must draw near to the Mighty One—in worship, in prayer, in reading the word, in fellowship, and in the sacraments. We must draw near to receive mercy and to find grace for all our needs. "Draw near" is in the present tense. That means we may come again and again. God's door is open and he wants to see us.

d. *He saves all who draw near to God the Father*

To whom do we draw near? To God the Father. We can come to God because our great high priest, Jesus Christ, has removed the barrier of sin. The veil has been torn from top to bottom, and nothing prevents us from coming to our Father in him.

e. *We come through Jesus Christ*

Hebrews 7:25 tells us this high priest is mighty to save us when we draw near to God "through him," meaning through Jesus. Jesus is the only way to the Father, as Christ himself declared: "I am the way and the truth and the life. No one comes to the Father except through me" (John 14:6). There is no other mediator, no other high priest, and no other savior. Peter proclaims, "Salvation is found in no one else, for there is no other name under heaven given to men by which we must be saved" (Acts 4:12). Self-salvation is impossible. All other religions are false in their claims to bring us to the true and living God. All worship outside of worshiping our heavenly Father in the name of Jesus Christ is the worship of demons (1 Cor. 10:20–21).

f. *He always lives to intercede*

This high priest always lives in heaven to intercede for his people. This aspect of the ministry of Jesus is often forgotten by the church. Jesus is always interceding to the Father in our behalf, especially when we stumble and sin.

Because Jesus prays to the Father on the basis of his atonement, his intercession is always effectual and we can enjoy great comfort. Our great high priest intercedes for us when we sleep and when we wake, when we work and when we come home, when we give birth and raise children, when we are sick and old, and when we face death.

This heavenly intercession is a continuation of what Jesus did on earth. He told Simon Peter, "Simon, Simon, Satan has asked to sift you as wheat. But I have prayed for you, Simon, that your faith may not fail. And when you have turned back, strengthen your brothers" (Luke 22:31–32). John 17 is an intercessory prayer of our Lord for his church. For instance, Jesus says, "I pray for them. I am not praying for the world, but for those you have given me, for they are yours" (v. 9). Then he says, "My prayer is not that you take them out of the world but that you protect them from the evil one" (v. 15).

Thank God, we have all been tempted to do many wrong things but have not done them because the Lord has been praying for us and has kept us from all kinds of troubles. We are a blessed people because our great high priest continuously intercedes for us.

7. A Qualified High Priest

"*Such a high priest meets our need—one who is holy, blameless, pure, set apart from sinners, exalted above the heavens*" (Heb. 7:26). This is the seventh way Jesus Christ is superior to Aaron. Because we were sinners under God's wrath, we needed a qualified high priest, one who is both holy God and holy man. Aaron did not and could not meet our need. No man can. But in the fullness of time, God sent his Son—holy, guileless, undefiled, separate from sinners, exalted into the heavens, our great high priest after the order of Melchizedek.

First, we note that Christ is without sin: "*Unlike the other high priests, he does not need to offer sacrifices day after day, first for his own sins, and then for the sins of the people. He sacrificed for their sins once for all when he offered himself*" (Heb. 7:27–28). The cross speaks about Jesus' sacrifice for our sins. Not only was he the priest making the offering, but he was also the victim—not a dumb, brute, unconscious animal, but the sinless Son of God. All the blood shed in the Old Testament was pointing forward to the bloodshedding of this great high priest on our behalf.

He offered himself to God once-for-all *(ephapax)*. This word appears several times in the epistle. By Christ's one sacrifice, he satisfied the demand of the Father for justice by suffering God's wrath on the cross for our sakes. No further sacrifice is necessary: all our sins—past, present, and future—are paid for in the once-for-all sacrifice of Jesus Christ. This means no work on our part is required to effect our salvation. Salvation is by grace alone through faith alone. In fact, any work on our part is an insult to Christ and his sacrifice, as well as to God the Father. Only believe in this One and his once-for-all offered sacrifice.

Truly, Jesus is our king of righteousness and peace, for he *is* our righteousness and peace. Having been justified by faith, we have peace with God (Rom. 5:1).

We must understand that we are all sinners, and our sin is pervasive. The essence of sin is enmity against God. We must not flatter ourselves by thinking otherwise. All are sinners, enemies of God, and under God's wrath. The law and the Aaronic priesthood cannot save us, but they can point us to Christ, who fulfilled the law in our place. He makes us perfect so that we can have fellowship with God. We are justified by God the Father on the basis of the high priestly work of his Son; thus, we are saved from God's wrath, which was endured by Jesus Christ alone in our place. Having gone to hell for us on the cross, he now calls us to draw near to God through faith in him. He calls us to draw near to him and be saved. Praise God for the eternal priesthood of our eternal Savior!

16

New Covenant Blessings

¹The point of what we are saying is this: We do have such a high priest, who sat down at the right hand of the throne of the Majesty in heaven, ²and who serves in the sanctuary, the true tabernacle set up by the Lord, not by man.

³Every high priest is appointed to offer both gifts and sacrifices, and so it was necessary for this one also to have something to offer. ⁴If he were on earth, he would not be a priest, for there are already men who offer the gifts prescribed by the law. ⁵They serve at a sanctuary that is a copy and shadow of what is in heaven. This is why Moses was warned when he was about to build the tabernacle: "See to it that you make everything according to the pattern shown you on the mountain." ⁶But the ministry Jesus has received is as superior to theirs as the covenant of which he is mediator is superior to the old one, and it is founded on better promises.

⁷For if there had been nothing wrong with that first covenant, no place would have been sought for another. ⁸But God found fault with the people and said: "The time is coming, declares the Lord, when I will make a new covenant with the house of Israel and with the house of Judah. ⁹It will not be like the covenant I made with their forefathers when I took them by the hand to lead them out of Egypt, because they did not remain faithful to my covenant, and I turned away from them, declares the Lord. ¹⁰This is the covenant I will make with the house of Israel after that time, declares the Lord. I will put my laws in their minds and write them on their hearts. I will be their God, and they will be my people. ¹¹No longer will a man teach his neighbor, or a man his brother, saying, 'Know the Lord,' because they will all know me, from the least of them to the greatest. ¹²For I will forgive their wickedness and will remember their sins no more." ¹³By calling this covenant "new," he has made the first one obsolete; and what is obsolete and aging will soon disappear.

Hebrews 8:1–13

There are sacerdotal Orthodox and Roman Catholic churches today with priests who follow after the pattern of the Levitical priesthood, which Jesus Christ came to abolish. They do not preach the bright light and life of the gospel, but function as shadow and symbol, even though the reality has now come in Jesus. Then there are Protestant churches that exist, not as shadows, but as deep darkness, in their refusal to preach and practice the clear word of God. By divine grace many have been able to come out from the shadow into the marvelous light of the gospel.

Due to persecution and suffering, the church of the Hebrews was tempted to go back to Judaism with its animal sacrifices and the perceived dignity of the Levitical priesthood. Similarly, many prominent evangelicals today are returning to the shadow of sacerdotal churches. They are enamored by the rituals of the Mass and by vestments, bells, incense, candles, traditions, and beautiful buildings.

In this letter, the author shows the foolishness of going back to the symbol and shadow of the Aaronic priesthood with its bloody sacrifices after experiencing the reality to which the shadow pointed. That reality is the superior priesthood of Jesus Christ, who ministers in a superior sanctuary as the mediator of the new covenant. It is utter mindlessness to abandon substance for shadows and forsake the new covenant blessings that flow from the ministry of Christ. Jesus Christ made the Aaronic priesthood obsolete. This system was aging and decaying when Christ came; it completely disappeared, as Jesus predicted, in AD 70.

The Superior Priesthood of Christ

"The point of what we are saying is this: We do have such a high priest, who sat down at the right hand of the throne of the Majesty in heaven, and who serves in the sanctuary, the true tabernacle set up by the Lord, not by man" (Heb. 8:1–2). In these verses, the author summarizes the chief point of this passage, declaring that in Jesus we have a superior high priest after the order of Melchizedek, the guarantor of a better covenant.

Hebrews 7 told us that the priesthood of Aaron was weak and useless, for it never made anyone perfect, it did not solve our sin problem or open the way to the Holy of Holies, and it could not bring a sinner into fellowship with God. So the sinless Son of God, by his one sacrifice of himself once-for-all-offered, made atonement for the sins of God's people. This high priest is mighty to save completely and for all time all those who come to God through him.

"*We do have such a high priest*" (v. 1). The writer uses the present tense, which means we possess him now. This high priest is with us and is for us. He said, "I am with you always, to the very end of the age" (Matt. 28:20). He is in us, our hope of glory (Col. 1:27). Yet he is also with the Father, interceding before him in our behalf on the basis of his atonement. The author says that this distinguished high priest is seated. In contrast, the Levitical priests never sat down; in fact, we find no mention of chairs in the tabernacle or temple. They could not sit because their work was never finished. Hebrews 10 tells us that the Aaronic sacrifices were an annual reminder of the sins of the people. But they could never make effective atonement for the people's sins because the priests themselves were sinners, subject to death, offering unconscious and unwilling animals as their substitute.

Jesus Christ, the sinless Son of Man, finished his work by offering himself in our place once for all. He cried from the cross, "*Tetelestai!* (It is finished!)" Having finished forever the work of atonement, Christ sat down: "After he had provided purification for sins, he sat down at the right hand of the Majesty in heaven" (Heb. 1:3). David says, "The LORD says to my Lord: 'Sit at my right hand until I make your enemies a footstool for your feet'" (Ps. 110:1). He sat down as both king and priest. Paul says this royal priest is seated "far above all rule and authority, power and dominion, and every title that can be given, not only in the present age but also in the one to come. And God placed all things under his feet and appointed him to be head over everything for the church, which is his body, and the fullness of him who fills everything in every way" (Eph. 1:21–23). Jesus Christ sat down, and we also, in a sense, are seated with him.

Verse 1 also says, "*[Jesus] sat down at the right hand of the throne of the Majesty in heaven.*" Christ is given the seat of privilege, honor, and all authority, and all things are subjected to him. He is the head of the church and fills the church with blessings. On

173

the right hand of the Father, the seated Christ "must reign until he has put all his enemies under his feet" (1 Cor. 15:25). All our resistance to the will of God can never succeed.

Christ is seated, reigning and interceding in the presence of God himself: "For Christ did not enter a man-made sanctuary that was only a copy of the true one; he entered heaven itself, now to appear for us in God's presence" (Heb. 9:24). Jesus ascended to the Father's right hand to minister in a superior sanctuary. He ascended not only as Son, Lord, and King, but also as Son of Man, high priest, and Savior. He ascended as one person in two natures, the unique God-man.

So the author says that Christ *"serves in the sanctuary, the true tabernacle set up by the Lord, not by man"* (Heb. 8:2). The earthly temple was only a copy, a shadow cast by the true heavenly sanctuary. Moses built the earthly tabernacle according to the pattern shown to him on the mountain, but it was imperfect and impermanent. It was simply a type and symbol of the heavenly sanctuary. It pointed to the heavenly country, the city with foundations whose maker and builder is God. It pointed to the unshakable kingdom of God and to God himself.

The Jewish people took pride in the tabernacle, first, and later in the temple, thinking these places of worship guaranteed their own security and salvation. But the earthly tabernacle was destroyed and the temple burned. The heavenly sanctuary, however, where our Lord Jesus Christ serves as our great high priest, lasts forever. When Christ was on earth, he was not a priest but a layman and was prevented by law from ministering in the temple. Now, however, he ministers in heaven in the real sanctuary, a sanctuary not made with human hands but pitched by the Lord himself.

The time of shadow is over and the age of reality has come in Jesus Christ. It is foolish to yearn for symbols, vestments, incense, candles, gold, silver, Gothic structures, and the clergy-laity distinction. Away with such carnal things! We have a high priest seated in heaven who ministers in the heavenly, God-built sanctuary.

Hebrews 12 gives us a glimpse of the spiritual nature of this sanctuary and of true New Testament worship: "But you have come to Mount Zion, to the heavenly Jerusalem, the city of the living God. You have come to thousands upon thousands of angels in joyful assembly, to the church of the firstborn, whose names are written in heaven. You have come to God, the judge of all men, to the spirits of righteous men made perfect, to Jesus the mediator of a new covenant, and to the sprinkled blood that speaks a better word than the blood of Abel" (vv. 22–24). We have left the old way of worship and have come by the Spirit and faith to the heavenly Jerusalem, where we worship God in the light of the gospel.

A Superior Mediator

"The ministry Jesus has received is as superior to [that of the Aaronic priests] as the covenant of which he is mediator is superior to the old one, and it is founded on better promises" (Heb. 8:6). In the heavenly sanctuary, the Lord Jesus serves as our mediator of the new covenant. When Jesus Christ guarantees our salvation and mediates between God and us, we have nothing to worry about.

A mediator is a go-between, an arbitrator between two estranged parties—in this case, between holy God and sinful men. Defending the interests of both, he brings about a win-win situation. Jesus defended God's justice and holiness even as he secured the eternal salvation of us sinners from God's wrath: "For this reason Christ is the mediator of a new covenant, that those who are called may receive the promised eternal inheritance—now that he has died as a ransom to set them free from the sins committed under the first covenant" (Heb. 9:15). Because of Christ's mediation, we can never fall short of our eternal inheritance, the everlasting rest of the saints.

Jesus Christ is our "atonemaker," a term used by William Tyndale. He made atonement by fully keeping God's law in his life and death. He thus defended God's justice and holiness, so God now can justify sinners, not in spite of his holiness, but in harmony with it. Christ lived and died to defend God's holiness and to save sinners.

Christ died for our sins: "But when this priest had offered for all time one sacrifice for sins, he sat down at the right hand of God" (Heb. 10:12). Every high priest must offer a sacrifice. What did Christ offer? He offered himself (Heb. 9:28) by shedding his blood and offering his body (Heb. 9:12; 10:10). He did so once-for-all, defending both our interest and God's. Now God can be just in justifying all who believe in him. In the heavenly sanctuary, Christ now makes intercession in our behalf based on the singularity of his own sacrifice. He is both our guarantor and mediator. And the Father's answer to the Son's intercession for us is always "Yes."

Our salvation does not depend on anything in this world, especially not on our feelings, which change like the weather. Our salvation rests on Christ's mediatorship and atonement accomplished by his vicarious sacrifice.

The Superior New Covenant Blessings

"For if there had been nothing wrong with that first covenant, no place would have been sought for another. But God found fault with the people and said: 'The time is coming, declares the Lord, when I will make a new covenant with the house of Israel and with the house of Judah'" (Heb. 8:7–8). The old covenant was faulty, imperfect, and temporary; yet God himself instituted it. The fault is not in God but in us. Paul said, "What the law was powerless to do because of our flesh [our sinfulness], God did" (Rom. 8:3, author's translation).

The Sinaitic covenant emphasized Israel's obligation to God. When God established this covenant with Israel on Mount Sinai, they agreed to keep it, declaring, "Everything the LORD has said we will do. . . . We will do everything the Lord has said: we will obey" (Exod. 24:3, 7).

But notice what God says about his people: *"They did not remain faithful to my covenant"* (Heb. 8:9). The problem was not the covenant but human sinfulness. So God dealt the unbelieving rebel Israelites throughout their history. During the forty years in the wilderness, most of them were killed by God. After they entered Canaan, God destroyed more and cast others into exile.

It was always God's plan, not an afterthought, to bring about a new priesthood after the order of Melchizedek and to establish a new covenant, (see Ps. 110; Jer. 31). By design, then, the Aaronic priesthood and the law were temporary. The purpose of this temporary Sinaitic covenant was to bring consciousness of our sin and moral inability so that we may realize our need for Christ.

In the seventh century BC, God declared through Jeremiah his intent to bring about a new covenant that would be permanent and effectual. This new covenant was established by Jesus Christ our mediator. It solved our sin problem once and for all and so enables us to enter the presence of God that we may worship him in spirit and in truth and have fellowship with him forever. In Hebrews 8:8–12 the author quotes Jeremiah 31:31–34 in full; this is the longest Old Testament quotation in the New Testament. This new covenant is an authoritative declaration of God. Three times we are told, "declares the Lord," and seven times God says, "I will," confirming that he will perform what he has promised. So we read, "I will accomplish," "I will establish," "I will put," "I will write," "I will be," "I will forgive," and "I will not remember their sins."

Blessings and Characteristics of the New Covenant

The author emphasizes three new covenant characteristics and blessings in this quote from Jeremiah 31:31–34: God implants his law in our hearts, he gives us knowledge of him, and he blots out all our sins.

1. *"I will put my laws in their minds and write them on their hearts"* (Heb. 8:10).

God implants his law into our hearts so that it becomes our nature to love God and his law and to do his will. If we do not delight in doing God's law, it is an indication to us that we must call upon the name of the Lord and be saved.

The law given on Sinai was written on stones, not on human hearts. But man's problem is that as a sinner he naturally rebels against God's law. He hates it in his heart and his mind refuses to accept it, exchanging its truth for a lie. He always chooses evil and his affections are always for evil.

We read about this total depravity of man in Genesis 6:5: "Every inclination of the thoughts of his heart was only evil all the time," and Jeremiah 17:9: "The heart is deceitful above all things, and desperately wicked: who can know it?" (KJV). Jesus himself located sin not outside but inside our human nature: "From within, out of men's hearts, come evil thoughts, sexual immorality, theft, murder, adultery, greed, malice, deceit, lewdness, envy, slander, arrogance, and folly" (Mark 7:21–22). Paul also speaks about the total depravity of the human heart:

> As it is written: "There is no one righteous, not even one; there is no one who understands, no one who seeks God. All have turned away, they have together become worthless; there is no one who does good, not even one." "Their throats are open graves; their tongues practice deceit." "The poison of vipers is on their lips." "Their mouths are full of cursing and bitterness." "Their feet are swift to shed blood; ruin and misery mark their ways, and the way of peace they do not know." "There is no fear of God before their eyes." (Rom. 3:10–18)

Our problem is never external and environmental. Our problem is internal rottenness, and the only solution is a new heart, a new mind, a new will, and new affections. We need nothing less than to be regenerated by the Holy Spirit. This is not a decisional salvation, but a salvation based on God implanting his law in our hearts. We need spiritual resurrection, the life of God in the soul of man. We need God to write his moral laws on a new heart.

When we are regenerated, we will naturally delight in God's laws and do them. We will eagerly study God's law with our minds, we will gladly choose with our wills to do it, and we will wholeheartedly love it and hate evil. Salvation does not mean we get rid of God's law and become antinomian. There is nothing wrong with the law. In fact, the law is the transcript of God's nature to which he wants us to conform.

So God implants his law in us, that we may know it, will it, and love it. When we are born of God, our minds want to know God, our wills will be yielded to God's will, and our affections will love God and hate evil. Grace enables us to do God's law and thus honor him. Anyone who disobeys God's law dishonors God. We cannot disobey God's moral law and glorify him at the same time, because the law reflects God's nature.

Before we became Christians, we lacked ability to obey God, but the new covenant enables us to love God and keep his commandments. God's law is now our inner principle. The Lord spoke about this through Ezekiel: "They will return to [the land of Israel] and remove all its vile images and detestable idols. I will give them an undivided heart and put a new spirit in them; I will remove from them their heart of stone and give them a heart of flesh. Then they will follow my decrees and be careful to keep my laws. They will be my people, and I will be their God" (Ezek. 11:18–20). Our problem is our wicked, deceitful mind, will, and affections. We need nothing less than a new heart. God himself performs that miracle in his people: "I will give you a new heart and put a new spirit in you; I will remove from you your heart of stone and give you a heart of flesh. And I will put my Spirit in you and move you to follow my decrees and be careful to keep my laws" (Ezek. 36:26–27). Our problem is moral depravity, and God's answer is regeneration. He himself gives us a new heart, a new attitude, a new nature, and a new power.

True Christianity is thus not anti-law. Paul exhorts, "Let no debt remain outstanding, except the continuing debt to love one another, for he who loves his fellowman has fulfilled the law. The commandments, 'Do not commit adultery,' 'Do not murder,' 'Do not steal,' 'Do not covet,' and whatever other commandment there may be, are summed up in this one rule: 'Love your neighbor as yourself'" (Rom. 13:8–9). Christianity does not tell us to forget about the law; rather, it enables us to love and obey it.

In Hebrews 13 the pastor tells his church how they should live: "May the God of peace, who through the blood of the eternal covenant brought back from the dead our Lord Jesus, that great Shepherd of the sheep, equip you with everything good for doing his will, and may he work in us what is pleasing to him, through Jesus Christ, to whom be glory for ever and ever. Amen" (Heb. 13:20–21). Paul speaks similarly: "Continue to work out your salvation with fear and trembling, for it is God who works in you to will and to act according to his good purpose" (Phil. 2:12–13). We please God by keeping his moral law.

2. *"I will be their God, and they will be my people. No longer will a man teach his neighbor, or a man his brother, saying, 'Know the Lord,' because they will all know me, from the least of them to the greatest"* (Heb. 8:10b–11).

The second characteristic of this new covenant is that God gives us knowledge of him. This means new covenant people will know God directly and enjoy fellowship with him. They will love the Lord with all their heart, soul, mind, and strength. There is an initial experiential knowledge brought about by the Spirit's regeneration, followed by a continuing desire to know God and have fellowship with him. Our desire is to know God from the Scriptures, as taught by the Spirit.

We are told that all his people will know and love the Lord—Israel and Judah, Jews and Gentiles, the least and the greatest. They will have intimacy with God and worship him. Such delight in God is a sign of the new covenant.

The Lord says he will be our God and do for us what only God can do for us, and we will be his people, loving him, doing his will, and having fellowship with him. Jesus describes this relationship of the Father with his people: "Now this is eternal life: that they may know you, the only true God, and Jesus Christ, whom you have sent" (John 17:3).

God delights in his people, and his people delight in their God. There is no more idolatry. The hearts of the saints find their everlasting rest in fellowship with God.

3. *"For I will forgive their wickedness and will remember their sins no more"* (Heb. 8:12).

How is it possible for sinful people to have fellowship with the holy God? God promises to blot out our sins: *"Because I will be merciful to their unrighteousness and I will remember their sins no more"* (author's translation). David declared, "Blessed is he whose transgressions are forgiven, whose sins are covered. Blessed is the man whose sin the Lord does not count against him and in whose spirit is no deceit" (Ps. 32:1–2). He also prayed, "Have mercy on me, O God, according to your unfailing love; according to your great compassion blot out my transgressions" (Ps. 51:1).

In this new covenant that the Lord himself established based on the high priestly ministry of Jesus, all our sins are blotted out. Not even one remains, whether it is a sin of the past, the present, or the future. No longer do we experience a crushing load of sin on our backs. No longer are we slaves to sin and in bondage to our wills. No longer are we found guilty and subject to the wrath of God. A new day of God's favor is dawning and we are entering into an eternal spring season of God's smiling upon us.

New Covenant Blessings

On the basis of blood being shed on the mercy seat, the publican cried out, "Be merciful to me, the sinner" (Luke 18:13). Now we know it is not the blood of animals, but the blood of Jesus Christ himself that is sprinkled there. Because Christ has satisfied God's justice, God says he will therefore be merciful to our wickedness.

"*I . . . will remember their sins no more*" (Heb. 8:12). "Remember" in this context means God could act against the sinner on the basis of his sins and send him to hell. But God is saying he will never remember our sins. We are saved forever.

God has washed, sanctified, and justified us because of the sacrifice of Christ on our behalf. Throughout the Old Testament the Lord spoke of this glorious blessing from the new covenant: "I, even I, am he who blots out your transgressions, *for my own sake*" (Isa. 43:25, italics added). The new covenant is fulfilled by God, not because of anything in us that is commendable or good, but for his own sake. He blots out and remembers our sins no more. Isaiah declares, "[The Lord says,] 'I have swept away your offenses like a cloud, your sins like the morning mist.' . . . Sing for joy, O heavens, for the Lord has done this" (Isa. 44:22–23). And Micah asks, "Who is a God like you, who pardons sin and forgives the transgression of the remnant of his inheritance? You do not stay angry forever, but delight to show mercy. You will again have compassion on us; you will tread our sins underfoot and hurl all our iniquities into the depths of the sea" (Mic. 7:18–19).

God promises to blot out all our sins and remember them no more: "'Come now, let us reason together,' says the Lord. 'Though your sins are like scarlet, they shall be as white as snow; though they are red as crimson, they shall be like wool'" (Isa. 1:18). What is the reason? "[Jesus] was pierced for our transgressions, he was crushed for our iniquities; the punishment that brought us peace was upon him, and by his wounds we are healed" (Isa. 53:5). Now we enjoy a better priesthood, a better covenant, better promises, and a better sanctuary. All our sins are blotted out, not in spite of God's justice and holiness, but in harmony with it, due to the work of our mediator.

What about You?

Do you belong to this new covenant that Jesus ratified by his blood? Jesus said, "This cup is the new covenant in my blood, which is poured out for you" (cf. Matt. 26:28; Mark 14:24; 1 Cor. 11:25). This new covenant made the old one obsolete. When Christ was crucified, the veil that prevented people from coming into the Holy of Holies was torn from top to bottom.

Have you trusted in Jesus Christ alone for your eternal salvation? Does he say to you, "I will forgive your wickedness and remember your sins no more?" Jesus came to fulfill the covenant in our stead, that those who trust in him may partake of its blessings. Such people have a new nature that delights in God and his law; thus, they glorify God by loving and doing God's will by grace. The Holy Spirit dwells in them, enabling them to love God with a new heart, a new mind, a new will, and new affections.

What, then, shall we do? Consider Jesus. Fix your eyes on Jesus, the author and finisher of our faith, the apostle and the high priest of the new covenant. He died for us, was buried, and was raised on the third day according to the Scriptures. He ascended into heaven and is seated on the right hand of God the Father. As royal priest, he is given all power and authority. He rules and reigns as royal priest in God's presence, the heavenly sanctuary.

Consider him who lives forever to intercede for us before the Father. In him is forgiveness and salvation. His answer is always yes. Consider him as our guarantor and mediator, and you shall be filled with all hope, power, and peace to live for God's glory in joy inexpressible both here and hereafter.

17
A Clear Conscience

¹Now the first covenant had regulations for worship and also an earthly sanctuary. ²A tabernacle was set up. In its first room were the lampstand, the table and the consecrated bread; this was called the Holy Place. ³Behind the second curtain was a room called the Most Holy Place, ⁴which had the golden altar of incense and the gold-covered ark of the covenant. This ark contained the gold jar of manna, Aaron's staff that had budded, and the stone tablets of the covenant. ⁵Above the ark were the cherubim of the Glory, overshadowing the atonement cover. But we cannot discuss these things in detail now.

⁶When everything had been arranged like this, the priests entered regularly into the outer room to carry on their ministry. ⁷But only the high priest entered the inner room, and that only once a year, and never without blood, which he offered for himself and for the sins the people had committed in ignorance. ⁸The Holy Spirit was showing by this that the way into the Most Holy Place had not yet been disclosed as long as the first tabernacle was still standing. ⁹This is an illustration for the present time, indicating that the gifts and sacrifices being offered were not able to clear the conscience of the worshiper. ¹⁰They are only a matter of food and drink and various ceremonial washings—external regulations applying until the time of the new order.

¹¹When Christ came as high priest of the good things that are already here, he went through the greater and more perfect tabernacle that is not man-made, that is to say, not a part of this creation. ¹²He did not enter by means of the blood of goats and calves; but he entered the Most Holy Place once for all by his own blood, having obtained eternal redemption. ¹³The blood of goats and bulls and the ashes of a heifer sprinkled on those who are ceremonially unclean sanctify them so that they are outwardly clean. ¹⁴How much more, then, will the blood of Christ, who through the eternal Spirit offered himself

unblemished to God, cleanse our consciences from acts that lead to death, so that we may serve the living God!

Hebrews 9:1–14

The people of the world have many peculiar "problems." The most popular problem today is global warming. It used to be global cooling; before that, it was the population explosion. But the real problem of every sinner is his filthy conscience. We need to know how to get rid of our guilt and gain a clear conscience.

Throughout history people have tried to cleanse their consciences in many ways. The ancient Ammonites used to throw their children into the fire in worship of their god Molech, while Hindus would throw their children into rivers to appease wrathful deities. In modern times, young people strap bomb belts around themselves and self-destruct, killing "infidels" in the process. Some people flagellate themselves in religious frenzy, while others walk over fiery coals, crucify themselves, or practice severe asceticism. Those with money give great sums to charitable causes. Yet none of these behaviors can truly cleanse a guilty conscience.

God instituted the Levitical priesthood with its bloody sacrifices to deal with the sins of his people. But even these God-instituted bloody sacrifices did not provide cleansing for filthy consciences. The blood of goats and bulls and the ashes of heifers utterly failed to cleanse the conscience of the worshiper (Heb. 9:9, 13). The ceremonial law, however, had a purpose: it pointed to a better sacrifice that *could* cleanse human filthy consciences. This better sacrifice, offered by a better priest once for all to God, was the blood of Jesus Christ. Thus, the author implies in this passage that it would be foolish for anyone to go back to the imperfect worship of Judaism, which was only a shadow of the good things that came in Christ.

If you are burdened with a guilty conscience, I have good news for you. You can be delivered from the penalty and power of sin today, instantly and eternally. Why carry this crushing load when a way has been established for its eternal disposition?

The Earthly Tabernacle

The earthly sanctuary of which the author was speaking (v.1) was not designed to give us a good conscience and usher us into the intimate presence of God. The tabernacle Moses was ordered to construct consisted of an outer room called the Holy Place and an inner room called the Holy of Holies. The author calls it an earthly sanctuary, contrasting it with the true heavenly sanctuary where Jesus ministers in the presence of God.

The Holy Place was furnished on the south side with a seven-branched lampstand made of about seventy-five pounds of gold. Solomon's later temple had ten lampstands. On the north side was a table on which twelve loaves of bread were placed on each Sabbath in two rows of six, representing the twelve tribes of Israel. On the west side, in front of the second thick veil that barred people from the presence of God, there was the altar of incense. Our author places the altar of incense in the Holy of Holies because of its association with the ministry that occurred there, especially the high priest's sprinkling of the blood of the sin offering upon and in front of the mercy seat above the ark (1 Kings 6:22). It may be that on the Day of Atonement the altar of incense was moved to the inner room of the Holy of Holies, but all other days it remained in the Holy Place.

The most important piece of furniture, which was placed in the Holy of Holies, was the ark, in which were the golden jar of manna, the rod of Aaron that budded, and the two tablets of the covenant, which contained the Ten Commandments. The ark disappeared when the temple was destroyed in 587 BC. According to the historian Tacitus, it was still missing in 63 BC, when Pompey forced his way into the second temple.

This ark had a cover made of gold with two cherubim on each side. Their outstretched wings overshadowed this atonement cover, the *hilasterion*, or mercy seat. God's presence was above this mercy seat, as we read in Psalm 80:1: "Hear us, O Shepherd of Israel, you who lead Joseph like a flock; you who sit enthroned between the cherubim, shine forth!" The mercy seat was interposed between the law in the ark and the holy God above it. The idea is that the blood of the sin offerings sprinkled on the mercy seat came between the lawbreakers and the holy God, making God propitious and merciful toward them. Thus God would forgive the sins of the worshipers on the basis of his own plan of salvation, which included the death of a substitute.

An Imperfect Ministry

This ministry of the priests and the high priest, however, was not designed to make the worshipers perfect or cleanse their consciences. The priests would enter the Holy Place daily for services, ensuring that the lamps were dressed, the wicks trimmed, and the oil poured. All seven lights were to be lit and shining day and night. In the book of Revelation, Jesus likens the lampstands to local churches, which are the light of the world.

The priests also made sure that the altar of incense was burning with incense morning and evening. That is the duty Zechariah was doing when the angel Gabriel appeared to him (Luke 1:8–11). The priests also replenished the table of showbread with twelve fresh loaves in two rows of six on each Sabbath day, giving the old bread to the priests and their families to eat.

According to Leviticus 16, the high priest could go past the thick veil into the Holy of Holies only once a year. This was an extremely hazardous duty. It could be that the two older sons of Aaron were consumed by the fire from the Holy of Holies because they dared to enter when they were not supposed to (Lev. 10).

Once a year, on the tenth day of the seventh month (Tishri), a day known as Yom Kippur, or the Day of Atonement, the high priest would go into the Holy of Holies. Yet even his right to go in was not inherent. Being a sinner, he had to first enter with the blood of a bull as a sin offering for himself and for his household. Then he could go in a second time with the blood of a goat for the sin of the whole people. He would take a censer full of burning coals and two handfuls of incense to burn, thereby covering the mercy seat with a cloud of incense so that he would not see it and die.

The work of the high priest was lonely; no one could assist him. It was also hard, for he had to offer many sacrifices on the Day of Atonement. When the priest entered in the prescribed manner, he would sprinkle the blood of the sin offerings on top of the mercy seat and in front of it for the forgiveness of the sins of ignorance. This was all designed by God himself to be in force until Jesus Christ came: "For the life of a creature is in the blood, and I have given it to you to make atonement for yourselves on the altar; it is the blood that makes atonement for one's life" (Lev. 17:11).

This bloody sacrifice of animals, however, did not cleanse the people's consciences or make them perfect; rather, it pointed to the sacrifice of Jesus Christ, offered to God on the cross. It is the sacrifice of Christ alone that can cleanse our consciences instantly and eternally. The author of Hebrews says that all the blood of all the animals, though ineffectual in making atonement for our sins, teaches us about salvation through the sacrifice of another, Jesus the Messiah.

Therefore, the ministry of the Levitical priests in the earthly sanctuary did not result in the cleansing of anyone's conscience. Nor did it justify the worshipers so that they could appear before God in the Holy of Holies. The thick veil remained, and the people had to worship the holy God at a distance.

The system was incapable of perfecting the conscience of a worshiper. We read in Hebrews 9:9, *"This is an illustration for the present time, indicating that the gifts and sacrifices being offered were not able to clear the conscience of the worshiper."* Verse 8 tells us what this system was teaching: *"The Holy Spirit was showing by this that the way into the Most Holy Place had not yet been disclosed as long as the first tabernacle was still standing."* God set the Levitical system in place only until *"the time of the new order"* (v. 10), when God would set everything straight by the sacrifice of his Son on the cross.

Yet there were some benefits through this system. The Levitical system cleansed the sinner outwardly, physically, and socially. As long as individuals observed the laws and participated in the sacrificial system of worship, they were not cut off from the covenant community. Old Testament believers, however, were saved by their faith in the coming Messiah, which the sacrificial system foreshadowed. Jesus declared, "Your father Abraham rejoiced at the thought of seeing my day; he saw it and was glad" (John 8:56). Abraham saw it by faith, as did Moses: "By faith he left Egypt, not fearing the king's anger; he persevered because he saw him who is invisible" (Heb. 11:27). By faith these Old Testament believers saw that the sacrificial system was pointing to a Messiah who would come and make an effectual and justifying sacrifice.

Hebrews 11 reveals the faith of these Old Testament saints: "For [they were] looking forward to the city with foundations, whose architect and builder is God. . . . All these people were still living by faith when they died. They did not receive the things promised; they only saw them and welcomed them from a distance. And they admitted that they were aliens and strangers on earth. . . . They were longing for a better country—a heavenly one. Therefore God is not ashamed to be called their God, for he has prepared a city for them" (vv. 10, 13, 16). These people lived by faith in the sacrifice of the Messiah who would come and die in their place. They looked forward to the justifying and conscience-cleansing sacrifice of the promised Messiah.

The author says in Hebrews 9:9 that the Levitical sacrificial system was a parable, an illustration of the coming new covenant. It was a signpost, not the reality itself. It pointed to the good things that came with Jesus Christ (Heb. 9:11), which include a good conscience.

Only Christ Can Cleanse Our Conscience

Only the person and work of Christ can cleanse our filthy, guilty consciences. The Levitical priesthood failed to accomplish this, as Philip E. Hughes says:

> The *conscience* is properly man's inner knowledge of himself, especially in the sense of his *answerability* for his motives and actions in view of the fact that he, as a creature made in the image of God, stands before and must give an account of himself to his Creator. As a sinner, who has failed to keep the loving standard of God's law, he has an inner consciousness of his guilt and of his need for cleansing and restoration. The levitical ceremonial [law] was incompetent to provide that perfection of reconciliation, that completeness of justification before God, which the sinner so radically needed.[1]

In Hebrews 9:14 we learn that the blood of Christ alone accomplishes this cleansing: *"How much more, then, will the blood of*

---

1 Philip E. Hughes, *Commentary on Hebrews*, 324.

A Clear Conscience

Christ, who through the eternal Spirit offered himself unblemished to God, cleanse our consciences." The author of this letter had himself experienced it: "Pray for us. We are sure that we have a clear conscience and desire to live honorably in every way" (Heb. 13:18).

Our great problem is not global warming, but a filthy conscience. Jesus explains, "For from within, out of men's hearts, come evil thoughts, sexual immorality, theft, murder, adultery, greed, malice, deceit, lewdness, envy, slander, arrogance and folly. All these evils come from inside and make a man 'unclean'" (Mark 7:21–23).

We need a clean heart, a new heart, a heart of flesh that delights in God's laws. And we need something better than the blood of bulls and goats to purge our filthy consciences. Thank God for his own plan of salvation through the death of another. When God sees Christ's blood shed on the mercy seat, he forgives us sinners who have broken his holy law. "God presented him as a sacrifice of atonement, through faith in his blood. He did this to demonstrate his justice . . . so as to be just and the one who justifies those who have faith in Jesus" (Rom. 3:25–26). God's only Son is the sacrifice of atonement; he himself is the mercy seat upon which his own blood was sprinkled to atone for our sins.

The author of Hebrews tells us about the multitude of benefits that result from Christ's sacrifice: *"When Christ came as high priest of the good things that are already here . . ."* (Heb. 9:11). Jesus Christ has prepared for us a feast of good things. He entered the true tabernacle, the heavenly Most Holy Place of God's presence, as our high priest after the order of Melchizedek, having obtained eternal redemption by his blood (v. 12). He paid the price we owed by his death on the cross. He shed his blood to redeem us from our slavery to sin and Satan and bring us into God's kingdom: "Since the children have flesh and blood, he too shared in their humanity so that by his death he might destroy him who holds the power of death—that is, the devil—and free those who all their lives were held in slavery by their fear of death" (Heb. 2:14–15).

By his bloody death in our place, by his one sacrifice once-for-all offered, Christ has set us free forever! Our consciences have been cleared and cleansed by the blood of Christ; nothing else could do it. The author argues that if the blood of animals could cleanse the people externally, how much more will the blood of Christ cleanse our conscience from all the guilt of our sins (Heb. 9:13–14).

We are living in the day of fulfillment of God's promise of salvation: "No matter how many promises God has made, they are 'Yes' in Christ. And so through him the 'Amen' is spoken by us to the glory of God" (2 Cor. 1:20). The old system became obsolete when Christ sacrificed himself in our place on the cross (Heb. 8:13).

The Argument

The core of the author's argument is found in verses 11 through 13. First, he says, "*When Christ came.*" This is speaking about the incarnation. The word *Christos* means Messiah, Anointed One: "The Spirit of the Sovereign LORD is on me, because the LORD has anointed me" (Isa. 61:1; cf. Luke 4:18). Two thousand years ago the anointed Savior came to fulfill God's promise of salvation.

Second, he says Christ came "*as high priest,*" not after the order of Aaron, but after the order of Melchizedek, on the basis of his indestructible life. Not only is Christ the perfect high priest, but he is also the perfect victim. He did not take the blood of another; he shed his own blood. The sacrifice he offered was unblemished and spotless (v. 14). The author also speaks elsewhere about Jesus as the sinless high priest and sinless victim (Heb. 4:15; 5:8–9; 7:26).

Then we are told this high priest offered *himself*, not an animal. On the cross he obeyed God the Father by offering himself as a sacrifice to God in our place: "He sacrificed for their sins once for all when he offered himself" (Heb. 7:27). No repetition is necessary; Christ's one sacrifice is effectual forever.

Christ offered himself spotlessly, rationally, and voluntarily: "Christ loved the church and gave himself up for her" (Eph. 5:25). Jesus himself says, "I am the good shepherd. The good shepherd lays down his life for the sheep" (John 10:11).

All three persons of the Godhead were involved in this great work of salvation. To propitiate God's wrath against us, the sinless Son of God interposed himself between God and sinners. Christ offered himself to God by the power of the Holy Spirit (Heb. 9:14). The Father smote him in our place, and the Son submitted to this smiting. Christ died for our sins and suffered God's wrath. The Holy Spirit sustained him in this suffering, just as he sustained Jesus throughout his ministry. Verse 12 says that Christ thereby obtained eternal redemption for us.

Here, then, we see the infinite superiority and eternal worth of the person of Jesus and his sacrifice. His work is finished forever to the satisfaction of God the Father. The eternal Son obtained for us everlasting freedom from all bondage. If the Son sets us free, we are truly free from sin, guilt, and hell.

The Efficacy of Christ's Blood

The blood of Christ alone is God's answer to an accusing conscience and an accusing devil. John writes, "They overcame [Satan] by the blood of the Lamb and by the word of their testimony" (Rev. 12:11). No other cleansing agent in the whole world can give us a good conscience. The sacrifice of Jesus Christ alone cleanses the filthy consciences of both Jews and Gentiles. By it alone we resist the devil.

While the Levitical system was not able to make a human conscience clean, the sacrifice of Christ can: "Therefore, [Christ] is able to save completely those who come to God through him" (Heb. 7:25).

To cleanse our consciences means to clear them of guilt. It is a forensic, declarative act, says Geerhardus Vos.[2] God pronounces that we are clean on the basis of the alien righteousness of Jesus Christ. It is not something happening within, but it is a legal status: "He who knew no sin became sin for us that we might become the righteousness of God in him" (2 Cor. 5:21, author's translation). God made Christ for us to be wisdom, righteousness, sanctification, and redemption (1 Cor. 1:30). The moment we trust in him, we are instantly and eternally saved, cleansed, and freed.

The shed blood of Christ alone clears the guilty. On the basis of the blood of Christ, the Father declares us to be just. Christ's blood removes the guilt of sin, which keeps us from coming to God and worshiping in his presence. The shed blood of Christ is the basis of our justification, sanctification, and glorification: "Because by one sacrifice he has made perfect forever those who are being made holy" (Heb. 10:14). The sacrifice of Christ cleanses our conscience from dead works, the works we did while sinners, of which we must repent (Heb. 6:1; 9:14). Dead works are our

---

2   Vos, *Teaching of the Epistle to the Hebrews*, 57–58.

sins. They lead us into everlasting ruin and death because the soul that sins shall die (Ezek. 18:20). But a believer in Christ's sacrifice is justified and declared not guilty. He is given a new nature that now causes him to turn from sin and perform good works (Eph. 2:10).

Good Things in Christ

The author says Christ came "*as high priest of the good things that are already here*" (Heb. 9:11). Brothers and sisters, we have a great feast of good things in Jesus Christ. We have forgiveness of sins (Heb. 8:12), justification (Heb. 10:14), sanctification (Heb. 10:14), and fellowship with God (Heb. 10:22). We are told repeatedly, "Draw near." The thick veil that barred us from the presence of God has been torn and removed. As we trust in Christ and his sacrifice, we can now come with confidence into the very presence of God to find mercy and to receive grace in time of need (Heb. 4:16).

Let us rejoice because of this great gospel. It is a feast of good things. Let us come to eat and drink, praise and rejoice in the presence of our God and Savior. He gives us a good conscience (Heb. 9:14), knowledge of God (Heb. 8:11), the guarantee of salvation (Heb. 7:22), victory over Satan and our fear of death (Heb. 2:14–15), and confidence that when our time to die comes, we will go into his very presence. Our high priest, Jesus Christ, is at the right hand of God interceding for us effectually and continually (Heb. 7:25).

Cleansed to Serve God

What is the purpose of having a clear conscience? Why does God save us and bring us to his presence? Notice the last clause of verse 14: "*that we may serve the living God.*" True happiness is to serve the living God all our lives. Now we are royal priests. The veil that barred us from God has been taken away by Christ, and we may now come with boldness to worship God and offer spiritual sacrifices.

We are royal priests with sacrifices to offer: "Offer your bodies as living sacrifices, holy and pleasing to God—this is your spiritual act of worship" (Rom. 12:1); "You also, like living stones, are being built into a spiritual house to be a holy priesthood, offering spiritual sacrifices acceptable to God through Jesus Christ. . . . You are a chosen people, a royal priesthood, a holy nation, a people belonging to God, that you may declare the praises of him who called you out of darkness into his wonderful light" (1 Pet. 2:5, 9); "Through Jesus, therefore, let us continually offer to God a sacrifice of praise—the fruit of lips that confess his name. And do not forget to do good and to share with others, for with such sacrifices God is pleased" (Heb. 13:15–16).

We are to serve God all our life: "Whether you eat or drink or whatever you do, do it all for the glory of God" (1 Cor. 10:31). There is joy in serving Jesus.

The apostle John discloses the final fulfillment of our service: "No longer will there be any curse. The throne of God and of the Lamb will be in the city, and his servants will serve him" (Rev. 22:3). That is what life is designed for—eternal service to God by his redeemed creatures. This is the definition of pure, unadulterated, everlasting happiness.

B. F. Westcott says, "Purity is not the end but the means of the new life. The [goal] of restored fellowship is energetic service to Him Who alone lives and gives life."[3] The purpose of redemption is not autonomy, antinomianism, or the evil of independence. In light of our salvation and Christ's resurrection from the dead, Paul writes, "Therefore, my dear brothers, stand firm. Let nothing move you. Always give yourselves fully to the work of the Lord, because you know that your labor in the Lord is not in vain" (1 Cor. 15:58). John Calvin says, "We are not cleansed by Christ so we can immerse ourselves continually in fresh dirt, but in order that our purity may serve the glory of God."[4]

By nature, we all have filthy consciences and are cut off from God because of our sins. But, thanks be to God, Christ came and died for our sins. We can now be instantly and eternally cleansed of all guilt to serve God in utter happiness on the basis of his sacrifice.

---

3   Westcott, *Epistle to the Hebrews*, 263.
4   Quoted by Philip E. Hughes, *Commentary on Hebrews*, 362.

18

The Blessings of Good Friday

¹⁵*For this reason Christ is the mediator of a new covenant, that those who are called may receive the promised eternal inheritance— now that he has died as a ransom to set them free from the sins committed under the first covenant.*

¹⁶*In the case of a will, it is necessary to prove the death of the one who made it,* ¹⁷*because a will is in force only when somebody has died; it never takes effect while the one who made it is living.* ¹⁸*This is why even the first covenant was not put into effect without blood.* ¹⁹*When Moses had proclaimed every commandment of the law to all the people, he took the blood of calves, together with water, scarlet wool and branches of hyssop, and sprinkled the scroll and all the people.* ²⁰*He said, "This is the blood of the covenant, which God has commanded you to keep."* ²¹*In the same way, he sprinkled with the blood both the tabernacle and everything used in its ceremonies.* ²²*In fact, the law requires that nearly everything be cleansed with blood, and without the shedding of blood there is no forgiveness.*

²³*It was necessary, then, for the copies of the heavenly things to be purified with these sacrifices, but the heavenly things themselves with better sacrifices than these.* ²⁴*For Christ did not enter a man-made sanctuary that was only a copy of the true one; he entered heaven itself, now to appear for us in God's presence.* ²⁵*Nor did he enter heaven to offer himself again and again, the way the high priest enters the Most Holy Place every year with blood that is not his own.* ²⁶*Then Christ would have had to suffer many times since the creation of the world. But now he has appeared once for all at the end of the ages to do away with sin by the sacrifice of himself.*

Hebrews 9:15–26

The Bible is a bloody book. It speaks of killing millions of animals whose deaths had sacramental and symbolic significance. But all of this blood was not able to cleanse the human conscience from its guilt. Such bloody sacrifices never brought a person into fellowship with God.

Good Friday speaks about the death, not of an animal, but of a human, and yet more than a human. It speaks about One who is very God and very man, one who knew no sin, yet who died because of sin. Not only did the Father give him up, but Christ gave himself up because he loved us. The death of Jesus Christ is unique, for it alone can open the door to heaven for us by canceling our sin and its penalty.

Finding True Happiness

I recently heard about an unusual graduate program designed to find out what makes people happy. The spokesperson said that researchers do not know enough about what gives people hope, energy, enjoyment, and value to life. They are looking for an answer in behavioral psychology. These researchers want to find an answer in man, but the answer has already been revealed in the Bible. The gospel is the answer to the question, "What makes people happy?"

True happiness comes to us as a result of what happened on the hill of Calvary on Good Friday. Jesus stated, "The thief comes only to steal and kill and destroy; I have come that you may have life, and have it to the full" (John 10:10). Jesus alone can give us abundant happiness. "God so loved the world that he gave his one and only Son" (John 3:16). Jesus loved us and gave himself for us on the cross. Isaac, the one and only son of Abraham, did not have to die. God provided a substitute, a ram caught in the thicket. But the Son of God died in our place; there was no substitute for him. The sinless One died for our sins so that we may live with God in eternal happiness. In him alone we find grace, which causes us to rejoice always.

I do not need a doctoral research program to find out what makes me happy. What happened long ago on Good Friday can make us all happy. But this happiness comes to us only on

The Blessings of Good Friday

the basis of God's covenant, concerning which Hebrews 9 has much to say.

The Covenant Structure

"In the case of a will, it is necessary to prove the death of the one who made it, because a will is in force only when somebody has died; it never takes effect while the one who made it is living" (Heb. 9:16–17). The New International Version uses the word "will" in verses 16–17, but the Greek word is really "covenant" (*diathēkē*), the same word used in verse 15 and Hebrews 7:22. The idea of covenant is important in this section; therefore, let us first examine the structure of the covenant discussed here.

When God enters into a covenant with man, it is always based on grace. God takes the initiative to impose covenantal terms on his creatures to establish a loving relationship with them. That is why the heart of the covenant is, "I will be their God, and they will be my people" (Heb. 8:10). A covenant is a relational agreement designed for our enjoyment and based on our loving obedience to God. Those who violate it, however, must die.

A covenant was always ratified by the shedding of blood, as illustrated in Genesis 15. Animals were cut in half and arranged so that there was a pathway between the split animals. Usually both parties would walk through the carcasses, calling a curse of death upon themselves if they were found delinquent in keeping the terms of the covenant. But when God established his covenant with Abraham in Genesis 15, only God went through that path. This ceremony showed that God himself in Jesus Christ would die in place of sinful man.

John Murray says such a covenant "is a sovereign dispensation of God's grace. It is grace bestowed and a relation established."[1] It is divinely devised, administered, confirmed, and executed. When we study the Abrahamic covenant (Gen. 12, 15, 17), which is the basis of both the Mosaic covenant (Exod. 19–24) and the new covenant of which Jeremiah spoke (Jer. 31:31–34), we notice the following features:

---

1 Murray, *Covenant of Grace*, 19.

1. Certain promises are given: "I will be your God and you will be my people." The heart of the covenant is a love relationship between God and man.
2. It is characterized by divine monergism—God alone executes the covenant for the enjoyment of his obedient people.
3. It is characterized by perpetuity; it is an everlasting covenant.
4. God pronounces a curse upon himself if he does not perform the covenant for the blessing of his people, just as he confirmed his covenant to Abraham by a self-maledictory, covenant-ratifying procedure.
5. Man must obey the covenant stipulations if he is to enjoy God's blessings. Love for God is expressed by obedience to his commands (John 14:15).
6. Such a covenant would be ratified by the death of animals representing the two parties to the agreement, God and man. So animals would be killed and blood shed to ratify the covenant. This ratification ceremony highlighted the fact that the party who violates the covenant must die. But God cannot lie; thus, he cannot violate his covenant. It is man who violates the covenant and, therefore, it is man who must die. That is why we see rivers of blood. The Bible speaks so much about blood because we did not keep God's covenant.

We all violate God's covenant because we are all born sinners who practice sin daily. Fallen man is morally crippled and unable to keep God's law. But in God's own eternal plan, instead of having the actual violators die for their violations, God himself, the innocent party, decided to die in the place of sinful man.

Yet God is immortal. How, then, can he die? God's Son had to become man to die our death that we may live. "The wages of sin is death" (Rom. 6:23). Adam had to die, for he sinned against the God who said to him, "The day you eat thereof, you must die" (Gen. 2:17). All of us are born dead spiritually and will die physically. Unless we trust in this One who died in our place, we will also die an eternal death, called "the second death" in the Bible. We can research all we want about happiness, but we will never experience it outside of Christ. Hebrews 9:27 reminds us that it is appointed for man once to die and then face judgment.

Since the fall of Adam, multitudes of animals have been killed until Good Friday, the day Jesus died in place of sinners. Yet the blood of bulls and goats could never cleanse our defiled consciences and make us holy to enjoy fellowship with a holy God, who demands, "Be holy, because I am holy" (Lev. 11:44).

Holiness is an essential precondition for happiness, because holiness brings about eternal enjoyment of the presence of God.

Thank God for the divine principle of substitution and for his divinely qualified substitute, the sinless Son of God! All the animal sacrifices in the history of redemption pointed to Christ as the solution to our sin problem. As mediator of the covenant, he made a new and better covenant, for he ensured that the interests of both parties were secured. Jesus Christ not only vindicated God's justice and holiness, but he also saved sinners like us by his death once-for-all offered to God.

Christ's obedience and righteousness in life and death defends God's holiness and saves us from our eternal destruction. Paul writes, "God presented him as a sacrifice of atonement, through faith in his blood. He did this to demonstrate his justice, because in his forbearance he had left the sins committed beforehand unpunished—he did it to demonstrate his justice at the present time, so as to be just and the one who justifies those who have faith in Jesus" (Rom. 3:25–26).

The choice is now clear. Every sinner must either die and face eternal judgment, or trust in Jesus Christ alone, who died in the place of every sinner who repents and believes.

Keeping the Covenant

"*Without the shedding of blood there is no forgiveness*" (Heb. 9:22). This is the key verse in this chapter. To keep the covenant, blood must be shed.

When the Mosaic covenant was ratified, blood was shed upon the altar and upon the people (Exod. 24:3–8). The Hebrews author reminds us that as Moses sprinkled blood on the people, he declared, "*This is the blood of the covenant, which God has commanded you to keep*" (Heb. 9:20). Without the death of a substitute, there is no forgiveness, no cleansing of conscience, no worship, no fellowship with God, and no salvation. A person may give away all his wealth, but that cannot cause his sins to be forgiven. Even our own physical death cannot save us. We are sinners, unfit to make a perfect, God-pleasing sacrifice of atonement.

To fulfill the covenant, someone must die. But who? The Old Testament promised a suitable substitute, the Messiah, who would make our filthy consciences as white as snow (Isa. 1:18) and bear our sins in his death (Isa. 53). Jesus Christ is our mediator and guarantor of good things. His mission was to bring many sons from shame to glory, from death to life: "Since the children have flesh and blood, he too shared in their humanity so that by his death he might destroy him who holds the power of death—that is, the devil—and free those who all their lives were held in slavery by their fear of death" (Heb. 2:14–15). On Good Friday the holy Jesus died as our substitute, making atonement for our sins. Thus he became the mediator of the new covenant.

On the night he was betrayed, Jesus declared: "This cup is the new covenant in my blood, which is poured out for you" (Luke 22:20). It was not the blood of animals but Christ's own blood that was poured out for the salvation of everyone who believes in him. All our misery, shame, degradation, and hopelessness is due to sin and guilt. The blood of Christ alone can bring forgiveness. So Jesus said, "This is my blood of the covenant, which is poured out for many for the forgiveness of sins" (Matt. 26:28).

Praise God, a fit substitute has died in our place! Paul used a bold expression in his farewell to the Ephesian elders, "Keep watch over yourselves and all the flock of which the Holy Spirit has made you overseers. Be shepherds of the church of God, *which he bought with his own blood*" (Acts 20:28, italics added). Now we understand why only one went through the split carcasses. God shed his own blood in the death of Jesus Christ, and the church is bought with that blood. Because we violated God's law, we deserve only death. Yet it is not we, but God, who died. Christ died in our place for our benefit, salvation, and everlasting joy. This is true happiness.

"For this reason Christ is the mediator of a new covenant, that those who are called may receive the promised eternal inheritance—now that he has died" (Heb. 9:15). A death has occurred—the death that the covenant demanded. Hebrews 9:26 declares: *"But now he has appeared once for all at the end of the ages to do away with sin by the sacrifice of himself."* In Hebrews 13:12 we read, "And so Jesus also suffered outside the city gate to make the people holy through his own blood." Through the blood of Christ we have been made holy and acceptable to God, and now we can have fellowship with him. Everyone who trusts in the death of Christ is holy and can appear

with confidence and a good conscience in the very presence of God to enjoy unending happiness. A unique death has occurred that will solve our misery, depression, anxiety, and fear.

Jesus told his disciples, "For even the Son of Man did not come to be served, but to serve, and to give his life as a ransom for many" (Mark 10:45). The price of our redemption was the sacrificial death of Christ. He paid that price on Good Friday on the hill of Calvary in the midpoint of time that we may live and be blessed. His death was not optional but was demanded by God in his covenant. So Jesus self-consciously makes this statement: "Did not the Christ have to suffer these things and then enter his glory?" (Luke 24:26). It was divinely determined in the covenant of redemption, and agreed to by the Son of God in eternity. Christ *must* die.

We were the Barabbases, waiting for the moment of our execution. But Jesus died in our place; therefore, we were set free. Barabbas was set free physically; everyone who trusts in Christ is set free physically, spiritually, and eternally, to live in total happiness with God.

Paul says that because a death was necessary, Christ "became obedient to death—even death on a cross!" (Phil. 2:8). God the Son became man and was obedient in life and in death. In Romans Paul asks who can condemn those who trust in Christ. He is challenging all of creation, including the devil and the demons. But no one can condemn those who are in Christ. The devil is the accuser of the brethren, but not even he can condemn us. Then Paul gives the reason: "Christ Jesus, who died—more than that, who was raised to life—is at the right hand of God and is also interceding for us" (Rom. 8:34).

A death has occurred, blood has been shed, and we are sprinkled clean. Moses sprinkled blood upon the Israelites when he ratified the Mosaic covenant. But now a new covenant is established. Christ himself died in our place and his blood is shed upon us. Paul says, "He was delivered over to death for our sins and was raised to life for our justification" (Rom. 4:25). We are saved, cleansed, and happy in Jesus.

The Covenant Blessings

Hebrews 9:11 says that "Christ came as high priest of the good things that are already here." Because of this new covenant, every

Christian's guilt and death has been taken away, and we are now invited to enjoy good things in Christ Jesus.

The author spoke earlier about some of the good things that we who once lived in darkness now experience: enlightenment, a share in the Holy Spirit, a taste of the goodness of God's word (Heb. 6:4–5); regeneration, fellowship, forgiveness of all sins (Heb. 8:10–12); a good conscience (Heb. 9:14); and eternal redemption (Heb. 9:12). When he came down from heaven, Jesus Christ brought us these good things, blessings that we never could have earned. It is a feast of good things, to which we are invited to come.

"For this reason Christ is the mediator of a new covenant, that those who are called may receive the promised inheritance—now that he has died as a ransom to set them free from the sins committed under the first covenant" (Heb. 9:15). If a person is not called, he has no part in God's good things. God calls his people effectually in the preaching of the gospel. Salvation is limited to those who are called. They are the elect, the chosen ones: "For those God foreknew he also predestined to be conformed to the likeness of his Son, that he might be the firstborn among many brothers. And those he predestined, he also called; those he called, he also justified; those he justified, he also glorified" (Rom. 8:29–30). Hebrews 3:1 addresses us as "sharers of the heavenly calling," a calling that is from heaven and to heaven.

This calling is not limited to national Israel. God told Abraham, "In thee shall all families of the earth be blessed" (Gen. 12:3, KJV). How do we know if we are called? If we repent and believe on the Lord Jesus Christ, we are called. We will feel the pull of the Holy Spirit in our souls and come to God's feast. We will bring nothing, for salvation is by grace through faith, but come clothed in the perfect free righteousness of Christ.

Note the language of the New American Standard Version: *"And for this reason He is the mediator of a new covenant, in order that since a death has taken place for [bringing about] the redemption of the transgressions that were committed under the first covenant, those who have been called may receive the promise of the eternal inheritance"* (Heb. 9:15). Christ brought about "the redemption of the transgressions." The word "redemption" intimates that we are in a prison about to be killed, and the only way out is for someone to pay the redemption price. It tells us that there is a redeemer who paid that price to set us free from our slavery and death. Jesus Christ is that redeemer—he paid that price. "Redemption of the transgressions" means redemption from *all* sins—past, present and future. In the language of Hebrews, we have been perfected because our sin has been put away.

The moment we trust in Christ, all our sins, guilt, and punishment are taken away, and we are brought out from prison into the glorious liberty of the children of God. We are delivered from slavery to freedom, from darkness to light, from death to life, and from hell to heaven. Jesus sets us free. The price of our redemption is the death of Christ.

Jesus gives us freedom from the penalty, the power, and, eventually, from the presence of sin. How can we still wallow in sin, if we have been set free! If we are true Christians, God is working in us both to will and to do his good pleasure, and we are to work out our salvation with fear and trembling (cf. Phil. 2:12–13). Sanctification is a cooperative venture wherein we fight sin, resist the devil, believe, pray, read the word of God, and obey Christ. Christians have been redeemed to serve Christ. We have been set free from Satan's dominion, from our fear of death, and from all condemnation: "Therefore, there is now no condemnation for those who are in Christ Jesus" (Rom. 8:1). No one can bring an accusation against the child of God. By dying in our place, Christ has set us free.

Christ's death for our redemption is the negative statement of Hebrews 9:15; the positive statement is that believers receive the promise of eternal salvation, *"the promised eternal inheritance."* All of our sins have been forgiven and we are now heirs of God and joint-heirs with Christ. We have been adopted as sons and daughters of God. Jesus Christ came that we wretched people might become rich, lacking in nothing. God called us that we may receive the promised eternal inheritance.

God performs what he promises because he cannot lie. The Bible says everyone who calls upon the name of the Lord *will* be saved. In fact, Hebrews 6 says that God made his promise even stronger by an oath. Because he could not make an oath by anyone superior to him, he swore by himself, that we may have strong consolation. People promise all kinds of things, but then change their minds. But God is not a man. What he promises, he performs. Therefore, when you read the Scriptures, believe what God is saying and let your whole life hang on his promises. He who promises eternal salvation can be trusted.

God promises us an *eternal* inheritance. Peter writes, "Praise be to the God and Father of our Lord Jesus Christ! In his great mercy he has given us new birth into a living hope through the resurrection of Jesus Christ from the dead, and into an inheritance that can never perish, spoil or fade—kept in heaven for you, who through faith are shielded by God's power until the coming of the salvation that is ready to be revealed in the last time" (1 Pet. 1:3–5). As children of God, we have a rich inheritance that cannot rust, perish, spoil, fade, or be stolen. Our treasure is kept safe for us in heaven.

Earthly riches tend to develop wings and fly away (Prov. 23:5). But what God has promised is eternal, unchanging, and everlasting. We are rich forever in God. Jesus said, "I give them eternal life, and they shall never perish" (John 10:28).

Hebrews 9:16–17 declares, *"In the case of a will, it is necessary to prove the death of the one who made it, because a will is in force only when somebody has died; it never takes effect while the one who made it is living."* Our Lord, the testator, died, and he has a will, a covenant. Yet not only did he die, but he also rose again. We can say, therefore, that he is the executor as well as the testator and now he distributes blessings one after another to us, his beneficiaries. He daily loads us with good things, giving us grace upon grace sufficient to live a Christian life.

Is your name in his covenant? If so, you have an eternal inheritance. Not only will we receive it when we get to heaven, but we also receive it here as a foretaste. And we shall receive it in all its fullness when he comes again.

Beneficiaries of God

Thus, we are beneficiaries of God's covenant, which is in force because our testator died on the cross. Now he lives to distribute blessings to his people.

The inheritance Christ gives us is *his*. It is an infinite, heavenly, imperishable, joy-giving inheritance, and we rejoice in receiving it. Christ died, that we may live. Christ died, and we are made rich: "For you know the grace of our Lord Jesus Christ, that though he was rich, yet for your sakes he became poor, so that you through his poverty might become rich" (2 Cor. 8:9). Christ died, and we are made alive. Christ died, and our gloom is gone forever. Thus, we can say with Paul, that we are "sorrowful, yet always rejoicing" (2 Cor. 6:10).

This inheritance will probably not include much gold or a powerful position in this fallen world. We cannot guarantee such things. But we can guarantee this: eternal enjoyment of God in his very presence. The thick veil that kept us out has been torn asunder, and we can now come into God's presence to rejoice in intimate relationship with him. Augustine correctly said that our hearts are restless until they find their rest in God. Our inheritance is that rest of ever-increasing, never-ending happiness in the presence of God.

We find this description of heavenly bliss in Revelation:

> "Hallelujah! For our Lord God Almighty reigns. Let us rejoice and be glad and give him glory! For the wedding of the Lamb has come, and his bride has made herself ready. . . ." Then I saw a new heaven and a new earth, for the first heaven and the first earth had passed away, and there was no longer any sea. I saw the Holy City, the new Jerusalem, coming down out of heaven from God, prepared as a bride beautifully dressed for her husband. And I heard a loud voice from the throne saying, "Now the dwelling of God is with men, and he will live with them. They will be his people, and God himself will be with them and be their God. He will wipe every tear from their eyes. There will be no more death or mourning or crying or pain, for the old order of things has passed away." (Rev. 19:6–7; 21:1–4)

This is our inheritance! There will be a new heaven and a new earth, where God will dwell with his people. In Revelation 22 we read, "No longer will there be any curse. The throne of God and of the Lamb will be in the city, and his servants will serve him. They will see his face" (vv. 3–4). This is the intimate communion we look forward to: we shall see God's face.

Our inheritance in Christ is one of justification and sanctification. If God has justified us, he will sanctify us. He will give us power over sin so that we will live a victorious Christian life by his grace. Jesus is our justification, sanctification, and glorification. He who saved us will keep us from sinning and will give us victory.

Our inheritance is one of eternal salvation. The eternal judgment that was ours is gone, taken by Christ in his person on the cross. He is the author of eternal salvation for all who obey him (Heb. 5:9).

Our inheritance is one of blessing. The biblical definition of blessing is to see God face to face and to live with him forever. True happiness is belonging to the kingdom of God, which is righteousness, peace, and joy in the Holy Spirit (Rom. 14:17). This inheritance is for all those who trusted in the Messiah before the coming of Christ, and for all those who have trusted in him after his death and resurrection. The moment we trust in Christ, he takes care of our sins so that we can go to God and have fellowship with him.

This inheritance is for all the called ones of God, whether Jew or Gentile. Everyone who calls upon the name of the Lord will be saved instantly. The only thing that prevents us from calling upon the name of the Lord is love for sin instead of love for the Savior who died for our sins.

The latter part of Hebrews 9:24 says, "*He entered heaven itself, now to appear for us in God's presence.*" In the Greek, it is "now to appear in the face of God." This speaks of the Son's communion with the Father in our behalf. So Christ is now in heaven in our behalf making intercession for us (Heb. 7:25). He must do so because we live in a fallen world. Sin is still in us, Satan is loose, and the world is against us. But Christ is ever-interceding before the Father to keep us safe.

Roman Catholicism teaches that Christ is daily offering himself anew before God. That is not true, as this chapter confirms. Christ's once-for-all offering of himself was eternally sufficient. John MacArthur writes:

> The idea of the perpetual offering of Christ is a heretical doctrine that for many centuries has contradicted this and the many other clear biblical teachings about the finished work of Christ. It maintains that inasmuch as the priesthood of Christ is perpetual and sacrifice is an essential part of priesthood, therefore the sacrificial offering of Christ must also be perpetual. Ludwig

The Blessings of Good Friday

Ott, a Roman Catholic theologian, explains this perpetual sacrifice dogma. . . . [He says,] "The holy Mass . . . is a true and proper sacrifice. It is physical and propitiatory, removing sins and conferring the grace of repentance. Propitiated by the offering of this sacrifice, God, by granting the grace of the gift and the gift of Penance, remits trespasses and sins however grievous they may be." In other words, God's satisfaction regarding sin depends upon the weekly mass. That is why attending mass is so important to Catholics.[2]

The truth is, Jesus Christ offered his sacrifice once and for all in history on Calvary's hill, and its effect is eternal. What, then, is he doing in heaven? He is interceding for us so that we may be kept from all evil.

What about the sin still remaining in us? Though we are justified, can we lose our salvation? No, our salvation is secure, for he has given us eternal life. His effectual intercession ensures that we will be preserved and will persevere to the end in the faith. I believe in both the session and the intercession of Christ. Session refers to his kingship; intercession refers to his high priesthood in our behalf. Our heavenly King and Priest gives us power to exercise power over sin and Satan so that we can resist the devil, and he shall flee from us.

Thus, we do not need the intercession of Mary or anyone else. Jesus himself is the only intercessor, and he stands in the presence of God. "Christ Jesus who died—more than that, who was raised to life—is at the right hand of God and is also interceding for us" (Rom. 8:34).

"*But now he has appeared once for all at the end of the ages to do away with sin by the sacrifice of himself*" (Heb. 9:26). The term "do away" is rich in meaning. As our substitute on Calvary's cross, Jesus did away with, canceled, obliterated, expunged, rendered null and void, and blotted out our transgressions, our guilt, our punishment, our death, our hell forever. There is no other way to be saved other than trusting in Christ and his substitutionary death.

Leviticus 17:11 says that the blood is given by God for our atonement. It is not ultimately the blood of animals but the blood of Christ. Christ is God's gift to us to make atonement for us. And because Christ blotted out our sins, God does not see or remember our sins. It is as if we had never sinned.

---

2   MacArthur, *Hebrews*, 241.

Yes, a death has taken place. But because of that death, we are a happy people! Our burden is gone. "Blessed is he whose transgressions are forgiven, whose sins are covered. Blessed is the man whose sin the LORD does not count against him and in whose spirit is no deceit" (Ps. 32:1–2). God does not count our sins against us because he counted them against his own Son. We have been set free, and if the Son sets us free, we are free indeed. We need not fear, especially death: "Death has been swallowed up in victory.... The sting of death is sin, and the power of sin is the law. But thanks be to God! He gives us the victory through our Lord Jesus Christ" (1 Cor. 15:54, 56–57). We can rejoice, knowing that "neither death nor life . . . nor anything else in all creation [is] able to separate us from the love of God that is in Christ Jesus our Lord" (Rom. 8:38–39).

19

The Second Coming of Jesus Christ

^{26b}*But now he has appeared once for all at the end of the ages to do away with sin by the sacrifice of himself.* ²⁷*Just as man is destined to die once, and after that to face judgment,* ²⁸*so Christ was sacrificed once to take away the sins of many people; and he will appear a second time, not to bear sin, but to bring salvation to those who are waiting for him.*

Hebrews 9:26b–28

Can you imagine that the God of the Bible used a flood to destroy all but eight people for their wickedness? Can you imagine that this same God used fire to destroy all but three of the people of Sodom and Gomorrah for their immorality? It is true: God punishes sinners, not only in their lifetimes, but also at their deaths and at the final judgment.

The God revealed in the Scriptures is a moral God who both saves and punishes. Educated fools often speak of a "closed universe," declaring that God is shut out from the universe and has nothing to do with it. However, the truth is that ours is an open universe in which God acts in history, and all people shall face him in due time, either as Savior or as Judge. Philosophical materialism cannot save anyone from having to face the infinite, personal God.

Have you ever wondered where your parents, relatives, and friends are who have died? Are they enjoying salvation in God's presence, or are they experiencing eternal torment away from

God? In God's plan, there is salvation for those who trust in Jesus but judgment for those who reject him.

Paul speaks about God as Judge:

> God is just: He will pay back trouble to those who trouble you and give relief to you who are troubled, and to us as well. This will happen when the Lord Jesus is revealed from heaven in blazing fire with his powerful angels. He will punish those who do not know God and do not obey the gospel of our Lord Jesus. They will be punished with everlasting destruction and shut out from the presence of the Lord and from the majesty of his power on the day he comes to be glorified in his holy people and to be marveled at among all those who have believed. This includes you, because you believed our testimony to you. (2 Thess. 1:6–10)

May God help each of us to heed the gospel call and be saved from the coming wrath of God.

The First Coming of Christ

These verses in Hebrews 9 speak about the second coming of Christ to bring salvation and judgment. Before we speak about this second coming, let us look at the first coming of Jesus, as the Hebrews author does in Hebrews 9:26b. The purpose of Christ's incarnation was to cancel our sins through his sacrificial suffering and death (Isa. 53:10–12).

The author tells us that the eternal Son of God entered history in human flesh over two thousand years ago "*at the end of the ages*" (Heb. 9:26b). This is the climax of history, what Hebrews 1:2 calls "these last days." Christ ushered in the messianic age to which all the prophets had pointed. The infinite became finite, the immortal became mortal, God became man.[1]

The eternal Son became man that he may die. The Hebrews author speaks clearly about the purpose of the incarnation: "Since the children have flesh and blood, he too shared in their humanity so that by his death he might destroy him who holds the power of death—that is, the devil—and free those who all

---

[1] See John Murray, *Collected Writings of John Murray: Volume Two, Select Lectures in Systematic Theology* (Edinburgh: Banner of Truth Trust, 1977), 132.

their lives were held in slavery by their fear of death. . . . For this reason he had to be made like his brothers in every way, in order that he might become a merciful and faithful high priest in service to God, and that he might make atonement for the sins of the people" (Heb. 2:14–15, 17).

Every sinner is a slave to Satan and death, but Christ died to set us free from such slavery. Because of Adam's sin, every child of Adam comes into the world spiritually stillborn. We enter this world as sinners to live lives of sin and experience eternal death. Paul speaks of this: "Sin entered the world through one man, and death through sin, and in this way, death came to all men. . . .The wages of sin is death. . . . In Adam all die" (Rom. 5:12; 6:23; 1 Cor. 15:22).

Every man is born a sinner, except Jesus, who came into history to defeat sin. He accomplished this by suffering in our behalf. Christ himself bore our sins away, paying for them by his death in our place. He came as the Lamb of God who takes away the sin of the world by his sacrifice of himself once offered on the altar of the cross. He suffered the just wrath of God that was against us due to our sins and guilt. The full cup of God's wrath that was ours was given to him. Jesus drank the foaming wine of divine wrath to the last drop, leaving nothing for us. He came as our kinsman-redeemer, substitute, and representative to blot out our sins. Christ freely accepted our sins and guilt that the Father put on him. He endured our punishment of death and was crucified and buried. But on the third day God raised him up from the dead. The resurrection of Jesus Christ is the proof that God accepted Christ's death as atonement for our sins. By his death, our sins have been buried in the depths of the ocean. He threw them behind his back and remembers them no more. Our sins have been paid for and removed from our shoulders.

Though we were weary in sin, we heard Christ's call: "Come to me, all you who are weary and burdened, and I will give you rest" (Matt. 11:28). He came to put away our sins. Paul writes: "God was reconciling the world to himself in Christ, not counting men's sins against them" (2 Cor. 5:19). Because God is holy and just, he must count our sins. He counts our sins either against us or against his own Son. He must do so, that he may be just and the justifier of those who believe in Jesus (see Rom. 3:26). "God made him who had no sin to be sin for us, so that in him we might become the righteousness of God" (2 Cor. 5:21). When our sins are imputed to Jesus, his righteousness is put into our account.

Christ came the first time to cancel our sins, and now our sin, with all its penalty and power, is gone: "Therefore, there is now no condemnation for those who are in Christ Jesus" (Rom. 8:1). He dealt with our sin, both its root and its branches. Death is gone for us forever, and we are given eternal life. The infinite holiness of the person of Jesus demands the infinite worth of his atonement. Christ's atonement is effective eternally for all who trust in him. We have been justified by faith and have peace with God. We have been admitted to the kingdom of God, which is righteousness, peace, and joy in the Holy Spirit (Rom. 14:17).

Death is terrible and certain. But when Christ pronounced from the cross, "It is finished," our sins and death were dealt with forever. Jesus came into history the first time to cancel sin. His mission was to bring many sons from the pit of shame to the glory of heaven (Heb. 2:10). Peter also speaks about this: "For Christ died for sins once for all, the righteous for the unrighteous, to bring you to God" (1 Pet. 3:18). In Adam we were banished from God's presence, but through Christ we can now draw near to God.

The Second Coming of Jesus

Christ is coming again to end history. History is not cyclical, as the Greeks and Hindus believe. History had a beginning and will have an end. Jesus Christ is the Lord of history. His first coming ushered in the last days, and his second coming will mark their end.

"*Just as man is destined to die once, and after that to face judgment...*" (Heb. 9:27). The Hebrews writer says that it is appointed for men once to die, and then he uses the Greek word *krisis*, from which we have the English word "crisis." There is a twofold purpose to Christ's second coming: the first part is *krisis*. There is a crisis awaiting every unbeliever, from which there is no escape. *Krisis* is the process of judgment, which ends in condemnation and hell. It is the eternal judgment of all who refuse to repent and believe in Jesus. Such people mock him, spit on him, beat him, and treat with contempt his offer of peace and reconciliation with God. But though these people reject Christ, he is going to come again to bring about a crisis from which they cannot escape.

However, Christ is also coming to bring the fullness of salvation for his people, those who eagerly await him. The Bible says we are saved, we are being saved, and we will be saved. When Christ comes again, we will be resurrected and given a glorious body like unto his glorious body. We shall see him, commune with him, and enjoy the fullness of salvation that is awaiting us.

Christ's mission is to bring many sons to glory, and he is coming again to do that. We will dwell with God in a new heaven and a new earth of eternal joy, where there will be no pain, tears, or parting.

The text says it is *appointed* for men to die once and then face judgment. Who makes the appointment? God himself. This is not an appointment like one we would make with a doctor, one that can be canceled or rescheduled for a more convenient time. Adam sinned, and in him all died. We *must* die. Do not believe the evolutionary hypothesis that says that death is based on natural processes. Death is based on divine decree and appointment.

This revelation refutes certain popular ideas. First, it refutes the idea of reincarnation. All are appointed *only once* to die. It also refutes the notion of evolutionary atheists who say that our death is *final*, like that of an animal, and that there is nothing afterwards. Death is followed by a final judgment in which we will have to give an account to God.

This revelation also refutes the notion that after someone dies we can help that person achieve salvation by giving money to the church, by performing some good work, or by asking saints to pray for that person. All these ideas are false. Each person will "receive what is due him for the things done while in the body, whether good or bad" (2 Cor. 5:10). That is why now is the accepted time, now is the day of salvation.

Not only will God keep the appointment he has made, but so will all sinners. Though they die, the day is surely coming when God will raise them up from the dead to face him who died on the cross. Jesus himself made this point: "[The Father] has given him authority to judge because he is the Son of Man. Do not be amazed at this, for a time is coming when all who are in their graves will hear his voice and come out—those who have done good will rise to live, and those who have done evil will rise to be condemned" (John 5:27–29). He whom men have rejected will be the judge; it is the decree of the Father. When he summons, all will come.

There is a crisis of eternal death awaiting people. In 1777 Samuel Johnson wrote, "Depend on it. When a man knows he is to be hanged in a fortnight, it concentrates his mind wonderfully." We have only a limited number of days to live. It is appointed for every man to die once. For us who have trusted in Christ, the terror of death is gone. We die in faith and appear before the presence of God in glory. But realize that our times are in God's hands, not ours. We have no control over our birth or death. It may be today that we die. Old and young must die. May this truth concentrate our minds wonderfully. The psalmist says, "Teach us to number our days aright, that we may gain a heart of wisdom" (Ps. 90:12).

Have you been thinking about Christ's second coming, which was the blessed hope of the early church? Jesus spoke about it: "Do not let your hearts be troubled. Trust in God; trust also in me. In my Father's house are many rooms; if it were not so, I would have told you. I am going there to prepare a place for you. And if I go and prepare a place for you, I will come back and take you to be with me that you also may be where I am" (John 14:1–3).

At his first coming, Jesus died on the cross and canceled our sin by suffering for it himself. But he also rose from the dead and went through the heavens to the presence of God, where he is seated on God's right hand as King of kings and as our high priest, ever interceding for us.

Soon Christ shall descend to this planet again: "For the Lord himself will come down from heaven, with a loud command, with the voice of the archangel and with the trumpet call of God, and the dead in Christ will rise first" (1 Thess. 4:16). Paul writes elsewhere: "But our citizenship is in heaven. And we eagerly await a Savior from there, the Lord Jesus Christ, who, by the power that enables him to bring everything under his control, will transform our lowly bodies so that they will be like his glorious body" (Phil. 3:20–21). The disciples were admonished, "Men of Galilee, why do you stand here looking into the sky?

The Second Coming of Jesus Christ

This same Jesus, who has been taken from you into heaven, will come back in the same way you have seen him go into heaven" (Acts 1:11).

What are some of the characteristics of this second coming? It will be *personal*. The same Jesus who ascended will come back (Acts 1:11). It will be *visible*, not secret—every eye shall see him (Rev. 1:7; Matt. 24:30–31). Jesus was manifested to the world in the first coming in humiliation, but he is going to be manifested in the second coming in glory. Several Greek words used to describe the second coming give this idea, including *apokalupsis* (unveiling), and *epiphaneia* (appearing).

Christ's second coming will also be *glorious*: "When the Son of Man comes in his glory, and all the angels with him, he will sit on his throne in heavenly glory" (Matt. 25:31). No longer will anyone mock Jesus and treat him with contempt by plucking out his beard, beating him, and crucifying him. Christ is going to come again in glory.

The second coming will be *purposeful*. Jesus is coming not only to save but also to judge. Paul writes of the judgment to come: "But because of your stubbornness and unrepentant heart, you are storing up wrath against yourself for the day of God's wrath, when his righteous judgment will be revealed. . . . This will take place on the day when God will judge men's secrets through Jesus Christ, as my gospel declares" (Rom. 2:5, 16). When he comes, men will cry out to the mountains and hills to fall on them and hide them, because the wrath of the Lamb has come (Rev. 6:15–17).

Matthew 25:31–46 and Revelation 20:11–15 are among the many passages where we learn of this twofold purpose of judgment and salvation. We must surrender any superficial or cultural understanding we have of Jesus and replace it with the revelation we receive from the Holy Scriptures. At the end of all things, "every knee shall bow . . . and every tongue confess that Jesus Christ is Lord, to the glory of God the Father" (Phil 2:10-11). Every enemy shall be put under his feet.

> He's coming soon,
> he's coming soon;
> with joy we'll welcome his returning.

Why do we welcome him with joy and not sorrow? Because Christ has canceled the sins of those who believe. By his sacrificial suffering and death, he bore our sins away. He died our death, suffered our wrath, and set us free from guilt and death. His second coming, therefore, is not a tragedy; it will be our jubilee and coronation. Jesus is coming to save those who are waiting for him.

When soldiers are away at war, many have wives waiting for them to come home. They may be separated for months or even years. During this time, some wives prove unfaithful to their husbands. In fact, some hope that their husbands will not return. But then there are others who are waiting and praying: "O God, spare him and bring him safely home." They are reading their husbands' letters over and over again, fixing up the house, and doing everything for that day when their husbands return.

Christ is coming for those who hope in him and eagerly await him. He came first to atone for the sins of those who are given to him to save. Those whose sins he atoned for will repent and trust in him, and will wait for him with patient jubilation. They will not wait idly, but they will be laboring for the Lord as they anticipate his return. When they speak, they will talk about their wonderful bridegroom who died for them. As the bride of Christ, they will love not the world but their heavenly Bridegroom and wait patiently for his coming. Such people will not dirty their wedding dresses with sin as they wait.

As Christians, we long for the second coming of Christ. Before his martyrdom, Paul wrote, "For I am already being poured out like a drink offering, and the time has come for my departure. I have fought the good fight, I have finished the race, I have kept the faith. Now there is in store for me the crown of righteousness, which the Lord, the righteous Judge, will award to me on that day—and not only to me, but also to all who have longed for his appearing" (2 Tim. 4:6–8). Christ is not coming again to atone for sin. He did that in his first coming. He is coming to judge all rebels and to grant full salvation to those who have trusted in the way of the cross. He is coming that he may be with his saints forever.

What Are You Waiting For?

Are you eagerly awaiting Christ's second coming? Are you waiting for him in holiness, righteousness, love, hope, and labor? Are you loving Jesus by reading his love letter to you, which is the word of God? Do you show your love for him by obeying his commands? Does prayer give you pleasure and worship exhilarate you? Are you careful with your wedding dress, or are you dragging it through the mud? Are you crying out, "*Marana tha*; Come, Lord Jesus"?

The end of history is coming. Peter exhorts, "Since everything will be destroyed in this way, what kind of people ought you to be? You ought to live holy and godly lives as you look forward to the day of God and speed its coming. That day will bring about the destruction of the heavens by fire, and the elements will melt in the heat. But in keeping with his promise we are looking forward to a new heaven and a new earth, the home of righteousness" (2 Pet. 3:11–13). John says, "Everyone who has this hope in him purifies himself, just as he is pure" (1 John 3:3).

In the parable of the ten virgins Jesus gives a sober warning:

> At midnight the cry rang out, "Here's the bridegroom! Come out to meet him!" Then all the virgins woke up and trimmed their lamps. The foolish ones said to the wise, "Give us some of your oil; our lamps are going out." "No," they replied, "there may not be enough for both us and you. Instead, go to those who sell oil and buy some for yourselves." But while they were on their way to buy the oil, the bridegroom arrived. The virgins who were ready went in with him to the wedding banquet. And the door was shut. Later, the others also came. "Sir! Sir!" they said. "Open the door for us!" But he replied, "I tell you the truth, I do not know you." Therefore keep watch, because you do not know the day or the hour. (Matt. 25:6–13)

Are you a foolish virgin, a false professor, with no oil in your lamp? Or are you a wise virgin who brought enough oil for the long wait? If we are the bride of Christ, we will love our Bridegroom with all our heart and wait patiently for him, being always ready to meet him. My prayer is that you may hear from our glorious Bridegroom, "Thou good and faithful bride, enter into the joy of your beloved Lord," and not, "Depart from me, you evildoer!"

There is an appointment with God that we all must keep. The first coming of Christ provides us with an escape from God's wrath, and those who trust in Jesus shall fear neither death nor Christ's second coming. Like the wise virgins, they will rejoice at the midnight cry: "Here is the Bridegroom! Come out to meet him!" But though all shall see him, the vast majority will weep and wail when Christ comes again.

There is no salvation outside of Jesus. Death can come any time; Jesus can come back at any moment. Now is our time to repent, believe in him, and be eternally saved. Now is our time to live a holy life and wait eagerly for his appearing. May God help us to do so as we wait for the second coming of Jesus Christ!

20

Who Can Forgive Sins?

¹*The law is only a shadow of the good things that are coming—not the realities themselves. For this reason it can never, by the same sacrifices repeated endlessly year after year, make perfect those who draw near to worship.* ²*If it could, would they not have stopped being offered? For the worshipers would have been cleansed once for all, and would no longer have felt guilty for their sins.* ³*But those sacrifices are an annual reminder of sins,* ⁴*because it is impossible for the blood of bulls and goats to take away sins.*

⁵*Therefore, when Christ came into the world, he said: "Sacrifice and offering you did not desire, but a body you prepared for me;* ⁶*with burnt offerings and sin offerings you were not pleased.* ⁷*Then I said, 'Here I am—it is written about me in the scroll—I have come to do your will, O God.'"* ⁸*First he said, "Sacrifices and offerings, burnt offerings and sin offerings you did not desire, nor were you pleased with them" (although the law required them to be made).* ⁹*Then he said, "Here I am, I have come to do your will." He sets aside the first to establish the second.* ¹⁰*And by that will, we have been made holy through the sacrifice of the body of Jesus Christ once for all.*

¹¹*Day after day every priest stands and performs his religious duties; again and again he offers the same sacrifices, which can never take away sins.* ¹²*But when this priest had offered for all time one sacrifice for sins, he sat down at the right hand of God.* ¹³*Since that time he waits for his enemies to be made his footstool,* ¹⁴*because by one sacrifice he has made perfect forever those who are being made holy.* ¹⁵*The Holy Spirit also testifies to us about this. First he says:* ¹⁶*"This is the covenant I will make with them after that time, says the Lord. I will put my laws in their hearts, and I will write them on their minds."* ¹⁷*Then he adds: "Their sins and lawless acts I will remember no more."* ¹⁸*And where these have been forgiven, there is no longer any sacrifice for sin.*

Hebrews 10:1–18

People die each day, many suddenly and unexpectedly. Sudden destruction awaits us all unless our sins are forgiven. We do not even know what awaits us today, but we do know that it is appointed for man once to die and then comes judgment (Heb. 9:27). Let us therefore consider this most important issue of how our sins can be forgiven.

Who Can Forgive Our Sins?

According to the Bible, the infinite, personal God created all things. Yet God's crowning creation, man, sinned against his Maker, and now all of Adam's descendants are born sinners and practice sin daily. Because of our sins, we are storing up wrath against ourselves until the day of wrath, when God will judge all men's secrets in righteousness.

How can we get rid of our sins? We cannot forgive them ourselves, nor can we forgive the sins of our neighbors. David confessed, "Against thee, thee only, have I sinned, and done what is evil in thy sight" (Ps. 51:4, KJV). All sin is transgression against God and his moral law. Unless God himself forgives us, we are without hope and doomed to destruction. If we die still in our sins, we will enter eternal death.

Yet the Bible also tells us that God is "compassionate and gracious, slow to anger, abounding in love. . . . He does not treat us as our sins deserve or repay us according to our iniquities" (Ps. 103:8, 10). Our gracious God has a plan to save us through the sacrifice of a substitute. God revealed to Moses that through a sin offering the guilt of the community could be taken away: "For the life of a creature is in the blood, and I have given it to you to make atonement for yourselves on the altar; it is the blood that makes atonement for one's life" (Lev. 17:11). Adam sinned, and he must die an eternal death. The soul that sins must die (Ezek. 18:20). But God ordained the death of a substitute to take away the guilt of our sins.

Thanks be to God for this heavenly doctrine of the substitutionary atonement! This is the gospel we must continue to gladly and boldly preach. It is said that on a church building there once was a sign: "We preach Christ crucified." As time went on, ivy grew up and covered the sign until it read: "We preach Christ." The ivy grew more until the sign read, "We preach." This is true of so many churches today. They begin by preaching the glorious gospel of Jesus Christ and him crucified. Gradually, as people become sophisticated and ashamed of the cross, they teach a human Christ. As they become still more refined, they stop preaching even a human Christ and simply talk about themselves.

We must preach Jesus Christ and him crucified, for he is the only way of salvation. Hebrews 10:1–18 speaks of the good news of Christ's atoning death in behalf of sinful man. From this passage we want to examine the following: the law, the gospel, and how our sins can be forgiven.

The Law

"*The law is only a shadow of the good things that are coming—not the realities themselves. For this reason it can never, by the same sacrifices repeated endlessly year after year, make perfect those who draw near to worship*" (Heb. 10:1). The Mosaic law required that bulls and goats be sacrificed to make atonement for the sins of the people, especially on the Day of Atonement. But this system of animal sacrifice, although divinely instituted, was only a preparatory, interim measure. It was only a sign, not the destination. The sacrificial system foreshadowed the "good things" of our eternal salvation.

The author confesses in Hebrews 7:19, "For the law made nothing perfect." It could neither cleanse people of their guilt nor make them able to freely draw near to God. These repeated sacrifices only served to remind them of their sins. Hebrews 10:4 discloses the truth about the Mosaic system: "*It is impossible for the blood of bulls and goats to take away sins.*"

Animal sacrifice was powerless to bring about forgiveness of our sins. It was only a teaching device, pointing to a better, human substitute. How could irrational, unwilling animals be fit substitutes for man, who was created in the image of God? Understanding this, David prayed, "You do not delight in sacrifice, or I would bring it; you do not take pleasure in burnt offerings" (Ps. 51:16). The prophet Samuel declared, "Does the LORD delight in burnt offerings and sacrifices as much as in obeying the voice of the Lord? To obey is better than sacrifice, and to heed is better than the fat of rams" (1 Sam. 15:22). Brute beasts cannot turn away the wrath of God against us.

Paul also understood this: "For what the law was powerless to do in that it was weakened by the sinful nature, God did by sending his own Son in the likeness of sinful man to be a sin offering" (Rom. 8:3). We need a sinless human substitute for human sinners, one who is both God and man, to atone for the sins of the whole world.

The Gospel

"*Therefore, when Christ came into the world . . .*" (Heb. 10:5). "Therefore" means in view of the impotence of the Mosaic sacrificial system. God promised long ago to send us a fit substitute; the gospel declares that Jesus Christ came as that substitute. Psalm 40:6–8, which is quoted in Hebrews 10:5–7, promises a better substitute, a heavenly one. It is speaking about the incarnation of the Son of God.

Jesus came to atone for our sins. What God required was not the blood of millions of animals, but a human being who would honor him by fully obeying his law. We needed a second Adam to undo the evil of the first, so Christ came into the world from the bosom of the Father. Verses 7 and 9 begin with the word "*Idou,*" meaning, "Behold! Look! See!" Something wonderful happened in the midpoint of time: the incarnation of the eternal Son of God. In view of the failure of the Mosaic system, God's Son came and took on human flesh to become the fit substitute for us sinners.

Psalm 40 speaks of this incarnation of the eternal Son: "a body you have prepared for me" (v. 6, Septuagint). The Father's eternal plan, accomplished by the incarnate Son, is the salvation of all his elect sinners. God's will was that his Son perfectly obey God's law in our place and die on the cross. The apex of Christ's obedience was seen as he hung on the cross for the sin of the world. He absorbed the wrath of God due us.

The Father prepared for Christ a perfect human body. The angel Gabriel told Mary, "The Holy Spirit will come upon you, and the power of the Most High will overshadow you. So the holy one to be born will be called the Son of God" (Luke 1:35). The Son of God became perfect man. "Such a high priest meets our need—one who is holy, blameless, pure, set apart from sinners, exalted above the heavens" (Heb. 7:26). John tells us, "The Word became flesh and made his dwelling among us. We have seen his glory, the glory of the One and Only, who came from the Father, full of grace and truth" (John 1:14). Paul says, "But when the time had fully come, God sent his Son, born of a woman, born under law, to redeem those under law, that we might receive the full rights of sons" (Gal. 4:4).

Jesus Christ came into the world to save sinners. He knew this was his purpose because it had been written of him in the Law, the Prophets, the Psalms, and the Writings. The Old Testament promised a fit substitute to die in our place to make atonement for our sins. So Jesus explained, "This is what is written: The Christ will suffer and rise from the dead on the third day, and repentance and forgiveness of sins will be preached in his name to all nations, beginning at Jerusalem" (Luke 24:46–47).

Forgiveness of Sins

In this body prepared by the Father, Jesus came to do his Father's will, and to do so without fail. Isaiah 50:5–8 speaks of the Son's obedience: "The Sovereign LORD has opened my ears, and I have not been rebellious; I have not drawn back. I have offered my back to those who beat me, my cheeks to those who pulled out my beard; I did not hide my face from mocking and spitting. Because the Sovereign LORD helps me, I will not be disgraced. Therefore have I set my face like flint, and I know I will not be put to shame. He who vindicates me is near." Jesus himself declared, "My food is to do the will of him who sent me and to finish his work. . . . For I have come down from heaven not to do my will but to do the will of him who sent me" (John 4:34; 6:38).

God's will was to save us by Christ's perfect obedience in our place. Jesus said, "The one who sent me is with me; he has not left me alone, for I always do what pleases him" (John 8:29). He later declared, "I am the good shepherd. The good shepherd lays down his life for the sheep. . . . The world must learn that I love the Father and that I do exactly what my Father has commanded me" (John 10:11; 14:31). At Gethsemane, as he bore the sin of the world, he prayed, "Father, if you are willing, take this cup from me; yet not my will, but yours be done" (Luke 22:42). That will was to accomplish salvation for his people by his substitutionary atonement.

The ultimate cause of our salvation is the Father's will, which the Son fulfilled by the sacrifice of himself on the cross. Freely and willingly, unlike brute animals, Jesus loved the church and gave himself for her. The sinless Son of God, our great high priest, offered himself as the perfect offering as our substitute. We will not experience even an infinitesimally small part of God's wrath; he suffered it all in our place.

Christ's sacrifice put an end to the Mosaic sacrificial system that could not atone for anyone. "Christ is the end of the law so there may be righteousness for everyone who believes" (Rom. 10:4). The Father accepted his Son as an atoning sacrifice for our sins; now forgiveness flows from the cross. By the sacrifice of Christ, he abolished the first covenant to establish the new covenant of grace. As Jesus declared at the Last Supper, "This cup is the new covenant in my blood, which is poured out for you" (Luke 22:20).

The author tells us, "Without the shedding of blood there is no forgiveness" (Heb. 9:22). Then he writes, *"It is impossible for the blood of bulls and goats to take away sins"* (Heb. 10:4). Therefore, blood must be shed, but whose? It must be the blood of Jesus Christ. Because Christ shed his blood on the cross for our sins, there is now forgiveness for all who come to him in faith: *"And by that will, we have been made holy through the sacrifice of the body of Jesus Christ once for all"* (Heb. 10:10).

Jesus died, rose from the dead, and is seated with the Father: *"But when this priest had offered for all time one sacrifice for sins, he sat down at the right hand of God"* (Heb. 10:12). The writer tells us in verse 11 that the Aaronic priests always stood because their work was never finished. But Christ by his death finished the work of atonement and is now seated in the most honored place at God's right hand. From the utter shame of the cross, he ascended to sit in the seat of greatest heavenly glory. Jesus himself spoke of this to the Sanhedrin: "But I say to all of you: In the future you will see the Son of Man sitting at the right hand of the Mighty One and coming on the clouds of heaven" (Matt. 26:64).

Many sacrifices offered by many priests for many centuries failed to atone for our sins. Now one priest by one perfect sacrifice, offered once for all on the cross, has atoned for all the sins of all God's people. Jesus announced from the cross, "It is finished." He accomplished his mission.

The Good Things of Salvation

"The law is only a shadow of the good things that are coming" (Heb. 10:1). What are the "good things" of salvation?

1. *Christ destroyed our death by his death.* He said, "I have come that they may have life, and have it to the full. . . . I give them eternal life, and they shall never perish" (John 10:10, 28). Even if our enemies kill us, they are only assisting us in going sooner into the presence of God. The death of Christ has freed us from our fear of death.

2. *God forgives our sins.* This is another blessing that flows from this one perfect sacrifice of Christ. In Hebrews 5:8–9 we read, "Although he was a son, he learned obedience from what he suffered and, once made perfect, he became the source of eternal salvation." In speaking of Christ's first coming, the author says, "But now he has appeared once for all at the end of the ages to do away with sin" (Heb. 9:26). Jesus came to blot out sins. In the fourth century Athanasius explained that the Savior "put on a body so that in the body he might find death and blot it out." Christ destroyed death by his death.

In 2 Corinthians 5 we find a glorious Holy Spirit-inspired declaration of our salvation: "Therefore, if anyone is in Christ, he is a new creation; the old has gone, the new has come!" (v. 17). God wants to see the new in us, not the same old rebellion and stubbornness. "God was reconciling the world to himself in Christ, not counting men's sins against them" (v. 19).

"The law is only a shadow of the good things" (Heb. 10:1). We are no longer in shadow; good things have come in Jesus Christ. We taste them, we eat them, and we enjoy them. "How beautiful . . . are the feet of those who bring good news" (Isa. 52:7). The gospel proclaims good things for us in Jesus Christ, the One who is good.

3. *God made us perfect.* Hebrews 10:14 tells us, *"By one sacrifice he has made perfect forever those who are being made holy."* This statement is in the perfect tense. Not only did Christ make us perfect, but we are also perfect now, and we shall be perfect in the future. This is speaking about justification. You may say, "But I still have sin in me." Take heart: Christ's death on the cross is the cause of both our justification and our sanctification. He who justifies us will necessarily also sanctify us. In fact, he is transforming us even now. Not only does God declare us righteous, but he also transforms us by writing his law in our hearts so that we will love it and do it by the power of the indwelling Holy Spirit.

What about the future? Hebrews 9:28 says, "So Christ was sacrificed once to take away the sins of many people; and he will appear a second time, not to bear sin, but to bring salvation to those who are waiting for him." We shall be glorified. Jesus Christ will give us a body like unto his own glorious body. Even the very presence of sin will be gone, and we shall all be conformed to the image of Christ.

4. *We no longer have a guilty conscience* (Heb. 9:14; 10:2). Satan may accuse us, but we can resist him successfully because the blood of Jesus Christ has cleansed us from all our sins. Having forgiven our sins, God remembers them no more.

5. *The Holy Spirit testifies to us* (Heb. 10:15). The Holy Spirit ministers to us both from the Scripture and by testifying to our spirits that we are children of God. As we read the word of God, we eat it, grow by it, and delight in it. A person cannot be a Christian without daily reading the Bible, for it is the food for God's people. "Man does not live on bread alone but on every word that comes from the mouth of the LORD" (Deut. 8:3).

6. *Our sins are forgiven and, therefore, forgotten* (Heb. 10:18). Only God in Jesus Christ can forgive our sins; there is no other religion by which we can be saved. Having our evil consciences taken care of by the blood of Jesus Christ, we can now come to God. So the author says, "Come, pray to him. Worship him. Draw near to God, that you may find mercy and grace for time of need."

7. *He defeats our enemies.* Hebrews 10:13 says, *"Since that time he waits for his enemies to be made his footstool."* If we fail to repent and trust in Jesus alone, we remain at enmity with him. And soon he shall defeat all his enemies. The Father told the Son, "Sit at my

right hand until I make your enemies a footstool for your feet" (Ps. 110:1). Either we will be seated with him or we will feel the pressure of his feet on our necks. We must think very seriously: Are we Christ's enemies, or are we his surrendered subjects?

Partial surrender is no surrender. God only accepts complete and total surrender. In this conflict, the enemies of Christ always lose: "He will punish those who do not know God and do not obey the gospel of our Lord Jesus. They will be punished with everlasting destruction and shut out from the presence of the Lord and from the majesty of his power on the day he comes to be glorified in his holy people and to be marveled at among all those who have believed" (2 Thess. 1:8–10). Jesus Christ has received all authority in heaven and on earth. He is the victor.

May God help us to rejoice in this forgiveness of sins, this great salvation, and this free access to God. May we worship him in spirit and truth, and rejoice in his presence, experiencing his justification and sanctification even while we await our glorification. May we rejoice that the Holy Spirit is even now ministering to us from the Scripture, revealing that there is forgiveness of sins, and may we be saved through Christ's death for our sins.

21
Worship of the Saints

> [19]*Therefore, brothers, since we have confidence to enter the Most Holy Place by the blood of Jesus,* [20]*by a new and living way opened for us through the curtain, that is, his body,* [21]*and since we have a great priest over the house of God,* [22]*let us draw near to God with a sincere heart in full assurance of faith, having our hearts sprinkled to cleanse us from a guilty conscience and having our bodies washed with pure water.* [23]*Let us hold unswervingly to the hope we profess, for he who promised is faithful.* [24]*And let us consider how we may spur one another on toward love and good deeds.* [25]*Let us not give up meeting together, as some are in the habit of doing, but let us encourage one another—and all the more as you see the Day approaching.*
>
> Hebrews 10:19-25

The theme of Hebrews 10:19-25 is the worship of the saints. This does not mean that we worship saints; rather, it is speaking about the saints' worship of God.

In the previous section, we learned that God has made us perfect and holy in Christ. Our sin problem, which kept us from God, has been solved forever. In Hebrews 9:22 we read that without the shedding of blood there is no remission of sins. Yet we also read that "it is impossible for the blood of bulls and goats to take away sins" (Heb. 10:4). Therefore, the Mosaic sacrificial system failed to deal with our sins. Rather, it pointed to the new covenant, which Christ established by the shedding of his own blood for our sins on the cross. As Jesus said, "This is my blood of the covenant, which is poured out for many for the forgiveness of sins" (Matt. 26:28).

Because of our sins, we were supposed to die, but Christ died instead. By dying our death, he took away our sins. Now those who trust in him are called saints; they alone are invited to worship and serve God. This section begins with "Therefore." The author is giving his logic that since Christ has cleansed and sanctified us, we can now draw near to God.

In the wilderness the Israelites had to worship God from a distance because God is holy and they were sinners. Even after they came to the Promised Land, they were still kept outside the temple. But since Jesus our great high priest made his perfect sacrifice, all believers can go directly into God's presence. Once we were driven away from the presence of God, but now we are brought near to him in Christ.

From this text, we want to examine why we are now able to come near to God and three exhortations of what we should do in light of these reasons.

God Gives Us Confidence

"Therefore, brothers, since we have confidence to enter the Most Holy Place by the blood of Jesus, by a new and living way opened for us through the curtain, that is his body . . . let us draw near to God" (Heb. 10:19–20, 22). What has God done for us so that we can now draw near and worship him? First, he gives us confidence. The Greek word is *parrēsia*, boldness.

As children of God, we have confidence. If we have trusted in Jesus Christ, then we are holy brothers, beloved of God. Our sins have been blotted out and we have been adopted into the family of God. Because of that, we have a God-given right to draw near to God. Just as the children of the president of the United States always have confidence to enter the Oval Office, so we as God's children have the privilege to come into the throne room of God. Through Jesus Christ both Jews and Gentiles have access to the Father by one Holy Spirit (Eph. 2:18).

What is the ground of this confidence? The blood of Jesus. Without the shedding of blood, there is no forgiveness. Christ's blood, however, was shed to open the way to the Father. Paul says, "Now in him and through faith in him we may approach God with freedom and confidence" (Eph. 3:12). Jesus Christ inaugurated for our benefit the way into God's presence. It is called "the way of his flesh."[1] This way of Christ's incarnation is a new way that did not exist before. It was inaugurated when Christ died on the cross. At that point, the veil that separated God from his people was torn apart forever and this new way was opened. No longer are there any restrictions or barriers between us and God. Now all believers are welcome to come into the Father's presence in the Holy of Holies of the heavenly sanctuary.

This way is a living way; the way of the cross leads to eternal life. Jesus Christ who died now lives an indestructible life (Heb. 7:16). "Jesus lives forever. . . . Therefore, he is able to save completely those who come to God through him" (Heb. 7:24–25).

Jesus tells us, "I am the way and the truth and the life. No one comes to the Father except through me" (John 14:6). In the Mosaic system, this way into the Holy of Holies was not open to us (Heb. 9:8). But it has been opened up by the death and the resurrection of Jesus Christ our Lord. Christ is the new and living way, the only way, to come to the Father.

Our Great High Priest Is Over God's Church

"Since we have a high priest over the house of God, let us draw near God" (Heb. 10:21–22). The second reason we can worship God is that our great high priest, the sinless Son of God, who is a high priest after the order of Melchizedek and greater than Moses, Aaron, the temple, and Solomon, is *over* the house of God. In other words, he is the head of the church: "But Christ is faithful as a son over God's house. And we are his house" (Heb. 3:6).

Peter writes, "As you come to him, the living Stone—rejected by men but chosen by God and precious to him—you also, like living stones, are being built into a spiritual house to be a holy priesthood, offering spiritual sacrifices acceptable to God through Jesus Christ" (1 Pet. 2:4–5). We are God's temple and his priests. And over this spiritual house is our great high priest, Jesus Christ. Paul speaks of the same idea: "Consequently, you are no longer foreigners and aliens, but fellow citizens with God's people and members of God's household, built on the foundation of the

---

1   Westcott, *Epistle to the Hebrews*, 322.

apostles and prophets, with Christ Jesus himself as the chief cornerstone. In him the whole building is joined together and rises to become a holy temple in the Lord. And in him you too are being built together to become a dwelling in which God lives by his Spirit" (Eph. 2:19–22).

As our head, Christ directs, protects, provides, and intercedes for us. He arrived in heaven in our behalf to help us: "We have this hope as an anchor for the soul, firm and secure. It enters the inner sanctuary behind the curtain, where Jesus, who went before us, has entered on our behalf. He has become a high priest forever, in the order of Melchizedek" (Heb. 6:19–20). Christ our forerunner made the way so that we can follow him. He is in God's presence for our benefit, and he escorts us there so that we can boldly approach the throne of grace.

We Must Draw Near

"Let us draw near to God" (Heb. 10:22). In view of these reasons, the author now exhorts us to do three things. First, we must draw near to God, not once a year as the Aaronic high priests did, but continuously, as indicated by use of the present tense. We must come to God daily in prayer, reading the word, singing, repenting, and giving thanks. We must come to God in private and public worship.

You may ask, "But who can ascend the hill of the Lord? Who may stand in his holy place?" Psalm 24 answers the question: "He who has clean hands and a pure heart, who does not lift up his soul to an idol or swear by what is false. He will receive blessing from the LORD and vindication from God his Savior" (vv. 3–5). Only those who are pure in heart may enter God's presence. "Blessed are the pure in heart, for they will see God" (Matt. 5:8). We see God as we draw near through our holy Jesus. God invites us to come now and see him by faith.

Our problem is that we are full of sin and have an evil conscience. But thank God, Christ ascended as the Holy One for us: "No one has ever gone into heaven except the one who came from heaven—the Son of Man" (John 3:13). Jesus came down and accomplished the will of God by shedding his blood for the forgiveness of our sins. Having ascended the holy hill of the Lord,

Christ entered the presence of God and is seated at his right hand in heaven. By faith we are now united with Christ; we therefore have ascended with him and are seated in heavenly places with him. We are not stranded and left to fend for ourselves. He is holy, and in him we have been made holy.

Hebrews 4 tells us, "Therefore, since we have a great high priest who has gone through the heavens, Jesus the Son of God, let us hold firmly to the faith we profess. . . . Let us then approach the throne of grace with confidence, so that we may receive mercy and find grace to help us in our time of need" (vv. 14, 16). In times of temptation, warfare, persecution, or martyrdom, as well as in daily life, we need God's mercy and grace.

Therefore, do not be afraid to draw near to God; you shall not die! The wrath against us has been absorbed fully by our glorious substitute. Draw near with confidence. Come to Jesus, and through him, come to the Father: "You have come to Mount Zion, to the heavenly Jerusalem, the city of the living God. You have come to thousands upon thousands of angels in joyful assembly, to the church of the firstborn, whose names are written in heaven. You have come to God, the judge of all men, to the spirits of righteous men made perfect, to Jesus the mediator of a new covenant, and to the sprinkled blood that speaks a better word than the blood of Abel" (Heb. 12:22–24). Even now, both Jews and Gentiles are drawing near to God through Jesus by faith.

"Let us draw near to God with a sincere heart" (Heb. 10:22). Do not come like Nadab and Abihu, who were consumed by the holy God. Come with an undivided heart. Come without any doubt. Do not be hypocritical, like Achan, Demas, Simon Magus, or Ananias and Sapphira, all of whom came to God in a wrong way. We must approach God with a true heart. David prayed, "Surely you desire truth in the inner parts" (Ps. 51:6). Elijah asked, "How long will you waver between two opinions? If the Lord is God, follow him; but if Baal is God, follow him" (1 Kings 18:21). Double-minded people cannot come into God's presence.

"Let us draw near to God . . . in full assurance of faith" (Heb. 10:22). Elsewhere, the writer says, "Anyone who comes to [God] must believe that he exists and that he rewards those who earnestly seek him" (Heb. 11:6). God always fulfills what he promises. His promises are to be trusted because they are the promises of God

himself. And in addition to his promises, God has also given us an oath: "God did this so that, by two unchangeable things in which it is impossible for God to lie, we who have fled to take hold of the hope offered to us may be greatly encouraged" (Heb. 6:18).

We must come to God with fullness of faith, which comes by hearing the word of God. This means we must read the word daily, hear God's word preached, listen to the testimonies of God's faithfulness to his people, and be encouraged by God's answers to our prayers. James says, "Come near to God and he will come near to you" (James 4:8).

"Let us draw near to God . . . having our hearts sprinkled to cleanse us from a guilty conscience" (Heb. 10:22). The Mosaic system could not cleanse the consciences of the worshipers, but the new covenant inaugurated by Jesus can. Christ's blood gives a clean conscience to those who trust in his person and his work. No more do we experience the torment of sin and its guilt! Our fear is blotted out, and we are set free to serve God.

Peter says that we "have been chosen according to the foreknowledge of God the Father, through the sanctifying work of the Spirit, for obedience to Jesus Christ and sprinkling by his blood" (1 Pet. 1:2). John writes, "If we confess our sins, he is faithful and just and will forgive us our sins and purify us from all unrighteousness" (1 John 1:9). The blood of Jesus justifies and sanctifies us so that we can draw near to God.

"Let us draw near to God . . . having our bodies washed with pure water" (Heb. 10:22). This final qualification may be speaking about water baptism. In Ezekiel 36:25 the Lord speaks about pure water: "I will sprinkle clean water on you, and you will be clean; I will cleanse you from all your impurities and from all your idols." Ananias told Paul, "And now what are you waiting for? Get up, be baptized and wash away your sins, calling on his name" (Acts 22:16). Having been cleansed inwardly, those who are drawing near are also baptized outwardly in the name of the Father, Son, and Holy Spirit, confirming the interior work of God. Therefore, we can now draw near with a clean conscience. We may come to God with a true heart and in fullness of faith, confessing sin and confessing Christ. We can come to God to receive help to resist the devil and live a victorious Christian

life. The Father is waiting for us, as is Jesus, our great high priest. Clean people may draw near to God to worship.

Hold Fast to Your Confession

"Let us hold unswervingly to the hope we profess" (Heb. 10:23). The second exhortation is to hold fast to our confession of faith in Christ. Calvin said that hope is a child of faith and is nourished by faith.[2] The objective content of hope is our eternal salvation. In view of the two reasons we spoke about, we must also persevere in faith and hope. Do not throw away the gospel for the sake of a cup of soup. Hold on to Christ, especially in the midst of temptations, persecutions, and difficulties. Be a martyr for your faith, if needs be. Deny yourselves, take up the cross, and follow Jesus.

In Hebrews 11 we read about some people who held on to their faith: "Others were tortured and refused to be released, so that they might gain a better resurrection. Some faced jeers and flogging, while still others were chained and put in prison. They were stoned; they were sawed in two; they were put to death by the sword. They went about in sheepskins and goatskins, destitute, persecuted and mistreated" (v. 35–37). In 2 Corinthians Paul speaks several times about the severe trials and persecutions he experienced. Yet he fought the fight, kept the faith, ran the race, and died in faith.

Hold on to your faith in sickness, in poverty, and in the face of torture and death. What can death do to us? Christ has conquered death by his death. In Christ, death has become our servant. To live is Christ and to die is gain (Phil. 1:21). Jesus has given us eternal life, and we shall never perish (John 10:28).

We must hold on! Notice the conditions laid out in these verses: "But Christ is faithful as a son over God's house. And we are his house, *if we hold on* to our courage and the hope of which we boast. . . . We have come to share in Christ *if we hold firmly till the end* the confidence we had at first" (Heb. 3:6, 14). False professors may start out testifying about their faith in Christ and being active in the church. But in due time, they fall away.

---

[2] Cited by Philip E. Hughes, *Commentary on Hebrews*, 414.

The Hebrews writer exhorts, "We want each of you to show this same diligence to the very end, in order to make your hope sure" (Heb. 6:11). Be faithful and hopeful till death. Ours is a living hope that never fails nor makes us ashamed.

To what are we to hold on unswervingly? *"To the hope we profess."* We must confess our hope so that all of God's elect will hear and be saved. Jesus said, "I tell you, whoever acknowledges me before men, the Son of Man will acknowledge him before the angels of God. But he who disowns me before men will be disowned before the angels of God" (Luke 12:8–9). Confess your faith to the world. Do not turn to the right or to the left of this gospel. As pilgrims, let us move steadily on to the heavenly city, resisting all temptations and distractions that issue from a hopeless, miserable world.

We should hold fast to our confession of hope because the One who promised us eternal salvation is trustworthy. Satan is a liar, but our Savior is truth and so keeps his promises. He is the same yesterday, today, and forever. Others may forsake us, but God tells us, "Never will I leave you; never will I forsake you" (Heb. 13:5).

Spur One Another On

"Let us consider how we may spur one another on toward love and good deeds" (Heb. 10:24). A rider spurs his horse so that the horse will do what he wants it to do. In this third exhortation, the writer is saying, "Let us continuously consider, think about, ponder, study, and fix our minds on ways to inspire and incite one another to love and good deeds."

Christianity primarily demands thinking, not feeling. The author has already called the Hebrews to concentrated mental activity: "Therefore, holy brothers, who share in the heavenly calling, *fix your thoughts* on Jesus" (Heb. 3:1, italics added). First, then, we are to focus our minds on Jesus. We are to study God's word that we may love and trust Christ.

We are also to think of others. He who thinks of Jesus cannot neglect God's people. There is no solo Christianity. The church is a family; therefore, we look after one another. As brothers and sisters, we live and die for one another: "This is how we know what love is: Jesus Christ laid down his life for us, and we ought to lay down our lives for our brothers. If anyone has material possessions and sees his brother in need but has no pity on him, how can the love of God be in him?" (1 John 3:16–17). The early church came together and loved one another, even selling their real estate and placing the money at the apostles' feet to provide for the people of God (Acts 2:42–47; 4:32–35).

As members of the family of God, we love both our Father and his children. When people are in love, they want to be with each other. Nothing can keep lovers apart. They think up ways to be together. Love knows no obstacles. It is the same in the family of God. We come from far and wide to worship and have fellowship with the people of God. We know each other's needs and take care of them. When one member suffers, we all suffer; when one rejoices, we all rejoice. We think up ways to spur one another on to love. Love is evident everywhere—a love that translates into deeds done to help God's people. We spend our time, talents, and money to help others, especially the household of God.

At various times Jesus urged his disciples to consider and learn from creation, whether from the ravens, the lilies of the field, or the ants. So also we are to study the people of God, getting together so that we can know our brothers and sisters and help meet their needs, whether spiritual, economic, physical, marital, or familial. We are to rebuke, correct, teach, and instruct one another, and to spur each other on, provoking and stimulating each other to love God.

"*Let us not give up meeting together, as some are in the habit of doing, but let us encourage one another—and all the more as you see the Day approaching*" (Heb. 10:25). Some forsake the assembling together of the saints because of trials, persecution, or arrogance. Matthew 24:12 says that in the last days the love of many will grow cold. First John 2:19 speaks of false brothers who went out from the church because they did not really belong to it. But true people of God will never forsake the assembly of the saints. He who loves God will love God's people. True people of God are not like the Dead Sea, which is stagnant because it has no outlet; rather, they are channels of blessings, with rivers of living water flowing out of their innermost being to help others.

The Hebrews author previously wrote, "See to it, brothers, that none of you has a sinful, unbelieving heart that turns away from the living God. But encourage one another daily, as long as it is called Today, so that none of you may be hardened by sin's deceitfulness" (Heb. 3:12–13). In Ephesians Paul prays that we "may have power, *together with all the saints*, to grasp how wide and long and high and deep is the love of Christ" (Eph. 3:18, italics added).

God's love book consists of his people. Each one is a page. We cannot understand the love of God without belonging to his church. We cannot fully know the love of God apart from his saints. Therefore, we are responsible and accountable to one another. We are commanded, "Submit yourselves to one another out of reverence for Christ" (Eph. 5:21). We must get together to encourage one another and build one another up through our ministries. We must know who has lost his job, who is sick, or who is wandering from God's way, and we must help those people. We must get together to correct and refresh each other. Paul writes, "May the Lord show mercy to the household of Onesiphorus, because he often refreshed me and was not ashamed of my chains. On the contrary, when he was in Rome, he searched hard for me until he found me. May the Lord grant that he will find mercy from the Lord on that day! You know very well in how many ways he helped me in Ephesus" (2 Tim. 1:16–18).

Let us, therefore, get together in large groups, in small groups, and on a one-to-one basis to help one another, so that we may *together* draw near to God and hold on to the confession of our hope without swerving. May we get together often to encourage one another in love and good deeds, and actively follow the example of Jesus Christ who came not to be ministered unto but to minister and give his life as a ransom for many. May we serve Christ by serving his holy people, and may we do so even more frequently "as we see the Day approaching"—the day when we shall see God face to face, either at our death or at his second coming.

22
Warning against Apostasy

²⁶*If we deliberately keep on sinning after we have received the knowledge of the truth, no sacrifice for sins is left, ²⁷but only a fearful expectation of judgment and of raging fire that will consume the enemies of God. ²⁸Anyone who rejected the law of Moses died without mercy on the testimony of two or three witnesses. ²⁹How much more severely do you think a man deserves to be punished who has trampled the Son of God under foot, who has treated as an unholy thing the blood of the covenant that sanctified him, and who has insulted the Spirit of grace? ³⁰For we know him who said, "It is mine to avenge; I will repay," and again, "The Lord will judge his people." ³¹It is a dreadful thing to fall into the hands of the living God.*

Hebrews 10:26-31

Hebrews 10:26–31 is a warning about apostasy, given not to pagans, but to those in the church. In one sense, only those who claim to be God's people can become apostate. *Aposteinai* in Greek means "to stand away from." Apostasy, therefore, means to stand away from Christ and his gospel and to stand opposed to the living God.

Who Is an Apostate?

An apostate is one who, though he may have heard and believed the gospel and even experienced the power of the Holy Spirit in his life in a non-regenerative way, yet in due time turns against the gospel and becomes an enemy of Jesus Christ.

There is the potential for apostasy in every church of God. Every church consists of those who are eternally chosen and truly regenerate, and those who may have made credible confessions of faith but are not true believers. In due time, the feet of those in the latter group will slip and they shall prove themselves to be unregenerate apostates.

We find examples of apostates in both the Old and New Testaments. Saul, the first king of Israel, became an apostate, as did Judas, one of the twelve apostles. Hebrews 3 and 4 describes the apostasy of the Israelites in the wilderness. Though God had promised them rest, the majority of them did not enter into it "because of their unbelief." The author therefore warns, "See to it, brothers, that none of you has a sinful, unbelieving heart that turns away from the living God" (Heb. 3:12). In Hebrews 6:4–6 the author declares about such people, "It is impossible for [them] . . . if they fall away, to be brought back to repentance, because to their loss they are crucifying the Son of God all over again and subjecting him to public disgrace." Apostates must experience the covenant curse of everlasting destruction. The bottom of hell is reserved, not for pagans, but for professing Christians who abandon the gospel and become enemies of Christ and his cross.

God judges us according to the knowledge we have. The greater our knowledge, the greater our responsibility and the greater our punishment if we commit apostasy. Jesus himself laid down this principle in Luke 12:47–48: "That servant who knows his master's will and does not get ready or does not do what his master wants will be beaten with many blows. But the one who does not know and does things deserving punishment will be beaten with few blows."

Reasons for Apostasy

The Bible gives us a number of reasons why people deliberately turn away from the living God.

1. *Persecution.* Jesus himself warned about this: "Then you will be handed over to be persecuted and put to death, and you will be hated by all nations because of me. At that time many will turn away from the faith and will betray and hate each other"

(Matt. 24:9–10). Jesus calls such people "rocky soil" because they turn away from the gospel when trouble comes (Matt. 13:20–21).

2. *Worldliness.* Paul writes, "Demas, because he loved this world, has deserted me" (2 Tim. 4:10). Jesus speaks about "thorny soil" Christians who become apostate because of the worries of life, the pleasures of sin, and the deceitfulness of riches (Matt. 13:22). Worldliness can creep into us, especially in a society such as ours, where we are constantly barraged with the idea that more is always better. The apostle John warns, "Do not love the world or anything in the world. If anyone loves the world, the love of the Father is not in him. For everything in the world—the cravings of sinful man, the lust of his eyes and the boasting of what he has and does—comes not from the Father but from the world. The world and its desires pass away, but the man who does the will of God lives forever" (1 John 2:15–17).

3. *Influence of false teachers in the church.* Jesus said, "Many false prophets will appear and deceive many people" (Matt. 24:11). Paul warns, "For the time will come when men will not put up with sound doctrine. Instead, to suit their own desires, they will gather around them a great number of teachers to say what their itching ears want to hear" (2 Tim. 4:3). Many church people today only want to hear pleasant things and be entertained. But false teaching leads to apostasy.

4. *Neglect of the means of grace.* The Hebrews writer asks, "How shall we escape if we ignore such a great salvation?" (Heb. 2:3). To neglect the means of grace is to neglect God's word, prayer, fellowship, and worship. In the same epistle, the author cautions, "Let us not give up meeting together, as some are in the habit of doing" (Heb. 10:25). When we do not feel like going to church, we have a very serious problem and may be on the verge of apostasy.

5. *Clinging to mindless traditionalism.* No matter what our religious background, when we hear the gospel, we must reject extra-biblical traditions that do not lead to salvation and commit ourselves to following Christ alone. New wine cannot be contained in the old wineskins of mindless traditionalism.

How do we know if we are falling away? Professor Gerald Hawthorne writes, "There is no objective evidence that one who has made his Christian confession and has been baptized is indeed a Christian, other than the daily perseverance in love and good works, that is, a persistence in the very essence of what his confession implies."[1] The Bible urges us to make our calling and election sure and to examine ourselves to see whether we are in the faith (2 Pet 1:10; 2 Cor. 13:5).

Professor John Frame's view on apostasy can be summarized as follows: Those who are *eternally* chosen will also be historically chosen, meaning they will be part of the visible church on earth. Such people shall persevere to the end. But those who are *only* historically chosen, including unregenerate children brought up in the church, shall not persevere.[2] Many in Israel were not eternally chosen, and so they perished. This is also true in the church age. Paul declares: "For those God foreknew he also predestined to be conformed to the likeness of his Son, that he might be the firstborn among many brothers. And those he predestined, he also called; those he called, he also justified; those he justified, he also glorified" (Rom. 8:29–30). In view of this, let us examine two points from Hebrews 10:26–31: apostasy and judgment.

Anatomy of Apostasy

"*If we deliberately keep on sinning after we have received the knowledge of the truth, no sacrifice for sins is left*" (Heb. 10:26). The first word of verse 26 should be "For," because the author is giving his logic for what he intimated in verse 25, where he warned those who were habitually neglecting the means of grace of public worship and fellowship. Now he emphasizes that these people were not sinning out of ignorance, but knowingly, defiantly, and highhandedly.

Numbers 15 condemns such deliberate sinning: "Anyone who sins defiantly, whether native-born or alien, blasphemes the LORD and that person must be cut off from his people. Because he has despised the LORD's word and broken his commands, that person must surely be cut off; his guilt remains on him (vv. 30–31).

Not only does such a person sin defiantly, but he also sins daily. The Greek expression is in the present tense: "*If we deliberately*

---

1 Gerald F. Hawthorne, "The Letter to the Hebrews," in *A New Testament Commentary*, G.C.D. Howley, ed. (Grand Rapids: Zondervan, 1969), 560.
2 Frame, *Salvation Belongs to the Lord*, 177–178, 223–228.

keep on sinning." Sin becomes one's habit. We must keep in mind that the Bible does not teach sinless perfection in this life. True Christians do sin, but not defiantly and continually. And so we oppose the Novatians of the third century, who taught that God does not forgive post-baptismal sins. John writes, "If we claim to be without sin, we deceive ourselves and the truth is not in us. If we confess our sins, he is faithful and just and will forgive us our sins and purify us from all unrighteousness.... My dear children, I write this to you so that you will not sin. But if anybody does sin, we have one who speaks to the Father in our defense—Jesus Christ, the Righteous One. He is the atoning sacrifice for our sins" (1 John 1:8–9; 2:1–2). Paul declares, "Brothers, if someone is caught in a sin, you who are spiritual should restore him gently. But watch yourself, or you also may be tempted" (Gal. 6:1).

Apostates, on the other hand, sin deliberately, defiantly, and daily. They willingly walk out of light into pitch darkness. John's gospel gives us the anatomy of such apostasy in the example of Judas. As an apostle who believed in Jesus and experienced the Holy Spirit in some measure, Judas preached the gospel, healed the sick, and cast out demons. But John tells us that he had already come under the devil's influence at the time of the Last Supper: "The evening meal was being served, and the devil had already prompted Judas Iscariot, son of Simon, to betray Jesus" (John 13:2). Verse 27 says the devil entered Judas, taking complete control, and in verse 30 we are told that Judas went out, leaving the holy communion, "and it was night." Judas turned away from the brightness of walking with Christ and chose to walk with the devil.

John writes of such apostates, "They went out from us, but they did not really belong to us. For if they had belonged to us, they would have remained with us; but their going showed that none of them belonged to us" (1 John 2:19). Such people can be leaders, teachers, and fellow church members. But in reality, they are false brothers, apostates, and unregenerate. They are historically but not eternally chosen. They are children of the devil.

Note the phrase: *"after we have received the knowledge of the truth"* (Heb. 10:26). This phrase means that such people have received the full revelation of the gospel, which Jesus Christ has disclosed to us. Earlier, the author wrote, "In the past God spoke to our forefathers through the prophets at many times and in various ways, but in these last days he has spoken to us by his Son" (Heb. 1:1-2). Christian apostates have received God's final revelation in Jesus Christ and clearly know his person and work. They hear the full gospel, yet they reject God's power unto salvation.

Throughout this epistle, the author warns against ignoring such knowledge:

> We must pay more careful attention, therefore, to what we have heard, so that we do not drift away. For if the message spoken by angels was binding, and every violation and disobedience received its just punishment, how shall we escape if we ignore such a great salvation? This salvation, which was first announced by the Lord, was confirmed to us by those who heard him. God also testified to it by signs, wonders and various miracles, and gifts of the Holy Spirit distributed according to his will. . . . It is impossible for those who have once been enlightened, who have tasted the heavenly gift, who have shared in the Holy Spirit, who have tasted the goodness of the word of God and the powers of the coming age, if they fall away, to be brought back to repentance. (Heb. 2:1-4; 6:4-6)

"How much more severely do you think a man deserves to be punished who has trampled the Son of God under foot?" (Heb. 10:29). Not only do apostates engage in deliberate sin, but they also come to treat Jesus Christ with extreme disgust and contempt, rejecting his deity and sinless humanity. They grind him underfoot—this One who is greater than angels, Moses, Aaron, Melchizedek, Solomon, and the temple. We are told not to throw pearls before swine lest they trample them under their feet; here we see the pearl of Christ and his gospel being so despised and trampled.

"How much more severely do you think a man deserves to be punished . . . who has treated as an unholy thing the blood of the covenant that sanctified him?" (Heb. 10:29). Such people also consider Christ's blood to be filthy. They call unclean the heaven-sent blood that justifies and sanctifies us and brings about the forgiveness of all our sins, the blood that cleanses our consciences and secures us admittance into the presence of God, the blood that is the only divine provision to cleanse us. This is utter contempt for the work of Christ. Apostates consider the blood of Jesus to be the same as that of common men and reject its eternal efficacy to save sinners. They are sophisticated

people who reject the cross and the doctrine of substitutionary atonement, although it was the blood of Christ that ushered in the new covenant blessings of a new heart, knowledge of God, and total forgiveness of sins.

"How much more severely do you think a man deserves to be punished . . . who has insulted the Spirit of grace?" (Heb. 10:29). Apostates also insult the Spirit of grace, whose responsibility it is to apply Christ's redemption to sinners by granting them grace. They insult the Holy Spirit who dwells in the church and blesses Christians (cf. Hebrews 2:4; 6:4; 9:14; and 10:15). Such grieving of the third person of the Trinity is the sin that cannot be forgiven, as Jesus himself says: "Anyone who speaks a word against the Son of Man will be forgiven, but anyone who speaks against the Holy Spirit will not be forgiven, either in this age or in the age to come" (Matt. 12:32). John calls this the sin that leads to eternal death (1 John 5:16). The church is told not to pray for such a person because he is doomed to destruction; it is impossible for him to repent.

Apostates thus show contempt for all three persons of the Godhead. They are known for their insolent self-assertion against the almighty God.

What will happen to such people? Let me illustrate with a story from my own childhood. When I was a boy growing up in South India, one of us would always have to stay home on Sundays to watch our home and livestock. One Sunday when it was my turn, a neighbor came and started singing in a mocking manner a song about the Holy Spirit: "O God, set me on fire by the Spirit of God." As he was singing, I looked up and noticed his house was on fire. When he saw it, this man stopped mocking and ran to save his home, but it was too late. His house was totally consumed. Though we may not experience such immediate consequences, we must be careful not to insult the Spirit of grace, for God will surely judge apostates.

God's Judgment of Apostates

Having examined the nature of apostasy, let us now consider God's judgment of apostates. The greater our knowledge, the greater our responsibility; and, therefore, the greater the judgment God will mete out on those who fall away from the truth. The cross of Christ declares both God's love and his holiness. God must judge sin, either in Jesus Christ or in those who defy him. He who neglects the gospel will be judged by Christ.

We find several references to eternal judgment throughout this epistle: "instruction about baptisms, the laying on of hands, the resurrection of the dead, and *eternal judgment*" (6:2); "Just as man is destined to die once, and after that to face *judgment*" (9:27); "But only a fearful expectation of *judgment*" (10:27); "It is mine to avenge; I will *repay*" (10:30); "Marriage should be honored by all and the marriage bed kept pure, for God will *judge* the adulterer and all the sexually immoral" (13:4).

"If we deliberately keep on sinning after we have received the knowledge of the truth, no sacrifice for sins is left" (Heb. 10:26). This verse tells us that for such apostates, no sacrifice for sins remains because they have rejected the only sacrifice God would accept on our behalf. When we reject his atonement, no sacrifice is left for us. The one who rejects Jesus is doomed forever; it is impossible to redeem such an apostate. He will eventually die a miserable death and enter hell to await an even more horrible eternal punishment. Such a person has *"only a fearful expectation of judgment and of raging fire that will consume the enemies of God"* (Heb. 10:27). Deep within every unbeliever is a fearful expectation of judgment coming, because there is a God-consciousness in every human being. We all know we must eventually face God.

God himself is the judge of all men (Heb. 12:23). Jonathan Edwards spoke from Deuteronomy 32:35 about sinners in the hands of an angry God. He said in due time their foot shall slip. God is love, but he is also holy; he is Savior, but he is also Judge.

When God came to Mount Horeb, the mountain itself began to quake and was set ablaze. The people were frightened, and "the sight was so terrifying that Moses said, 'I am trembling with fear'" (Heb. 12:21). Yet most people do not fear God because Satan has blinded their eyes so that they do not see the glory of God in the face of Jesus Christ (2 Cor.4:4).

How important it is that we recognize the awesomeness of the Lord! Our God is a *"raging fire that will consume the enemies of God"* (Heb. 10:27). Leviticus 10 describes how Nadab and Abihu were *consumed* by fire that came out from God. The holiness of

Warning against Apostasy

God came and destroyed these priests, even as it later destroyed the 250 allies of Korah (Num. 16:35). It is time for us to adjust our view of God and worship him in the beauty of his holiness. "Raging fire" means God is essentially holy. Surrender to him and be saved, or oppose him and be consumed by his holiness.

Moses refers to the fire of God's holiness several times: "You came near and stood at the foot of the mountain while it blazed with fire. . . . You saw no form of any kind the day the LORD spoke to you at Horeb out of the fire. . . . For the LORD your God is a consuming fire, a jealous God. . . . Has any other people heard the voice of God speaking out of fire, as you have, and lived? . . . From heaven he made you hear his voice to discipline you. On earth he showed you his great fire, and you heard his words from out of the fire" (Deut. 4:11, 15, 24, 33, 36). Do we see God as a consuming fire? If we do, the fear of God will keep us from sinning (Exod. 20:20). Simply put, a sinning person has no fear of God.

Few churches today speak about sin and judgment. But consider this picture of hell painted by the prophet Isaiah: God's people "will go out and look upon the dead bodies of those who rebelled against [God]; their worm will not die, nor will their fire be quenched, and they will be loathsome to all mankind" (Isa. 66:24). Jesus himself spoke of unbelievers being thrown "into the fiery furnace, where there will be weeping and gnashing of teeth" (Matt. 13:42). Revelation 20:15 tells us that anyone whose name is not found in the book of life will be "thrown into the lake of fire."

"*Anyone who rejected the law of Moses died without mercy on the testimony of two or three witnesses*" (Heb. 10:28). Referring to Deuteronomy 17, the author then argues from the lesser to the greater: If the one who defied the Mosaic law died, how much worse punishment will those get who received the fullness of the revelation of the gospel and rejected it? In other words, those who rejected Moses received physical death, but those who reject Christ will reap eternal death. The author used this argument earlier: "For if the message spoken by angels was binding, and every violation and disobedience received its just punishment, how shall we escape if we ignore a such great salvation?" (Heb. 2:2–3).

"For we know him who said, 'It is mine to avenge; I will repay,' and again, 'The Lord will judge his people'" (Heb. 10:30). Citing Deuteronomy 32:35–36, the writer gives proof for the utter judgment of the apostate. The habit of this author is to cite Scripture; and when Scripture speaks, all argument ends, because the author of Scripture is God himself. So finally, he concludes, "It is a dreadful thing to fall into the hands of the living God" (Heb. 10:31). The eternal God is not a figment of human imagination. As the Creator of all, he is also necessarily the Judge of all. It is terrifying to fall into his hands.

No one can run away from the living God. We all must face him; there is no escape. Even suicide will not solve our sin problem, for all who remain pagans and apostates go to hell the moment they die.

How to Avoid Apostasy

In light of this teaching, what must we do, especially if we have been falling away? We should emulate David who, although he sinned terribly, chose to cast himself upon the Lord, saying, "I am in deep distress. Let us fall into the hands of the LORD, for his mercy is great" (2 Sam. 24:14). Let us repent truly and believe in Jesus the Son of God and in his blood that cleanses us from all sins and justifies and sanctifies us. He will save us and help us to live a holy life to the end. Beware of people like Korah, Achan, Saul, Judas, Demas, and others who would entice us to join in their apostasy. Above all, take heed of God's word that speaks about the coming apostasy (Matt. 24:10–13; 1 Tim. 4:1–8; 2 Tim. 3:1–5; 1 John 2:18–27). Recognize that our lives are not under our control; God may demand our souls even this night. Let us, therefore, enter the ark of God's salvation, run to the city of refuge, and be safe forever. If we do not, we shall fall into the hands of the Sovereign Judge, and no mountain can hide us from his fearsome wrath.

It will be terrifying beyond description for all who are cast into the lake of fire on the day when Christ judges those who treated him with contempt. Jesus himself said, "Do not be afraid of those who kill the body but cannot kill the soul. Rather, be afraid of the One who can destroy both soul and body in hell" (Matt. 10:28).

Warning against Apostasy

But if you have trusted in Christ and are walking carefully, fear not! He shall keep you from falling (John 6:39–40; 10:27–30). Consider the promise of Jude 24: "To him who is able to keep you from falling and to present you before his glorious presence without fault and with great joy—to the only God our Savior be glory, majesty, power and authority, through Jesus Christ our Lord, before all ages, now and forevermore! Amen."

'Twas grace that taught my heart to fear
and grace my fears relieved.

23
Saints' Endurance

[32]Remember those earlier days after you had received the light, when you stood your ground in a great contest in the face of suffering. [33]Sometimes you were publicly exposed to insult and persecution; at other times you stood side by side with those who were so treated. [34]You sympathized with those in prison and joyfully accepted the confiscation of your property, because you knew that you yourselves had better and lasting possessions. [35]So do not throw away your confidence; it will be richly rewarded. [36]You need to persevere so that when you have done the will of God, you will receive what he has promised. [37]For in just a very little while, "He who is coming will come and will not delay. [38]But my righteous one will live by faith. And if he shrinks back, I will not be pleased with him." [39]But we are not of those who shrink back and are destroyed, but of those who believe and are saved.

Hebrews 10:32–39

How often have we started a project with great eagerness, only to become weary and give up before it is completed. Then we live with a guilty conscience. We needed endurance and perseverance to finish the project!

Some people consider the Christian life to be like a hundred-meter dash, an exercise requiring only a brief burst of energy. But the Christian life is a race that lasts one's lifetime and requires strict training. A true child of God will endure to the very end. The writer to the Hebrews says, "Let us throw off everything that hinders and the sin that so easily entangles, and let us run with perseverance the race marked out for us" (Heb. 12:1). And Paul exhorted Timothy to endure hardship like a soldier, an athlete, and a farmer (2 Tim. 2:3–6).

A large part of modern evangelism is synthetic, tailored to today's superficial atmosphere. Preachers say, "Accept Jesus, and all your problems will go away. No obedience or suffering is necessary. You will have health, wealth, and power here in this life and eternal happiness in heaven." True Christianity, however, is following Christ and suffering with him, if needs be. Jesus calls us to deny ourselves, take up the cross daily, and follow him. Why the cross? Because the world will do to us what it did to Jesus if we belong to him.

In Hebrews 10:26–31 the author warned against turning away from Christ and turning to a false gospel, especially to avoid persecution. Now in verses 32 through 39 he speaks of our need to patiently endure in the midst of severe trials. He encourages his readers by telling them to remember their past faithfulness in suffering as well as Christ's sufferings for them, to know God and his word, to hold on to their confidence, to recognize that endurance comes through suffering, and to continue doing God's will.

Remembering Past Faithfulness

"Remember those earlier days after you had received the light, when you stood your ground in a great contest in the face of suffering" (Heb. 10:32). The Hebrews were in danger of apostasy to avoid persecution. They were tempted to reject Jesus for Moses and the gospel for the rituals of Judaism. To help them remain firm in their faith, the author now exhorts them to remember their own past faithfulness and suffering for the gospel. He has already encouraged them: "God is not unjust; he will not forget your work and the love you have shown him as you have helped his people and continue to help them" (Heb. 6:10). In the past these people had loved the gospel and sacrificially helped God's people who were suffering for the gospel. Now the author exhorts them to remember their past faithfulness and to persevere.

We must remember the past, as Jesus exhorted the Ephesian church to do when they fell from their first love: "Remember the height from which you have fallen! Repent and do the things you did at first" (Rev. 2:5). Married couples should remember the love they first had for each other and let that help them live in love now. So also we should remember our first love for Jesus and let that help us live in love for him now. We love him because he first loved us, and he loves us still.

The Hebrew Christians experienced great sufferings as soon as they were converted. In AD 33 Stephen was stoned to death; ten years later, James, the brother of John, was beheaded by King Agrippa I, the grandson of Herod the Great. Around AD 62, during the reign of the high priest Annas II, James the Just, the pastor of the Jerusalem church and the brother of Jesus, was stoned to death. Believers were made a public spectacle as they endured reproach and persecution from both Gentiles and Jews. Some were even thrown to the lions as entertainment for the Romans.

Not only were these Hebrew Christians to remember how they personally suffered for the gospel, but they were also to remember how they suffered and sympathized with others who were persecuted and imprisoned for their faith. In those days prisoners were punished, not pampered. They were given little provision and had to depend on others for help. These Hebrew Christians helped their brothers in prison, grieving and praying with them, and bringing them clothing, books, food, and other necessities. It was dangerous for them to do these things, for they themselves could also be arrested and tortured. Yet they were ready to suffer for the gospel.

Paul wrote several times about experiencing such kindness from his fellow believers during his imprisonments: "Greet Priscilla and Aquila, my fellow workers in Christ Jesus. They risked their lives for me. Not only I but all the churches of the Gentiles are grateful to them" (Rom. 16:3–4); "May the Lord show mercy to the household of Onesiphorus, because he often refreshed me and was not ashamed of my chains. On the contrary, when he was in Rome, he searched hard for me until he found me. May the Lord grant that he will find mercy from the Lord on that day! . . . When you come, bring the cloak that I left with Carpus at Troas, and my scrolls, especially the parchments" (2 Tim. 1:16–18; 4:13).

In Hebrews 13:3 the author exhorts, "Remember those in prison as if you were their fellow prisoners, and those who are mistreated as if you yourselves were suffering." Jesus also spoke about this aspect of the Christian life:

> The King will say, . . . "For I was hungry and you gave me something to eat, I was thirsty and you gave me something to drink, I was a stranger and you invited me in, I needed clothes and you clothed me, I was sick and you looked after me, I was in prison and you came to visit me." Then the righteous will answer him, "Lord, when did we see you hungry and feed you, or thirsty and give you something to drink? When did we see you a stranger and invite you in, or needing clothes and clothe you? When did we see you sick or in prison and go to visit you?" The King will reply, "I tell you the truth, whatever you did for one of the least of these brothers of mine, you did it for me." (Matt. 25:34-40)

The Hebrew writer also urges his readers to remember how they joyfully accepted the confiscation of their properties for the sake of the gospel. The public baptism of the Hebrew Christians invited Jewish persecution, for the Jews saw these people as traitors and outlaws, without any legal protection. Their houses and properties were taken, and many lost their businesses, for no one wanted to do business with Christians. No wonder the Jerusalem church always remained poor and in continual need of help. Yet they accepted the loss of all material things with joy, which is a fruit of the Spirit. Because they were filled with the Spirit, they rejoiced in such deprivations and persecutions.

Jesus spoke about such joy to his disciples: "Blessed are you when men hate you, when they exclude you and insult you and reject your name as evil, because of the Son of Man. Rejoice in that day and leap for joy, because great is your reward in heaven" (Luke 6:22). The apostles experienced it: "The apostles left the Sanhedrin, rejoicing because they had been counted worthy of suffering disgrace for the Name" (Acts 5:41). After they were beaten up and thrust in the Philippian prison, Paul and Silas prayed and sang hymns to God in the middle of the night (Acts 16:25).

The Hebrew church joyfully endured physical and psychological suffering, economic deprivation, and rejection by family and friends. Church historian Eusebius referred to this passage from Hebrews 10 when writing about the condition of the Alexandrian church in the middle of the third century. In addition to much more brutal assaults and tortures, the following incident is narrated:

> Then, with one accord, all rushed upon the houses of the pious, and whomsoever of their neighbours they knew, they drove thither in all haste, and despoiled and plundered them, setting apart the more valuable of the articles for themselves: but the more common and wooden furniture they threw about and burnt in the roads, presenting a sight like a city taken by the enemy. But the brethren [withdrew], and gave way, and like those to whom Paul bears witness, they also regarded the plunder of their goods with joy.[1]

As Christians, we should not be surprised when faced with trials and persecutions. Rather, we should expect these things and endure them with joy. A true Christian, one who is born of God and indwelt by the Holy Spirit, will endure sufferings with joy to the end of his life. Ours is the way of the cross, as it was for Jesus:

> Therefore, since we are surrounded by such a great cloud of witnesses, let us throw off everything that hinders and the sin that so easily entangles, and let us run with *perseverance* the race marked out for us. Let us fix our eyes on Jesus, the author and perfecter of our faith, who for the joy set before him the cross, scorning its shame, and sat down at the right hand of the throne of God. Consider him who endured such opposition from sinful men, so that you will not grow weary and lose heart. (Heb. 12:1–3)

Let us remember the sufferings of Jesus for our salvation and our own sufferings in the past that we may continue in the way of suffering to the end.

Knowing God

"You sympathized with those in prison and joyfully accepted the confiscation of your property, because you knew that you yourselves had better and lasting possessions" (Heb. 10:34). We must know

---

1 Eusebius, *The Ecclesiastical History of Eusebius Pamphilus* (Grand Rapids: Baker Books, 1990), 257–258.

God and know the Scriptures so that we can joyfully endure suffering and persevere in the Christian life.

Christians endure suffering through knowledge, not feeling. They exercise their minds to know the true gospel and their covenant Lord. They are inspired to endure sufferings because they know that even now they have better and everlasting possessions. They know that God is their portion and that they are God's. Because their spiritual eyes have been opened, they know who God is, who man is, and the nature of the world and the devil. They know there is a heaven and a hell.

Those without such knowledge will not last long in the Christian life. Jesus tells us, "The knowledge of the secrets of the kingdom of heaven has been given to you, but not to them" (Matt. 13:11). Knowledge of God helps us to hope, believe, and endure our sufferings with joy. Unbelievers are morally incapable of knowing God, but Christians are those who have received the knowledge of the truth (Heb. 10:26). So Paul writes, "The god of this age has blinded the minds of unbelievers, so that they cannot see the light of the gospel of the glory of Christ, who is the image of God. For we do not preach ourselves, but Jesus Christ as Lord, and ourselves as your servants for Jesus' sake. For God, who said, 'Let light shine out of darkness,' made his light shine in our hearts to give us the light of the knowledge of the glory of God in the face of Christ" (2 Cor. 4:4–6).

What is the result of knowing God? "Not only so, but we also rejoice in our sufferings, because we know that suffering produces perseverance; perseverance, character; and character, hope" (Rom. 5:3–4). Our knowledge of God results in our loving God more. It prevents us from trusting in ourselves or in the things of this world. James exhorts us, "Consider it pure joy, my brothers, whenever you face trials of many kinds, because you know that the testing of your faith develops perseverance" (James 1:2–3). God has a plan and a purpose. He has chosen us to be holy and blameless in his sight. And he is going to achieve that purpose by whatever means he chooses to use.

In Psalm 73 we find the psalmist unhappy because everyone else was prospering and he was not. Then he went to the temple and God caused him to change his mind. We must learn to pay attention to what God is trying to achieve in our lives through suffering. Then we can say with the psalmist: "Whom have I in heaven but you? And earth has nothing I desire besides you. My flesh and my heart may fail, but God is the strength of my heart and my portion forever" (Ps. 73:25-26).

Through sufferings God teaches us that only in his presence is there fullness of joy and on his right hand, pleasures forevermore. Through sufferings he shows us that we have no permanent home here, but we are on our way to the heavenly city and country that Abraham and others yearned for: "For [Abraham] was looking forward to the city with foundations, whose architect and builder is God. . . . Instead, they were longing for a better country—a heavenly one. Therefore God is not ashamed to be called their God, for he has prepared a city for them" (Heb. 11:10, 16).

Our treasure is God, not gold. We possess the pearl of great price; no thief can steal it, no moth or rust can destroy it, and nothing in all creation can separate us from it. If we have such knowledge of God, we will rejoice in sufferings.

Thus Paul writes, "I pray also that the eyes of your heart may be enlightened in order that you may know the hope to which he has called you, the riches of his glorious inheritance in the saints, and his incomparably great power for us who believe" (Eph. 1:18-19). We must exercise our minds to understand God and his plan for us and for this world so that we may endure hardship with joy, knowing that we possess eternal life.

Holding On to Your Confidence

"So do not throw away your confidence; it will be richly rewarded" (Heb. 10:35). The writer now encourages the Hebrews not to foolishly throw away their confidence. God had saved them and they had already suffered so much for the gospel; therefore, they should not foolishly throw away their confidence, but persevere, fearlessly holding fast to their confession, because they are closer to their salvation than when they first believed.

The writer had already spoken of the need for perseverance in Hebrews 3: "But Christ is faithful as a son over God's house. And we are his house, if we hold on to our courage and the hope of which we boast. . . . We have come to share in Christ if we hold firmly till the end the confidence we had at first" (vv. 6, 14). Now he again exhorts them to not cast away their precious confession of Jesus and their confidence. They must not quit their Christian walk because of suffering and the enticement of sin. They should not be like Esau, who sold his birthright for a cup of soup.

My grandson has confidence in approaching me because it is his right to call me "Grandpa." So also we have confidence toward God and his Son Jesus Christ: "Yet to all who received him, to those who believed in his name, he gave the right to become children of God—children born not of natural descent, nor of human decision or a husband's will, but born of God" (John 1:12–13).

God is our heavenly Father. Listen to the language of Paul: "But when the time had fully come, God sent his Son, born of a woman, born under law, to redeem those under law, that we might receive the full rights of sons. Because you are sons, God sent the Spirit of his Son into our hearts, the Spirit who calls out, 'Abba, Father'" (Gal. 4:4–6). The word "Abba" in Aramaic means "Daddy." That is why Jesus taught us to pray, "Our Father," or, "Our Daddy." This intimate relationship is our confidence.

We must persevere in our Christian walk. The author is warning us against becoming weary and losing everything. We must not grow weary in our marriages, in our jobs, or in any other aspect of our Christian lives. We must heed the words of Hebrews 12:3: "Consider him who endured such opposition from sinful men, so that you will not grow weary and lose heart." We must not quit and cast away our confidence as something that is worthless.

When God regenerates a person's heart, that person will never lose his salvation. God will change him from glory to glory until he reaches the perfect glory of the eternal state. Apostasy only proves that a person was never truly a regenerate citizen of heaven. A true Christian always perseveres to the end.

Jesus spoke of this:

> Brother will betray brother to death, and a father his child; children will rebel against their parents and have them put to death. All men will hate you because of me, but he who stands firm to the end will be saved. . . . At that time many will turn away from the faith and will betray and hate each other, and many false prophets will appear and deceive many people. Because of the increase of wickedness, the love of most will

grow cold, but he who stands firm to the end will be saved. (Matt. 10:21–22; 24:10–13)

A true Christian is sealed with the Holy Spirit as a sign of security, ownership, and value. The Holy Spirit himself guarantees our final perseverance. So Paul writes, "[I am] confident of this, that he who began a good work in you will carry it on to completion until the day of Christ Jesus" (Phil. 1:6). People may quit, but Christ will not. What he works in us, we work out, and finally he will bring us safely home. No matter what happens, whether our spouses walk out or our children reject us or our employer abandons us or we become deathly ill, we must look to Jesus. He alone can give us grace to rejoice in the midst of all troubles.

"Rocky soil" Christians and "thorny soil" Christians are, in the final analysis, unregenerate (see Matt. 13:1–23). Though they may simulate spiritual graces for a while, they do not persevere and will not receive the great reward. In time they will cast away their inauthentic confidence and prove themselves to be unregenerate covenant-breakers and false Christians, like Judas and Demas. But by God's power, the regenerate will persevere and endure to the end of their lives. Only those who endure to the end are regenerate.

How do we persevere? Jesus himself keeps the regenerate from falling away (Jude 24). Jesus told Peter, "Simon, Simon, Satan has asked to sift you as wheat. But I have prayed for you, Simon, that your faith may not fail" (Luke 22:31–32). Jesus prays that the faith of his people may not fail. We will be brought into the very presence of God without fault and with great jubilation. He saves us from beginning to end!

Peter writes, "Praise be to the God and Father of our Lord Jesus Christ! In his great mercy he has given us new birth into a living hope through the resurrection of Jesus Christ from the dead, and into an inheritance that can never perish, spoil or fade—kept in heaven for you, who through faith are [being] shielded by God's power until the coming of the salvation that is ready to be revealed in the last time" (1 Pet. 1:3–5). The word for "shielded" is a present participle: even now we are being shielded by God.

Are you merely simulating Christianity? Is your faith external only? If you are unregenerate, you will find it hard to love and obey God. But if you are born of God, it will be your joy to do his will.

Enduring Patiently

"You need to persevere so that when you have done the will of God, you will receive what he has promised" (Heb. 10:36). Modern people do not have much patience. We pamper our children, and they too grow up without patience. But here we learn that we need patient endurance to live the Christian life.

Those who become "Christians" through false evangelism are not able to endure the hardship of the Christian life. Expecting a life of ease and prosperity, they are shocked by trials and persecutions.

Scripture is very clear about how we may obtain the endurance we need. We lack endurance because we do not experience suffering. So God works in us the virtue of endurance by causing us to suffer: "Not only so, but we also rejoice in our sufferings, because we know that suffering produces perseverance" (Rom. 5:3). I do not pray for suffering, nor should you. But whether we pray or not, God's commitment to us is to make us holy and blameless so that we can be presented to him without fault and in all glory. Therefore, he ordains sufferings to produce perseverance: "Consider it pure joy, my brothers, whenever you face trials of many kinds, because you know that the testing of your faith develops perseverance" (Jas. 1:2).

We should not be surprised when suffering comes to us. Jesus said, "I have told you these things, so that in me you may have peace. In this world you will have trouble. But take heart! I have overcome the world" (John 16:33). Since Paul was a true evangelist, he was careful to let people know about this hard truth: "We must go through many hardships to enter the kingdom of God" (Acts 14:22). We may not like suffering, but God's plan is to glorify us through it.

No believer is exempt from suffering: "In fact, everyone who wants to live a godly life in Christ Jesus will be persecuted" (2 Tim. 3:12). If we do not live godly lives, we will not experience persecution. It is our difference from the world that causes persecution to come. The world hates holy people; darkness despises light. Paul writes, "We sent Timothy . . . to strengthen and encourage you in your faith, so that no one would be unsettled by these trials. You know quite well that we were destined for them" (1 Thess. 3:2–3). Trials are the destiny of every Christian.

Endurance is the ability to stand under severe pressure by the power of the Holy Spirit. Paul writes: "No temptation has seized you except what is common to man. And God is faithful; he will not let you be tempted beyond what you can bear. But when you are tempted, he will also provide a way out so that you can stand up under it" (1 Cor. 10:13). We want to claim that our difficulties are unique, but they are not. And God will give us grace sufficient to stand up under all pressures, so we have no excuse.

Christian history is replete with examples of those who endured suffering. Stephen and James endured stoning, Peter endured crucifixion, and Paul endured beheading. Some were torn asunder and eaten by wild animals in the arena, while others were covered with pitch and set ablaze to give light in the garden of Nero. True people of God have suffered much throughout history and still suffer and die today in many parts of the world. They endure because God is with them and in them.

If you are tempted to self-pity, read about the trials Paul endured (2 Cor. 4, 6, 11, and 12). Yet he wrote, "I can do all things through Christ who strengthens me" (Phil. 4:13, NKJV). Elsewhere he says, "Therefore I will boast all the more gladly about my weaknesses, so that Christ's power may rest on me" (2 Cor. 12:9). As we go through suffering, we must remember that the trial is not the only thing that is present in our life. The power of God is also resting upon us so that we can stand up under it.

How, then, do we prepare to endure? Study the Scriptures and pray. Draw near to God to receive mercy and find grace for our time of need. Remember our past faithfulness. Read histories of God's martyrs. Cultivate strong fellowship with God's people. Keep in mind what is awaiting us at our death or at the soon coming of Christ: *"You yourselves [have] better and lasting possessions"* (Heb. 10:34). We are very rich in Christ because we have indestructible spiritual possessions. *"Do not throw away your confidence; it will be richly rewarded"* (Heb. 10:35). We must keep this in mind, especially as we go through the valley of the shadow of death. Either we are going to fix our eyes on our pain, or we will fix them on Jesus. When we do the latter, we will leap for joy in our trials.

"*But we are not of those who shrink back and are destroyed, but of those who believe and are saved*" (Heb. 10:39). The idea of suffering and physical death should not throw us into confusion. Believers who die enter into the saints' everlasting rest.

I pray that we will seek God and his promises, not a life of comfort and ease. Hebrews 11:6 says, "Without faith it is impossible to please God, because anyone who comes to him must believe that he exists and that he rewards those who earnestly seek him." God richly rewards those who diligently seek him, whether young or old. What does it profit if we fling away our confidence out of fear of the world or because of the seduction of sin? What does it profit if we gain the whole world and lose our souls? If we lose our confidence, we lose everything. The just live moment by moment by faith in God's promise.

Doing God's Will

"*You need to persevere so that when you have done the will of God, you will receive what he has promised*" (Heb. 10:36). It is only when we have actually done the will of God that we receive our reward. God wants us to finish the race, fight the good fight, and keep the faith. It is like a Christian husband and wife who have vowed to love one another. They have made a covenant and must continue to perform that covenant until death separates them.

An unregenerate person will not do the will of God. He may promise to do so, but he can never carry it out from the heart. He is a synthetic, plastic Christian who experiences no interior change. He is a pagan sitting in the church.

Jesus always did the will of God: "During the days of Jesus' life on earth, he offered up prayers and petitions with loud cries and tears to the one who could save him from death, and he was heard because of his reverent submission. Although he was a son, he learned obedience from what he suffered and, once made perfect, he became the source of eternal salvation for all who obey him" (Heb. 5:7–9). He said to the Father, "Here I am—it is written about me in the scroll—I have come to do your will, O God" (Heb. 10:7). Hebrews 1:3 speaks of Christ doing the will of God by his atoning death: "The Son is the radiance of God's glory and the exact representation of his being, sustaining all things by his powerful word. *After he had provided purification for sins*, he sat down at the right hand of the Majesty in heaven" (italics added).

As God's children, we also must do our Father's will. Then we will receive our reward. It is wonderful to hear the final words of one who has lived a godly life. Such a person can declare, "It is finished; I have done the will of God," as he is ushered into the presence of God to receive his inheritance. And God will help us to do his will: "May the God of peace, who through the blood of the eternal covenant brought back from the dead our Lord Jesus, that great Shepherd of the sheep, equip you with everything good for doing his will, and may he work in us what is pleasing to him, through Jesus Christ, to whom be glory for ever and ever. Amen" (Heb. 13:20–21).

God works his will into us, and we work it out. The One who is in us is greater than the devil who is in the world. God is in us, and we are in God. The Christian journey is a journey with our triumphant Christ. He says, "Follow me," and as his sheep, we do so—some through the flood, some through the fire, but all through the blood of Christ. We all travel with Jesus the victor in the way of the cross. And he will bring all his elect safely to the presence of our heavenly Father.

Jesus Christ is conqueror par excellence, having conquered hell and death, the world and the devil, on our behalf. In him we are more than conquerors (Rom. 8:37). We are the justified who live by faith in our Christ.

"'*But my righteous one will live by faith. And if he shrinks back, I will not be pleased with him.' But we are not of those who shrink back and are destroyed, but of those who believe and are saved*" (Heb. 10:38–39). Here the writer is quoting Habakkuk 2:4, which says, "See, he is puffed up; his desires are not upright—but the righteous will live by his faith." Habakkuk was speaking about Babylon and the wicked Jews. In the Hebrew text, the word translated "puffed up" or "swollen" can also be translated "hemorrhoid." We find the same word throughout 1 Samuel 5–6. The Philistines took the ark of God to Ashdod, Gath, and Ekron, and God brought upon them tumors—"hemorrhoids in their secret parts" (1 Sam. 5:9, KJV). These mighty people could not sit down without pain. God thus pictures an arrogant, self-sufficient Christian as a hemorrhoid. The opposite of such hemorrhoids are those who are righteous—the people of God. Such people are humble. They are always dependent on God, not on themselves or on their supposed achievements, brilliance, and beauty. The fear of God is the hallmark of godliness. The just shall live by faith.

The author concludes, *"But we are not of those who shrink back and are destroyed, but of those who believe and are saved"* (Heb. 10:39). We could say, "We are not of those who swell up." Jesus Christ saves us from beginning to end. Because he prays for us, we will persevere till the end, and we will be able to say with Paul, "I have fought the good fight, I have finished the race, I have kept the faith. Now there is in store for me the crown of righteousness, which the Lord, the righteous Judge, will award to me on that day—and not only to me, but also to all who have longed for his appearing" (2 Tim. 4:7–8).

May God help us to make our calling and election sure. May we be humble and Christ-centered, quick to hear and do the will of God exactly, immediately, and with great joy. In the days ahead, may we prove by our lives that we are truly more than conquerors in Jesus Christ, a people who have nothing to fear, even though we may walk through the valley of the shadow of death. Yes, our trials may multiply, but we know God's purpose is to produce perseverance, character, and hope in the glory of God. Jesus Christ is coming again, and he will bring us into a new heaven and a new earth, to enjoy joy celestial and happiness eternal.

24
Faith of Our Fathers

¹*Now faith is being sure of what we hope for and certain of what we do not see.* ²*This is what the ancients were commended for.*

³*By faith we understand that the universe was formed at God's command, so that what is seen was not made out of what was visible.*

Hebrews 11:1-3

Hebrews 11 defines faith and illustrates it through the lives of those who lived by faith. In the previous chapter, the author quoted God's words from Habakkuk 2: "My righteous one will live by faith." Then he exhorted, "But we are not of those who shrink back and are destroyed, but those who believe and are saved" (Heb. 10:38-39). In Hebrews 11 the author says, "Without faith it is impossible to please God" (v. 6). To be saved, we *must* believe on the Lord Jesus Christ. The Bible declares that he who *believes* has eternal life.

The author previously said that the Israelites perished in the wilderness because they did not believe the gospel (Heb. 3:19). Because they were disobedient (Heb. 3:18), and did not mix the word of God with faith (Heb. 4:2), they did not enter into God's rest. Even today people are restless because of their unbelief in the gospel.

We want to examine the definition of faith, the substance of faith, the commendation of faith, and the understanding of faith.

The Definition of Faith

"*Now faith is being sure of what we hope for and certain of what we do not see*" (Heb. 11:1). Biblical faith is not faith in ourselves, nor is it faith in faith itself. The object of biblical faith is God and his Son. Biblical faith, therefore, first requires knowledge of this One in whom we believe. Faith comes by hearing the gospel preached clearly. We must know that Jesus died on the cross for our sins according to the Scriptures, that he was buried, that he was raised on the third day according to the Scriptures, that he appeared to many, and that he is seated on the right hand of the Father. We must realize that Christ alone is the King of kings and Lord of lords, the head of the church, and that he is coming again to judge the living and the dead and to save his people with the fullness of salvation.

Peter preached this gospel on the day of Pentecost, and three thousand believed and were saved. Paul preached the same message to a group of women in Philippi, and God opened the heart of Lydia so that she believed. The Philippian jailer heard the gospel, believed, and was saved in the middle of the night. True faith requires information. That is why every Christian must proclaim the gospel by life and word. The purpose of our lives in this world is to point others to the Savior.

Second, we must agree with this information about Jesus Christ. Cognition must lead to conviction. When we hear the gospel, we must understand the gospel intellectually and agree not only that it is true, but also that it is personally applicable to us. We must say, "I need Jesus to save me."

Yet even that is not true saving faith. Conviction must finally lead to commitment. Roman Catholics have taught that faith is mere mental assent to the gospel, and many of today's evangelicals heartily agree with that position. They say that we do not have to commit our lives to Jesus or live the gospel life, that mental agreement to the facts of the gospel is sufficient. Mere mental assent, however, is the faith of demons. Demons believe that God exists, and tremble (Jas. 2:19). Demons are quite orthodox in their faith, but they will never repent and commit themselves to serve the true and living God.

Those who hear the gospel must move from cognition to conviction, and then to commitment to Christ. They must commit to live for him forever. The Reformers had a saying: "*Fides est fiducia,*" or "Faith is trust." Biblical faith is the entrustment of all that we are and have to Jesus Christ now and forevermore.

Faith means that we move the focus of our life from ourselves to Jesus Christ. Faith declares Jesus Christ is Lord of our life. Faith in its essence is committing ourselves to Christ that we may be saved. We rest not in who we are but in the person and work of the almighty Savior.

True saving faith, unlike the devil's faith of mental assent, will always and necessarily issue in good works of obedience. James declares, "Faith without works is dead" (Jas. 2:20, KJV). Faith without works only simulates the spiritual grace of faith. It is plastic, artificial, and demonic. Paul says that true faith expresses itself in love (Gal. 5:6). Jesus says, "If you love me, you will obey what I command" (John 14:15). True believers devote themselves to doing what is good. Faith works and perseveres to the end.

Scripture teaches that genuine, saving faith is a supernatural gift that cannot be produced by humans; rather, it is a consequence of the miracle of regeneration. It is the faith of our fathers—Abraham, Moses, Gideon, Peter, Paul, Luther, Calvin, Knox, Wesley, Whitefield, Spurgeon, Lloyd-Jones, and others. It is a faith that expects and endures trials gladly.

Such faith is faith in God, and it is through this faith that we inherit what has been promised (Heb. 6:1, 12). By this faith and in its full assurance we can draw near to God in worship (Heb. 10:22). It is a faith that knows we have better and abiding possessions, so that we can gladly suffer the loss of all things, including our very lives (Heb. 10:34). This faith is not a one-time occurrence; it is a living and continuing trust in Jesus. Daily faith and repentance are foundational to the Christian life.

The Substance of Faith

What is the substance of saving faith? The author gives us a partial definition: "*Faith is the [hupostasis] of things longed for, of things future, and the [elenchos] of things not seen*" (Heb. 11:1, author's paraphrase). *Hupostasis* can have both an objective and a subjective sense. The New International Version translates the noun subjectively: "Now faith *is being sure* of what we hope for," while the King James Version chooses the objective meaning: "Faith *is the substance* of things hoped for" (italics added). Both meanings are valid because the objective provides the subjective.

This gift of supernatural faith is the foundation of things hoped for. It substantiates the objective future reality we hope for in the present. *Hupostasis* means that which "stands under." It is speaking about a rock-solid, sure foundation. The word was found in ancient papyri to mean something that guarantees a transaction. Hebrews 11:1 can thus be translated, "Faith is *the title deed* to things hoped for."

Faith provides a firm ground to stand on while we await the fulfillment of God's promises. By faith we can be sure that all of God's promises to us will be fulfilled. Faith is assurance in the present. It gives the object hoped for a present power in the soul as if it were already possessed. Faith gives us a vision of things future. It is like a telescope that enables us to see distant objects and be energized by that sight to live our lives in the present. Paul says, "We live by faith, not by sight" (2 Cor. 5:7). By faith we see spiritual realities now and deal with the present in the light of that reality. Matthew Henry says, "Faith demonstrates to the eye of the mind the reality of those things which cannot be discerned by the eye of the body."[1] Paul declares, "So we fix our eyes not on what is seen, but on what is unseen" (2 Cor. 4:18).

Such statements may seem contradictory, but they are true of faith. Hebrews 11:1 tells us we can see by faith what is unseen by our eyes. Faith sees and hopes in the unseen.

Next we read that faith is the *elenchos* of things not seen. The word *elenchos* has the objective meaning of "proof," "guarantee," or "evidence." Faith is proof of the unseen things God has promised and the evidence of things future. Faith demonstrates to us things unseen; we therefore have a sure conviction. We are certain and assured of the unseen things that we shall see in the future.

Although faith leads us to know realities beyond the ability of unaided reason to discover, faith also employs reason. The Greeks thought faith was the characteristic of the uneducated and unsophisticated. But biblical faith is not blind. It does not require a leap in the dark or the sacrifice of our intellect. Biblical faith

---

1 Quoted by Pink, *Exposition of Hebrews*, 652.

is reasonable because it rests on the greatest possible reason—the infinite, personal God and his word. Therefore, we as believers in Jesus Christ declare, "God said it, I believe it, and that settles it." We place our trust in a God who cannot lie. Concerning Abraham, the author says that God promised and confirmed his promise with an oath "so that, by two unchangeable things in which is impossible for God to lie, we . . . may be greatly encouraged" (Heb. 6:17–18).

Noah had never seen any rain, let alone a flood. Yet when God said he was going to destroy the world by a flood and told Noah to build an ark, he did so, believing what God said was true: "By faith Noah, when warned about things not seen, in holy fear built an ark to save his family" (Heb. 11:7).

The writer says, "All these people were still living by faith when they died. They did not receive the things promised; they only saw them and welcomed them from a distance" (Heb. 11:13). Faith sees the invisible, and the believer is certain that God will do what he has promised.

God told Abraham to go and sacrifice his son. Abraham obeyed God, and the Hebrews author explains why: "Abraham reasoned that God could raise the dead" (Heb. 11:19). Abraham believed that as soon as the sacrifice was done, God would raise his son from the ashes because God had promised a nation and a messiah through Isaac, the son of promise. By faith he reasoned that God cannot lie and so he can be trusted.

Paul speaks more about the faith of Abraham: "He is our father in the sight of God, in whom he believed—the God who gives life to the dead and calls things that are not as though they were. . . . Without weakening in his faith, he faced the fact that his body was as good as dead—since he was about a hundred years old—and that Sarah's womb was also dead" (Rom. 4:17, 19). Abraham looked upon these things that were visible and interpreted them in the light of God's promise of a son. What, then, was his response? "Yet he did not waver through unbelief regarding the promise of God, but was strengthened in his faith and gave glory to God, being fully persuaded that God had power to do what he had promised" (vv. 20–21).

Observe how Moses exercised his faith: "By faith he left Egypt, not fearing the king's anger." Moses left Egypt, with all its glories, power, and position. "He persevered because he saw him who is invisible" (Heb. 11:27). Faith is substance, proof, demonstration, evidence. Faith sees the invisible and is energized by that sight to obey God.

Faith sees the mighty operations of God in the fulfillment of his promises. Jesus said to Martha, "Did I not tell you that if you believed, you would see the glory of God?" (John 11:40). Paul describes his impending death: "For I am already being poured out like a drink offering, and the time has come for my departure. I have fought the good fight, I have finished the race, I have kept the faith. Now there is in store for me the crown of righteousness, which the Lord, the righteous Judge, will award to me on that day—and not only to me, but also to all who have longed for his appearing" (2 Tim. 4:6–8). This is the substance of faith. It is not shifting sand, but a solid rock upon which we can stand. It is the conviction and certainty that God will do what he has promised.

The Commendation of Faith

"*This is what the ancients were commended for*" (Heb. 11:2). The author is saying that the faith of the Hebrew church is like that of "the ancients." The word means "elders"; it has the same meaning as "forefathers" (Heb. 1:1). The people of God are one, and they are all characterized by this constant: they all possess saving faith that is living, persevering, sacrificing, and death-defying.

Notice that God himself commended the elders for their faith. Our testimonies about ourselves do not matter. These ancients were certified by God, which is the greatest testimony we can have.

The one thing that characterizes all believers throughout history is this faith without which it is impossible to please God. The author illustrates such faith through the examples of Abel, Enoch, Noah, and others, all of whom lived by faith in the promises of God. They were sure of things future and convinced of things they did not yet see with their physical eyes. They trusted implicitly in God's promises. By their lives of faith, they bore witness to God's goodness; therefore, God commended them and bore witness to them by recording their names in the holy

Scriptures: "By faith Abel offered God a better sacrifice than Cain did. By faith he was *commended* as a righteous man, when God spoke well of his offerings. . . . By faith Enoch was taken from this life, so that he did not experience death; he could not be found, because God had taken him away. For before he was taken, he was *commended* as one who pleased God. . . . These were all *commended* for their faith" (Heb. 11:4, 5, 39, italics added).

Do you live by faith? Do you witness to God's goodness by living according to the word? If you live for God's glory, he will testify concerning you on the last day: "Well done, good and faithful servant! . . . Come and share your master's happiness!" (Matt. 25:21, 23). He so testified concerning his own Son, "This is my beloved Son, in whom I am well-pleased; hear ye him" (Matt. 17:5, KJV). Jesus lived by faith and always pleased his Father. When tempted, he obeyed God, not the devil (Matt. 4:1–11). I urge you to live such a life that God may commend you and invite you into his eternal kingdom.

The Understanding of Faith

"By faith we understand that the universe was formed at God's command, so that what is seen was not made out of what was visible" (Heb. 11:3). How do we understand the origin of the universe? The author says we do so by faith. The author now speaks of his faith and the faith of his church, especially in relation to cosmology and cosmogony.

There was no human witness to creation. God asked Job, "Where were you when I laid the earth's foundation? Tell me, if you understand" (Job 38:4). Only by faith in God's revelation can we understand how the world was made. God reveals it to us in Genesis, and we must study this divine disclosure with all our intellect, that we may understand divine cosmogony and cosmology. Modern people may laugh at it because they look upon faith and understanding as being mutually exclusive. But faith and understanding complement each other.

A Christian should never sacrifice his mind. Rather, he should use his intellect to its full capacity to study God's revelation both in the Scriptures and in creation. No philosopher or scientist can speak correctly of the origin of the universe if he rejects the biblical revelation. By faith God's people understand intellectually that the universe was created by divine command. God's word is powerful, creative, and formative. It always accomplishes the purpose for which it is sent (Isa. 55:11).

"*By faith we understand.*" No doubt the author is referring to Genesis 1:3, 6, 9, 11, 14, 20, 24 and 26, where the phrase "and God said" speaks of the creation of the world. The whole universe came into existence at his command: "By the word of the Lord were the heavens made, their starry host by the breath of his mouth. . . . For he spoke, and it came to be" (Ps. 33:6, 9).

Earlier the author wrote, "But in these last days he has spoken to us by his Son, whom he appointed heir of all things, and through whom he made the universe" (Heb. 1:2). And not only did God make the universe, but he also upholds it by the word of his power (Heb. 1:3). The powerful word that brought forth the universe also maintains and preserves everything in it, including us.

Paul spoke about Christ's role in creation: "For by him all things were created: things in heaven and on earth, visible and invisible, whether thrones or powers or rulers or authorities; all things were created by him and for him" (Col. 1:16; cf. John 1:3).

God intends that all people understand that he created everything by his powerful word: "For since the creation of the world God's invisible qualities—his eternal power and divine nature—have been clearly seen, being understood from what has been made, so that men are without excuse" (Rom. 1:20). It is not that unbelievers do not know about God. They are enemies of God who suppress the truth and exchange it for a lie so that they do not have to bow down and serve this great God.

People do not recognize God's role in creation because of sin. Unbelievers are dead in trespasses and sins. Untouched by the Spirit of the living God, their minds are not quickened. God has revealed these things to us by his Spirit (1 Cor. 2:10). Paul writes, "We have not received the spirit of the world but the Spirit who is from God, that we may understand what God has freely given us. . . . The man without the Spirit does not accept the things that come from the Spirit of God, for they are foolishness to him. and he cannot understand them, because they are spiritually discerned" (1 Cor. 2:12, 14).

We whose eyes have been opened by the mighty operation of the Holy Spirit understand from Scripture that the universe was created and maintained by the word of God. The visible universe was not made out of what is visible; what is seen was not made out of what is seen. The author is teaching us that the universe was not made out of pre-existing matter.

When Plato spoke of cosmogony, he said the creator fashioned the world by pre-existing, formless matter. Philo the Jew also believed this view. But here our author is deliberately denying Platonic and Philonic cosmogonies and cosmologies. He denies the eternality of matter and the Greek thought that matter is evil. He denies the dualistic view of good and evil. He denies pantheism and affirms the Creator/creature distinction. He also denies all present day explanations of the universe, including the evolutionary hypothesis and the big bang theory, which require pre-existing matter. The author affirms that God alone created the universe out of nothing by his creative, powerful command.

The universe is not a self-existent reality but the work product of the self-existing, self-sufficient, infinite, personal triune God of the Scriptures. That is why only believers in Jesus Christ understand the true origin of the universe. Those who say in their hearts that there is no God may call us fools, but the Scripture calls them fools (Ps. 14:1). An unbeliever cannot affirm the true origin of the universe. He knows the truth, but he suppresses it.

Not only did God create the universe by his powerful word, but he also recreates us by his powerful word, making us new creations in Christ. Paul writes, "For God, who said, 'Let light shine out of darkness,' made his light shine in our hearts to give us the light of the knowledge of the glory of God in the face of Christ" (2 Cor. 4:6). To us who were dead in our sins he said, "Let there be light," and light flooded into our souls. Our eyes were opened, we saw the reality that we are sinners and that God is holy, and we cried out, "O God, have mercy upon us!"

James writes, "He chose to give us birth through the word of truth, that we might be a kind of firstfruits for all he created" (Jas. 1:18). Peter states, "For you have been born again, not of perishable seed but of imperishable, through the living and enduring word of God" (1 Pet. 1:23).

Jesus as well spoke about this re-creative activity of God: "I tell you the truth, a time is coming and has now come when the dead will hear the voice of the Son of God, and those who hear will live" (John 5:25). Everyone who is in Christ Jesus is a new creation. The old is gone and the new has come (2 Cor. 5:17).

Have you experienced the miracle of re-creation? Have you been given the gift of godly repentance and saving faith? Then you will understand and believe all the miracles of the Scriptures. You will not question the biblical account of the origin of the universe or the resurrection of Christ.

I have no problem believing every miracle in the Bible, because they all are reasonable. The mighty, infinite God is the reasonable explanation for each of them. When we exercise faith in God, we will understand the divine revelation. Then we will be sure of things hoped for and certain of things yet unseen. Then we will know that nothing can separate us from the love of God, that our bodies are the temple of the Holy Spirit, that Jesus Christ is with us always, that he is the same yesterday, today, and forever, and that we are going to heaven to be with him forever. In his presence there is fullness of joy and on his right hand, pleasures forevermore. This Savior is coming again, and he will make a new heaven and a new earth by his powerful word for us to dwell in with him, and he will give us a body like unto his own glorious body.

By faith we also know that there is going to be a final judgment. Every unbeliever will be cast into hell, the lake of fire, irrevocably entering eternal punishment. By faith we see and understand these things. By faith we understand from Scripture not only the origin of the first creation, but also the new creation. May God, therefore, help us to be his new creations, that we may show love by faithful obedience to God's word and give witness to God's goodness in this world.

25
Happiness Is Pleasing God

⁴*By faith Abel offered God a better sacrifice than Cain did. By faith he was commended as a righteous man, when God spoke well of his offerings. And by faith he still speaks, even though he is dead.*

⁵*By faith Enoch was taken from this life, so that he did not experience death; he could not be found, because God had taken him away. For before he was taken, he was commended as one who pleased God.* ⁶*And without faith it is impossible to please God, because anyone who comes to him must believe that he exists and that he rewards those who earnestly seek him.*

Hebrews 11:4–6

Godliness is pleasing God, which results in our happiness. The Westminster Shorter Catechism asserts that the chief end of man is "to glorify God and enjoy him forever." Paul speaks in Romans 1 about the problem of pagans who suppress God's truth in wickedness. If ungodliness is our problem, then the solution is godliness that produces a righteous life. Happiness is godliness, and godliness is pleasing God by doing his will.

Godliness means to please God through living by faith in God's word. Those who obey God's word are witnesses to God in the world. In this study we want to look at two such people, Abel and Enoch (Heb. 11:4–6).

Not only do we witness to God when we live by faith, but God also witnesses to us. He commends us, saying, "Thou good and faithful servant, enter into the joy of the Lord."

The author of Hebrews has already spoken about what will happen to those who do not believe God and do not persevere to the end: "If he shrinks back, I will not be pleased with him" (Heb. 10:38). In Hebrews 11 he gives a list of some who lived by faith in God and thus received God's approval: "This is what the ancients were commended for" (v. 2). It does not matter what man says about us. What ultimately matters is, does *God* commend us?

Either we live to please ourselves, or we live to please God. But we must not be deceived; pleasing ourselves is really pleasing the devil. Concerning the forbidden fruit, Eve said, "It is good for food, good for the eyes, and good to make us wise; therefore, it is good for me." Then she took and ate. She pleased herself, but, in reality, she was pleasing the devil. Every time we disobey, we think we are pleasing ourselves, but we are really serving Satan. There are only two masters in this world: God and the devil. Yet God rules the devil and will dispose of him and all of God's enemies in due time (see Rev. 20).

Are you a self-centered person who makes decisions on the basis of what gives you pleasure? Jesus calls us to deny ourselves daily. Denying ourselves means death to self-will. It means to say no to ourselves and yes to Jesus Christ. Jesus calls us to take up the cross and follow him. A Christian does not trust in himself; he is told to believe on the Lord Jesus Christ. A Christian is not self-focused and self-pleasing. He is Christ-centered, Christ-focused, and Christ-pleasing, even to the point of martyrdom.

The Example of Abel

"By faith Abel offered to God a better sacrifice than Cain did. By faith he was commended as a righteous man, when God spoke well of his offerings. And by faith he still speaks, even though he is dead" (Heb. 11:4). Abel lived by faith. Biblical faith is not faith in faith or faith in ourselves; it is faith in God and his word. It is not faith in a god of human creation, a postulate of our minds. Hebrews 11:6 declares that those who come to God *must* believe that he exists—it is a logical and moral necessity. We must believe in this independent, moral being who is the cause of all creation. Biblical faith is not faith in a god that we can discover through scientific research or learn about through philosophical reasoning; rather, it is faith in the God who has revealed himself to us in the Scriptures.

Happiness Is Pleasing God

Everyone who comes to God must believe not only that he exists, but also that he cares for us and rewards those who diligently seek him (Heb. 11:6). We must believe in God, the Creator and Redeemer. This Sovereign King revealed himself to us through the prophets and finally through his Son Jesus Christ (Heb. 1:1–3). We must believe in this infinite, personal, holy, compassionate God who revealed himself to Moses as "I AM WHO I AM." This uncreated, self-sufficient God not only created us but also preserves us so that even now we breathe and our minds work. In his sovereign will, we will die, whether of cancer or some other frailty of the body. But physical death is not the end of us: "It is appointed for man to die once and after this comes judgment" (Heb. 9:27, NASB). So Paul exclaims, "Now to the King eternal, immortal, invisible, the only God, be honor and glory forever and ever" (1 Tim. 1:17).

Faith is the *sine qua non*, the indispensable condition, of every believer. The phrase "by faith" is repeated in Hebrews 11 to refer to all named believers. "By faith" does not mean making a one-time declaration of faith when we first become Christians. It means trusting God throughout our lives. We live by faith in this life and in the life to come. Paul says that faith, along with hope and love, abides (1 Cor. 13:13). He who believes in God trusts implicitly in his promises regarding the future, no matter how great those promises are, just as Abraham and Sarah believed God's promise to give them a son, even though their bodies were as good as dead. God always performs what he promises. He is the ever-existing "I AM."

Cain and Abel both brought sacrifices to God. Yet God was pleased only with Abel's sacrifice (Gen. 4:3–5). Abel offered an acceptable sacrifice, a better sacrifice, and he did so by faith (Heb. 11:4). Cain, on the other hand, offered his sacrifice in unbelief. John describes Cain as a son of the devil, one "who belonged to the evil one" (1 John 3:12). Jude warns of "the way of Cain" (Jude 11), which is the way of self-will and self-trust. Being a child of the devil, Cain would not please God by offering him a sacrifice with a pure heart. He would not follow the way of the word, the way of revelation. Cain never said, "Thy will be done," but always, "My will be done."

A true worshiper worships God with a pure heart and brings the sacrifice God prescribes. "The LORD detests the sacrifice of the wicked, but the prayer of the upright pleases him" (Prov. 15:8). How many people's worship is not accepted because it does not come from a pure heart and is not offered in the prescribed way! Because Cain's sacrifice was detestable to God, it was rejected and Cain became dejected. Divine approbation brings true happiness, but when we seek to please ourselves, we become miserable. Cain's countenance fell and he was unhappy the rest of his life. He became a restless, God-forsaken wanderer.

"*By faith Abel offered God a better sacrifice*" (Heb. 11:4). Abel's heart was pure because he trusted in God, not only as Creator but also as Redeemer. He knew that he himself was born a sinner, guilty and deserving only of death. But he also knew of God's mercy and the principle of substitution because he had been told how God had killed innocent animals and clothed his parents with their skins. The blood of the animals that was shed for the forgiveness of Adam and Eve's sin points to the blood shed by Jesus Christ on the cross. God symbolically dressed Adam and Eve in his righteousness when he clothed them with animal skins, replacing their self-made fig-leaf garments.

By his sacrifice Abel was confessing that he was a sinner who could not save himself. Yet he also knew that God is merciful and had provided a substitute who died in his place that he might live. Abel understood that "without the shedding of blood there is no forgiveness of sins" (Heb. 9:22).

Abel sacrificed *by faith* and brought a God-pleasing sacrifice. Now we know that faith comes by hearing the word (Rom. 10:17), so God must have told Adam and his family how they should worship. I believe they even knew about blood sacrifices because God himself in mercy and patience asked Cain, "If you do what is right, will you not be accepted?" (Gen. 4:7).

Worshiping by faith, Abel brought the right bloody sacrifice. But Cain denied his guilt and his need for salvation. He refused to do what is right. "What is right" is what God says is right, not what we say: "There is a way that seems right to a man, but in the end it leads to death" (Prov. 14:12). Cain refused to offer a bloody sacrifice with a believing heart. He would not kill a lamb as an acceptable offering to God for his salvation, though he later showed no qualms in shedding the blood of his own brother.

Abel believed God and sacrificed the right way as revealed to him, the way of a substitute, which pointed to the Lamb of God who takes away the sin of the world. This man of faith *"was commended as a righteous man, when God spoke well of his offerings"* (Heb. 11:4). Jesus also called Abel righteous (Matt. 23:35) and said he was a prophet and the first martyr (Luke 11:51). When all others stand against God, we must live by faith and stand for God and truth. God is pleased with such people and will commend them.

"By faith [Abel] still speaks, even though he is dead" (Heb. 11:4). Abel still speaks to us through the Scriptures and, as it were, from heaven, where he dwells with God. He is telling us to believe God and his word, to believe in the substitutionary atonement of Jesus, and to believe in Christ, the only Savior.

The Hebrews author says Abel offered *"a better sacrifice"* and that *"God spoke well of his offerings"* (Heb. 11:4). We know that Abel's sacrifice was approved while Cain's was rejected. How was this approval evidenced? Theodotion, a second-century theologian, writes about fire coming down from heaven and consuming Abel's sacrifice but not Cain's. Because the Scripture often speaks of God's showing approval by sending divine fire to consume a sacrifice (cf. Lev. 9:24; Judg. 6:21; 1 Kings 18:38; 1 Chron. 21:26; 2 Chron. 7:1), we have no problem believing that God demonstrated in such a supernatural way his approval of Abel, who by faith pleased him.

Today we are no longer asked to offer bloody sacrifices; rather, we are asked to offer the whole of our lives as a living sacrifice: "Therefore, I urge you, brothers, in view of God's mercy, to offer your bodies as living sacrifices, holy and pleasing to God—this is your spiritual act of worship. Do not conform any longer to the pattern of this world, but be transformed by the renewing of your mind. Then you will be able to test and approve what God's will is—his good, pleasing and perfect will" (Rom. 12:1–2).

How is your sacrifice? Does God approve of your life and decision-making? Are you living by faith? Are you living according to God's will? Paul exhorts, "Do your best to present yourself to God as one approved, a workman who does not need to be ashamed and who correctly handles the word of truth" (2 Tim. 2:15). A man approved and commended by God is a happy man. May we so please God and be happy!

The Example of Enoch

"*By faith Enoch was taken from this life, so that he did not experience death; he could not be found, because God had taken him away. For before he was taken, he was commended as one who pleased God*" (Heb. 11:5). Enoch is another person who lived by faith in God and his word. The Genesis account says, "Enoch walked with God" (Gen. 5:24). The Septuagint translation says, "Enoch pleased God." We can conclude that Enoch pleased God by walking with him. In fact, God was so pleased with Enoch that he took him from earth to heaven without requiring him to experience death. When we read the long genealogy in Genesis 5, we notice the refrain: "and he died." But concerning Enoch this refrain is not recorded, for he did not die. God took him into his presence that he might enjoy everlasting happiness.

Elijah also experienced such translation, and we are told that every Christian who is alive when Christ comes again will be translated without seeing death: "For the Lord himself will come down from heaven, with a loud command, with the voice of the archangel and with the trumpet call of God, and the dead in Christ will rise first. After that, we who are still alive and are left will be caught up together with them in the clouds to meet the Lord in the air. And so we will be with the Lord forever" (1 Thess. 4:16–17). If Christ does not come during our lifetime, he will send the chariots of heart attack, cancer, and other debilities of the flesh to usher us to heaven. We must not worry; when we walk with God, death cannot interrupt this fellowship. "Neither death nor life . . . will be able to separate us from the love of God that is in Christ Jesus our Lord" (Rom. 8:38–39).

The Genesis account does not specifically mention the faith of Enoch. But Hebrews 11:6 gives us the key: "*Without faith it is impossible to please God.*" The Hebrews writer also says that God testified to Enoch before his translation that he pleased God: "*For before he was taken, he was commended as one who pleased God*" (Heb. 11:5). Therefore we can conclude that Enoch lived by faith as he walked with God. Enoch pleased God, and God rewarded him by taking him to be with him forever. He sought the Lord diligently, with all his heart, soul, mind, and strength. Solomon exhorted the people to seek God wholeheartedly

(2 Chron. 6:36–39). David too speaks of such wholehearted seeking: "One thing I ask of the LORD, this is what I seek: that I may dwell in the house of the LORD all the days of my life, to gaze upon the beauty of the LORD and to seek him in his temple" (Ps. 27:4).

God rewards those who earnestly seek him, but we should not conclude that this reward is something we earn; it is always of grace. In Isaiah we read, "See, the Sovereign LORD comes with power, and his arm rules for him. See, his reward is with him, and his recompense accompanies him. . . . The LORD has made proclamation to the ends of the earth: 'Say to the Daughter of Zion, "See, your Savior comes! See, his reward is with him, and his recompense accompanies him"'" (Isa. 40:10; 62:11). What is this reward? Is it gold, glory, or a longer life? No, God gives us more than gold. As he told Abraham, "I am your very great reward" (Gen. 15:1).

Our reward is God himself. We are created to be happy in God. The psalmist says, "In thy presence is fullness of joy; at thy right hand there are pleasures forevermore" (Ps. 16:11, KJV). Elsewhere he says, "Then will I go to the altar of God, to God, my joy and my delight. I will praise you with the harp, O God, my God" (Ps. 43:4). If we cannot say what the psalmist said, then we are idolaters who are not seeking God with all our heart.

Again, the psalmist exclaims, "Whom have I in heaven but you? And earth has nothing I desire besides you. My flesh and my heart may fail, but God is the strength of my heart and my portion forever" (Ps. 73:25–26). Like Paul, we do not seek gold or the glories of this world; we seek God, who alone makes us happy. Jesus teaches, "Blessed are the pure in heart, for they will see God" (Matt. 5:8). Seeing God will be sheer terror for many people, but not for a true child of God.

The Genesis account says Enoch "walked with God." This means Enoch agreed with God, for two cannot walk together unless they are in agreement (Amos 3:3). This means Enoch desired to be holy, for the Lord commands, "Be ye holy for I am holy" (cf. Lev. 11:44, 45; 19:2; 20:7; 1 Pet. 1:15–16). It means he acknowledged God as Lord and himself as God's obedient servant, ready to hear and do the will of God. We are told Enoch walked with God for three hundred years. His walk was not for a day, but for his entire life.

Enoch's walking with God means he communed with God. He was a praying person, always talking to God. It also means he talked to others about God. Enoch preached to the people of the antediluvian community about God and his righteousness (Jude 14–15). "He walked with God" means he made each decision for the glory of God, one step and one decision at a time. It also means he was a friend of God. Jesus said his disciples were his friends (John 15:15). Friends talk and communicate.

The Christian life is described as walking with God. Like Enoch, we also are to be led by the Spirit and by Scripture all our life. Happiness is pleasing God by walking with him, as the hymn goes:

> Each step I take I know that he will guide me;
> to higher ground he ever leads me on,
> until some day the last step will be taken.
> Each step I take just leads me closer home.

Death is not fearful for a believer; it is coming home.

God communicated to Enoch before his translation that Enoch had pleased him. What assurance of salvation! We can imagine what he said: "Enoch, you have done well. You have pleased me and trusted me. Now I am going to reward you. You shall not experience death; I will just take you home with me."

Paul speaks about the assurance that comes from pleasing God: "The Spirit himself testifies with our spirit that we are God's children" (Rom. 8:16). Jesus also teaches: "Whoever has my commands and obeys them, he is the one who loves me. He who loves me will be loved by my Father, and I too will love him and show myself to him. . . . If anyone loves me, he will obey my teaching. My Father will love him, and we will come to him and make our home with him" (John 14:21, 23). This is happiness, this is fellowship with God, this is truly a trouble-free life. Why should we be troubled when God himself dwells with us and shows himself to us?

I pray that we will stop our restless seeking of happiness and peace in the things of this world. God created us to find happiness only through fellowship with him. May we, therefore, seek first the kingdom of God and his righteousness. May we seek

Happiness Is Pleasing God

to please God in all that we do. Then we will know in the core of our being that we are God's children and we will experience the inexpressible joy of the Lord that comes only from walking with God.

26
Living in the Present by Faith

> By faith Noah, when warned about things not yet seen, in holy fear built an ark to save his family. By his faith he condemned the world and became heir of the righteousness that comes by faith.
>
> Hebrews 11:7

The life of Noah clearly illustrates the connection between faith in God and obedience to God. In the book of Genesis, four chapters are dedicated to the story of Noah and the ark, but the Hebrews writer gives him only one verse. In the Genesis account no reference is given to the faith of Noah. In fact, the word "faith" does not appear in Genesis. Yet Noah's life was characterized by obedient faith in God. The spoken word of God was his Bible.

Noah was the last in the godly line of Adam through Seth. When he was born, six of his ancestors were still living: Enosh, Kenan, Mahalel, Jared, Methuselah, and Lamech. They all died before the flood. But we are told that Noah found grace in the eyes of the Lord—a grace that justified him (Gen. 6:8).

Noah was righteous in life and blameless in his dealings with other people. Like Enoch, he walked in holy communion with God and obeyed all of God's commandments (Gen. 6:22; 7:5). In this chapter we want to examine the faith of Noah, the work of Noah, and the justification of Noah.

The Faith of Noah

"*By faith Noah* . . ." (Heb. 11:7). The author of Hebrews is saying in effect that Noah lived his entire life by faith. "Without faith it is impossible to please God" (Heb. 11:6). We can go further and say that without faith it is impossible to be saved from sin. Noah pleased God through his obedience and was saved from death in the flood. That is why we can say that Noah lived by faith.

Noah lived by faith in God and his objective word. A child who believes in his father will obey his father's word. Noah lived by faith in the God who created the universe out of nothing, having been told about him by his forefathers (cf. Gen. 1:1; Heb. 11:3). He believed in a holy God who hates sin and communicates his will to man concerning how he should live. Noah knew he was a sinner, but repented of his sins and trusted in the Messiah who was to come to save sinners. He worshiped God by offering bloody sacrifices according to God's instruction: "Then Noah built an altar to the LORD and, taking some of all the clean animals and clean birds, he sacrificed burnt offerings on it" (Gen. 8:20). Noah understood that without the shedding of blood there is no forgiveness of sins (Heb. 9:22).

Noah did not believe in a manmade god. He believed in the God who had revealed himself to his fathers and to him. He lived by the faith that comes by hearing God's word. He stood alone by faith when everyone else lived in enmity toward God. Genesis 6:5 describes the wicked generation in which Noah lived: "The LORD saw how great man's wickedness on the earth had become, and that every inclination of the thoughts of his heart was only evil all the time."

In the midst of this corrupt generation, one person stood alone, loving and serving God: "Now the earth was corrupt in God's sight and was full of violence [lawlessness]. God saw how corrupt the earth had become, for all the people on earth had corrupted their ways. So God said to Noah, 'I am going to put an end to all people, for the earth is filled with violence because of them. I am surely going to destroy both them and the earth'" (Gen. 6:11–13).

Noah lived according to the specific revelation God gave him, that in 120 years God would destroy all the people of the world by a flood. The Hebrews author speaks of this: "*By faith Noah, when warned about things not yet seen* . . ." (Heb. 11:7).

We read elsewhere of such warnings from God: "Moses was warned when he was about to build the tabernacle: 'See to it that you make everything according to the pattern shown you on the mountain'" (Heb. 8:5). Such direct, specific communication also came to the Magi: "And having been warned in a dream not to go back to Herod, they returned to their country by another route" (Matt. 2:12). And God gave a specific oracle to Joseph, the legal father of Jesus: "But when [Joseph] heard that Archelaus was reigning in Judea in place of his father Herod, he was afraid to go there. Having been warned in a dream, he withdrew to the district of Galilee" (Matt. 2:22).

Hebrews 12:25 warns: "See to it that you do not refuse him who speaks. If they did not escape when they refused him who warned them on earth, how much less will we, if we turn away from him who warns us from heaven?" Today we are warned, not by some personal communication, but by the entire body of revelation given to us in the Scripture. We must govern ourselves in the light of this infallible communication from God: "All Scripture is God-breathed and is useful for teaching, rebuking, correcting and training in righteousness, so that the man of God may be thoroughly equipped for every good work" (2 Tim. 3:16).

Noah was warned "of things not yet seen." These things included the universal flood that would destroy every wicked person of that generation, and instructions for building an ark (Gen. 6:13–17).

Faith is thus faith in God's revelation. In Noah's day, God's revelation was given orally; now we have it in written form. Jesus Christ himself lived by such faith. He said, "It stands written," referring to God's authoritative word (Matt. 4:1–11). As God's Son, he honored his Father by doing his revealed will. This is precisely where Eve failed. She should have told Satan, "It is spoken, and I stand under the authority of God's oracle."

Noah did not act on the basis of a hunch, but on the basis of God's objective word. God's word is still authoritative for everyone, especially for God's people. Noah was given a revelation concerning things not yet seen, things 120 years into the future. If we had been given such a warning, we might have said, "That may be true, but I don't have to worry about it right now. These things won't happen for a long time. Maybe I will start building in a century or so." But Noah moved with fear right away and began to build. In fact, in the Greek text of Hebrews 11:7 the idea of warning and obedience are simultaneous. God requires immediate, exact, and glad obedience of his children. Delay and denial are not part of true faith.

God's revelation had to do with something unprecedented, something "unreasonable," without any historical analogy. There had never been a flood, let alone rain, on the earth before: "When the LORD God made the earth and the heavens—and no shrub of the field had yet appeared on the earth and no plant of the field had yet sprung up, for the LORD God had not sent rain on the earth and there was no man to work the ground, but streams came up from the earth and watered the whole surface of the ground" (Gen. 2:4–6). Now Noah was being told there was going to be a flood 120 years in the future that would cover the whole inhabited earth and destroy everyone except Noah and his family. He was to build a boat, with specific instructions to use gopher wood and coat it with pitch, to put in a door, and to make three decks. This ark was to be 450 feet long, 75 feet wide, and 45 feet high, without an anchor, mast, sail, or steering wheel. It was to be built on dry land in a landlocked area. This was the unreasonable, unprecedented revelation that came to Noah.

The Obedient Work of Noah

"By faith Noah . . . in holy fear built an ark" (Heb. 11:7). The author next shows us how Noah obeyed God's word. He says that Noah, when warned of things not yet seen, moved with anxious, godly earnestness, and began building the ark. As soon as he heard God's word, Noah put it into action.

In the Hebrew text of Genesis 6, there is only one command given—to build the ark (Gen. 6:14). Noah began to do this immediately, because he was acting in faith. Faith has its reason: the infinite, personal God behind the word. Noah's faith in God motivated him to obey immediately. Faith's reasoning argues from the ability of God to do everything he has promised.

Abraham was also given an "unprecedented, unreasonable" oracle by the true God (Gen. 22). In the middle of the night God told him to take his only son Isaac, the son he loved, and kill him as a sacrifice to God to demonstrate Abraham's surpassing love for God. Moved with holy fear, Abraham got up very early the next morning and went to sacrifice Isaac. The Hebrews writer gives us the reason behind Abraham's action: "Abraham reasoned that God could raise the dead, and figuratively speaking, he did receive Isaac back from death" (Heb. 11:19). Abraham believed that God was able to raise Isaac from his ashes in order to fulfill his promises.

Noah's life literally fulfilled the description of faith given in Hebrews 11:1. Faith sees things future as already present. Such a view energizes us to do the will of God and to live by God's word in the present. Faith gives us the substance of things hoped for and the proof of things not seen. Faith is like a telescope that brings things distant and future to the near and present, that we may be inspired by it to live for God.

By faith Noah saw the promised deluge destroying all the wicked people of his generation, and he saw himself and his family being saved by divine grace. Therefore, he acted in faith and constructed the ark for the salvation of his family. Faith works in the light of God's revelation. Faith is active, not passive.

Faith without present obedience is dead faith. It is the devil's faith and its destiny is the same as that of the devil—eternal destruction in the lake of fire. If we do not act justly, then our claim to be justified is mere presumption and our faith is dead (James 2:14–17). Matthew Henry says, "Faith first influences our affections and then our actions."[1]

Noah had authentic faith and therefore moved with godly fear and paid heed to God's word. When I see people without any reverence and holy fear, I realize they have nothing to do with genuine saving faith. We are exhorted by Paul, the great champion of salvation by sovereign grace, to work out our salvation with fear and trembling (Phil. 2:12–13). Godly fear causes us to avoid evil and inspires us to do God's will gladly.

---

1   Quoted by Pink, *Exposition of Hebrews*, 684.

Paul himself was moved with a holy fear of God and lived daily in obedience to the will of God. He writes, "For we must all appear before the judgment seat of Christ, that each one may receive what is due him for the things done while in the body, whether good or bad. Since, then, we know what it is to fear the Lord, we try to persuade men" (2 Cor. 5:10–11). Jesus also revered God the Father: "During the days of Jesus' life on earth, he offered up prayers and petitions with loud cries and tears to the one who could save him from death, and he was heard because of his reverent submission" (Heb. 5:7).

Hebrews 12:28 speaks of such godly fear: "Therefore, since we are receiving a kingdom that cannot be shaken, let us be thankful, and so worship God acceptably with reverence and awe." In Psalm 2:11–12 we are exhorted, "Serve the Lord with fear and rejoice with trembling. Kiss the Son, lest he be angry and you be destroyed in your way, for his wrath can flare up in a moment. Blessed are all who take refuge in him." The curse of this generation is that we treat God as a buddy. Oh, that we would fear him as the psalmist did: "My flesh trembles in fear of you; I stand in awe of your laws" (Ps. 119:120).

Several times in the book of Malachi, the Lord makes a clear distinction between those who fear him and the rest of that miserable generation: "Cursed is the cheat who has an acceptable male in his flock and vows to give it, but then sacrifices a blemished animal to the Lord. 'For I am a great king,' says the Lord Almighty, 'and my name is to be feared among the nations'" (1:14); "My covenant was with him, a covenant of life and peace, and I gave them to him; this called for reverence and he revered me and stood in awe of my name" (2:5); "So I will come near to you for judgment. I will be quick to testify against sorcerers, adulterers and perjurers, against those who defraud laborers of their wages, who oppress the widows and the fatherless, and deprive aliens of justice, but do not fear me" (3:5); "Then those who feared the Lord talked with each other, and the Lord listened and heard" (3:16); "But for you who revere my name, the sun of righteousness will rise with healing in its wings" (4:2).

Thus, people who have saving faith will fear God and earnestly do his will. Faith has two aspects—an invisible, internal aspect and a visible, external aspect. Faith in its internal aspect trusts

God with the heart. It is a faith that affects our affections. Our internal attitude is energized by our trust in God's veracity and unchangeableness. But if we trust God with our hearts, then our faith will also become visible through our deeds. We will do the will of God immediately, exactly, and gladly. Jesus said, "If you love me, you will obey what I command" (John 14:15). Invisible faith is made visible through what we do.

In Mark 2 we read about four people who believed that Jesus was able and willing to heal their paralyzed friend. They carried him to the house where Jesus was ministering and saw that the house was full, with people crowding outside. But they refused to go back. They went to the roof, made a hole in it, and lowered the man down through it into the very presence of Jesus. We read next: "When Jesus saw their faith . . ." (Mark 2:5). Faith is visible. In this case, their internal attitude was made visible by taking this wretch of a man to Jesus. All their actions, including digging a hole in the roof of someone's house, were a result of faith working.

Faith in Jesus Christ scales all walls. So Noah believed in his heart that God is and that he is the Savior of those who diligently seek him. He demonstrated his faith by building a huge ark in a dry land. And all the while the ark was being built, Noah was preaching to the wicked antediluvian people in two ways—by his actions in building the ark and by his words. He told them God was going to destroy the world in 120 years. He warned them that because God hates evil, his judgment was surely coming, and all wicked people would be destroyed, though nothing like this had ever happened before. He also told them that the only way of salvation is through repentance and faith in God. He urged them to repent, believe, and join him in worshiping and serving the true and living God. Noah exhorted them to live holy lives and be saved by the ark (cf. 1 Pet. 3:19–20; 2 Pet. 2:5).

How did the people respond? They mocked Noah and his message. I am sure they called him an unscientific, non-materialist fool who believed in an infinite, personal God of judgment. "Old man," they would insist, "there is no judgment, no God, and no morality. Live it up! Eat, drink, and be merry. In a few hundred years, we will die, and that will be it."

The one hundred and twenty years eventually came to an end. The last week arrived and God said that in seven days the flood would come. Notice, we do not read about any clouds. The sky was still clear. There was nothing different, and no one believed Noah, including his employees. Then the animals began to come by a divine summons and they entered the ark. The people saw this, yet they still refused to come and enter the ark.

Finally, the last day came. Noah and his seven family members entered the ark, and the Lord shut the door. Then, just as God had warned, the flood came. Noah was proven right, and the world was proven wrong. The people ran to the ark, but they could not enter. They climbed on the roofs of their houses and to the tops of the trees. They fled to the hills and the mountains, but they could not escape the floodwaters of God's judgment. The wicked mockers all died, but Noah and his family were saved.

There is a blessing for those who live by faith and obey God's word. Remember the story of Peter working all night and catching nothing? In the morning Jesus told him to pull the boat into the deep waters and once again let down the net. At first Peter protested, but then he said, "But because you say so, I will let down the nets," and he and his friends caught a boatful of fish (Luke 5:4–7). To the ten lepers Jesus said, "Go, show yourselves to the priests," and as they went, they were healed (Luke 17:11–19). Elisha told the Syrian general Naaman, who was a leper, "Go, wash yourself seven times in the Jordan, and your flesh will be restored and you will be cleansed." Naaman refused at first, because he was a powerful and mighty man and he did not like this simple gospel. He was, however, persuaded by his servants to dip himself seven times. When he came up the seventh time, he was healed (2 Kings 5).

What must we do to be saved? The answer is simple: "Believe in the Lord Jesus, and you will be saved—you and your household" (Acts 16:31). The Philippian jailer believed and was saved the same night. Jesus Christ is King of kings and Lord of lords. He does not beg, plead, or cajole; rather, he commands all people everywhere to repent and be saved.

The Righteousness of Noah

"By his faith he condemned the world and became heir of the righteousness that comes by faith" (Heb. 11:7). Our author concludes

this verse by saying that Noah became an heir of "the righteousness that comes by faith." If we are theologically sensitive, we can see how this verse harmonizes with the central message of the Bible that justification is according to faith, not works.

Genesis 6:8 told us that "Noah found favor [grace] in the eyes of the Lord." All are born sinners and practice sin, and Noah was no exception. But Noah found grace and it was the basis for his righteousness. Noah was not justified by his obedient work of building the ark. He was saved by grace—unmerited favor. He, like us, merited hell and eternal death, but God freely gave him heaven and eternal life. That is what grace is all about.

God's grace justified Noah and he became a preacher of righteousness in his generation (2 Pet. 2:5). When everyone else was practicing wickedness, he was shining as light in their midst. He was saved by grace through faith. This is precisely the Pauline doctrine we discover in the epistles to the Romans and the Galatians.

The author of Hebrews says that Noah became an heir of righteousness by faith, not on the basis of his own good works. Earlier, he used the word "heir" in Hebrews 1:2 in reference to God appointing his Son to be the heir of all things. He also used it to speak of believers: "Are not all angels ministering spirits sent to serve those who will inherit salvation?" (Heb. 1:14). Righteousness is not something we earn; it is a gift, the Father's free disposition of salvation. We also read that we are heirs of God's promises of salvation (Heb. 6:12, 17).

Paul also speaks extensively of salvation and justification: "What shall we conclude then? Are we any better? Not at all! We have already made the charge that Jews and Gentiles alike are all under sin" (Rom. 3:9). He goes on to say, "For all have sinned and fall short of the glory of God" (Rom. 3:23). Paul believes in the pervasiveness of sin; we are born sinners and practice sin. There is no way, therefore, that we can do anything to please God and merit his salvation. So Paul declares, "This righteousness from God comes through faith in Jesus Christ to all who believe" (Rom. 3:22). The doctrine of Paul and that of the author of Hebrews is the same. Noah became an heir of righteousness according to faith.

The Bible speaks about justification by grace through faith: we are saved by grace through faith, not based on anything we have done. This righteousness that is according to faith manifests itself in sanctification, which is acting in obedience to God's will. Thus, a justified Noah obeyed God by building the ark. His doing so was evidence that Noah had become an heir of righteousness according to faith, not according to any meritorious works of his own. Sanctification proves justification by grace through faith. If we do not see sanctification expressed by obedience to God, we cannot be assured that a person is saved. The only way to know if a person is truly justified is to look for visible evidence of sanctification.

Modern evangelicalism glories in a justification without sanctification. But we must not separate that which God has joined together. God has linked justification with sanctification, and when modern people separate the two, they are doing a devilish work. Modern evangelicalism glories in a faith without works and a salvation in which Jesus Christ is Savior but not Lord. Many flock to churches that preach such heresy. But to glory in a salvation in which Jesus Christ is not Lord is to glory in a dead faith, in the devil's faith, in a faith whose destiny is the destiny of the devil. To such people the Lord will say on that great day, "Depart from me, you workers of iniquity." Such people are not heirs of righteousness according to faith.

Noah was not only justified by faith, but he also lived by faith in God's word. He walked with God in blamelessness and righteousness. He lived by faith in God's word and did God's will *because* he was justified. Noah's life thus illustrates the principle of Hebrews 10:38: "But my righteous one will live by faith," meaning by faith in God and his word. He became an heir of righteousness according to faith. Noah knew he was justified. This is not speaking of a future possession of righteousness. Righteousness is a present possession of all who have trusted in Jesus Christ alone for their eternal salvation. We are justified and have been given righteousness. Having been justified by faith, we now experience peace with God (Rom. 5:1). We enjoy now assurance of salvation.

What about You?

Are you justified by grace through faith now? Are you an heir of God's promise of salvation? Are you an heir of righteousness according to faith? Do you live daily in obedience to God's will? Do you witness by deed and by word, as Noah did when the vast majority of men lived in utter wickedness? Remember, only eight people were saved from the flood; and when God burned up Sodom and Gomorrah, only three were saved. Few are going to be saved when Christ comes again (cf. Matt. 7:13–14).

If we are Christians, we are the light of the world, the salt of the earth, and the hope of the world. Therefore, we must declare the gospel, for faith comes to the sinner by hearing the gospel. We have the same word Noah preached. In fact, we have the Bible, the whole written word of God. Therefore, as heirs of righteousness, we must boldly proclaim the gospel, warning people that destruction and judgment are coming when Jesus Christ returns.

Jesus is the Sovereign Lord and heir of all things and the upholder of the universe. He never begs or pleads, but commands us to surrender completely to him, that we may be saved and become an heir of the righteousness that is by faith. He declares, "All authority in heaven and on earth has been given to me. Therefore go and make disciples of all nations, baptizing them in the name of the Father and of the Son and of the Holy Spirit, and teaching them to obey everything I have commanded you" (Matt. 28:18–20). At the house of Cornelius, Peter said, "He commanded us to preach to the people and to testify that he is the one whom God appointed as judge of the living and the dead" (Acts 10:42).

When Paul was brought to Areopagus Hill in Athens and was interviewed by philosophers and the city councilmen, he proclaimed, "In the past God overlooked such ignorance, but now he commands all people everywhere to repent. For he has set a day when he will judge the world with justice by the man he has appointed. He has given proof of this to all men by raising him from the dead" (Acts 17:30–31).

We may wonder why Christ has not yet come. Jesus himself gives the reason: "This gospel of the kingdom will be preached in the whole world as a testimony to all nations, and then the end will come" (Matt. 24:14). This is the same message Noah proclaimed. He spoke for 120 years before judgment came. It has now been two thousand years since Christ's first advent. This "delay" tempts us to think nothing is going to happen and that the biblical promise of judgment is a mere myth. In fact, people have used the phrase "it is like the second coming" to speak about something that will not happen.

But read the warning given by Peter:

> First of all, you must understand that in the last days scoffers will come, scoffing and following their own evil desires. They will say, 'Where is this "coming" he promised? Ever since our fathers died, everything goes on as it has since the beginning of creation. . . .' The Lord is not slow in keeping his promise, as some understand slowness. He is patient with you, not wanting anyone to perish, but everyone to come to repentance. But the day of the Lord will come like a thief. The heavens will disappear with a roar; the elements will be destroyed by fire, and the earth and everything in it will be laid bare." (2 Pet. 3:3–4, 9–10)

The second coming of Christ may seem as incredible to us as the great flood did to the people of Noah's time. How can something happen that has never happened before? It is so unscientific and unreasonable. But the flood did come, and Christ, too, will surely come on the appointed day.

There is no difference between the people of Noah's day and ours. Jesus himself said in the context of his teaching on eschatology, "As it was in the days of Noah, so it will be at the coming of the Son of Man. For in the days before the flood, people were eating and drinking, marrying and giving in marriage, up to the day Noah entered the ark; and they knew nothing about what would happen until the flood came and took them all away. This is how it will be at the coming of the Son of Man" (Matt. 24:37–39).

If you are not a Christian, I urge you to enter the ark now and be saved, that you may become an heir of righteousness by faith before your door of opportunity is shut by God, either by his coming or by your death. If you are saved, I pray that you live by faith in God's word as Noah did, not by your own ideas. Christians follow Jesus Christ; he does not follow us, and we are to make all of our decisions for his glory based on his word. That is what it means to live by faith. If you are confused, it means you do not want to do what God wants you to do. The moment you agree to obey God, the cloud goes away and everything is clear.

Living in the Present by Faith

If we really are saved and believe that Jesus is coming again to judge the world, that knowledge will affect our lives. Peter writes, "Since everything will be destroyed in this way, what kind of people ought you to be? You ought to live holy and godly lives as you look forward to the day of God and speed its coming" (2 Pet. 3:11–12). John says the same thing: "Dear friends, now we are children of God, and what we will be has not yet been made known. But we know that when he appears, we shall be like him, for we shall see him like he is. Everyone who has this hope in him purifies himself, just as he is pure" (1 John 3:2–3). The second coming of Christ is not a theoretical idea that we can read about and forget. The gospel must govern our thinking, our priorities, our finances, our going and coming—every aspect of our lives. If we are heirs of righteousness by faith, it should spur us to holy living. God's people will be holy, while others pretend to be holy. But the latter will be told, "You are workers of iniquity."

May God help us to believe in the eternal, personal, moral God whose revelation in the Bible is completely true. May we believe in the Lord Jesus Christ for our salvation, and demonstrate our justification through sanctification. May we live by faith daily as Noah did. As he believed in the flood, may we believe in the second coming of Christ and live holy lives, speeding his coming as we wait for him, declaring, "Amen, come Lord Jesus."

27
The Fiery Trial of Our Faith

⁸*By faith Abraham, when called to go to a place he would later receive as his inheritance, obeyed and went, even though he did not know where he was going. ⁹By faith he made his home in the promised land like a stranger in a foreign country; he lived in tents, as did Isaac and Jacob, who were heirs with him of the same promise. ¹⁰For he was looking forward to the city with foundations, whose architect and builder is God. ¹¹By faith Abraham, even though he was past age—and Sarah herself was barren—was enabled to become a father because he considered him faithful who had made the promise. ¹²And so from this one man, and he as good as dead, came descendants as numerous as the stars in the sky and as countless as the sand on the seashore.*

¹³All these people were still living by faith when they died. They did not receive the things promised; they only saw them and welcomed them from a distance. And they admitted that they were aliens and strangers on earth. ¹⁴People who say such things show that they are looking for a country of their own. ¹⁵If they had been thinking of the country they had left, they would have had opportunity to return. ¹⁶Instead, they were longing for a better country—a heavenly one. Therefore God is not ashamed to be called their God, for he has prepared a city for them.

¹⁷By faith Abraham, when God tested him, offered Isaac as a sacrifice. He who had received the promises was about to sacrifice his one and only son, ¹⁸even though God had said to him, "It is through Isaac that your offspring will be reckoned." ¹⁹Abraham reasoned that God could raise the dead, and figuratively speaking, he did receive Isaac back from death. ²⁰By faith Isaac blessed Jacob and Esau in regard to their future. ²¹By faith Jacob, when he was dying, blessed each of Joseph's sons, and worshiped as he leaned on the top of his staff. ²²By faith Joseph, when his end was near, spoke about the exodus of the Israelites from Egypt and gave instructions about his bones.

Hebrews 11:8–22

At some point in every Christian's life, his or her faith will be severely tested.

Such trials reveal whether we are false believers or authentic people of God. As we continue our study of authentic faith we now want to look at the life of Abraham so that we will not be discouraged when we face trials, including our final trial—the valley of the shadow of death. A true believer can rejoice in such tribulations, knowing that God has a purpose in permitting us to go through such fiery ordeals.

When asked, "What must I do to be saved from God's wrath against me, a sinner?" the Bible declares, "Believe on the Lord Jesus Christ." If we believe, then we are saved forever, given eternal life, and adopted as God's beloved child. God becomes our heavenly Father, and Jesus Christ is our sure Redeemer.

If we have made such a profession of faith in Christ, God will test that faith to see if it is persevering and obedient. Concerning our salvation Peter writes, "In this you greatly rejoice, though now for a little while you may have had to suffer grief in all kinds of trials. These have come so that your faith—of greater worth than gold, which perishes even though refined by fire—may be proved genuine and may result in praise, glory and honor when Jesus Christ is revealed. . . . Dear friends, do not be surprised at the painful trial you are suffering, as though something strange were happening to you. But rejoice that you participate in the sufferings of Christ, so that you may be overjoyed when his glory is revealed" (1 Pet. 1:6–7; 4:12–13). A true believer will deny himself, take up the cross, and follow Jesus Christ wherever he leads. And sometimes he will lead us through fiery trials.

True faith and obedience are as inseparable as the sun and light. A true believer lives and dies by faith. It is a faith that does God's works. Abraham suffered the fiery trial of faith, and his faith was proven genuine. He is given the most attention in Hebrews 11 because of the greatness of his faith. Abraham's faith was tested in at least four different ways, including the most painful way imaginable.

The First Test: Following God

"By faith Abraham, when called to go to a place he would later receive as his inheritance, obeyed and went, even though he did not know where he was going" (Heb. 11:8). Abraham's first test came when God asked him to leave his idols and familiar surroundings and go to Canaan.

Abraham was an idol worshiper like his parents. He lived in Mesopotamia, in the city of Ur, located in what is now Iraq. To the cultured men of that time, city life was the highest form of civilized existence. Abraham was already a rich man, a mighty prince. He did not leave Ur of the Chaldees like a migrant worker seeking a job in Canaan. He was living a life of great security and pleasure. But the God of glory appeared to him and demanded that he leave his country, his relatives, and his father's house to go to a land that God would reveal to him (Gen 12:1). Abraham was to leave all of his certainty and comfort behind and trust in God.

John Calvin says that "it is no ordinary trial of faith to give what we have in hand in order to seek what is afar off and unknown to us."[1] But as soon as God commanded him, Abraham obeyed and left, not knowing where he was going. Abraham's decision resulted from his faith. It is faith in the Lord of glory and in his word.

We can imagine Abraham saying, "God has spoken, so I will leave my country, my kindred, and my father's house. I do not know where I am going, but I do not need to know. God knows, and he will go before me." Thus Abraham went out from Ur, as his descendants would go out many centuries later from Egypt, to the land of Canaan. Abraham trusted in the naked word of God.

We must understand Abraham's background to fully appreciate this act of faith. His parents did not believe in God. He knew no prophets and had no Bible to consult. Yet Abraham lived by faith and obeyed the One who called him. Faith is a journey into the unknown with God, who knows all things. God asked Abraham to leave his country, and this man of true faith obeyed. Abraham's faith was tried, and he passed the test.

---

1 Quoted by Philip E. Hughes, *Commentary on Hebrews*, 466–467.

The Second Test: Living and Dying as a Pilgrim

"By faith he made his home in the promised land like a stranger in a foreign country; he lived in tents, as did Isaac and Jacob, who were heirs with him of the same promise. For he was looking forward to the city with foundations, whose architect and builder is God" (Heb. 11:9–10). The second trial of Abraham's faith was to live in Canaan without personally experiencing the fulfillment of the great promises given to him that he would possess the land.

When God led Abraham to Canaan, he told him he would receive it as his inheritance (Gen. 12:7; 13:14–17). Abraham was seventy-five years old when he arrived in Canaan with his wife Sarah. He went on to live in Canaan for one hundred years, yet he never possessed even a foot of ground in Canaan as his inheritance (Acts 7:5).

Nevertheless, Abraham believed God. He stayed in Canaan, not in permanent buildings as he had in Ur, but in tents, along with his son Isaac and later his grandson Jacob, fellow heirs of the promises of God. As a nomad and an immigrant, he moved from place to place. In fact, when Sarah died at one hundred and twenty-seven years of age, Abraham had no place to bury her. He said to the Hittite leaders of the land, "I am an alien and a stranger among you. Sell me some property for a burial site here so I can bury my dead" (Gen. 23:4). Thus he bought the cave of Machpelah from Ephron the Hittite for four hundred shekels of silver.

Before Abraham left for this unknown land, God had given him a great promise: "I will make you into a great nation and I will bless you; I will make your name great, and you will be a blessing. I will bless those who bless you, and whoever curses you I will curse; and all peoples on earth will be blessed through you" (Gen. 12:2–3).

Where were these blessings God had promised? By the time Abraham died, there was still no land and no nation. Yet Abraham never sought to return to his fatherland to live the secure, comfortable life he had known before. That would have been unbelief in the God who spoke to him. He lived by faith in God and in God's future fulfillment of all his promises: "But my righteous one will live by faith. And if he shrinks back, I will not be pleased with him" (Heb. 10:38). Abraham did not shrink back, but continued to have faith that God's promises would be fulfilled.

Not only did Abraham live by faith, but he also died by faith: *"All these people were still living by faith when they died"* (Heb. 11:13). To die a good death we must live by faith. Oh, what tragedy when people die in unbelief! Jesus Christ said to the unbelieving Jews: "I told you that you would die in your sins; if you do not believe that I am the one I claim to be, you will indeed die in your sins" (John 8:24).

Unbelievers die in their sins. But Hebrews 11:13 tells us there is another way to die—to die in faith in God. Believers die trusting that the Lord will come to fulfill all his promises. Jacob exhibited such faith: "Then [Jacob] said to Joseph, 'I am about to die, but God will be with you and take you back to the land of your fathers. . . . I look for your deliverance, O Lord'" (Gen. 48:21; 49:18). Later, when it was his turn to die, Joseph spoke in faith to his brothers, "I am about to die. But God will surely come to your aid and take you up out of this land to the land he promised on oath to Abraham, Isaac and Jacob" (Gen. 50:24).

Abraham and his descendants lived and died in faith: *"By faith Isaac blessed Jacob and Esau in regard to their future. By faith Jacob, when he was dying, blessed each of Joseph's sons, and worshiped as he leaned on the top of his staff. By faith Joseph, when his end was near, spoke about the exodus of the Israelites from Egypt and gave instructions about his bones"* (Heb. 11:20–22). They were all looking for God to come and fulfill his great promises of salvation. They died by faith in God's promises of future deliverance.

When they died, they had not received the fullness of salvation, but they believed that the words of the God of glory would be fulfilled. By faith *"they only saw [the things promised] and welcomed them from a distance"* (Heb. 11:13). Jesus said, "Abraham rejoiced at the thought of seeing my day; he saw it and was glad" (John 8:56). By faith Abraham saw his own future offspring Jesus.

The vibrant, authentic faith of these believers brought what was future to the present and energized them to live as strangers in this world. They refused to conform to the world, for they were being transformed by their faith in God's promises. Abraham, Isaac, Jacob, and Joseph all lived by faith. They lived fully in the world, yet they were not of the world. What was the motivation behind their pilgrim lives? They were *"looking forward to the city with foundations, whose architect and builder is God"* (Heb. 11:10).

The Third Test: Children

"By faith Abraham, even though he was past age—and Sarah herself was barren—was enabled to become a father because he considered him faithful who had made the promise. And so from this one man, and he as good as dead, came descendants as numerous as the stars in the sky and as countless as the sand on the seashore" (Heb. 11:11–12). Abraham's third trial of faith concerned having children. The God of glory promised to make Abraham into a great nation and give him a multitude of children (Gen. 12:2; 13:16). By the time Abraham was in his eighties he had not a single offspring, so he appointed his servant Eliezer to be his heir. Yet God came to him again in Canaan and promised a multitude of children (Gen. 15:4–5). More than a decade passed, and still Abraham had no son through Sarah. But the Lord appeared to him again and affirmed that he and Sarah would be the parents of many nations (Gen. 17:4, 16).

How could this be? His sterile wife was now ninety years old. She herself confessed, "I am worn out" (Gen. 18:12). Sarah was aged and barren; her husband, who was almost one hundred years old, was no longer able to father children. In Hebrews 11:12 the author uses a perfect passive participle to describe Abraham: he was *nenekrōmenou,* meaning "as good as dead," or "in a state of death." Paul uses the same word in Romans 4:19. But Abraham believed God and, together with Sarah, received power from the living God to father Isaac because he considered him faithful who promised (Heb. 11:11; cf. Rom. 4:17–21).

We read in Hebrews 11:11: *"By faith Abraham, even though he was past age—and Sarah herself was barren—was enabled to become a father because he considered him faithful who had made the promise."* Abraham received the power to beget Isaac because he understood who God was and what he could do.

Abraham believed that the "God who gives life to the dead and calls things that are not as though they were" was competent to fulfill his promises. And truly God did raise up Sarah and Abraham from death. Thus we read that from one dead man and one dead woman, by God's supernatural power of resurrection, came an innumerable multitude of people (Heb. 11:12). Abraham's faith was tested and proven genuine. He believed God and received children just as God promised.

The Final Test: Sacrificing Isaac

"*By faith Abraham, when God tested him, offered Isaac as a sacrifice. He who had received the promises was about to sacrifice his one and only son, even though God had said to him, 'It is through Isaac that your offspring will be reckoned'*" (Heb. 11:17–18). The final and most demanding test of Abraham's faith was the call to sacrifice Isaac. When Isaac was a teenager, God came to Abraham in the middle of the night and told him to kill his son and burn him up in worship. God's demand was clear: he did not ask that Abraham sacrifice his servant Eliezer or his son Ishmael. God wanted Isaac to be sacrificed, and God wanted Abraham to do it as a demonstration of his total love and devotion to God. Just as Jesus asked Simon Peter if he loved him more than anything else (John 21:15–17), so God was asking, "Abraham, do you love me more than Isaac your son, your only son of promise, the son whom you love?" Abraham's answer was yes. Like Abraham, we are to love God with all our heart, soul, mind, and strength. We cannot serve two masters. God will not tolerate idolatry of any kind.

Now Abraham knew God's promise full well, that his offspring would be reckoned through Isaac (Gen. 21:12). The Messiah who would save Abraham and the world was to come through Isaac. But the demand also was clear. God himself told Abraham that Isaac must be killed and burned up. God's demand and promise to Abraham were in apparent conflict.

What are we to do when God's command appears to clash with God's covenant promises? First, we must affirm that God is not a God of contradictions. If God promised to give Abraham descendants, including the Messiah, through Isaac, he would fulfill that promise. If God demanded that Isaac be sacrificed, then that sacrifice could not nullify God's covenant promise.

This apparent contradiction of promise and demand was resolved: "*Abraham reasoned that God could raise the dead, and figuratively speaking, he did receive Isaac back from death*" (Heb. 11:19). Christians are called not to live an emotional life but an intelligent life, a life that demands our full powers of thought. Abraham reasoned that to fulfill his promise God must raise Isaac from the ashes. Abraham knew from his own experience that God was able to do so, for he had already raised "dead" Sarah and Abraham so that Isaac could be born. Now he reasoned that God must also be able to raise Isaac from the dead.

Christianity demands reasoning ability. When faced with this seemingly insurmountable problem, Abraham thought carefully. Finally his mind focused on the infinite, personal, almighty God, who is completely competent to raise the dead. Genesis 22:5 reveals Abraham's thought process. He told his servants, "Stay here with the donkey while I and the boy go over there. We will worship and then *we will come back to you*" (italics added). Abraham rose early in the morning and cut the wood to use in burning up his son Isaac. He walked three days to Mount Moriah, and as he walked he reasoned until he came to this resolution of the conflict: God must raise Isaac up from the dead, and he surely would.

Our duty is to obey God's clear word, for God is altogether holy and reliable. He is the God of glory, not a dumb idol. Abraham reasoned that God had proved reliable so far; thus, he must and would raise Isaac to fulfill his covenant promises.

As Abraham was about to kill Isaac, God intervened and stopped him. Then God provided a ram for sacrifice, which pointed forward to the future son of Abraham, Jesus Christ. But Jesus was not spared from death. He died and was buried, and on the third day he rose from the dead as the Savior of all who believe in him.

The Lord commanded Abraham not to lay a hand on the boy because, in purpose and intention, Abraham had already sacrificed Isaac, and God was satisfied. The Lord told him, "Now I know that you fear God, because you have not withheld from me your son, your only son" (Gen. 22:12). Abraham passed the test. He loved God more than Isaac, as God himself certified.

The Secret of Abraham's Faith

What was the secret of Abraham's faith? In verse 10 we read, "For he was looking forward to the city with foundations, whose

The Fiery Trial of Our Faith

architect and builder is God." Abraham truly trusted in God. He was not looking to God for health, wealth, and power in this world. He was not looking to build a city in Canaan and dwell there. Yes, Abraham was looking for a city, but it was the city of God—a heavenly city designed and built by God himself, a city that cannot be conquered and destroyed, an everlasting city with foundations (cf. Ps. 87:1).

That is why Abraham did not return to Ur of the Chaldees or join Lot in going to live in Sodom. Because he was longing for a home country, he dwelt in tents and lived as a stranger and pilgrim: *"People who say such things [admitting they are aliens and strangers on earth] show that they are looking for a country of their own"* (Heb. 11:14). He was longing for a heavenly city that is better than all the impermanent cities of this world.

Like Jesus, Abraham considered all the glories and splendors of the kingdoms of this world as less than nothing. Jesus asked, "What good will it be for a man if he gains the whole world, yet forfeits his soul?" (Matt. 16:26). Paul speaks in the same fashion: "What is more, I consider everything a loss compared to the surpassing greatness of knowing Christ Jesus my Lord, for whose sake I have lost all things. . . . Not that I have already obtained all this, or have already been made perfect, but I press on to take hold of that for which Christ Jesus took hold of me. . . . Forgetting what is behind and straining toward what is ahead, I press on toward the goal to win the prize for which God has called me heavenward in Christ Jesus" (Phil. 3:8, 12–14).

In Hebrews 12 we find a description of this city: "But you have come to Mount Zion, to the heavenly Jerusalem, the city of the living God" (v. 22). Look also at verse 28: "We are receiving a kingdom that cannot be shaken." Unlike all the cities of the world, this God-ruled city is unshakable. It is the rock spoken of by the prophet Daniel—the kingdom of God that comes down from heaven and destroys every city and kingdom of this world (Dan. 2:34–35, 44–45).

We are fools if we put our hope in the cities of this world: "For here we do not have an enduring city, but we are looking for the city that is to come" (Heb. 13:14). All the kingdoms and cities of the world are shakable; the city of God alone is unshakable. *"For [God] has prepared a city for them"* (Heb. 11:16).

This city is already prepared for our enjoyment that we may dwell in it with God. Paul writes, "'No eye has seen, no ear has heard, no mind has conceived what God has prepared for those who love him'—but God has revealed it to us by his Spirit" (1 Cor. 2:9–10).

God has prepared a city for his people. If you are going through trials, listen to the comforting words of Jesus Christ: "Do not let your hearts be troubled. Trust in God; trust also in me. In my Father's house are many rooms; if it were not so, I would have told you. I am going there to prepare a place for you. And if I go and prepare a place for you, I will come back and take you to be with me that you also may be where I am" (John 14:1–3). He is speaking about the city of God, which is the very presence of God, the place of everlasting happiness.

The final destiny of the people of God is to dwell with God. Jesus declares, "Whoever has my commands and obeys them, he is the one who loves me. He who loves me will be loved by my Father, and I too will love him and show myself to him. . . . If anyone loves me, he will obey my teaching. My Father will love him, and we will come to him and make our home with him" (John 14:21, 23). Jesus elsewhere tells us, "Then the King will say to those on his right, 'Come, you who are blessed by my Father; take your inheritance, the kingdom prepared for you since the creation of the world'" (Matt. 25:34).

The Hebrews writer thus exhorts us, "Therefore, holy brothers, who share in the heavenly calling, fix your thoughts on Jesus, the apostle and high priest whom we confess" (Heb. 3:1). Lift up your eyes to the hills, to the heavenly country, to the heavenly city. Lift up your eyes and see Jesus, as Stephen saw him (Acts 7:55–56). "Let us fix our eyes on Jesus, the author and perfecter of our faith" (Heb. 12:2). Paul writes, "I consider that our present sufferings are not worth comparing with the glory that will be revealed in us" (Rom. 8:18); "Therefore we do not lose heart. Though outwardly we are wasting away, yet inwardly we are being renewed day by day. For our light and momentary troubles are achieving for us an eternal glory that far outweighs them all. So we fix our eyes not on what is seen, but on what is unseen. For what is seen is temporary, but what is unseen is eternal" (2 Cor. 4:16–18). Our citizenship is in heaven.

The city of God is God and his people. It is living forever with God: "Now this is eternal life: that they may know you, the only true God, and Jesus Christ, whom you have sent" (John 17:3). It is God dwelling with man and man with God. John writes: "I saw the Holy City, the new Jerusalem, coming down out of heaven from God, prepared as a bride beautifully dressed for her husband. And I heard a loud voice from the throne saying, 'Now the dwelling of God is with men, and he will live with them. They will be his people, and God himself will be with them and be their God. He will wipe every tear from their eyes. There will be no more death or mourning or crying or pain, for the old order of things has passed away'" (Rev. 21:2–4). This is the new heaven and new earth, wherein righteousness dwells. "Blessed are the pure in heart, for they will see God" (Matt. 5:8).

"*Instead, they were longing for a better country—a heavenly one. Therefore God is not ashamed to be called their God, for he has prepared a city for them*" (Heb. 11:16). Here the writer says that God was so proud of Abraham, Isaac, and Jacob because they lived by faith in him that he is not ashamed to be called their God. God will honor those who honor him. God loves to be known as our God.

Our inheritance is not Ur of Chaldees or Sodom or wherever we now live. God is our inheritance, and we are his. Someday we too will dwell with God in the new heavens and the new earth, in the city of God. Henry Francis Lyte wrote:

> It is not for me to be seeking my bliss
> and building my hopes in a region like this;
> I look for a city which hands have not piled,
> I pant for a country by sin undefiled.[2]

May God help us to trust in Christ, that we too may live with him forever in everlasting bliss.

---

[2] Quoted by Bruce, *Epistle to the Hebrews*, 300.

28

The Faith of Moses

23By faith Moses' parents hid him for three months after he was born, because they saw he was no ordinary child, and they were not afraid of the king's edict. 24By faith Moses, when he had grown up, refused to be known as the son of Pharaoh's daughter. 25He chose to be mistreated along with the people of God rather than to enjoy the pleasures of sin for a short time. 26He regarded disgrace for the sake of Christ as of greater value than the treasures of Egypt, because he was looking ahead to his reward. 27By faith he left Egypt, not fearing the king's anger; he persevered because he saw him who is invisible. 28By faith he kept the Passover and the sprinkling of blood, so that the destroyer of the firstborn would not touch the firstborn of Israel.

Hebrews 11:23-28

We are continuing our study about the nature of faith from Hebrews 11. Christians are saved by faith, but not a mere intellectual faith. True saving faith is active and it works. In Hebrews 11:23-28, the author speaks about Moses' active, working faith.

Moses was a man of great faith, which made him a man of decision and mighty deeds. Today the Pharaoh who persecuted the children of Israel is not celebrated. But Moses, who defied Pharaoh and renounced his own princely status and privileges for the sake of God and his covenant people, is honored by Jews, Christians, and Muslims throughout the world. Moses honored God, and God honored him. "Those who honor me I will honor" (1 Sam. 2:30).

Stephen describes Moses as one who "was educated in all the

wisdom of the Egyptians and was powerful in speech and action" (Acts 7:22). We could imagine him receiving Ph.D.s in multiple subjects, such as art, architecture, administration, military science, and theology. Just as he later chose the brilliant Saul of Tarsus to be a mighty apostle, so God chose this highly educated man to lead his people out of Egypt.

The Source of Moses' Faith

The source of Moses' faith was his parents (Heb. 11:23). Before he was born, a decree came from the king that all male Hebrew infants were to be thrown into the Nile River. Pharaoh's agents roamed throughout the country, searching for pregnant women or newborn males so that they could take the babies and dispose of them. Satan was bent on destroying Israel, but Satan cannot succeed against God's plan. If God is for his people, who can prevail against them?

Moses was an extraordinarily beautiful child. Stephen says the infant Moses was "acceptable to God" or "favored by God" (Acts 7:20). It appears that his parents were given a supernatural revelation that he would deliver Israel from Egyptian slavery. His parents, therefore, had faith that God would preserve Moses, despite the king's threats, for they knew God had a plan for their son. Faith in God overcomes all fears. If we are afraid, we are not believing. Why should we fear a mere king when the King of kings is for us?

By faith in God and his revelation, Moses' parents hid him in the house for three months after he was born. Then they placed him in the Nile River among the reeds in a basket coated with tar and pitch to make it watertight. The Holy Spirit was guiding these parents to act in faith. This is what faith is: obeying God and his clear word, not following one's own subjective ideas.

God ordained the steps of Pharaoh's daughter to come to the river at just the right time. When she saw the basket, she was intrigued and opened it. At just the right time the baby let out a cry and Pharaoh's daughter fell in love with him. She called Miriam, Moses' sister, to find a nurse for the baby. God thus ordained that Moses' own mother would be paid to take care of him until he had grown. We can imagine that Moses' parents taught him about the God of Israel and God's covenant with Israel, just as Timothy's mother and grandmother taught him to be pious (2 Tim. 1:5). When Moses was brought back to the princess, she adopted him, giving him legal rights in the palace of Egypt.

The faith of Moses' parents in God's special revelation enabled them to defy the king's decree and hide their son. They took the chance that their entire family might be killed if Moses was discovered, yet they chose to believe that God Almighty would preserve both Moses and them. These parents chose to obey God rather than the wicked Pharaoh. Thus the Hebrew Moses, by God's design, became a royal prince in Pharaoh's court. He grew up in all splendor and wisdom to eventually serve as God's deliverer of Israel.

By Faith Moses Refused

"By faith Moses, when he had grown up, refused to be known as the son of Pharaoh's daughter" (Heb. 11:24). As Moses grew up in the palace, God's Spirit was upon him. His parents had taught him the basics of the history of Israel; now God directed him to do further research. He began to learn of Abraham, Isaac, and Jacob, and of God's everlasting covenant with the people of Israel. He learned how Joseph came to Egypt and became prime minister, saving Egypt and Israel from severe famine. He learned of God's promise to Abraham to deliver Israel from Egypt and bring them back to Canaan four hundred years after going there. He learned of the specific prophecies of Jacob and Joseph concerning the deliverance from Egypt: "Then Israel said to Joseph, 'I am about to die, but God will be with you and take you back to the land of your fathers. . . . I look for your deliverance, O LORD'" (Gen. 48:21; 49:18). Later, Joseph told his brothers, "I am about to die. But God will surely come to your aid and take you up out of this land to the land he promised on oath to Abraham, Isaac and Jacob" (Gen. 50:24).

Moses discovered all of this through historical research. He was educated in all the wisdom of Egypt, and he might also have visited his family and the elders of Israel to further his studies in Israelite history. As a result of the latter, Moses placed his faith in the God of Israel and God's covenant with his people. He began to identify himself not as an Egyptian, but as an Israelite with a clear mission of delivering his people from Egyptian oppression. After he grew up and became great in stature and wisdom, he renounced his royal status—the palace life, his power, and his limitless wealth—because he had faith in the God of Israel and his plan for redeeming his people.

Was Moses foolish to say no to the Egyptian world and all its splendor? After all, was not the crown of Egypt within his reach? His action could be compared to forgoing the presidency of the United States to preach the gospel of Jesus. But Moses was like Jesus, who rejected Satan's offer of all the glories of the kingdoms of the world, choosing instead the death of the cross.

By Faith Moses Chose

By faith Moses *"chose to be mistreated along with the people of God rather than to enjoy the pleasures of sin for a short time"* (Heb. 11:25). By faith in the God of Israel and his plan for the salvation of the Israelites, Moses chose righteousness and eternal life rather than royalty, worldly power, fashion, treasures, and the fleeting pleasures of the sin of Egypt. He deliberately chose to suffer along with the people of God. He chose the way of the cross, with its danger, beatings, scorn, reproach, and privation. Instead of Egypt, Moses chose the city with foundations whose builder and maker is God.

By Faith Moses Considered

By faith Moses *"regarded disgrace for the sake of Christ as of greater value than the treasures of Egypt"* (Heb. 11:26). Faith is not a leap into the dark; rather, it thinks, considers, and reasons. Moses used his mind to make his decision. He weighed all the issues, considering all the status and pleasure he could enjoy in Egypt. Then he looked at God's final judgment, and considered God, his people, his salvation, and his Christ. Moses chose disgrace for the sake of Christ because he understood that this disgrace was of greater value than all the treasure Egypt could offer. Jesus asked, "What good will it be for a man if he gains the whole world, yet forfeits his soul?" (Matt. 16:26). May God help us to use our minds and understand what is real and abiding, and choose God's glorious plan of salvation over the pleasures of sin for a season.

Moses chose Christ and his people, his eternal life, and his treasure in heaven. In contrast, Esau chose a cup of soup; Achan chose a little silver and gold; Lot's wife chose Sodom and its nightlife; Judas chose thirty pieces of silver; Demas chose the fame, power, and wealth of this world; the rich young ruler chose his great wealth; and the Gadarenes chose their pigs. Sadly, all of these people chose to love the things of this world rather than Christ and his salvation.

The choices we make in this life are important because they determine our eternal destiny. Joseph chose to please God instead of enjoying the pleasure of fornication. Shadrach, Meshach, and Abednego chose to die rather than to worship an image of the Babylonian king. Daniel chose to pray to the true God and so was thrown into the lion's den. Jesus chose to die on the cross for our salvation rather than to obtain the glories of this world by worshiping Satan.

How do you make your decisions? What are you considering? Upon what are you fixing your eyes? Hear the call of Jesus: "Deny yourself, take up the cross, and follow me." The disciples of Jesus left all and followed him even to death. Where he leads, we must follow.

I urge you to join Moses and follow Jesus, who alone can give you eternal life. Forsake the pleasures of sin so that you can enjoy the everlasting and satisfying pleasures of God.

Reason of Faith

"He regarded disgrace for the sake of Christ as of greater value than the treasures of Egypt, because he was looking ahead to his reward" (Heb. 11:26). Why did Moses leave all and follow Christ and his people, renouncing the royalty, power, and pleasures of Egypt for the reproach of Christ and a life of suffering and scorn? Why did he leave Egypt, not fearing the wrath of the king? Moses did all these things because he was a man of faith. By faith in God and

in his revelation, he saw something infinitely greater than Egypt and all the wonders of creation. He saw God himself—the God of glory who created all things out of nothing.

The Hebrews writer says that the first reason why Moses acted as he did was *"because he was looking ahead to his reward."* In the Greek it is, "because he was continually looking upon his reward." We will not forsake Egypt unless we see something else of greater value. Moses' eyes were constantly fixed on his reward, which was his great salvation and fellowship with God. Like Abraham, Moses by faith was looking forward to the eternal city where God dwells with his people in everlasting joy.

The Greek text says that Moses looked away from the momentary allurements of this world and looked continuously to his heavenly reward of fellowship with the living God. Moses focused on the God who called out to him from the burning bush; the God whose name is "I AM WHO I AM"; the God of great power who by means of ten plagues defeated the gods of the Egyptians and drowned Pharaoh's army in the Red Sea; the God who led Israel through the wilderness by the pillars of cloud and fire; the God who spoke to Moses face to face; the God with whom Moses engaged in sweet fellowship for eighty days without eating or drinking; the God who was his sole delight and to whom he prayed, "Now show me your glory" (Exod. 33:18). We are fools if we prefer the fleeting pleasures of sin over the eternal God who is a rewarder of those who diligently seek him.

The second reason for Moses' behavior is found in Hebrews 11:27: *"He persevered because he saw him who is invisible."* In the Greek it is: "For he endured by continually seeing him who is invisible." The key to perseverance is to see God: "Anyone who comes to him must believe that he exists and that he rewards those who earnestly seek him" (Heb. 11:6). How can we be afraid if we see God, who is for us, with us, and in us? The writer earlier exhorted, "Therefore, holy brothers, who share in the heavenly calling, fix your thoughts on Jesus, the apostle and high priest whom we confess" (Heb. 3:1). We must see Jesus seated on the throne as Sovereign Lord of the universe. If we are undergoing fiery trials of temptation and affliction, we will receive inspiration and strength by looking to Jesus: "Let us fix our eyes on Jesus, the author and perfecter of our faith, who for the joy set before him endured the cross, scorning its shame, and sat down at the right hand of the throne of God. Consider him who endured such opposition from sinful men, so that you will not grow weary and lose heart" (Heb. 12:2–3).

We need to look away from the things of this world and look to the Son, who "is the radiance of God's glory and the exact representation of his being, sustaining all things by his powerful word. After he had provided purification for sins, he sat down at the right hand of the Majesty in heaven" (Heb. 1:3). Paul tells us what we should meditate upon: "Since, then, you have been raised with Christ, set your hearts on things above where Christ is seated at the right hand of God. Set your minds on things above, not on earthly things" (Col. 3:1–2).

Do you have sufferings and troubles? Look to Christ. Paul writes, "I consider that our present sufferings are not worth comparing with the glory that will be revealed in us" (Rom. 8:18). He then says, "No, in all these things we are more than conquerors through him who loved us. For I am convinced that neither death nor life . . . nor anything else in all creation, will be able to separate us from the love of God that is in Christ Jesus our Lord" (Rom. 8:37–39).

When some people cannot sleep, they get up, open their safes, and look at all their financial documents until they feel secure once again. Their wealth is their god, and they love to fix their eyes on it. But we are to look to God in all his glory, mercy, and love. Do not be like Lot and his wife, who chose Sodom (Gen. 13). Be like Abraham, to whom God appeared and said, "Lift up your eyes" (Gen. 13:14). As the hymn exhorts,

> Turn your eyes upon Jesus,
> look full in his wonderful face;
> and the things of earth will grow strangely dim
> in the light of his glory and grace.

When Stephen was being stoned, he looked up and saw heaven opened and Jesus standing at the right hand of God (Acts 7:56). This sight enabled him to endure martyrdom by stoning. Paul speaks of "a man in Christ who fourteen years ago was caught up to the third heaven . . . to paradise. He heard inexpressible things"

(2 Cor. 12:2–4). I am sure that Paul was speaking about seeing the mighty, transcendent God seated on his throne. John also writes of a joyous heavenly vision: "After this I looked, and there before me was a door standing open in heaven. And the voice I had first heard speaking to me like a trumpet said, 'Come up here, and I will show you what must take place after this.' At once I was in the Spirit and there before me was a throne in heaven with someone sitting on it" (Rev. 4:1–2).

What are you looking at? We are all looking at something. I pray we will be like Moses and look away from the things of this world and look up to God.

By Faith Moses Kept the Passover

"By faith [Moses] kept the Passover and the sprinkling of blood" (Heb. 11:28). This tells us that Moses knew that he and all of the Israelites were sinners. He knew the wages of sin is death, but he also knew that God gives eternal life by grace through the death of a fit substitute. Moses believed in the gospel of the Passover and acted on it by faith. He and his people obeyed every detail of God's instruction, applying the blood of the lamb to the sides and tops of the doorframes. As a result, the firstborn sons of Israel were saved from the destroyer who passed over their homes (Exod. 12).

Paul says, "For Christ, our Passover lamb, has been sacrificed" (1 Cor. 5:7). Through the death of Christ, our sin problem is eliminated, our guilt erased, and our hell done away with. Rejoice and be glad! We are the people of the Lamb of God who died for our sins. We have been saved from destruction and saved to serve God.

Have you believed the gospel like Moses? Have you renounced the glories of this world to follow Jesus? A man is known by the choices he makes. Have you considered and chosen Christ and his people? Have you left Egypt for the heavenly Canaan, or are you still clinging to this world? Elijah asked, "How long will you waver between two opinions? If the Lord is God, follow him; but if Baal is God, follow him" (1 Kings 18:21). We cannot afford to be undecided. What fascinates you—God or the world? Paul writes,

The Faith of Moses

Do not be yoked together with unbelievers. For what do righteousness and wickedness have in common? Or what fellowship can light have with darkness? What harmony is there between Christ and Belial? What does a believer have in common with an unbeliever? What agreement is there between the temple of God and idols? For we are the temple of the living God. As God has said: "I will live with them and walk among them, and I will be their God, and they will be my people." "Therefore come out from them and be separate, says the Lord. Touch no unclean thing and I will receive you." "I will be a Father to you, and you will be my sons and daughters, says the Lord Almighty." (2 Cor. 6:14-18)

I set before you today life and death. I beseech you to choose life. Choose Christ and his holy people, as Moses did, that we may together travel on to our eternal home, the city of the living God.

29

The "Foolishness" of Christian Faith

²⁹*By faith the people passed through the Red Sea as on dry land; but when the Egyptians tried to do so, they were drowned.* ³⁰*By faith the walls of Jericho fell, after the people had marched around them for seven days.* ³¹*By faith the prostitute Rahab, because she welcomed the spies, was not killed with those who were disobedient.*

Hebrews 11:29–31

Chapter 11 of Hebrews continues to emphasize the central importance of faith. No one can be saved except by faith, which is trust in God and his sure word. There is no effectual do-it-yourself salvation; God alone can do the impossible and save sinners. How do we get saving faith? We must hear the word of God proclaimed with authority.

But not all who hear the word of God believe it. In fact, to those who are perishing, God's wisdom is considered to be foolishness. Paul declares, "We preach Christ crucified: a stumbling block to Jews and foolishness to Gentiles" (1 Cor. 1:23). He also writes, "The man without the Spirit does not accept the things that come from the Spirit of God, for they are foolishness to him" (1 Cor. 2:14). But true foolishness is the "wisdom" of man that excludes God. Paul asks, "Where is the wise man? Where is the scholar? Where is the philosopher of this age? Has not God made foolish the wisdom of the world?" (1 Cor. 1:20). Thank God, he opened our eyes to see his wisdom and our foolishness. God granted us faith to believe in the "foolishness" of the gospel and be saved forever.

Saving faith believes continuously; it is not a one-time occurrence. The Christian life is an ongoing living by faith in God and his word and acting on that word in every new situation. Hebrews 11:29–31 speaks about the "foolishness" of the Christian faith, especially as seen in the faith of Israel in crossing the Red Sea on the way to Canaan, the faith of Israel in causing the walls of Jericho to fall, and the faith of Rahab that secured her salvation.

By Faith Israel Crossed the Red Sea

"By faith the people passed through the Red Sea as on dry land; but when the Egyptians tried to do so, they were drowned" (Heb. 11:29). Faith is not a leap in the dark or an irrational, subjective hunch. Faith rests securely in God and his propositional revelation. In Exodus 14 we discover that Pharaoh changed his mind after he let the people of Israel leave Egypt. People change their minds all the time. This is true not only of unbelievers but also of believers. They will say, "Jesus is Lord," but later change their minds. They will tell their spouses, "I will love you until death puts us apart," and then change their minds. They will join a church only to change their minds later. They will agree to bring up their children in the nurture and admonition of the Lord, and then change their minds. God, however, does not change his mind. We can rest in that truth.

Pharaoh changed his mind and pursued the departing Israelites with his chariots and his well-trained army. Now the Israelites had a serious problem. Before them was the Red Sea; behind them was the Egyptian army with its chariots. They were terrified and began to murmur against Moses.

In Exodus 14:13–14 Moses spoke to the people as God's prophet. He began, "Do not be afraid. Stand firm." The Israelites were to believe in the God who had promised to deliver them from Egypt and take them to a land flowing with milk and honey. Moses continued, "Stand firm and you will see the deliverance the Lord will bring you today. The Egyptians you see today you will never see again." When God comes, he judges those who do not believe in him and saves those who do. Finally Moses concluded, "The Lord will fight for you; you need only to be still."

The Lord himself then instructed Moses, "Tell the Israelites to go forward" (v. 15, NRSV). But how could they go forward? The

Red Sea was in front of them. Here we must note a principle: when God delivers us, he will always tell us to go forward. He never tells us to go backward because of potential enemies or obstacles. He is not ignorant of the future, like the god of open theism. It is not as if God did not know there was a Red Sea or the Amalekites or a wilderness or anticipate the problems they would face at Marah or the lack of food in the desert or how hard it would be to cross the Jordan River at flood stage.

God understands all things. Isaiah says he knows the end from the beginning (Isa. 46:10). He instructed Moses, "Raise your staff and stretch out your hand over the sea to divide the water so that the Israelites can go through the sea on dry ground" (Exod. 14:16). Through this miracle God gained glory for himself. Three times in this passage God says he will gain glory (Exod. 14:4, 17, 18). Jesus Christ gains glory for himself by salvation and by judgment; God gains glory because he triumphs in every situation. We ourselves are to the praise of his glorious grace (Eph. 1:6, 12, 14). The church is for his glory. Even hell is for his glory.

God's instruction to Moses sounds foolish. This is the offense of the gospel, which sounds foolish to natural man. How could God dry up the sea for the Israelites to go through? How could God defeat the mighty Egyptian army and its chariots? Such questions are appropriate if we are speaking about a god who is bound by nature. But our God is a God of miracles. He created the whole world out of nothing and sustains it by the word of his power. We breathe because he enables us to do so.

The God of Israel is the Creator of heaven and earth. Faith is reasonable when we realize who our God is. All enemies shall fall dead before him. Jesus said the gates of hell will not prevail against the church that he builds. All obstacles shall be removed when God moves. He delivers us from the city of destruction and leads us forward to the city of God. He defeats all of our enemies because our enemies are his enemies. Therefore, do not be afraid, but believe in our triumphant God and go forward.

And so first the angel of the Lord moved between the Egyptian army and Israel (Exod. 14:19–20). God was now between his people and their enemies. There was total darkness for the Egyptians but brilliant light for the Israelites. Then the Lord made a dry pathway for his people and they passed through the

Red Sea (Exod. 14:21–22). Oh, what security is ours in God! Our enemies cannot touch us without first defeating our God. We are in Christ and held up by his hands. Who can snatch us out of those hands? Neither death nor life nor anything else can separate us from God's everlasting love. We are in all things more than conquerors through him who loved us, who loves us, and who will love us forever.

The Egyptians were defeated and drowned; not one survived: "That day the LORD saved Israel from the hands of the Egyptians, and Israel saw the Egyptians lying dead on the shore. And when the Israelites saw the great power the LORD displayed against the Egyptians, the people feared the LORD and put their trust in him and in Moses his servant" (Exod. 14:30–31). To God be the glory, great things he has done! Let us sing unto the Lord eternal praise: he has thrown down the horse and the rider (cf. Exod. 15:1). "During the last watch of the night the LORD looked down from the pillar of fire and cloud at the Egyptian army and threw it into confusion" (Exod. 14:24). God simply looked down. In the Hebrew "threw it into confusion" can mean "took off the wheels of their chariots." The Egyptians became stuck in the mud. One look is all that was necessary to defeat God's enemies.

If you are facing obstacles, I hope you will be encouraged by this teaching. Elsewhere we read, "'Not by might nor by power, but by my Spirit,' says the LORD Almighty" (Zech. 4:6). This mountain shall be removed, the sea shall dry up, and the walls shall come down for us, because we are God's and he loves us. Go forward, then, led by the Spirit in the paths of righteousness.

God's great victory at the Red Sea is celebrated throughout the Scripture. Isaiah himself learned from this great event and declared: "When you pass through the waters, [the LORD] will be with you; and when you pass through the rivers, they will not sweep over you. When you walk through the fire, you will not be burned; the flames will not set you ablaze" (Isa. 43:2). Saints of God, let us cross all of our Red Seas by faith.

By Faith the Walls of Jericho Fell

"By faith the walls of Jericho fell, after the people had marched around them for seven days" (Heb. 11:30). The king of Jericho

The "Foolishness" of Christian Faith

heard how the God of Israel had defeated the king of Egypt forty years earlier, and more recently how he had utterly defeated the Amorite kings Sihon and Og. Yet the king of Jericho thought that he would not be defeated. As he saw the Israelites approaching, he refused to surrender and sue for peace. He was very confident that he could triumph over the God of Israel.

Jericho was the gateway city to Canaan. It had fresh water and plenty of stored food. We read in Joshua 6:1 that the city was tightly shut up. The city was impregnable and the Jerichoites were in a war mode. As Joshua was inspecting the towering walls and wondering what to do, the commander of the army of Israel appeared to him (Josh. 5:13-15). He gave Joshua instructions that would sound quite foolish to those who do not believe in God: "See, I have delivered Jericho into your hands, along with its king and its fighting men. March around the city once with all the armed men. Do this for six days. Have seven priests carry trumpets of rams' horns in front of the ark. On the seventh day, march around the city seven times, with the priests blowing the trumpets. When you hear them sound a long blast on the trumpets, have all the people give a loud shout." And here is the gospel: "Then the wall of the city will collapse and all the people will go up, every man straight in" (Josh. 6:2-5).

Let us analyze this procession. The armed guard was told to go forward first, followed by seven priests blowing rams' horns, announcing the arrival of the King of kings to fight against the king of Jericho. Then came the central feature of this march—the ark of the covenant, carried by the priests. The ark is mentioned nine times here, demonstrating its central significance: God is with us! Then the rear guard was to follow the ark. The people were to circle the city once each of the first six days. On the seventh day, they were to circle seven times, and during the seventh circling of the seventh day, the priests were to sound a trumpet blast as a signal for all the people to shout. At that point, they anticipated the walls would crumble. The people were to make no sound until the last circling of the seventh day. They were to trust in God's promise to deliver the city to them. When they shouted, the walls would come down.

This gospel sounds foolish to us. The Jerichoites probably looked out at the Israelites marching around their city and laughed at them: "Look at these fools. They are doing nothing. They have no battering rams. They are just marching around." Yet this was the wisdom of God.

By faith the Israelites strictly obeyed God's directions, and finally, on the seventh day, the trumpets sounded, the people shouted, and the walls collapsed. God is a warrior who comes as the commander of the army of Israel. He wins every battle he fights. Who are we to stand against this infinite, personal, almighty God? If we are arrogant, we shall also fall in due time as the walls did. Not even the gates of hell can prevail against him and his people.

Let me ask you: Are you with God? Then he is with you, and you shall enjoy his victory. Believe, and every wall shall fall down, and we shall go forward to victory. As David said, "With [God's] help I can advance against a troop; with my God I can scale a wall" (Ps. 18:29).

By Faith Rahab Was Saved

"By faith the prostitute Rahab, because she welcomed the spies, was not killed with those who were disobedient" (Heb. 11:31). Rahab was a Gentile woman, a prostitute of Jericho. Yet, amazingly, Rahab was saved by grace from destruction. Paul tells us, "Where sin increased, grace increased all the more" (Rom. 5:20). There is no difference between Jew and Gentile, slave or free. "Whoever believes in him shall not perish but have eternal life" (John 3:16). Jesus said to the self-righteous Pharisees, "I tell you the truth, the tax collectors and the prostitutes are entering the kingdom of God ahead of you" (Matt. 21:31).

Rahab was saved because she welcomed the two spies, hid them, and sent them away safely. She did so because she believed in the God of Israel and his saving power. Jesus said, "He who receives you receives me, and he who receives me receives the one who sent me" (Matt. 10:40). Rahab welcomed and believed.[1]

No Israelite preached the gospel to this woman. She gleaned it from the news of forty years before and from that of recent

---

1 Rahab's faith is discussed more thoroughly in *Victory in Jesus: A Feast from Joshua* by P. G. Mathew (Davis, CA: Grace and Glory Ministries, 2007), 25–36.

times—news concerning the God of Israel and his triumph over his enemies: "We have heard how the LORD dried up the water of the Red Sea for you when you came out of Egypt, and what you did to Sihon and Og. . . . When we heard of it, our hearts melted" (Josh. 2:10–11). Faith comes by hearing the gospel. Rahab heard the gospel, believed it, and confessed: "I know that the LORD has given this land to you . . . for the LORD your God is God in heaven above and on the earth below" (Josh. 2:9, 11). The people of Jericho worshiped the moon god. But Rahab now acknowledged that the God of Israel was the true God who created the heavens and the earth and who had defeated the Egyptians.

Not only did Rahab believe and confess, but she also prayed. Notice, she asked for mercy, not justice, for she recognized that she was a wicked sinner: "Now then, please swear to me by the LORD that you will show kindness to my family, because I have shown kindness to you. Give me a sure sign that you will spare the lives of my father and mother, my brothers and sisters, and all who belong to them, and that you will save us from death" (Josh. 2:12–13). Salvation is rescue from eternal damnation. Rahab's prayer was answered: "'Our lives for your lives!' the men assured her. 'If you don't tell what we are doing, we will treat you kindly and faithfully when the LORD gives us the land.'" (v. 14). Then the men told her, "This oath you made us swear will not be binding on us unless, when we enter the land, you have tied this scarlet cord in the window through which you have let us down, and unless you have brought your father and mother, your brothers and all your family into your house" (vv. 17–18).

Faith obeys, just as Rahab obeyed the instructions of the spies. If we do not obey God, we have no saving faith. She tied the scarlet cord in the window, collected all her family, and remained in her house. Right after the collapse of the walls of Jericho, Joshua ordered, "Go into the prostitute's house and bring her out and all who belong to her, in accordance with your oath to her" (Josh. 6:22). Rahab was saved by her faith.

Jesus said, "From the days of John the Baptist until now, the kingdom of heaven has been forcefully advancing, and forceful men lay hold of it" (Matt. 11:12). Do not misinterpret this verse; it means that people are saved through saving faith. But we must be persistent and bold: "Ask and it will be given to you; seek and you will find; knock and the door will be opened to you" (Matt. 7:7). In the Greek it is, "Keep on asking, keep on seeking, and keep on knocking." We must not be timid when it comes to our salvation. That is why, when blind Bartimaeus was told to be quiet, he refused and shouted all the more: "Jesus, Son of David, have mercy on me!" As a result, a miracle took place that was greater than the sun standing still: Jesus stood still. Then he asked him, "What do you want me to do for you?" "I want to see," Bartimaeus answered, and Jesus healed him (Mark 10:46–52). Another Gentile, the Syro-Phoenician woman, asked Jesus to drive a demon out of her daughter. Jesus said, "It is not right to take the children's bread and toss it to their dogs." This woman did not deny her lowly status, but said, "Even the dogs eat the crumbs that fall from their masters' table." Jesus exclaimed, "Woman, you have great faith!" and God healed her daughter (Matt. 15:21–28).

The gospel comes to nobodies like Rahab, and they believe. Paul writes,

> Brothers, think of what you were when you were called. Not many of you were wise by human standards; not many were influential; not many were of noble birth. But God chose the foolish things of the world to shame the wise; God chose the weak things of the world to shame the strong. He chose the lowly things of this world and the despised things—and the things that are not—to nullify the things that are, so that no one may boast before him. (1 Cor. 1:26–29)

All the Jerichoites had heard the gospel as Rahab had, but they refused to believe and surrender to the King of kings. But because of her faith, Rahab was not destroyed. According to Scripture, she later married Prince Salmon of Judah and became the mother of Boaz, who married Ruth and was the grandfather of David. Thus Rahab the pagan prostitute found a place in the genealogy of Jesus Christ. God honored her. This is amazing grace.

Let Us Live by Faith!

In conclusion, let us consider four points that will encourage us to live by faith:

The "Foolishness" of Christian Faith

1. As Christians, we will all face fiery trials of faith in our lives; we cannot escape them. We may be terrified at first, but we must know that God is with us in all our trials. He is before us, behind us, and around us. He is for us, he is in us, and we are in him. We can be secure in God.

2. God will fight our battles for us. He is a warrior. War is his business. That is why he says to repent, for the kingdom of God is at hand. Therefore, let the Egyptian army pursue and let the gates of Jericho be tightly shut. God will win every war and gain glory for himself.

3. When God tells us, "Go forward," every Red Sea shall be split open to make a dry path for us and every wall of Jericho shall fall. When God is with us, we shall go forward through all battles until we reach the Celestial City. Let us, therefore, trust God and fear not. All his promises will be fulfilled. Only believe, and he will raise us up on the last day.

4. God's ways are different from ours. It is good to remember this when we think a command of God sounds foolish: "'For my thoughts are not your thoughts, neither are your ways my ways,' declares the Lord. 'As the heavens are higher than the earth, so are my ways higher than your ways and my thoughts than your thoughts'" (Isa. 55:8–9). God's ways are different, but they work salvation for us. To fools, God's ways are foolishness; but to us, they are the power of God. God does not want us to lean on our own understanding, but to wholly trust in his word. We are not to go unto Hagar to produce an Ishmael and call it God's son of promise (Gen. 16). Paul writes, "The weapons we fight with are not the weapons of the world. On the contrary, they have divine power to demolish strongholds. We demolish arguments and every pretension that sets itself up against the knowledge of God, and we take captive every thought to make it obedient to Christ" (2 Cor. 10:4–5). We must acknowledge that God is not dependent on natural laws. By the "foolishness" of God, Jesus walked on water, the virgin conceived, the dead were raised up, iron axheads floated, water became wine, the sea divided and became walls of water on the right and on the left, and the walls of Jericho fell.

Therefore, brothers and sisters, take heart! He who is in us is greater than he who is in the world. Our faith in God and his word is the victory that overcomes the world.

30
By Faith We Live and Die

³²*And what more shall I say? I do not have time to tell about Gideon, Barak, Samson, Jephthah, David, Samuel and the prophets,* ³³*who through faith conquered kingdoms, administered justice, and gained what was promised; who shut the mouths of lions,* ³⁴*quenched the fury of the flames, and escaped the edge of the sword; whose weakness was turned to strength; and who became powerful in battle and routed foreign armies.* ³⁵*Women received back their dead, raised to life again. Others were tortured and refused to be released, so that they might gain a better resurrection.* ³⁶*Some faced jeers and flogging, while still others were chained and put in prison.* ³⁷*They were stoned; they were sawed in two; they were put to death by the sword. They went about in sheepskins and goatskins, destitute, persecuted and mistreated—* ³⁸*the world was not worthy of them. They wandered in deserts and mountains, and in caves and holes in the ground.* ³⁹*These were all commended for their faith, yet none of them received what had been promised.* ⁴⁰*God had planned something better for us so that only together with us would they be made perfect.*

Hebrews 11:32–40

In our study of the life of faith, we notice a seeming contradiction in Hebrews 11:32–40. Verse 34 says that by faith God's people escaped the edge of the sword, while verse 37 says that by faith some were put to death by the sword. There is, however, no contradiction. As believers, we live by faith and also die by faith. We may experience God's miraculous deliverance from troubles, or we may die without a miracle. We must fully understand that Christ's teaching includes our suffering.

This particular passage is extremely important to give balance in our lives. The thrust of much modern evangelism is that by receiving Jesus into our hearts, we can not only avoid hell and go to heaven, but we can also avoid pain and enjoy health, wealth, and power in this life. Such notions are false, and those who preach them are false teachers.

This passage reinforces the truth that in God's sovereign plan, Christians do suffer and may even become destitute and homeless. In fact, Christians are destined to suffer more than others because of their confession of Christ. Jesus said, "If the world hates you, keep in mind that it hated me first. . . . In fact, a time is coming when anyone who kills you will think he is offering a service to God" (John 15:18; 16:2). Elsewhere he warned, "Then you will be handed over to be persecuted and put to death, and you will be hated by all nations because of me" (Matt. 24:9).

I grew up believing in miracles, and I still do. But I have adjusted my thinking in the light of God's word. In God's sovereign will, he may perform miracles for us, or he may not. Jesus demands that Christians deny themselves, take up their crosses daily, and follow him. In other words, we must come and die that we may live forever. Jesus does not promise to give us trouble-free and prosperous lives here on earth. He does promise, "I give them eternal life, and they shall never perish" (John 10:28). Yet it is also true that "Everyone who wants to live a godly life in Christ Jesus will be persecuted" (2 Tim. 3:12). In reference to his own possible martyrdom, Paul writes, "I eagerly expect and hope that I will in no way be ashamed, but will have sufficient courage so that now as always Christ will be exalted in my body, whether by life or by death. For to me, to live is Christ and to die is gain. . . . I am torn between the two: I desire to depart and be with Christ, which is better by far" (Phil. 1:20–21, 23).

Hebrews 11:32–40 tells us clearly that by faith Christians live for Christ and by faith we suffer and die for Christ. The eternal life that Christ gives us is a death-conquering life. We are more than conquerors; by faith we shall overcome the world.

Faith means that we can clearly see the invisible things of God. When we do so, the present, visible world loses its charm. Through faith we are enabled to forfeit life itself, if necessary, to gain that better world to come. Faith is the response of all who are conscious of their own nothingness and weakness. Such people rely totally on God.

By Faith We Live

"And what more shall I say? I do not have time to tell about Gideon, Barak, Samson, Jephthah, David, Samuel and the prophets, who through faith conquered kingdoms, administered justice, and gained what was promised; who shut the mouths of lions, quenched the fury of the flames, and escaped the edge of the sword; whose weakness was turned to strength; and who became powerful in battle and routed foreign armies. Women received back their dead, raised to life again" (Heb. 11:32–35).

The author first gives six examples in which God's people triumphed through miracles because of their faith.

1. *Gideon.* As a vast multitude of Midianites came to swallow up the Israelites, God commissioned Gideon to defeat them. The Spirit of the Lord came upon him and God asked him to reduce the size of his army. With only three hundred men, Gideon totally defeated the Midianites (Judg. 6–7).
2. *Barak.* Although timid and fearful, Barak believed the word of the Lord that Deborah spoke and led his infantry to defeat Sisera and his 900 iron chariots (Judg. 4–5).
3. *Samson.* Despite his many flaws, Samson defeated the Philistines by faith in Yahweh and the empowerment of the Holy Spirit (Judg. 13–16).
4. *Jephthah.* Here was another flawed man. Yet the Spirit of God also came upon him and he defeated the Ammonites through his faith in the God of Israel (Judg. 11).
5. *David.* The Spirit of the Lord came upon him even while he was a teenager and enabled him to triumph over the Philistine champion Goliath (1 Sam. 17). Later, he overthrew the armies of various kingdoms, as recorded in 2 Samuel.
6. *Samuel and all the prophets.* These saints also lived by faith and prophesied fearlessly, often risking their own lives. They experienced miracles and successes in their lives through the power of the Holy Spirit.

"[These] through faith conquered kingdoms, administered justice, and gained what was promised; who shut the mouths of lions" (Heb. 11:33). The Hebrews author says these believers by faith *"conquered kingdoms,"* meaning the kingdoms of their enemies, and *"administered justice,"* which could also be translated "practiced holiness." These people lived righteous lives and administered justice as God's agents. They *"gained what was promised"* regarding

the nation and land of Israel, although they did not see the fulfillment of the promise of the Messiah in their lifetimes. They could say with Joshua, "Now I am about to go the way of all the earth. You know with all your heart and soul that not one of all the good promises the LORD your God gave you has failed. Every promise has been fulfilled; not one has failed" (Josh. 23:14). By faith some also *"shut the mouths of lions."* Because he lived by faith and prayed to God, Daniel was thrown into the lions' den. But God protected him, and so we read, "Daniel answered, 'O king, live forever! My God sent his angel, and he shut the mouths of the lions. They have not hurt me, because I was found innocent in his sight. Nor have I ever done any wrong before you, O king.' The king was overjoyed and gave orders to lift Daniel out of the den. And when Daniel was lifted from the den, no wound was found on him, because he had trusted in his God" (Dan. 6:21–23).

"[These] quenched the fury of flames, and escaped the edge of the sword; whose weakness was turned to strength; and who became powerful in battle and routed foreign armies" (Heb. 11:34). By faith some *"quenched the fury of the flames."* This refers to Shadrach, Meshach, and Abednego, who were asked to violate God's law by worshiping a ninety-foot tall golden image. Because they lived by faith in God and his word, they refused to worship the image and were thrown into a fiery furnace. Notice their declaration of faith and how God miraculously spared them:

> Shadrach, Meshach and Abednego replied to the king, "O Nebuchadnezzar, we do not need to defend ourselves before you in this matter. If we are thrown into the blazing furnace, the God we serve is able to save us from it, and he will rescue us from your hand, O king. But even if he does not, we want you to know, O king, that we will not serve your gods or worship the image of gold you have set up. . . ." So these men, wearing their robes, trousers, turbans and other clothes, were bound and thrown into the blazing furnace. . . . Then King Nebuchadnezzar leaped to his feet in amazement and asked his advisors, "Weren't there three men that we tied up and threw into the fire?" They replied, "Certainly, O king." He said, "Look! I see four men walking around in the fire, unbound and unharmed, and the fourth looks like a son of the gods." Nebuchadnezzar then approached the opening of the blazing furnace and shouted, "Shadrach, Meshach and Abednego, servants of the Most High God, come out! Come here!" So Shadrach, Meshach and Abednego came

out of the fire, and the satraps, prefects, governors and royal advisors crowded around them. They saw that the fire had not harmed their bodies, nor was a hair of their head singed; their robes were not scorched, and there was no smell of fire on them. (Dan. 3:16–18, 21, 24–27)

The Hebrews author then speaks about those who by faith *"escaped the edge of the sword"* (v. 34). First Kings 19 speaks of Elijah escaping Jezebel's sword: "Now Ahab told Jezebel everything Elijah had done and how he had killed all the prophets with the sword. So Jezebel sent a messenger to Elijah to say, 'May the gods deal with me, be it ever so severely, if by this time tomorrow I do not make your life like that of one of them'" (vv. 1–2). But Jezebel could not kill Elijah, for the Sovereign God did not want him to be killed.

Then the author says that their *"weakness was turned to strength"* (v. 34). The classic illustration is that of Samson, whose great strength left him when he sinned (Judg. 16:19). But look at his final prayer: "O Sovereign LORD, remember me. O God, please strengthen me just once more" (Judg. 16:28). God heard his prayer and Samson killed three thousand Philistines in his death. Paul tells us, "When I am weak, then I am strong" (2 Cor. 12:10). When we are at our weakest, then our faith in God makes us very strong.

Next, we learn that such people became *"powerful in battle"* by divine enablement (v. 34). This was certainly true of David, who declared, "You armed with me with strength for battle; you made my adversaries bow at my feet. You made my enemies turn their backs in flight, and I destroyed my foes" (Ps. 18:39–40).

Some *"routed foreign armies"* (v. 34). In 2 Kings 19 we read about Sennacherib coming against Hezekiah and his God. In verses 10 through 13, this Assyrian king gave reasons why Hezekiah should not trust in Yahweh. Yet it only took one angel to destroy one hundred and eighty-five thousand Assyrian soldiers. As a result, Sennacherib went back to Assyria, where he was killed.

Next we are told, *"Women received back their dead, raised to life again"* (Heb. 11:35). We read of several women experiencing this miracle: the widow of Zarephath, whose son Elijah raised from the dead (1 Kings 17:17–24); the Shunammite woman, whose son

Elisha raised (2 Kings 4:18–37); the widow of Nain, whose son was raised by Jesus (Luke 7:11–17); Mary and Martha, whose brother Lazarus was resurrected by Jesus (John 11); and the widows of Joppa, who saw Peter raise their young friend Dorcas from the dead (Acts 9:36–42).

The Hebrews author cites miracle after miracle. If we stopped here, we might tend to think that the normal Christian life is solely one of miracles.

By Faith We Suffer and Die

"Others were tortured and refused to be released, so that they might gain a better resurrection. Some faced jeers and flogging, while still others were chained and put in prison. They were stoned; they were sawed in two; they were put to death by the sword. They went about in sheepskins and goatskins, destitute, persecuted and mistreated— the world was not worthy of them. They wandered in deserts and mountains, and in caves and holes in the ground" (Heb. 11:35–38).

As we read on, however, we see that by faith believers may also be called upon to suffer and even die without any miraculous intervention by God. In verse 35 we read, *"Others were tortured and refused to be released, so that they might gain a better resurrection."* The author may be referring to the persecution of the Jewish people during the terror-filled reign of Antiochus Epiphanes IV, the Seleucid king of the second century BC. During the Maccabean war of independence, he gave Jewish believers the choice to either violate the law of God or be tortured to death. This king devised various instruments of torture, including wheels, joint dislocators, bone crushers, catapults, braziers, thumbscrews, iron claws, wedges, and branding irons. His troops tortured people by tearing out their tongues, scalping them, mutilating them, or frying them over flames.

These believers were tortured because they refused to violate God's laws. Had they taken the opportunities offered them to recant, they could have lived comfortable lives. But God's people by faith refused to become apostates. Thus, in 2 Maccabees 6 we read about a ninety-year-old Bible teacher named Eleazar who was offered an opportunity to escape death if he would eat pig's meat. Eleazar refused, and on his own accord, and in certain hope of his resurrection, he went by faith to the instrument of torture and death. In 2 Maccabees 7 we read of the torture and death of seven sons and their mother during the same persecution. Each one asserted before their deaths that the King of the universe would raise them up to an everlasting renewal of life because they were dying for his laws. The mother herself encouraged her sons with the following words: "It is the Creator of the world, who shaped the beginning of man and devised the origin of all things, who will, in his mercy, give life and breath back to you again" (v. 23). All seven sons and their mother were tortured to death, one after the other. They did so to gain a better resurrection of everlasting life, which was the hope of all Old Testament saints.

"Some faced jeers and flogging, while still others were chained and put in prison" (Heb. 11:36). Here we are told that some believers by faith experienced mocking, beatings, chains, and imprisonment. There is no mention of God miraculously intervening and putting an end to their sufferings. That is why we must call any theology unbiblical which teaches that the Christian life is a life of miracles from beginning to end. I have heard of preachers speaking against medicine even while they themselves go to the doctors for treatment. This text refutes such nonsense. There are times when God in his sovereign will does intervene. After Herod Agrippa I put James to death by the sword, he planned also to kill Peter. But God miraculously intervened and Peter was released from jail by an angel (Acts 12).

"They were stoned" (Heb. 11:37). When Zechariah, the son of Jehoiada the priest, prophesied God's truth to King Joash, the king had him stoned to death (2 Chron. 24:20–22). Or consider the story of Naboth. To help Ahab obtain Naboth's land, Jezebel came up with a plan that included having Naboth stoned to death for a false charge of blasphemy (1 Kings 21).

"They were sawed in two" (Heb. 11:37). A pseudepigraphic writing, *The Martyrdom of Isaiah*, also cited in the patristic writings, says that the wicked king Manasseh sawed Isaiah in two with a wooden sword, slowly but surely rending his person in two for preaching the kingdom of God.

"They were put to death by the sword" (Heb. 11:37). Elijah says that Jezebel put God's prophets to death by the sword (1 Kings 19:10). During the reign of King Jehoiakim, a prophet named Uriah fled

to Egypt out of fear of the king. But Jehoiakim had him brought back and killed with the sword (Jer. 26:20–23). In New Testament times John the Baptist and James were beheaded. Notice, verse 34 says that some escaped the sword, but here we read that others were put to death by the sword. Why was there no divine intervention? The Bible's answer is that death is a promotion to the very presence of God. Therefore, while some escape the sword by faith, in God's sovereign plan others will die in that same faith.

"*They went about in sheepskins and goatskins, destitute, persecuted and mistreated*" (Heb. 11:37). This describes David's plight when he was persecuted by Saul. I have seen some preachers wearing diamond rings and designer suits, fooling people by telling them that this is the way God wants them to live. That is not what this text tells us. Are you unhappy with the square footage of your house? These believers did not have a settled place to live; they lived as homeless wanderers by faith. Are you looking for health, wealth, and power in this world? Here we are told that God's people have oftentimes been poor and destitute. By faith they had no food, shelter, or medical insurance. They were afflicted, ill-treated, and tormented. In Maccabean times, following the seizure of Jerusalem by the troops of Antiochus Epiphanes IV, pious Jews fled, only to find themselves destitute and hunted down.

A. W. Pink observes, "Oftentimes the faith which *suffers* is greater than the faith that can boast an open triumph."[1] So the author interjects: "*The world was not worthy of them*" (Heb. 11:38). These people were God's gifts to the world, but the world was not worthy of them. Jesus came to his own, but his own did not receive him (John 1:11). That is the destiny of God's people. We are the light of the world, the salt of the earth, and the hope of the world. Paul says we are "known, yet regarded as unknown" (2 Cor. 6:9). We are known to God, not to the world.

These were considered outlaws, unfit to live in civilized society: "*They wandered in deserts and mountains, and in caves and holes in the ground*" (Heb. 11:38). In 1 Kings 18:13 we read that Obadiah sheltered and fed one hundred prophets of God in two caves. And Jeremiah found himself literally in a deep hole in the ground (Jer. 38:6).

---

1   Pink, *Exposition of Hebrews*, 869.

The theology of health, wealth, power, and continual miracles is false and will fail us in times of trouble. We must live by faith and also suffer by faith, in the hope of the glory of God. We did not receive Jesus to obtain power and riches in this world. Yet we have been given everything we need in Christ, particularly death-defying eternal life. By faith God may give us great victories, but by his will he may also permit us to be tortured and killed. In Acts 19 we see God performing extraordinary miracles through Paul; yet, by God's sovereign will, Paul himself experienced great suffering, as he recounts in 2 Corinthians 11:23–28.

All of these people were living by faith and all of these things were in God's will. The Bible encourages us that in all things, God works for the good—that is, the eternal salvation—of those who love him (Rom. 8:28). He has given us eternal life that death cannot destroy. For us, to die is gain and to be with the Lord. To die is to be promoted to holy communion in heaven. If we suffer with him, we shall reign with him. Whether we live or die, our objective is to glorify God in our bodies.

In the meantime, we need grace and mercy daily to persevere. It is available to us because of the propitiatory sacrifice of Christ. Our sympathetic high priest is always ready to give us mercy and grace. So may we be encouraged to "approach the throne of grace with confidence, so that we may receive mercy and find grace to help us in our time of need" (Heb. 4:16).

Let Us Live and Die by Faith

Therefore, brothers and sisters, let us approach God's throne of grace with confidence and receive grace, both to live well and to die well. Let us be encouraged by the words of the Lord: "When you pass through the waters, I will be with you; and when you pass through the rivers, they will not sweep over you. When you walk through the fire, you will not be burned; the flames will not set you ablaze" (Isa. 43:2). This does not mean we will not die, but it means we cannot lose our eternal life.

We have a sympathizing God who is with us, both when we experience miracles and when we are tortured and put to death: "In all their distress he too was distressed, and the angel of his presence saved them. In his love and mercy he redeemed them;

he lifted them up and carried them all the days of old" (Isa. 63:9). Paul writes in the same vein in Romans 8:35–39.

United with Christ, we are in God and God is in us; therefore, it is impossible for any power to harm or destroy us. Paul admonishes, "No temptation has seized you except what is common to man. And God is faithful; he will not let you be tempted beyond what you can bear. But when you are tempted, he will also provide a way out so that you can stand up under it" (1 Cor. 10:13).

Christ's suffering was unique; ours is not. God is with us always, especially in our sufferings. He will give us grace to live and grace to suffer and die. God is our shield and our very great reward. Filled with the Spirit, we therefore can live by faith and die by faith, whether we experience miracles or not. All Old Testament saints were commended and approved by God, and all were living by faith when they died (Heb. 11:13). If God commends us, nothing else matters. They all persevered, though they did not see the promised Messiah in their lifetimes, but only by faith from afar. Now Christ has come, and we, together with these saints, are perfected through his propitiatory sacrifice. Nonetheless, we have not yet received the fullness of perfection, the redemption of our bodies. By faith we also are looking forward to the day when we will receive our Spirit-engineered bodies.

Paul writes, "I consider that our present sufferings are not worth comparing with the glory that will be revealed in us" (Rom. 8:18); "We will all be changed—in a flash, in the twinkling of an eye, at the last trumpet. For the trumpet will sound, the dead will be raised imperishable, and we will be changed" (1 Cor. 15:51–52); "For the Lord himself will come down from heaven, with a loud command, with the voice of the archangel and with the trumpet call of God, and the dead in Christ will rise first. After that, we who are still alive and are left will be caught up together with them in the clouds to meet the Lord in the air. And so we will be with the Lord forever. Therefore encourage each other with these words" (1 Thess. 4:16–18). Let us, then, live by faith, looking forward to the day of our glorification.

31
Christian Endurance

¹Therefore, since we are surrounded by such a great cloud of witnesses, let us throw off everything that hinders and the sin that so easily entangles, and let us run with perseverance the race marked out for us. ²Let us fix our eyes on Jesus, the author and perfecter of our faith, who for the joy set before him endured the cross, scorning its shame, and sat down at the right hand of the throne of God. ³Consider him who endured such opposition from sinful men, so that you will not grow weary and lose heart.

Hebrews 12:1-3

The author of Hebrews compares the Christian life to a footrace, one of the five contests of the pentathlon in the ancient Pan-Hellenic games. The footrace always came first. It was a contest not so much of speed as of stamina—stamina that required discipline, commitment, and endurance. The Christian life is not a life of passive luxuriation; rather, it is a marathon that begins the moment we believe savingly in Jesus Christ and lasts until we die.

The Christian runner has a firm resolve never to drop out of the race. Despite hardship, exhaustion, and severe pain, he exerts every effort to continue in the race until he crosses the finish line. He must exert every nerve, sinew, and muscle.

In the Greek, the race is called *agōna*, from which we get the word "agony." The Christian life is, in one sense, a life of agony, a life full of stress. It is not a life of passivity but of vigorous activity. The prophet Amos says, "Woe to them that are at ease in Zion" (Amos 6:1, KJV). Jesus calls us to deny ourselves, take up the cross daily, and follow him even to death. The evangelist who promises that our troubles will be over if we believe in Jesus is not telling the truth. Listen to Paul: "Endure hardship with us like a good soldier of Christ Jesus" (2 Tim. 2:3). Jesus himself assures us, "All men will hate you because of me, but he who stands firm to the end will be saved" (Matt. 10:22).

The cheap grace of easy believism is a fraud. Christians who receive Jesus just to get things can be compared to the second soil in the parable of the sower: "The one who received the seed that fell on rocky places is the man who hears the word and at once receives it with joy. But since he has no root, he lasts only a short time. When trouble or persecution comes because of the word, he quickly falls away" (Matt. 13:20–21). Much modern evangelism produces rootless and fruitless "Christians" who fail to run the race to the finish line.

The Christian life is a spiritual race that calls for physical and spiritual fitness. Paul says, "Train yourself to be godly. For physical training is of some value, but godliness has value for all things, holding promise for both the present life and the life to come" (1 Tim. 4:7–8). The author teaches the same thing in Hebrews 12:1–3.

These verses that describe our Christian race can be divided into two headings: the motivations and the methods.

Motivations of the Christian Race: The Great Cloud of Witnesses

"Therefore, since we are surrounded by such a great cloud of witnesses, let us . . . run with perseverance the race marked out for us" (Heb. 12:1). Our first motivation comes from the "great cloud of witnesses," referring, first, to the heroes of faith listed in Hebrews 11.

The picture is of us in an amphitheater, competing as runners. Tiers of seats rise around us like a cloud, and in those seats are those who have already finished their own races of faith in God. The idea is that now they are watching us run our own race, and they are not only watching, but also encouraging us and witnessing to us, shouting out through the pages of Scripture:

"Strain every nerve, sinew, and muscle! Do not give up! Keep running! Keep your eye on the finish line! Do not be distracted by the allurements of this world. The Messiah who helped us run and finish the race will help you also." Jesus finished his race when he died on the cross, saying, "It is finished" (John 19:30). He finished so that every elect child of God can also run and finish the race. So we are exhorted not to quit or shrink back. If we do, God will not be pleased with us.

"We are surrounded by such a great cloud of witnesses." By God's grace, these saints of the Old Testament, from righteous Abel to the believers in the Maccabean era, have already successfully finished their race. They all lived by faith and were all commended for their faith by the living God. Some experienced extraordinary miracles of deliverance, while others suffered greatly. Yet they all ended their lives living by faith. Some were stoned, others were sawn asunder, beheaded, tortured, or tormented, but they all ran the race of faith and are now in the presence of God. The author later refers to them again when he says, "But you have come to Mount Zion, to the heavenly Jerusalem, the city of the living God. . . . You have come to God, the judge of all men, *to the spirits of righteous men made perfect*" (Heb. 12:22–23, italics added).

As later believers, we are encouraged not only by the Old Testament saints, but also by those of the New Testament—Stephen, James, Peter, Paul, John, and a multitude of martyrs who also ran and finished the race. All of these have joined the Old Testament saints who died in faith. The encouraging words of their testimonies in the Scripture also give us motivation. We are also encouraged by the examples of the faithful champions of church history—Luther, Calvin, Tyndale, Hus, Wesley, Whitefield, Edwards, Spurgeon, Lloyd-Jones, and thousands of God's saints who finished the race and are with the Lord now. Read their biographies and writings, and you will be greatly edified.

We are encouraged by all who have gone before us in the Christian life. The author says of leaders of the Hebrew church who apparently had already died: "Remember your leaders, who spoke the word of God to you. Consider the outcome of their way of life and imitate their faith. Jesus Christ is the same yesterday and today and forever" (Heb. 13:7–8). And, finally, we also receive encouragement from those who are still running the race. That is why we should pay attention to the exhortations of godly pastors and others. All of these constitute a cloud of witnesses to encourage us to follow Jesus and arrive at the finish line in heaven.

Notice, we are not alone as we run. We are many. Christ's church is an international body of believers, and even in a local church we are not alone. As members of Christ's body, we need one another to run this race marked out for us. We are to bless, encourage, rebuke, exhort, and love one another. So the author writes, "See to it, brothers, that none of you has a sinful, unbelieving heart that turns away from the living God. But encourage one another daily, as long as it is called Today, so that none of you may be hardened by sin's deceitfulness" (Heb. 3:12-13). We must not quit the race. He also exhorts, "Let us consider how we may spur one another on toward love and good deeds. Let us not give up meeting together, as some are in the habit of doing, but let us encourage one another—and all the more as you see the Day approaching" (Heb. 10:24-25). The Christian life is not a solo life. If it were, Jesus would not have said, "I will build my church, and the gates of Hades will not overcome it" (Matt. 16:18). The Christian life is not just Jesus and me; it is Jesus and one another. Each one is to give great encouragement to the others to persevere in the faith.

This vast cloud of witnesses also wants us to finish our race because they have a stake in it. Without us, they cannot be perfected and enjoy the fullness of salvation (Heb. 11:39-40). They are waiting for the final installment of salvation, the redemption of their bodies. "So Christ was sacrificed once to take away the sins of many people; and he will appear a second time, not to bear sin, but *to bring salvation to those who are waiting for him*" (Heb. 9:28, italics added).

Motivations of the Christian Race: Jesus Christ

"Let us fix our eyes on Jesus, the author and perfecter of our faith" (Heb. 12:2). Not only are we motivated by the great cloud of witnesses, but we are also, and primarily, motivated to finish the race by looking unto Jesus himself. The Greek word for "looking," *aphorōntes*, has both a negative and a positive meaning. It demands

that we look away from all the distractions of this world—the lust of the flesh, the lust of the eyes, the boasting of things, the worries and pleasures of this life, and the deceitfulness of riches—and look only to our reward, Jesus Christ. We are to emulate Moses, who turned away from all the allurements of Egypt and persevered in running the race of faith because he saw him who is invisible (Heb. 11:26–27).

We cannot serve two masters, God and money. James says that a double-minded man is unstable in all his ways (James 1:8). We must have eyes only for Jesus. The Lord says, "Look unto me and be saved, all the ends of the earth" (Isa. 45:22, KJV).

Stephen ran the race of faith by seeing Jesus only. He was preaching about Jesus when he was stoned for his faith. "But Stephen, full of the Holy Spirit, looked up to heaven and saw the glory of God, and Jesus standing at the right hand of God. 'Look,' he said, 'I see heaven open and the Son of Man standing at the right hand of God'" (Acts 7:55–56). What a glorious way to finish one's race!

The Hebrews writer spoke earlier of seeing Jesus: "Therefore, holy brothers, who share in the heavenly calling, fix your thoughts on Jesus, the apostle and high priest whom we confess" (Heb. 3:1).

> Turn your eyes upon Jesus,
> look full in his wonderful face,
> and the things of this earth shall grow strangely dim
> in the light of his glory and grace.

Some modern athletes seek to gain strength from performance-enhancing drugs. Christians also seek to gain strength for our race, but we do so by looking to Jesus. "Those who look to him are radiant; their faces are never covered with shame" (Ps. 34:5).

We must look to Jesus only. The author tells us that Jesus is the Son, the heir of all things, and the creator and sustainer of all things. He is the great high priest after the order of Melchizedek and the effectual propitiatory sacrifice of atonement. Superior to the angels, Moses, and Aaron, he is the Prophet, Priest, and King. He is the forerunner who arrived in heaven as a trailblazer for us. He is our older brother and the author of our salvation, the new and living way into the very presence of God.

Here we are told that he is "*the author and perfecter of our faith*" (Heb. 12:2), meaning the cause and source of our faith, as well as the one who perfects our faith. Jesus gives us faith to trust, and he is also the object of our faith. Paul writes, "He who began a good work in you will carry it on to completion until the day of Christ Jesus" (Phil. 1:6). Jesus prayed for Peter that his faith would not fail (Luke 22:32), and he prayed for us in John 17. Our faith shall not fail because he prays it will not, and the Father hears his Son's intercessory prayer. Every elect believer shall arrive where Jesus arrived already for us.

Jesus is the source of our eternal salvation (Heb. 5:9), and, having himself lived a life of faith, he is our example par excellence. His persecutors derided him for his faith: "He trusts in God. Let God rescue him now if he wants him, for he said, 'I am the Son of God'" (Matt. 27:43). Christ is not asking only us to live by faith; he himself lived that way. He always trusted in God. He always obeyed his Father, saying, "Not my will but thine be done." The Hebrews writer says, "*For the joy set before him [he] endured the cross, scorning its shame, and sat down at the right hand of the throne of God*" (Heb. 12:2).

Jesus had to run the race alone. His disciples all left him, and even his Father abandoned him. He cried out from the cross, "My God, my God, why hast thou forsaken me?" (Matt. 27:46, KJV). As one accursed by God, he endured the most ignominious death of the cross, which was reserved for the vilest criminals of the Roman empire: "And being found in appearance as a man, he humbled himself and became obedient to death—even death on a cross!" (Phil. 2:8). He endured the wrath of God that was against us and went to hell in our place. He was despised, but he endured that shame because of the joy that was set before him by his Father.

What was the joy set before Jesus? It was the joy of pleasing his Father and being restored to fellowship with him. Jesus prayed, "Father, glorify your Son. . . . I am coming to you now" (John 17:2, 13). It was the joy of accomplishing redemption for us sinners and looking forward to eternal fellowship with his church. Jesus says the reason he loves the church and gave himself for her is "that my joy may be in you and that your joy may be complete" (John 15:11). His joy is for our joy.

Let us fix our eyes on Jesus, who loved us and died for us, "the righteous for the unrighteous" (1 Pet. 3:18). Spurgeon said, "The sight of the crown removes all weight from our crosses."[1]

Let us not focus on our fear, anxiety, or depression; rather, let us look to Jesus and be transported in ecstasy to the heavenlies. Look to him who lived the life of faith, endured the life of obedience, and finished the race. Look to him in heaven, as he sits and waits for us to finish our race, knowing that we shall finish it, for he who finished his race is also with us and in us. He will help us to run our race with patience until we meet him at the finish line.

Paul spurs us to continue to run the race: "Therefore, my dear friends, as you have always obeyed—not only in my presence, but now much more in my absence—continue to work out your salvation with fear and trembling, for it is God who works in you to will and to act according to his good purpose" (Phil. 2:12–13). Our author speaks of the same idea: "May the God of peace, who through the blood of the eternal covenant brought back from the dead our Lord Jesus, that great Shepherd of the sheep, equip you with everything good for doing his will, and may he work in us what is pleasing to him, through Jesus Christ, to whom be glory for ever and ever. Amen" (Heb. 13:20–21). We will run and we will arrive at the finish line. Seeing his beaming, smiling face will be glory for us all. Heaven shall resound with joy when we meet him.

"Consider him who endured such opposition from sinful men, so that you will not grow weary and lose heart" (Heb. 12:3). The author not only urges us to fix our eyes on Jesus, but he says we can be encouraged by considering Jesus and the sufferings he endured. When we compare our sufferings with his, we discover that there is no comparison. Because Jesus suffered God's wrath, we never will. The sinless Son of God suffered and died so that he could take us to heaven.

Therefore, when we are suffering, let us consider his suffering and be encouraged. Christ endured every opposition from sinners, who called him a Samaritan, Beelzebub, demon-possessed, and a glutton. They mocked him, beat him, plucked out his beard,

---

[1] C. H. Spurgeon, *The Metropolitan Tabernacle Pulpit, Vol. 34, 1888* (Pasadena, TX: Pilgrim Press, 1988), 440.

nailed him to the cross, and thrust a spear into his side. He endured all of these trials by himself, yet he does not let us suffer alone. Jesus promises, "Surely I am with you always, even to the very end of the age" (Matt. 28:20). The Hebrews author exhorts us to keep our lives "free from the love of money and be content with what [we] have," and then he gives the reason: "because God has said, 'Never will I leave you; never will I forsake you.' So we say with confidence, 'The Lord is my helper; I will not be afraid. What can man do to me?'" (Heb. 13:5–6). Jesus assures us, "In this world you will have trouble. But take heart! I have overcome the world" (John 16:33). John declares, "The one who is in you is greater than the one who is the world" (1 John 4:4). Our faith is the victory that overcomes the world.

How to Run the Christian Race

"Therefore, since we are surrounded by such a great cloud of witnesses, let us throw off everything that hinders and the sin that so easily entangles, and let us run with perseverance the race marked out for us" (Heb. 12:1). In light of these motivations, how should we run the Christian race? First, we must *"throw off everything that hinders"* or "lay aside every weight" (KJV). The word "weight," *ogkon*, means "tumor" or "swelling." It means an excess weight around our body. We are too fat with the things of this world. We must train ourselves in godliness and become fit, ridding ourselves of everything that has no spiritual value. We must ask this question about all we do: Does this help or impede my Christian race?

The Greek runners ran almost naked. Like them, we must lose all the worldly weight that impedes our life of faith. Let us get rid of all loose garments and adornments that cause us to stumble. Identify these weights and throw them out gladly and instantly. We must do so today, as the Holy Spirit reveals them, for they only impede us.

Jesus warns, "Be careful, or your hearts will be weighed down with dissipation, drunkenness and the anxieties of life, and that day will close on you unexpectedly like a trap" (Luke 21:34). And listen to what Paul says: "But whatever was to my profit I now consider loss for the sake of Christ. What is more, I consider everything a loss compared to the surpassing greatness of knowing

Christ Jesus my Lord, for whose sake I have lost all things. I consider them rubbish, that I may gain Christ" (Phil. 3:7–8).

We must also get rid of every kind of sin that so easily entangles us. Sin always impedes our Christian race (see Eph. 4:22ff.; 1 Peter 2:1, 11). We must identify all works of the flesh and besetting sins and throw them off as Paul did when a viper attached itself to his hand (Acts 28:5). He did not tolerate it; he immediately and forcefully threw it into the fire.

When Jesus spoke about the third soil, he said that the cares of this life, the deceitfulness of riches, the lust for other things, and the pleasures of this life choked the plants, making the soil unfruitful (Matt. 13:7, 22). Therefore, let us get rid of all gluttony, greed, pride, pornography, addiction to television and the Internet, consumerism, credit buying, laziness, wicked boyfriends or girlfriends, lust for fun, and sports addictions. Let us get rid of all of these sins, that we may be fit to run the Christian race. Run light!

The author says we must *"run . . . the race marked out for us"* (Heb. 12:1). We cannot choose the race we want. Our race is chosen and prescribed by God for us. It is the race revealed in the word of God, the path of righteousness, the narrow way that leads to eternal life. It is the highway of holiness (Isa. 35:8), the way of Jesus, which is defined by our confession, "Jesus Christ is Lord."

We must *"run with perseverance"* (Heb. 12:1). We can run with endurance when we look at all those who ran before us, and we can run with patience when we think about the life of Jesus on earth, especially his trial and crucifixion. Paul says, "For I resolved to know nothing . . . except Jesus Christ and him crucified" (1 Cor. 2:2). Elsewhere, he writes, "Brothers, I do not consider myself yet to have taken hold of it. But one thing I do: Forgetting what is behind and straining toward what is ahead, I press on toward the goal to win the prize for which God has called me heavenward in Christ Jesus" (Phil. 3:13–14).

We must see Jesus as we read and meditate daily on the Scriptures, for all of Scripture speaks of him. We must see him when we pray in faith and when we come together to worship God. We must see him when we listen to the preached word, when we fellowship with the saints, and when we celebrate the Lord's

Supper. We must see him in the hour of our death, standing at the right hand of God to welcome us into heaven.

The writer concludes this passage by saying that the purpose of looking away from worldly things to see Jesus, the crucified and reigning one, is so that we "*will not grow weary and lose heart*" (Heb. 12:3). Aristotle used the words for "become weary" and "lose heart," *kamnō* and *ekluō*, in reference to the collapse of a runner *after* he has run past the goal. He must not rest *before* passing the winning post.

Are you tired? Are you weary? I urge you to look to Jesus. Isaiah exhorts:

> Do you not know? Have you not heard? The LORD is the everlasting God, the Creator of the ends of the earth. He will not grow tired or weary, and his understanding no one can fathom. He gives strength to the weary and increases the power of the weak. Even youths grow tired and weary, and young men stumble and fall; but those who hope in the LORD will renew their strength. They will soar on wings like eagles; they will run and not grow weary, they will walk and not be faint. (Isa. 40:28–31)

Jesus endured the cross for the joy set before him. There is also joy set before us, which is the prospect of living with him forever in a world without sin, death, pain, or sorrow. "Blessed are the pure in heart, for they will see God" (Matt. 5:8). In his presence there is fullness of joy, and on his right hand, pleasures forevermore. Then there will be no more bad news. With God, there is only good news for his people. The cross is the gateway to the crown of joy and righteousness. The Bible says that if we suffer with him, we shall reign with him forevermore. Let us, therefore, look to Jesus and keep on running until the race is finished and we meet the Lord, that he may say to us, "Well done, my good and faithful servant. Enter into the joy of the Lord."

32

Our Father's Discipline

⁴*In your struggle against sin, you have not yet resisted to the point of shedding your blood.* ⁵*And you have forgotten that word of encouragement that addresses you as sons: "My son, do not make light of the Lord's discipline, and do not lose heart when he rebukes you,* ⁶*because the Lord disciplines those he loves, and he punishes everyone he accepts as a son."*

⁷*Endure hardship as discipline; God is treating you as sons. For what son is not disciplined by his father?* ⁸*If you are not disciplined (and everyone undergoes discipline), then you are illegitimate children and not true sons.* ⁹*Moreover, we have all had human fathers who disciplined us and we respected them for it. How much more should we submit to the Father of our spirits and live!* ¹⁰*Our fathers disciplined us for a little while as they thought best; but God disciplines us for our good, that we may share in his holiness.* ¹¹*No discipline seems pleasant at the time, but painful. Later on, however, it produces a harvest of righteousness and peace for those who have been trained by it.*

Hebrews 12:4–11

Hebrews 12:4–11 speaks about the discipline of our heavenly Father. Modern man, loaded with money, boasts about individual freedom and hates the idea of discipline. In fact, some ministers even teach that because Jesus kept the law, we no longer have to obey or be disciplined. I suppose they could also say that it is acceptable for us now to lie, steal, commit adultery, and murder because Jesus kept the law for us. How foolish such people are!

What is God's purpose in saving us from his wrath by the sacrifice of his Son? He did not do it to make us healthy, wealthy, or famous. Paul writes, "For he chose us in him before the creation of the world *to be holy and blameless in his sight*. . . . For those God foreknew he also predestined *to be conformed to the likeness of his Son*" (Eph. 1:4; Rom. 8:29, italics added). Peter admonishes, "As obedient children, do not conform to the evil desires you had when you lived in ignorance. But just as he who called you is holy, so *be holy in all you do*; for it is written: 'Be holy, because I am holy'" (1 Pet. 1:14–16, italics added).

In Hebrews 12:14 we are told that without holiness no man can see God. This beatific vision is the ultimate covenant blessing that we as redeemed creatures will experience. God's purpose in saving us is to make us holy so that we can experience holy communion with him. This will be our everlasting happiness. As sinful people we cannot experience fellowship with the thrice-holy God. But when Jesus saves us from our sins, he makes us perfect in holiness. Justification, then, necessarily leads to sanctification. As believers, we must deal with enemies, including the devil and this wicked world, until we die. Let us examine our heavenly Father's discipline, which he uses to make his authentic children holy.

What Is Discipline?

First, we want to look at the biblical definition of discipline. The Hebrews had become weary and lazy in their minds and were revolting against maturity. They had developed the habit of not assembling together to hear God's word and worship him. They were in danger of fainting and quitting Christianity altogether because of the sufferings and persecution they were experiencing. In this passage the author explains the disciplinary nature of sufferings in order to encourage these people to persevere in their Christian lives.

This is a problem we also face. Who likes discipline in this world of great economic development and global trade? Many people think they do not need God because they have money. Even the poorest in the United States are richer than most people in the world. And not even Christian families are in the habit of disciplining their children.

But God has not abandoned his plan of making us holy and blameless. He still disciplines his children to achieve that goal.

Our Father's Discipline

Ours is not a chance universe. God ordains sufferings for his people to form holy character in them. Thus, all the pain that we experience, whether physical, psychological, or spiritual, is ordered by God for our good. Whether our suffering comes from sickness, natural disasters, persecution, poverty, death of loved ones, divorces, rebellious children, enmity in families, or even martyrdom, God is in control. He uses all these things for our everlasting profit.

Therefore, God disciplines his people through painful sufferings: *"The Lord disciplines those he loves, and he punishes everyone he accepts as a son"* (Heb. 12:6). The word *paideia* (discipline) appears about eight times in this passage. *Paideia* refers to God's teaching and training his children in his ways. It is God enforcing his teaching through rebuke, correction, and remedial punishment so that we can grow up as men and women who are loyal to his covenant. He wants us to worship and serve him only so that we will enjoy covenant blessings, not covenant curses. *Paideia* is bringing a sinful child to maturity through the necessary devices of correction, direction, instruction, and compulsion in the form of chastisement to turn him away from wandering byways into the right way.

The goal of all divine education is to produce a man who lives in obedience to the will of God. Such a man will be truly happy and prosperous. The goal of our Father's discipline is to drive out godlessness and impart godliness, to drive out foolishness and impart wisdom. Discipline, therefore, is an essential element of our relationship with God.

God disciplines us through his delegated agents, beginning in the home through the father. Paul exhorts, "Fathers, do not exasperate your children; instead, bring them up in the training and instruction of the Lord" (Eph. 6:4). The word "training" here is also *paideia*. Christian fathers are to bring up their covenant children in the discipline of the Lord. The Lord disciplines our children through us. We are to act in God's behalf. If a father fails to discipline his children to become godly, this text tells us that he essentially hates them. Such a father sins against God, the church, society, and his own family.

The Bible, especially the book of Proverbs, is filled with teaching on discipline. Let us look at a number of texts:

Muscular Christianity

1. Proverbs 13:24: "He who spares the rod hates his son, but he who loves him is careful to discipline him." The function of the rod is to drive out foolishness and impart wisdom by enforcing God's teachings.
2. Proverbs 19:18: "Discipline your son, for in that there is hope; do not be a willing party to his death." If parents do not discipline their children biblically, they are in some way responsible for their eternal damnation. This is a serious charge.
3. Proverbs 22:15: "Folly is bound up in the heart of a child, but the rod of discipline will drive it far from him." Folly means godlessness, not mere stupidity. A fool says in his heart there is no God. We are conceived in sin, born in sin, and practice sin daily. We need the expulsive power of the rod to deal with our sin.
4. Proverbs 23:13–14: "Do not withhold discipline from a child; if you punish him with the rod, he will not die. Punish him with the rod and save his soul from death." Do not be emotional or insecure about disciplining your children. How many insecure parents do not discipline their children for fear the children may cry or dislike them! But there is no greater punishment than the eternal death of a person; judicious parental discipline helps save a child from eternal death.
5. Proverbs 29:15: "The rod of correction imparts wisdom, but a child left to himself disgraces his mother." The rod drives out godlessness and imparts wisdom. When we fail to administer the Lord's discipline, our children will disgrace us.
6. Deuteronomy 6:6–7: "These commandments that I give you today are to be upon your hearts. Impress them on your children." We ourselves first have to love God and his word so much that it will be on our hearts at all times. If we do not love God's discipline, we can never impart it to our children.
7. Deuteronomy 11:18–19: "Fix these words of mine in your hearts and minds; tie them as symbols on your hands and bind them on your foreheads. Teach them to your children." Modern people have television, the Internet, video games, and so many other distractions. But what we really need is godly parents to speak to their children about God and his word.
8. 1 Kings 1:5–6: "Now Adonijah, whose mother was Haggith, put himself forward and said, 'I will be king.' So he got chariots and horses ready, with fifty men to run ahead of him. (His father had never interfered with him by asking, 'Why do you behave as you do?')" David, like Eli before him, failed to discipline his sons, and it resulted in tragedy.
9. 2 Timothy 3:16–17: "All Scripture is God-breathed and is useful for teaching, rebuking, correcting and training in righteousness, so that the man of God may be thoroughly equipped for every good work." To be thoroughly equipped for every good work simply means to fully obey God. Notice that at least half of the actions in

this verse, rebuking and correcting, can be construed negatively. Many modern Christians do not like such negativity! Such "sensitive" people would say we must always smile and never say anything negative. However, that is not what God's word says.
10. Revelation 2:20–23; 3:19–20: Though earthly fathers may not discipline their sons, God disciplines his. Note the serious statements that Christ, the head of the church, made about the church of Thyatira:

> Nevertheless, I have this against you: You tolerate that woman Jezebel, who calls herself a prophetess. By her teaching she misleads my servants into sexual immorality and the eating of food sacrificed to idols. I have given her time to repent of her immorality, but she is unwilling. So I will cast her on a bed of suffering, and I will make those who commit adultery with her suffer intensely, unless they repent of her ways. I will strike her children dead. Then all the churches will know that I am he who searches hearts and minds, and I will repay each of you according to your deeds (Rev. 2:20–23).

The risen Lord reiterated his commitment to disciplining his people when he told the church of Laodicea: "Those whom I love I rebuke and discipline. So be earnest, and repent. Here I am! I stand at the door and knock. If anyone hears my voice and opens the door, I will come in and eat with him, and he with me" (Rev. 3:19–20).

Discipline in Hebrews 12

No doubt the recipients of this epistle were familiar with the biblical view of discipline. But they were getting tired of God's discipline and weary of suffering for the gospel. To encourage them, the author spoke in the previous chapter about the heroes of the Old Testament who by faith persevered to the end, including those who died cruel deaths for their faith at the hand of their tormentors. These Hebrew Christians were to learn from them and persevere, inspired by this cloud of witnesses surrounding them. They were also told how the Son of God endured the shameful death of the cross and the opposition of sinful men, scorning all shame for the joy that was set before him. They were to fix their eyes on Jesus that they would not become weary in their Christian lives (Heb. 12:1–3).

Now the author tells them that their struggle is nothing compared with that of past martyrs and especially compared to

Jesus' death on the cross: "*In your struggle against sin, you have not yet resisted to the point of shedding your blood*" (Heb. 12:4). To say that they have *not yet* shed blood for their faith implies that such a possibility exists in the future. The author therefore admonishes these believers to grow in strength in their struggle against sin. The figure is changing: he stops speaking about a footrace and now refers to a wrestling match, another game in the Pan-Hellenic pentathlon.

Our struggle against sin is like a wrestling match. The author says we must grow strong enough to be victorious even through martyrdom. To grow in strength, we must pay attention to the Scriptures, especially God's view of discipline as stated in Proverbs 3:11–12: "My son, do not despise the Lord's discipline and do not resent his rebuke, because the Lord disciplines those he loves, as a father the son he delights in." We become spiritually weak when we are not drawing strength from the Scriptures. We can be in the church and listen to all the preaching, yet profit nothing. If we neglect the word of God, we are like a corked, empty bottle thrown into a river of clean water.

Paul writes, "For everything that was written in the past was written to teach us, so that through endurance and the encouragement of the Scriptures we might have hope" (Rom. 15:4). The Hebrews had completely forgotten God's exhortation about his fatherly discipline of his children. In Proverbs 3:11–12, God addresses his children of every generation. We are beloved children of God, but God will never spoil or indulge us.

The Hebrews, however, had forgotten this teaching. As a result, they were not receiving any comfort from the Scriptures. Those who do not hear the word grow weary and lose heart. They misinterpret their sufferings and do not profit by them.

We are warned not to forget God's benefits (Ps. 103:2). The psalmist writes, "But they soon forgot what he had done and did not wait for his counsel. . . . They forgot the God who saved them, who had done great things in Egypt" (Ps. 106:13, 21). These Hebrews forgot God and his Scriptures. We forget the Lord when we do not pay attention to his word. The reason we forget is arrogance (see Deut. 8:14).

When we forget God's teaching, we will also respond wrongly to God's discipline. There are two ways we do this. First, we

Our Father's Discipline

may despise it: "*My son, do not make light of the Lord's discipline*" (Heb. 12:5). Some people treat suffering as nothing. Have you ever heard children say after they are disciplined, "That didn't hurt," and go and misbehave again?

In *The Problem of Pain* C. S. Lewis says, "God whispers to us in our pleasures, speaks in our conscience, but shouts in our pains: it is His megaphone to rouse a deaf world."[1] I would adjust that to say sufferings are God's megaphone to rouse his deaf church. Let us heed God's wake up call: "Blessed is the man whom God corrects; so do not despise the discipline of the Almighty" (Job 5:17).

The second wrong response to God's discipline is to become depressed and say it is too heavy: "*And do not lose heart when he rebukes you*" (Heb. 12:5). We either treat discipline as nothing, or we say it is too much, that God is punishing us beyond what we can bear. We say that God is hard and uncaring. But if we give way to depression and fail to respond correctly to God's painful discipline, we will not profit from our sufferings.

What, then, is the proper response? We should rejoice when God disciplines us and draw comfort from the biblical principle: "*The Lord disciplines those he loves, and he punishes everyone he accepts as a son*" (Heb. 12:6). If we are experiencing painful discipline, we can conclude that God is our heavenly Father and we are his sons, that God loves us with an everlasting love, and that we are not illegitimate. Although they supported them financially, Roman fathers would not discipline the children of their concubines, but only the sons of the legal wife, who were being prepared to be their heirs. Only disciplined children could enjoy privileges and communion with the father.

In the same way, God does not discipline illegitimate sons. Therefore, when we are undergoing discipline, we should submit gladly to it, knowing we are true sons and that it will help us become like our Father in heaven. God's discipline qualifies us to enjoy the eternal happiness of fellowship with him. It will make us perfect, even as our heavenly Father is perfect.

Micah exhorts, "Heed the rod and the One who appointed it" (Mic. 6:9). We are not to despise or be depressed about God's rod of

---

1 C. S. Lewis, *The Problem of Pain* (New York: Collier Books, Macmillan, 1962), 93.

discipline, but to heed it. Peter says, "Humble yourselves, therefore, under God's mighty hand" (1 Pet. 5:6). That means when God disciplines us, we must humbly accept it. Paul encourages us, "No temptation has seized you except what is common to man. And God is faithful; he will not let you be tempted beyond what you can bear. But when you are tempted, he will also provide a way out so that you can stand up under it" (1 Cor. 10:13).

"Endure hardship as discipline; God is treating you as sons. For what son is not disciplined by his father?" (Heb. 12:7). May we respond to hardship correctly and draw proper conclusions from it. We do not seek sufferings, but they come, and usually when we least expect it. Yet it is through those sufferings that our Lord disciplines us. It is the Lord who "scourges" us—that is the word used in verse 6. He uses his agents—parents, pastors, teachers, bosses, magistrates, and so on—but it is the Lord himself who is disciplining us. Therefore, let us respect and submit to God's agents, and worship God for his loving discipline.

Our Father's Beneficent Discipline

The discipline of our earthly fathers and our heavenly Father benefits us greatly. It is a father's duty to teach and discipline his children in the way of the Lord so that they may grow up to make wise decisions in life. How many young people make foolish decisions! The chief end of man is to glorify God and enjoy him forever, but the ability to make decisions for the glory of God comes through discipline. It is the father's duty to impart the fear of the Lord to his children so that they become like the godly man of Psalm 1. Such children will refuse to walk, stand, or sit with evil people. Their delight will be in the law of the Lord, and on his law they will meditate day and night. They will be like trees planted by streams of water whose leaves shall not wither and who bring forth fruit in their season. Whatever they do shall prosper. That is one purpose of God's discipline.

A father is to impress the covenant law upon the hearts of his children. It is his duty to love his children and teach them God's ways so that they may become godly, and it is the children's duty to submit to their father's discipline. The Hebrews writer says, *"Our [earthly] fathers disciplined us for a little while as they thought best*" (Heb. 12:10). Our sovereign God uses imperfect agents to discipline us. The writer says that if we submit to and respect our earthly fathers, how much more ought we to submit to and respect our heavenly Father who disciplines us in perfect wisdom that we might enjoy eternal life: *"How much more should we submit to the Father of our spirits and live!"* (Heb. 12:9). The ultimate covenant blessing is eternal life.

"God disciplines us for our good, that we may share in his holiness" (Heb. 12:10). We may not always understand the eternal benefits of suffering as we go through it. Certainly, God knows that discipline is painful. But God, like a good father, is not primarily concerned about our feelings; rather, he is focused on the final outcome—"that we may share in his holiness." So that we can become holy as he is holy, he prunes us as a gardener prunes a vine. Pruning is painful to the branch but it causes the branch to produce more fruit. Our heavenly Father continuously prunes us through discipline. Therefore, do not rebel against God's pruning. We can rejoice in tribulations, knowing we shall experience an abundant harvest of righteousness, peace, and joy later on.

Consider Joseph, whose own brothers put him into a pit and sold him as a slave. From Potiphar's house, he was thrown into a prison where he stayed for many years. After all his sufferings, he came to understand God's purpose and told his brothers, "You intended to harm me, but God intended it for good" (Gen. 50:20). Paul writes, "In all things God works for the good of those who love him" (Rom. 8:28). Discipline is for a good purpose—the salvation of our souls.

I hope we will not rebel against hardship but endure it. "Without holiness no one will see the Lord" (Heb. 12:14). The benefit of holiness comes to those who are trained by discipline to endure to the end. It is a universal truth that every son is disciplined; thus, every true child of God sooner or later will undergo the Father's discipline. A believer who hates holiness is not a child of God, but a hell-bound child of the devil.

The cure for our rebellious, disobedient wandering is divinely given affliction. The psalmist writes, "Before I was afflicted I went astray, but now I obey your word. . . . It was good for me to be afflicted so that I might learn your decrees" (Ps. 119:67, 71). In Psalm 94:12–13 we read, "Blessed is the man you discipline, O

LORD, the man you teach from your law; you grant him relief from days of trouble." James writes, "Consider it pure joy, my brothers, whenever you face trials of many kinds, because you know that the testing of your faith develops perseverance. Perseverance must finish its work so that you may be mature and complete, not lacking anything. . . . Blessed is the man who perseveres under trial, because when he has stood the test, he will receive the crown of life that God has promised to those who love him" (James 1:2–4, 12).

Even the pagan Aristotle wrote, "The roots of discipline are bitter, but its fruit is sweet."[2] Thomas Aquinas declared, "Outwardly discipline holds sorrow as it is endured, but inwardly it holds sweetness because of the good end that is intended."[3] Guido De Brés, the author of the Belgic Confession of Faith, was executed for his holy faith on May 31, 1567. Just before he was executed, he wrote, "O my God, now the time has come that I must leave this life and be with you. Your will be done. I cannot escape from your hands. Even if I could, I would not do it, for it is my joy to conform to your will."[4] Martin Luther proclaimed in his hymn:

> That Word above all earthly pow'rs,
>   no thanks to them, abideth;
> the Spirit and the gifts are ours
>   through him who with us sideth.
> Let goods and kindred go, this mortal life also;
> the body they may kill: God's truth abideth still;
> his kingdom is forever.

We are God's sons, so he disciplines us that we may share in his holiness and be with him forever in eternal joy. His own Son knew no sin, but learned obedience by the things he suffered.

If you are weary in suffering, look to Jesus: "Because he himself suffered when he was tempted, he is able to help those who are being tempted" (Heb. 2:18); "Let us then approach the throne of grace with confidence, so that we may receive mercy and find grace to help us in our time of need." (Heb. 4:16). God gives us grace as we are tried, and he promises to be with us. "Therefore he

---

2   Quoted by Philip E. Hughes, *Commentary on Hebrews*, 532.
3   Ibid.
4   Kistemaker, *Exposition of the Epistle to the Hebrews*, 379.

is able to save completely those who come to God through him, because he always lives to intercede for them" (Heb. 7:25). Let us respect all God's agents who administer discipline to us for our good. Let us describe ourselves as Paul did: "Dying, and yet we live on; beaten, and yet not killed; sorrowful, yet always rejoicing; . . . having nothing, and yet possessing everything" (2 Cor. 6:9–10).

33
The Danger of Apostasy

¹²*Therefore, strengthen your feeble arms and weak knees.* ¹³*"Make level paths for your feet," so that the lame may not be disabled, but rather healed.* ¹⁴*Make every effort to live in peace with all men and to be holy; without holiness no one will see the Lord.* ¹⁵*See to it that no one misses the grace of God and that no bitter root grows up to cause trouble and defile many.* ¹⁶*See that no one is sexually immoral, or is godless like Esau, who for a single meal sold his inheritance rights as the oldest son.* ¹⁷*Afterward, as you know, when he wanted to inherit this blessing, he was rejected. He could bring about no change of mind, though he sought the blessing with tears.*

Hebrews 12:12–17

Hebrews 12:12–17 warns us about the danger of apostasy. Apostasy means to stand away from something—in this case, to stand away from God, from life, from light, from wisdom, from hope, and from all that is good. An apostate person is the most miserable person in the world. Hell is full of apostates.

In some ways we are all tempted to become apostates. Five minutes into my regular treadmill exercise, I get discouraged and want to stand away from it. But I persevere for the full forty minutes. Some married people decide after a few years that they want to stand away from marriage, and they divorce, which is a form of apostasy. Others may have jobs they want to stand away from, and they find all sorts of reasons not to go to work. That is also apostasy. Some people join churches, only to stand away from them later on. May God help us to learn from this passage how to avoid the most serious form of apostasy—standing away from God.

In our previous studies we learned that the Lord pours out wrath on those who reject his Son and the salvation he accomplished on the cross. But God does not pour his wrath out upon those who believe in his Son. Our heavenly Father does not discipline unbelievers, but he disciplines his children, that they may share in his holiness and become like him. Divine discipline is proof of our heavenly Father's love and relationship to us. Therefore we must by grace endure our Father's discipline, though it is painful for the moment. The author of Hebrews tells us that we must do so in view of the future blessings such discipline will yield in our lives.

The author has likened the Christian life to a footrace. In view of the good design of God's loving discipline, he now exhorts us to strengthen our feeble hands and palsied, paralyzed knees and run the race until we reach the finish line. This is the practical application of the doctrine of discipline.

Strengthen Your Feeble Arms and Weak Knees

"Therefore, strengthen your feeble arms and weak knees. 'Make level paths for your feet,' so that the lame may not be disabled, but rather healed" (Heb. 12:12–13). The writer's first exhortation is to strengthen ourselves. In the Greek it reads, "Straighten up the drooping hands and paralyzed knees." In Luke 6 we read that Jesus on a Sabbath day commanded a man with a shriveled hand, "Stretch out your hand" (Luke 6:10). As the man obeyed this word of the Lord, his hand was completely restored. In fact, Paul tells us that one purpose of Scripture is to correct us (2 Tim. 3:16). Many people do not like rebuke and correction. But God gives us his word for that very purpose, so that we may be straightened up from our crookedness and restored.

The believers in this Hebrew church wanted to quit before finishing the race. They were in danger of becoming apostates. Therefore, the author exhorted them, "Consider [Jesus] . . . so that you will not grow weary and lose heart" (Heb. 12:3). Then he encouraged them from the book of Proverbs, "My son, do not make light of the Lord's discipline, and do not lose heart when he rebukes you" (Heb. 12:5). Now he exhorts them, *"Strengthen your feeble arms and weak knees"* (Heb. 12:12).

This phrase is an idiom used to describe people who are about to quit a race. Eliphaz used similar language when he spoke to Job: "Think how you have instructed many, how you have strengthened feeble hands. Your words have supported those who stumbled; you have strengthened faltering knees" (Job 4:3-4). Philo used this expression also to refer to those who rebelled against Moses in the wilderness because they wanted to quit and return to Egypt. And so the Jewish believers are now exhorted to receive strength from the teaching on God's discipline found in Proverbs 3 and keep running the Christian race.

In the Greek, the word for "straighten up" is a present imperative, something God commands us to do continuously. God is commanding us to run this race every day of our lives. If we quit, we are not children of God, for the elect of God will persevere to the end. We must not become weary and faint; God will help us.

There is also the suggestion here that the strong believers must help the weak ones, that they too may finish the race. The author spoke about this earlier: "But encourage one another daily, as long as it is called Today, so that none of you may be hardened by sin's deceitfulness" (Heb. 3:13). In Hebrews 10:24-25 he also exhorts, "And let us consider how we may spur one another on toward love and good deeds. Let us not give up meeting together, as some are in the habit of doing, but let us encourage one another—and all the more as you see the Day is approaching." Paul similarly speaks of the responsibility of the strong to the weak: "We who are strong ought to bear with the failings of the weak and not to please ourselves" (Rom. 15:1). He also says, "Brothers, if someone is caught in a sin, you who are spiritual should restore him gently. But watch yourself, or you also may be tempted" (Gal. 6:1). James teaches, "My brothers, if one of you should wander from the truth and someone should bring him back, remember this: Whoever turns a sinner from the error of his way will save him from death [i.e., eternal damnation] and cover over a multitude of sins" (James 5:19-20).

After we are told to strengthen our drooping hands and weak knees, the author says to *"make level paths for your feet"*

(Heb. 12:13) As we move forward in our Christian lives, we must choose straight, level, firm paths, not crooked paths that stray to the right or to the left. Such twisted ways dislocate ankles and prevent us from running the race. That would be apostasy.

The psalmist warns, "Those who turn to crooked ways the Lord will banish with the evildoers" (Ps. 125:5). Isaiah says about the wicked, "The way of peace they do not know; there is no justice in their paths. They have turned them into crooked roads; no one who walks in them will know peace" (Isa. 59:8). Here, then, we are told to make level paths for our feet and continuously walk on these paths that lead to eternal life. We must travel all of our life on the well-traveled ancient paths—the straight and narrow way of the word of God.

The Lord spoke through Jeremiah, "Stand at the crossroads and look; ask for the ancient paths, ask where the good way is, and walk in it, and you will find rest for your souls. But you said, 'We will not walk in it'" (Jer. 6:16). We must walk in the way of a godly father's wise instruction (Prov. 4). We must walk in the Way of Holiness Isaiah speaks about (Isa. 35:8–10). Do not turn aside to the right or to the left, lest you become an apostate. Follow Jesus, who opened up for us a new and living way to the Father.

Make Every Effort to Live in Peace

"Make every effort to live in peace with all men and to be holy; without holiness no one will see the Lord" (Heb. 12:14). If we want to avoid the danger of apostasy, we must be very diligent to seek peace and live in peace, especially with members of the Christian community. Again, the author uses a present imperative.

When Paul heard that there were divisions in the Corinthian church, he urged them to agree with each other and be united in heart and mind. The reason he gave is that Christ is not divided, implying that Christ's church should not be either (1 Cor. 1:10–13). Elsewhere he directs, "If it is possible, as far as it depends on you, live at peace with everyone" (Rom. 12:18). We should not be a source of trouble in our family or in God's church. Paul also writes, "Let us therefore make every effort to do what leads to peace and to mutual edification" (Rom. 14:19).

The Danger of Apostasy

Our God is called the God of peace (Heb. 13:20), who gives peace and established peace between God and man by the cross of Christ. Sin destroys peace because it is self-seeking at the expense of the welfare of the community. But love sacrifices for the welfare of others. How can we look at the cross of Christ and not be at peace with one another! We must be filled with the Spirit, who produces in us the fruit of the Spirit known as peace. Paul exhorts, "Make every effort to keep the unity of the Spirit through the bond of peace" (Eph. 4:3). May there be peace in our families, in the church, and in ourselves. Let us do everything to enjoy peace, though not at the expense of the gospel.

Make Every Effort to Be Holy

"Make every effort . . . to be holy; without holiness no one will see the Lord" (Heb. 12:14). The Hebrews writer next admonishes us to pursue holiness in all of life. It is another continuous command. Louis Berkhof defines sanctification as "that gracious and continuous operation of the Holy Spirit, by which He delivers the justified sinner from the pollution of sin, renews his whole nature in the image of God, and enables him to perform good works."[1] In justification, God declares us righteous. In sanctification, God makes us righteous.

Unlike justification or regeneration, sanctification is a process in which we actively cooperate with God, who sanctifies us. Our sanctification will never reach perfection in this life. Yet every authentic Christian will progressively increase in holiness and become more like Jesus. Paul writes, "It is God's will that you should be sanctified: that you should avoid sexual immorality; that each of you should learn to control his own body in a way that is holy and honorable. . . . For God did not call us to be impure, but to live a holy life" (1 Thess. 4:3, 7). John states, "Everyone who has this hope in him purifies himself, just as he is pure" (1 John 3:3). Peter says the same thing: "Since everything will be destroyed in this way, what kind of people ought you to be? You ought to live holy and godly lives as you look forward to the day of God and speed its coming" (2 Pet. 3:11–12).

---

1   Louis Berkhof, *Systematic Theology* (Grand Rapids: Eerdmans, 1965), 532.

Holiness is not optional. It is the essential condition of seeing God both now and in eternity: "*Without holiness no one will see the Lord*" (Heb. 12:14). In speaking of the second coming, the Hebrews writer says, "So Christ was sacrificed once to take away the sins of many people. And he will appear a second time, not to bear sin, but to bring salvation to those who are waiting for him" (Heb. 9:28). But without holiness no one shall see God, because an unholy man is an apostate. Thus, the writer exhorts, "Let us not give up meeting together as some are in the habit of doing. But let us encourage one another, and all the more as you see the Day [of Christ's second coming] approaching" (Heb. 10:25).

God warns, "My righteous one will live by faith. And if he shrinks back, I will not be pleased with him" (Heb. 10:38). Shrinking back is becoming apostate and living an unholy life. There is no salvation for those without sanctification. Antinomians shall not see God. On that day the Lord will tell them, "I never knew you. Away from me, you evildoers!" (Matt. 7:23).

Throughout the Old Testament God commands his people, "Be ye holy, for I am holy." This same requirement of holiness is found in John's description of the new Jerusalem: "Nothing impure will ever enter it, nor will anyone who does what is shameful and deceitful, but only those whose names are written in the Lamb's book of life. . . . Blessed are those who wash their robes, that they may have the right to the tree of life and may go through the gates into the city. Outside are the dogs, those who practice magic arts, the sexually immoral, the murderers, the idolaters and everyone who loves and practices falsehood" (Rev. 21:27; 22:14–15).

Let us, therefore, make the pursuit of holiness our great quest instead of seeking the American dream of money and the happiness that money can buy. And let us never forget that holiness is inextricably linked to God's discipline; without such discipline, we will never be sanctified.

See To It That No One Misses the Grace of God

"*See to it that no one misses the grace of God and that no bitter root grows up to cause trouble and defile many*" (Heb. 12:15). Here we find an interesting Greek word, *episkopountes*, which is translated, "See to it." This is a present participle declaring that all people of God are to function as overseers. We are to run the Christian race, pursuing peace and holiness, but we are not to run alone. We are to run the race together with others who are God's dear children. There is no "Jesus and me"; it is "Jesus and us," the church, the body of Christ, the family of God. We are responsible to the rest of God's children for their peace and holiness as well as our own.

It is true that the Lord has appointed apostles, prophets, evangelists, pastors, and teachers to prepare God's people for works of service so that the body of Christ may be built up and brought to maturity (Eph. 4:11–13). We thank God for the godly shepherds he has granted to the church. The Hebrews writer exhorts us: "Obey your leaders and submit to their authority. They keep watch over you as men who must give an account. Obey them so that their work will be a joy, not a burden, for that would be of no advantage to you" (Heb. 13:17). Yet Hebrews 12:15 teaches us that each believer has a responsibility to watch over not only himself but also others; he must be an *episkopos*. In one sense, then, each person in the body of Christ is a pastor and a watchman for the welfare of the entire community. Paul also speaks of this: "Do nothing out of selfish ambition or vain conceit, but in humility consider others better than yourselves. Each of you should look not only to your own interests, but also to the interests of others" (Phil. 2:3–4).

Each person must make sure that the community is biblically healthy, that there is no division, that there is peace, and that there is no heresy or evil in the midst. Cain was wrong when he said he was not his brother's keeper. In the church, we are our brothers' keepers, and we ourselves need the pastoral care provided by others to keep us from self-deception. "There is a way that seems right to a man, but in the end it leads to death" (Prov. 14:12). How many people are self-deceived, insisting that their ways are right! But they do not know that their ways will lead to death: "There are those who curse their fathers and do not bless their mothers; those who are pure in their own eyes and yet are not cleansed of their filth" (Prov. 30:11–12).

When we sin, we need other people to insist that we get rid of that sin so that we can go to heaven. Listen to the language of Jesus as he spoke to the church of Laodicea: "You say, 'I am rich;

I have acquired wealth and do not need a thing.' But you do not realize that you are wretched, pitiful, poor, blind and naked" (Rev. 3:17).

We should not tell those who exhort us to seek holiness to leave us alone and mind their own business. As fellow members of the body of Christ and the family of God, we cannot mind our own business when it comes to our brothers' problems. Individualism may be as American as apple pie, but it is not biblical. When I have problems, I hope people will not leave me alone, but will counsel me and help me to pursue peace and holiness.

Throughout this epistle we are exhorted to see to it that not even one person fails to experience the grace of God, or becomes apostate, turning away from Jesus to Moses, from the new covenant to the old, from life to death, from reality to shadow. We must take responsibility for one another: "Therefore, since the promise of entering his rest still stands, let us be careful that none of you be found to have fallen short of it. . . . Let us, therefore, make every effort to enter that rest, so that no one will fall by following their example of disobedience. . . . We want each of you to show this same diligence to the very end, in order to make your hope sure" (Heb. 4:1, 11; 6:11). To come short of the grace of God means to come short of salvation. Paul writes, "As God's fellow workers we urge you not to receive God's grace in vain" (2 Cor. 6:1).

Without grace, we become apostates. We need more grace and, thankfully, it is available. We have the Spirit of grace, the Spirit who gives us grace (Heb. 10:29). We have the word of God's grace (Acts 20:32). We can come to the throne of grace to receive mercy and find grace for all our needs (Heb. 4:16). Hebrews 13:9 tells us, "Do not be carried away by all kinds of strange teachings. It is good for our hearts to be strengthened by grace."

We need the strength of God's grace to run the race of the Christian life. Paul said that though he was given a thorn in the flesh, God told him, "My grace is sufficient for you" (2 Cor. 12:9). God's grace comes to us in many ways to meet our every need. The means of grace include reading the word of God daily, praying daily, worshiping regularly, having fellowship with the people of God frequently, receiving the Lord's Supper often, and listening carefully to the preached word. God gives grace to the humble, that we may grow in grace and in the knowledge of Jesus Christ.

Each one, therefore, is to watch over the others, that everyone may have grace and no one will become apostate.

See To It That No Bitter Root Springs Up

"See to it that no one misses the grace of God and that no bitter root grows up to cause trouble and defile many" (Heb. 12:15). The author here quotes Deuteronomy 29:18. A bitter root refers to a false brother who lives among God's people and pretends to be a Christian. Such a person may appear to be very charming and charismatic, but his true intentions are hidden, as a root. But sooner or later the plant will spring up and reveal its true nature.

Bitter people are like Korah, who influenced many to oppose Moses. They are like the ten spies who brought an evil report and defiled many, causing many to rebel and be killed. Such people can cause great trouble in the church, destroying its peace and holiness and staining many. They spread their apostasy like a contagious disease. The fruit they bear is not good, but bitter and poisonous. They go after the idols of pleasure and wealth. Always murmuring and complaining, they are like the majority of the Israelites in the wilderness who did not enter into God's rest because of unbelief.

As shepherds of God's people, we must keep our eyes open for the bitter roots of idolaters and troublemakers, those who have no interest in peace, holiness, or the word of God. They are heretics who practice their immorality in the church itself. Paul wrote to Timothy, "Avoid godless chatter, because those who indulge in it will become more and more ungodly. Their teaching will spread like gangrene. Among them are Hymenaeus and Philetus, who have wandered away from the truth. They say that the resurrection has already taken place, and they destroy the faith of some" (2 Tim. 2:16–18).

Bitter roots also include those who indulge in sexual sin. Thus the author warns, "*See that no one is sexually immoral*" (Heb. 12:16). Paul exhorted the Corinthians: "It is actually reported that there is sexual immorality among you, and of a kind that does not occur even among pagans. . . . When you are assembled in the name of our Lord Jesus and I am with you in spirit, and the power of our Lord Jesus is present, hand this man over to Satan, so that the sinful nature may be destroyed and his spirit saved on the day of the Lord" (1 Cor. 5:1, 4–5). Then he warns, "Don't you know that a little yeast works through the whole batch of dough?" (1 Cor. 5:6). We must be ever careful and vigilant.

Today many people treat immorality and fornication casually, like eating ice cream. We find this attitude even in the church. May God raise up young people like Joseph who said, "How could I do such a wicked thing and sin against God?" (Gen. 39:9). We must flee all sexual immorality, for the day is coming on which the Lord will judge the secrets of men's hearts. Later, the author writes, "Marriage should be honored by all, and the marriage bed kept pure, for God will judge the adulterer and all the sexually immoral" (Heb. 13:4). William Barclay, a liberal theologian, states, "If a young man loses his purity or a girl her virginity, nothing can ever bring it back. The choice was made and the choice stands."[2] Young people, keep in mind that our choices have eternal consequences.

It is our job as shepherds to keep the church pure of sexual immorality. The unrepentant sexually immoral person must be put out of the church. Church discipline should be vigorously practiced, especially today, when it is deliberately neglected out of fear.

"See that no one . . . is godless like Esau, who for a single meal sold his inheritance rights as the oldest son. Afterward, as you know, when he wanted to inherit this blessing, he was rejected. He could bring about no change of mind, though he sought the blessing with tears" (Heb. 12:16–17). Finally, the writer warns us to watch out for godless people like Esau. Such bitter-root people are always in the church. They manifest themselves as irreligious, secular hedonists who live to satisfy their bodily desires rather than pleasing God. The author likens them to Esau, who rejected his firstborn rights to the covenant blessings for material gain. He compared his spiritual privileges with a cup of soup and happily made the trade.

Not only was Esau the firstborn, but he was also circumcised, which was the sign of the covenant. Nonetheless, this covenant child became an apostate. Therefore, we must keep an eye on those

---

2 Quoted by Morris, "Hebrews," in vol. 12 of *Expositor's Bible Commentary*, 140.

in the church who are hedonists and secularists. Such people are fools, for they affirm the temporal world and deny God. They are materialists who have no interest in God and his word, but live only to indulge their bodily appetites. Such hedonists despise all discipline. They seek only pleasure and avoid pain. Like Judas, they sell Jesus for thirty pieces of silver. Like Achan, they break covenant for gold and silver. Like Demas, they abandon Jesus for the good things of this present world. The rich young ruler was miserable, yet he chose his wealth instead of the eternal life Jesus came to give.

Watch out, therefore, for secularists like Esau and do not be like them. They reject God and are rejected by God. Incapable of true repentance, they are pigs who trample underfoot the pearl of the gospel. They must be put out of the church before they destroy it.

Be vigilant, brothers and sisters. Be filled with the holy Scriptures and the Holy Spirit. Do not become apostate; rather, look to Jesus, who refused the devil's offer of all the glories of the kingdoms of this world. He endured the cross for the joy that was set before him. Fix your eyes on Jesus and appreciate the benefits of your present sufferings. They produce holiness, with which you will be able to see him on that day. Straighten out your drooping hands and weak knees, and receive the grace God wants to give you. Run the race, finish the course, be holy, and you shall see the Lord!

34
New Covenant Worship

¹⁸*You have not come to a mountain that can be touched and that is burning with fire; to darkness, gloom and storm;* ¹⁹*to a trumpet blast or to such a voice speaking words that those who heard it begged that no further word be spoken to them,* ²⁰*because they could not bear what was commanded: "If even an animal touches the mountain, it must be stoned."* ²¹*The sight was so terrifying that Moses said, "I am trembling with fear."*

²²*But you have come to Mount Zion, to the heavenly Jerusalem, the city of the living God. You have come to thousands upon thousands of angels in joyful assembly,* ²³*to the church of the firstborn, whose names are written in heaven. You have come to God, the judge of all men, to the spirits of righteous men made perfect,* ²⁴*to Jesus the mediator of a new covenant, and to the sprinkled blood that speaks a better word than the blood of Abel.*

Hebrews 12:18–24

In the last verses of chapter 12 the author gives his final warning to the Hebrews. First, though, he contrasts the worship at Mount Sinai, which was pure dread, with the joyful worship at Mount Zion that is the privilege of every believer in Christ and speaks of the great blessings of new covenant worship.

The Worship of Mount Sinai

"You have not come to a mountain that can be touched and that is burning with fire; to darkness, gloom and storm; to a trumpet blast or to such a voice speaking words that those who heard it begged that

no further word be spoken to them, because they could not bear what was commanded: 'If even an animal touches the mountain, it must be stoned.' The sight was so terrifying that Moses said, 'I am trembling with fear'" (Heb. 12:18-21).

The Hebrews wanted to go back to the old covenant of Judaism, to Mount Sinai, where God gave them the Ten Commandments. They wanted to turn their backs on the better, new, eternal covenant whose mediator and guarantor is Jesus, and go back to that which was obsolete, aging, and disappearing.

Mount Sinai was designed to frighten and terrify sinners, for it pointed to the infinite holiness of the living God and the infinite sinfulness of the sons of Adam. This all-holy mountain was a fearsome sight. We are told that it quaked and burned with fire and volcanic eruptions. There was darkness, gloom, and fiery storm and the warning of the trumpet blasts. There was the piercing noise of God's words. There were no people on this mountain, only holy angels.

Mount Sinai tells us, "Stay away, you sinners. Do not come here, neither you nor your animals. Do not touch the holy mountain, lest you die. And if an animal touches the mountain, it must be stoned to death. Stay away. You are not holy!" But who can keep the Ten Commandments? Even Moses the mediator was full of fear and trembling when he approached the mountain. How could he help anyone? Moses himself was a sinner who needed a savior.

Sinai is a mountain of judgment, not justification. Therefore, we must stand away from it and cry, "Unclean! Unclean!" He who comes to Mount Sinai is under the law and under a curse. Paul tells us that Sinai stands for the ministry of condemnation and death (2 Cor. 3). There is no comfort and rest for sinners on Mount Sinai.

When the people of Israel came and stood at the foot of Sinai, they cried out in terror to Moses: "The LORD our God has shown us his glory and his majesty, and we have heard his voice from the fire. Today we have seen that a man can live even if God speaks with him. But now, why should we die? This great fire will consume us, and we will die if we hear the voice of the LORD our God any longer. For what mortal man has ever heard the voice of the living God speaking out of fire, as we have, and survived?"

(Deut. 5:24–26). Their response was similar to that of the prophet Isaiah when he saw the thrice-holy God high and lifted up: "Woe to me! . . . I am ruined! For I am a man of unclean lips, and I live among a people of unclean lips, and my eyes have seen the King, the Lord Almighty" (Isa. 6:5). The psalmist also writes of such terror: "We are consumed by your anger and terrified by your indignation. You have set our iniquities before you, our secret sins in the light of your presence. All our days pass away under your wrath; we finish our years with a moan" (Ps. 90:7–9).

Sin and guilt cause us to tremble with fear. We must have some way to get rid of our human guilt forever that we might approach God. But there is no access to God in Judaism. The people of Israel had to stand far away from the Holy of Holies. The priests also stood far away. Only the high priest could approach the Holy of Holies behind the thick veil, only once a year and only with blood.

Do we want to go back to the law and its ministry of condemnation and death? Paul says concerning the law, "Therefore, no one will be declared righteous in his sight by observing the law; rather, through the law we become conscious of sin. . . . The law brings wrath. . . . The law was added so that the trespass might increase" (Rom. 3:20; 4:15; 5:20).

There is no salvation, peace, joy, or righteousness on Mount Sinai. For these we must go to Mount Zion—not the geographical Mount Zion of Jerusalem where the temple stood, but the heavenly Mount Zion.

The Worship of Mount Zion

"But you have come to Mount Zion, to the heavenly Jerusalem, the city of the living God. You have come to thousands upon thousands of angels in joyful assembly, to the church of the firstborn, whose names are written in heaven. You have come to God, the judge of all men, to the spirits of righteous men made perfect, to Jesus the mediator of a new covenant, and to the sprinkled blood that speaks a better word than the blood of Abel" (Heb. 12:22–24). Let us now look at the worship on Mount Zion. This passage describes seven blessings for the worshipers. Mount Zion stands for the gospel of grace. It is the city of the living God, the spiritual, heavenly Jerusalem to

which Jesus Christ ascended and where he is now seated on the right hand of the throne of God.

1. WE HAVE COME TO MOUNT ZION

"But you have come to Mount Zion, to the heavenly Jerusalem, the city of the living God" (Heb. 12:22). The Hebrews writer says we have come to Mount Zion by faith in Jesus Christ. The Greek text tells us we have come permanently to the city of the living God; we shall never go back to the mountain of death. If a person returns to Judaism, it means he never truly came to Mount Zion and his name is not written in heaven. No one who is born of God will go back. John says people went out from the church because they were not of it (1 John 2:19). No true child of God will become apostate because God will keep him faithful to the end.

Yet there is no difference between the God of Mount Sinai and the God of Mount Zion. He is the same infinitely holy God. How, then, can we come to Mount Zion? The answer is that God must change us. We have a fit mediator who has solved our sin problem forever. By the grace of God, Jesus Christ tasted death for every believer. By his death he destroyed our death and made atonement for our sins. We belong to the new covenant of which Jesus is the mediator, and in this new covenant we have been given a new nature. We are new creations in a new relationship with the triune God. All our sins are forgiven and forgotten. Since we have been made holy, we can enjoy communion with a holy God.

Unlike Mount Sinai, Mount Zion invites us to come to God the Father through Jesus Christ. Jesus himself said, "Come to me, all you who are weary and burdened, and I will give you rest" (Matt. 11:28). Mount Zion is the mountain of grace, life, peace, righteousness, and joy. We are invited to feast on this heavenly mountain: "The Spirit and the bride say, 'Come!' And let him who hears say, 'Come!' Whoever is thirsty, let him come; and whoever wishes, let him take the free gift of the water of life" (Rev. 22:17). May we therefore come to worship God with confidence as royal priests, having our consciences sprinkled clean by the blood of Jesus.

The Hebrews writer repeatedly tells us to come, draw near, and approach because there is unrestricted access for believers to the Mount Zion that is above. In Hebrews 4:16 he exhorts, "Let us then approach the throne of grace with confidence, so that we may receive mercy and find grace to help us in our time of need." And in Hebrews 7:24–25 he says, "Because Jesus lives forever, he has a permanent priesthood. Therefore he is able to save completely those who come to God through him, because he always lives to intercede for them." In Hebrews 10:19–22 he admonishes, "Therefore, brothers, since we have confidence to enter the Most Holy Place by the blood of Jesus, by a new and living way opened for us through the curtain, that is, his body, and since we have a great priest over the house of God, let us draw near to God with a sincere heart in full assurance of faith, having our hearts sprinkled to cleanse us from a guilty conscience and having our bodies washed with pure water."

Now we have come to Mount Zion, and we have come forever, never to go back to the terror of Mount Sinai. We come having been cleansed, clothed in the righteousness of Jesus Christ. We have come to the city where God dwells, to the city with foundations that Abraham was looking forward to, whose builder and maker is God (Heb. 11:10). By faith we have come to an indestructible, sinless city, a harmonious society where God dwells with holy people and holy angels.

As the earthly Zion was the meeting point for the tribes of Israel, so the heavenly Zion is the meeting point for the new Israel of God. John describes it this way: "Then I looked, and there before me was the Lamb, standing on Mount Zion, and with him 144,000 who had his name and his Father's name written on their foreheads" (Rev. 14:1). Whenever God's people come together, God is in their midst. Paul writes, "When you are assembled in the name of our Lord Jesus and I am with you in spirit, and the power of our Lord Jesus is present" (1 Cor. 5:4; cf. Matt. 18:20). When we assemble for worship, we are coming by faith to the heavenly Mount Zion, the city of the living God. What a privilege is ours in Jesus Christ!

2. We Have Come to Angels

"You have come to thousands upon thousands of angels in joyful assembly" (Heb. 12:22). The heavenly Jerusalem is filled with millions of holy, elect angels who delight in worshiping and

serving God and who rejoice in God's presence when even one sinner repents.

The psalmist writes, "Praise the LORD, you his angels, you mighty ones who do his bidding, who obey his word" (Ps. 103:20). Hebrews 2:2 tells us that angels were on Mount Sinai: "For if the message spoken by angels was binding . . ." They were, however, separated from sinful Israel. Now angels and saints are united in the worship of God. Paul indicates such holy angels are present in our worship services: "For this reason, and because of the angels, the woman ought to have a sign of authority on her head" (1 Cor. 11:10).

We do not worship these angels, but we worship God together with them. John writes, "At this I fell at his feet to worship him. But he said to me, 'Do not do it! I am a fellow servant with you and with your brothers who hold to the testimony of Jesus. Worship God!'" (Rev. 19:10). He also says, "Then I looked and heard the voice of many angels, numbering thousands upon thousands, and ten thousand times ten thousand. They encircled the throne and the living creatures and the elders. In a loud voice they sang: 'Worthy is the Lamb, who was slain, to receive power and wealth and wisdom and strength and honor and glory and praise!'" (Rev. 5:11–12).

Worship is not for the purpose of self-adulation or entertainment. It is worshiping the triune God. The angels and archangels gather with us to worship God, not in gloom and depression, but with great joy.

3. WE HAVE COME TO THE CHURCH OF THE FIRSTBORN

The author says we have come *"to the church of the firstborn, whose names are written in heaven"* (Heb. 12:23). We have come to all the redeemed of the Lord whose names are recorded in the book of life from all eternity. The Greek text tells us these names are recorded permanently. What great security that gives us!

Jesus Christ is called the firstborn (Heb. 1:6), the most excellent one, which is what being firstborn means. He is the firstborn among many brothers (Rom. 8:29), the firstborn over all creation (Col. 1:15), and the firstborn from the dead (Col. 1:18). Israel is called God's firstborn (Exod. 4:22), and we also are firstborn ones with rights because we are brothers of Jesus. We are born again, born of the Spirit, born from above (John 3:3–8). Jesus the firstborn is also heir of all things (Heb. 1:2), and we are joint heirs with him (Rom. 8:17). We are rich in Christ. Paul says that Jesus became poor that we might become rich (2 Cor. 8:9). Who cares for the riches, power, and fame of this world? God is our portion. Unlike Esau, we do not despise our firstborn rights, but value spiritual blessings.

Because our names are written in heaven in the Lamb's book of life, we too come to this church of the firstborn ones when we come to worship. Paul addressed one epistle: "To the church of God in Corinth, to those sanctified in Christ Jesus and called to be holy, together with all those everywhere who call upon the name of the Lord Jesus Christ—their Lord and ours" (1 Cor. 1:2). The church is not just a thousand people here, five hundred there, and twenty somewhere else. When we come together to worship, we are in a sense joining with all who worship Christ both in this world and in heaven—a vast multitude of people, brothers and sisters who call upon the name of the Lord in spirit and in truth and whose names are recorded in the book of life.

Daniel speaks about God's people being delivered—"everyone whose name is found written in the book" (Dan. 12:1). Jesus tells us, "Do not rejoice that the spirits submit to you, but rejoice that your names are written in heaven" (Luke 10:20). Paul writes, "Yes, and I ask you, loyal yokefellow, help these women who have contended at my side in the cause of the gospel, along with Clement and the rest of my fellow workers, whose names are in the book of life" (Phil. 4:3), and in Philippians 3:20 he tells us that such people's citizenship is in heaven. John speaks much about the book of life. For example, Revelation 21:27 says of the new Jerusalem, "Nothing impure will ever enter it, nor will anyone who does what is shameful or deceitful, but only those whose names are written in the Lamb's book of life" (see also Rev. 3:5; 13:8; 17:8; 20:12–15).

4. We Have Come to God the Judge

We *"have come to God, the judge of all men"* (Heb. 12:23). There is only one living God, the Father of our Lord Jesus Christ. All who do not believe in Jesus Christ are worshiping false gods. We cannot come to the true and living God without Jesus Christ.

By faith we have come to this God who is the Judge of all people, both the living and the dead. Abraham understood that God is a righteous Judge (Gen. 18:25). Peter also speaks of this (1 Pet. 2:23), as does Paul (2 Tim. 4:8). But thanks be to God, when he judges us he will not condemn us, but will justify us because we are even now justified: "Therefore, since we have been justified through faith, we have peace with God" (Rom. 5:1). Our sins, guilt, and punishment are imputed to him and his righteousness is imputed to us: "God made him who had no sin to be sin for us, so that in him we might become the righteousness of God" (2 Cor. 5:21). The Hebrews writer tells us, "And by that will, we have been made holy through the sacrifice of the body of Jesus Christ once for all. . . . Because by one sacrifice he has made perfect forever those who are being made holy" (Heb. 10:10, 14). In Hebrews 9:28 we read, "So Christ was sacrificed once to take away the sins of many people."

Jesus saves all who come to him through faith, but he will judge all who refuse to come to him in this way. "Without faith it is impossible to please God" (Heb. 11:6). Our God is the Judge of all; therefore, he also judges and condemns all false believers. No one can escape his judgment: "The word of God is living and active. Sharper than any double-edged sword, it penetrates even to dividing soul and spirit, joints and marrow; it judges the thoughts and attitudes of the heart. Nothing in all creation is hidden from God's sight. Everything is uncovered and laid bare before the eyes of him to whom we must give account" (Heb. 4:12–13). Hebrews 10:30–31 tells us: "For we know him who said, 'It is mine to avenge; I will repay,' and again, 'The Lord will judge his people.' It is a dreadful thing to fall into the hands of the living God."

5. We Have Come to the Spirits of Just Men Made Perfect

Next, the writer says we have come *"to the spirits of righteous men made perfect"* (Heb. 12:23). When we come to worship by faith, we are joining with all the saints who lived and died in faith in the Messiah as well as with the holy angels in worship of the living God. We are joining with Abel, Abraham, Paul,

Luther, Calvin, our godly parents, and others when we come to worship.

What happens to believers when they die? Paul says that to die is to be with Christ (Phil. 1:23). He also says that to depart is to go home to the Lord (2 Cor. 5:8). John writes: "Then I heard a voice from heaven say, 'Write: Blessed are the dead who die in the Lord from now on.' 'Yes,' says the Spirit, 'they will rest from their labor, for their deeds will follow them'" (Rev. 14:13). Those who die in the Lord are righteous because they believed in the Messiah: "But my righteous one will live by faith" (Heb. 10:38). At death God perfects believers and they are now without sin. They have entered into rest; there is no more pain and sorrow. In God's presence they await their bodily resurrection. So do not weep for believers who have gone before us in death. They are rejoicing in God's presence as they worship God together with us.

6. We Have Come to Jesus

The author says that when we come to worship by the Spirit, we are coming *"to Jesus the mediator of a new covenant"* (Heb. 12:24). Having accomplished our redemption on the cross, Christ is now seated on the right hand of the throne of God. Joseph was told, "You shall call his name Jesus, for he will save his people from their sins" (Matt. 1:21, NASB). The Hebrews writer puts emphasis on Jesus and his blood.

Mount Sinai is terrifying to those who do not have such a sinless mediator. Moses himself was terrified. But no such fear is warranted on Mount Zion, for now we have a fit mediator, the sinless Son of God: "Such a high priest meets our need—one who is holy, blameless, pure, set apart from sinners, exalted above the heavens" (Heb. 7:26). "Although he was a son, he learned obedience from what he suffered and, once made perfect, he became the source of eternal salvation for all who obey him" (Heb. 5:8–9). Jesus Christ tasted death for us all. He is our atonement. He is our older brother who knows us and we know him. He is our sympathizing high priest after the order of Melchizedek. He is the mediator of the new covenant that makes us new creatures, gives us a new relationship with God, and forgives all our sins, casting them to the bottom of God's ocean of forgetfulness. It is this Jesus, on the basis of his death and resurrection, who calls us sinners to come to him and rest.

7. WE HAVE COME TO THE SPRINKLED BLOOD OF CHRIST

Finally, the author says we have come *"to the sprinkled blood that speaks a better word than the blood of Abel"* (Heb. 12:24). Hebrews 9:22 declares, "Without the shedding of blood there is no forgiveness." But the blood of the Jewish sacrificial system could not take away sins: "The law is only a shadow of the good things that are coming—not the realities themselves. For this reason it can never, by the same sacrifices repeated endlessly year after year, make perfect those who draw near to worship . . . because it is impossible for the blood of bulls and goats to take away sins. . . . Day after day every priest stands and performs his religious duties; again and again he offers the same sacrifices, which can never take away sins" (Heb. 10:1, 4, 11). Only the blood of Christ can take away our sins: "How much more, then, will the blood of Christ, who through the eternal Spirit offered himself unblemished to God, cleanse our consciences from acts that lead to death, so that we may serve the living God!" (Heb. 9:14).

Paul tells us what the blood of Jesus does for us: "In him we have redemption through his blood, the forgiveness of sins. . . . But now in Christ Jesus you who once were far away have been brought near through the blood of Christ" (Eph. 1:7; 2:13). We have been reconciled to God through the sacrifice of Christ on the cross.

Mount Sinai says, "Do not come near, you sinners! The wrath of God is upon you." But, thank God, we have another mountain, Mount Zion, the city of the living God, the heavenly Jerusalem. There Jesus and his blood speak of grace and forgiveness for us.

The dying Stephen saw heaven opened and Jesus standing at the right hand of God. Jesus also says to us, "Come and live forever. Come and rejoice. Come and rest. Your sin problem has been solved on Calvary's cross. You are forgiven and justified forever. Come and commune with God."

Christians can rejoice because God brought us to Mount Zion through Jesus Christ. He shed his blood for us and now we live by grace. We deserved death, but he gave us life. We deserved hell, but he gave us heaven. He invites us to come and fellowship.

Therefore, we join with holy angels, the church of the firstborn, the spirits of just men made perfect, and all people on earth who are calling upon the name of the Lord as we serve and worship our God in godly fear and awe.

35
A Dreadful Warning

²⁵See to it that you do not refuse him who speaks. If they did not escape when they refused him who warned them on earth, how much less will we, if we turn away from him who warns us from heaven? ²⁶At that time his voice shook the earth, but now he has promised, "Once more I will shake not only the earth but also the heavens." ²⁷The words "once more" indicate the removing of what can be shaken—that is, created things—so that what cannot be shaken may remain.

²⁸Therefore, since we are receiving a kingdom that cannot be shaken, let us be thankful, and so worship God acceptably with reverence and awe, ²⁹for our "God is a consuming fire."

Hebrews 12:25-29

Having spoken about the worship of Mount Sinai and Mount Zion, the author concludes this chapter with a dire warning to his readers. Some people think that those living in the gospel age have it easy and that it does not matter how we live; God is now nice. But the greater the light, the greater our responsibility. The writer ends this section on a sober note: *"for our 'God is a consuming fire'"* (Heb. 12:29).

We are familiar with God's severe judgments in the Old Testament. When Elijah fled to Horeb, God instructed him to anoint Hazael (1 Kings 19:15), which he did through Elisha (2 Kings 8). When Elisha began to weep, Hazael asked why, and Elisha replied, "Because I know the harm you will do to the Israelites. . . . You will set fire to their fortified places, kill their young men with the sword, dash their little children to the ground, and rip open their pregnant women" (2 Kings 8:12). By divine ordination and commission, God deliberately anointed Hazael and let these things happen to his people who were engaged in Baal worship.

There is no difference, however, between the God of the Old Testament and the God of the New Testament. God cannot change. It is foolish to think that the New Testament God will do nothing to discipline his children. Modern man has created an image of our heavenly Father as an apathetic, passive father who, like many modern fathers, does not involve himself in the affairs of his children. Such fathers fail utterly in representing God to their families. The God of the Bible is not like that.

Elisha predicted Hazael's army would rip open pregnant women and dash children to the ground. Such frightful events also took place when the Romans destroyed Jerusalem in 70 AD. Jesus himself predicted it: "They will dash you to the ground, you and the children within your walls" (Luke 19:44). Such atrocities happened in God's universe and they will happen again by his divine ordination.

Greater revelation means greater responsibility. God has spoken in the past through the prophets in part, but now he has spoken finally and fully by his Son (Heb. 1:1–3). We must not refuse him who speaks; rather, we must count it a great privilege if God is still speaking to us because a time may come when he will stop. How terrible it would be to be in the church but receive nothing because God has stopped speaking to us! About such people Jesus says, "They may be ever seeing but never perceiving, and ever hearing but never understanding; otherwise they might turn and be forgiven" (Mark 4:12). Not hearing is a divine curse. Therefore, do not refuse or reject him who speaks, because he is Almighty God. He has spoken in the past, and he speaks again now.

God speaks continually to us from the Scriptures. It is a great joy to rise early each day and read the Bible. God also speaks to us through daily family worship. Some homes are like the altar in Samaria that was in ruins until Elijah repaired it (1 Kings 18:30). We must regularly read the Scriptures and pray, or our lives will be disorderly. God also speaks to us through his Holy Spirit, his

A Dreadful Warning

appointed ministers, parents and teachers, and other brothers and sisters in the body of Christ. We can refuse him and be condemned, or believe him and be saved. Jesus said, "My word is spirit and my word is life" (John 6:63). What a privilege it is to hear the word of God by which we can cross from death to life!

God is speaking to us today from Mount Zion, the heavenly Jerusalem, inviting us to his great wedding banquet. We must pay attention and realize who is speaking. Do not create excuses for not coming: "I have just bought a field, and I must go and see it. . . . I have just bought five yoke of oxen, and I'm on my way to try them out. . . . I just got married, so I can't come" (Luke 14:18-20). Excuse after excuse is given to him who speaks good news to us from heaven. How many people are engrossed in the affairs of this world—planting, harvesting, buying, selling, marrying and giving in marriage—while their altars lie in ruins? All they seek after is fun. Soon we will find out that life is not all fun, but it will be too late.

God's wrath will be poured out upon those who refuse him. No one can escape the Judge and Sovereign Lord of the universe. Therefore, I urge you to repent and be saved now while God is still speaking in grace. At Mount Sinai he spoke, and the earth shook. But a day is coming when God will shake both the earth and the heavens. No one will escape God's final cosmic shaking.

We all have experienced some shaking in our lives. But there is a final shaking coming, and who can endure it? Those who are tempted to go back to Judaism and the comforts of this world must pay heed to this dreadful warning. We cannot escape God's cosmic shaking, which is designed to prove what is unshakable: "But the day of the Lord will come like a thief. The heavens will disappear with a roar; the elements will be destroyed by fire, and the earth and everything in it will be laid bare. Since everything will be destroyed in this way, what kind of people ought you to be? You ought to live holy and godly lives as you look forward to the day of God and speed its coming" (2 Pet. 3:10-12).

There is a great shaking coming. The Hebrews writer quotes Psalm 102: "In the beginning, O Lord, you laid the foundations of the earth, and the heavens are the work of your hands. They will perish, but you remain; they will all wear out like a garment. You will roll them up like a robe; like a garment they will be changed. But you remain the same, and your years will never end" (Heb. 1:10–12). John tells us: "The world and its desires pass away, but the man who does the will of God lives forever" (1 John 2:17). The lust of the flesh, the lust of the eyes, and the boasting of things will all go away. Paul says, "For this world in its present form is passing away" (1 Cor. 7:31). Our world looks so strong and invincible. Some say it is eternal and will remain forever. But the cosmos is a created work of God and has been made subject to futility. In time, God will shake it all and then create a new heaven and a new earth, where he will dwell with his people in righteousness.

God will wipe out everything that is marred by sin. Daniel spoke of this to Nebuchadnezzar:

> You looked, O king, and there before you stood a large statue—an enormous, dazzling statue, awesome in appearance. The head of the statue was made of pure gold, its chest and arms of silver, its belly and thighs of bronze, its legs of iron, its feet partly of iron and partly of baked clay. While you were watching, a rock was cut out, but not by human hands. It struck the statue on its feet of iron and clay and smashed them. Then the iron, the clay, the bronze, the silver and the gold were broken to pieces at the same time and became like chaff on a threshing floor in the summer. The wind swept them away without leaving a trace. But the rock that struck the statue became a huge mountain and filled the whole earth. (Dan. 2:31–35)

> In my vision at night I looked, and there before me was one like a son of man, coming with the clouds of heaven. He approached the Ancient of Days and was led into his presence. He was given authority, glory and sovereign power; all peoples, nations and men of every language worshiped him. His dominion is an everlasting dominion that will not pass away, and his kingdom is one that will never be destroyed. (Dan. 7:13–14)

In the light of this future shaking, consider the teachings of Christ:

> Therefore everyone who hears these words of mine and puts them into practice is like a wise man who built his house on the rock. The rain came down, the streams rose, and the winds blew and beat against that house; yet it did not fall, because it had its foundation on the rock. But everyone who hears these words of mine and does not put them into practice is like a foolish man who built his house on sand. The rain came down,

the streams rose, and the winds blew and beat against that house, and it fell with a great crash. (Matt. 7:24–27)

Houses built on the sand of fallen human reason and arrogance will fall with a great crash when they are shaken. It happens to families and individuals if they do not build on the principles of the kingdom of God.

Although this created world will be shaken, the kingdom of God can never be shaken. God and his holy people shall inhabit the new heaven and the new earth. Jesus says of those who trust in him, "I give them eternal life, and they shall never perish; no one can snatch them out of my hand. My Father, who has given them to me, is greater than all; no one can snatch them out of my Father's hand" (John 10:28–29). We are unshakable because we trust in Jesus Christ. The one who trusts in him shall never be dismayed (cf. Isa. 28:16; 1 Pet. 2:6). Nothing in all the world is able to shake us.

What Must We Do to Be Saved?

In light of all these things, I urge you to not despise the gospel or him who speaks it to us. Do not despise the grace of God and the blood of Jesus. Do not avoid holiness, persecution, or chastisement. We must realize that there is no refuge for us in this world. God will smoke us out of any bush or cave or hole in the ground that we think will hide us: "Then the kings of the earth, the princes, the generals, the rich, the mighty, and every slave and every free man hid in caves and among the rocks of the mountains. They called to the mountains and the rocks, 'Fall on us and hide us from the face of him who sits on the throne and from the wrath of the Lamb! For the great day of their wrath has come, and who can stand?'" (Rev. 6:15–17).

Enter through the narrow gate. Seek first the kingdom of God and his righteousness. Strive to enter the unshakable kingdom of God, which Jesus says believers are receiving even now: "Do not be afraid, little flock, for your Father has been pleased to give you the kingdom. Sell your possessions and give to the poor. Provide purses for yourselves that will not wear out, a treasure in heaven that will not be exhausted, where no thief comes near and no moth destroys. For where your treasure is, there your heart will be also" (Luke 12:32–34). Join with those to whom the King says, "Come, you who are blessed by my Father; take your inheritance, the kingdom prepared for you since the creation of the world" (Matt. 25:34). When God shakes all things, the kingdom and those in the kingdom will alone remain. Nothing in all creation will shake them.

To refuse the gospel brings greater judgment than refusing the Mosaic covenant. Therefore, the Hebrews writer warns his readers several times: "We must pay more careful attention . . . to what we have heard, so that we do not drift away. For if the message spoken by angels was binding, and every violation and disobedience received its just punishment, how shall we escape if we ignore such a great salvation?" (Heb. 2:1–3). Then he writes, "It is impossible for those who have once been enlightened, who have tasted the heavenly gift, who have shared in the Holy Spirit, who have tasted the goodness of the word of God and the powers of the coming age, if they fall away, to be brought back to repentance, because to their loss they are crucifying the Son of God all over again and subjecting him to public disgrace" (Heb. 6:4–6).

What, then, should we do? Three times the writer tells us, "Today, if you hear his voice, do not harden your hearts" (Heb. 3:7, 15; 4:7). God is speaking from heaven. We must not refuse him, but humble ourselves under his mighty hand. This is the day of grace. Soon he may stop speaking to us. We may be in the church but hear nothing. We may be at our family devotions but receive no understanding. Beyond that, we will soon die and stand before the Judge. What will be our defense? If he has spoken but we have rejected his words, we will hear the shocking and shaking words, "I never knew you. Away from me, you evildoers!" (Matt. 7:23). Jesus says of such people, "Then they will go away to eternal punishment, but the righteous to eternal life" (Matt. 25:46).

The great shaking is coming. Let us run to Christ, trust in Christ, and be found in Christ. Let us follow Christ and be safe. In Psalm 15 the writer says that the man who lives a holy life "will never be shaken" (v. 5). Elsewhere the psalmist says, "I have set the LORD always before me. Because he is at my right hand, I will not be shaken" (Ps. 16:8). Even when troubles come, we will not be shaken.

The Hebrews writer concludes, *"Therefore, since we are receiving a kingdom that cannot be shaken, let us be thankful, and so worship God acceptably with reverence and awe"* (Heb. 12:28). We worship God acceptably by doing what pleases him. The chief end of man is to glorify God and enjoy him forever. Woe unto that person who sees all things under the rubric of fun. The purpose of our lives is to find out the will of God and do it. Paul writes, "So we make it our goal to please him, whether we are at home in the body or away from it" (2 Cor. 5:9); "And find out what pleases the Lord" (Eph. 5:10); "I have received full payment and even more; I am amply supplied, now that I have received from Epaphroditus the gifts you sent. They are a fragrant offering, an acceptable sacrifice, pleasing to God" (Phil. 4:18). Real pleasure comes to us when we do the will of God. Our goal is to find out what God's will is and commit ourselves to doing it, that we may enjoy stability when everything else is shaking.

The Hebrews writer warns us not refuse him who warns us from heaven, but to be thankful by hearing and serving God all of life in reverence and awe, for *"our 'God is a consuming fire'"* (Heb. 12:29). On the Mount of Transfiguration the Father said, "This is my Son, whom I love. Listen to him!" (Mark 9:7). Jesus said, "My sheep listen to my voice; I know them, and they follow me" (John 10:27). Are you his sheep? Do you hear his voice? I pray that you will, before your day of shaking comes.

36
Brotherly Love

¹Keep on loving each other as brothers. ²Do not forget to entertain strangers, for by so doing some people have entertained angels without knowing it. ³Remember those in prison as if you were their fellow prisoners, and those who are mistreated as if you yourselves were suffering.

Hebrews 13:1–3

This last chapter of Hebrews has an epistolary ending, exhorting the readers to apply what the author has been teaching. If we want blessing, we must not only *hear* but also *do* the word of God. Jesus spoke about people hearing yet not hearing, and seeing yet not seeing, lest they turn and be healed (Matt. 13:13–15). If we are under the power of the Holy Spirit, we will carefully hear and apply what God speaks to us.

In the previous chapter we were told that because these Hebrew believers were receiving an unshakable kingdom, they were to "be thankful, and so worship God acceptably with reverence and awe" (Heb. 12:28). They were to make every effort to pursue peace with all men and to be holy.

God wants his people to be holy. I once heard a woman on the radio say that while Judaism has a moral code, Christianity does not—because Jesus died on the cross we only need to believe to be saved. Sadly, many people who say they believe the Bible would agree. Some even say that because Jesus kept all God's laws, we do not have to keep any. But the Bible tells us, "Without holiness no one will see the Lord" (Heb. 12:14).

By grace the Hebrews had come, not to the terrifying Mount Sinai, but to Mount Zion, the city of the living God; to Jesus, the mediator of the new covenant; and to his sprinkled blood that justifies us, forgives all our sins, cleanses our consciences, and makes us able to draw near to God with great confidence. God enabled them to draw near to him as priests to offer acceptable sacrifices, which include a lifestyle that pleases God, for true worship is not just what we do on Sunday morning for an hour or two. True worship is living our whole life in a way that is pleasing to God. We are to offer our bodies as living sacrifices, holy and pleasing to God (Rom. 12:1), and glorify God in our bodies because we have been bought with a price, the blood of Christ (1 Cor. 6:19–20).

This chapter is filled with commands for believers. In the Greek these imperatives are in the present tense, meaning we must keep on doing them. In this study we will consider the first three commands: to live in brotherly love (*philadelphia*), showing our love in deeds to our local community; to demonstrate a love for strangers (*philoxenia*), especially believers who come to us from afar; and to love prisoners (*philodesmia*), God's people who are in prison because of Christ.

Philadelphia: Brotherly Love

"Keep on loving each other as brothers" (Heb. 13:1). Loving our brothers is not merely a New Testament idea; it is also found throughout the Old Testament. In Leviticus 19:18 we read, "Do not seek revenge or bear a grudge against one of your people, but love your neighbor as yourself. I am the LORD." In this context, neighbor means one of God's people. Only those who receive God's grace—only true believers—can love one another.

We are asked here, "Let brotherly love continue" (KJV). Brotherly love necessarily exists in a believing community because it is a fruit of the Spirit. We love one another because we belong to the family of God: God is our Father and Jesus Christ is our older brother. In Hebrews 2 we are told that we are brothers of our Lord and Savior Jesus Christ: "Both the one who makes men holy and those who are made holy are of the same family. So Jesus is not ashamed to call them brothers" (Heb. 2:11). Hebrews 3:6 tells us

Brotherly Love

we belong to the same family: "But Christ is faithful as a son over God's house. And we are his house, if we hold on to our courage and the hope of which we boast." Jesus himself says that God is our Father and we are all brothers (Matt. 23:8–9). The Hebrews writer calls us "holy brothers" (Heb. 3:1). As believers, we are filled with the Holy Spirit; therefore, we are *holy* brothers and sisters.

This love we are to have for all people is a gift of God; it is not self-generated. God has poured out his love into our hearts by the Holy Spirit in abundance that we may love God, love our brothers, and love even our enemies (Rom. 5:5). It is the love God demonstrated in sending his Son into the world to die on the cross for us and the love Christ showed for the church by giving himself up for her (John 3:16; Eph. 5:25). The Holy Spirit fills our hearts with this divine, sacrificial, abundant love so that we may love God and others, not only in word, but also through sacrificial deeds.

In light of God having sent his Son to die on the cross in our place, John writes, "Dear friends, since God so loved us, we also ought to love one another. No one has ever seen God; but if we love one another, God lives in us and his love is made complete in us" (1 John 4:11–12). Therefore, this *philadelphia* is not an option, but an obligation, albeit a delightful one, for believers. This is the new commandment Jesus gave to his disciples (John 13:34–35). It is the manifestation of this brotherly love that causes the world to recognize us as Christians. John also says it is the proof that we have passed from eternal death to eternal life (1 John 3:14).

We are to love one another, not according to our subjective standards, but according to God's objective standard. Jesus tells us, "As I have loved you, so you must love one another" (John 13:34). John says, "This is how we know what love is: Jesus Christ laid down his life for us. And we ought to lay down our lives for our brothers. If anyone has material possessions and sees his brother in need but has no pity on him, how can the love of God be in him? Dear children, let us not love with words or tongue but with actions and in truth" (1 John 3:16–18).

We must lay down our lives—our time, our money, our talents—for our brothers. The early church practiced such love spontaneously by the Spirit's direction: "All the believers were together and had everything in common. Selling their possessions and goods, they gave to anyone as he had need. . . . All the believers were one in heart and mind. No one claimed that any of his possessions was his own, but they shared everything they had. . . . There were no needy persons among them. For from time to time those who owned lands or houses sold them, brought the money from the sales and put it at the apostles' feet, and it was distributed to anyone as he had need" (Acts 2:44–45; 4:32–35). Such unity exists because of *philadelphia*.

God delights when his people love one another and live in unity. The psalmist exclaims, "How good and pleasant it is when brothers live together in unity! . . . For there the Lord bestows his blessing, even life forevermore" (Ps. 133:1, 3). There God presides to bless, save, heal, comfort, and teach his people.

Sinners, however, are self-centered, incapable of truly loving others sacrificially. Paul tells us the nature of all unbelievers: "At one time we too were foolish, disobedient, deceived and enslaved by all kinds of passions and pleasures. We lived in malice and envy, being hated and hating one another" (Titus 3:3). Unbelievers are hateful by nature and so they hate others. And, sadly, a backslidden believer is like an unbeliever. We read about such people in Proverbs 30:15: "The leech has two daughters. They cry, 'Gimme! Gimme!'" (author's paraphrase). Unbelievers and backsliders can be likened to black holes that swallow up everything near them. They are always miserable and depressed. They live in wintertime. There is no sunshine in them and they drain the energy of those who are around them.

Jesus warned about such lack of love in the church: "Because of the increase of wickedness, the love of most will grow cold" (Matt. 24:12). Self-centeredness is sin. A selfish person loves only himself; he cannot love anyone else. Jesus rebuked the church of Ephesus: "Yet I hold this against you: You have forsaken your first love," meaning love toward God and God's people. They had fallen from the height of their first love, and the resurrected Lord was warning them that they must remember from where they had fallen, repent, and come back to their first love, lest they experience his divine judgment (Rev. 2:4–5). Christ had no criticism for the church of Philadelphia, however, because its members kept his word and commandments. The church of Philadelphia was approved by the Lord, the head of the church (Rev. 3:7–13).

Brotherly Love

The church of the Hebrews had manifested brotherly love in the past: "God is not unjust; he will not forget your work and the love you have shown him as you have helped his people and continue to help them" (Heb. 6:10). But in Hebrews 10 the author has to exhort them to remember their prior works, an indication that their first love had cooled:

> Remember those earlier days after you had received the light, when you stood your ground in a great contest in the face of suffering. Sometimes you were publicly exposed to insult and persecution; at other times you stood side by side with those who were so treated. You sympathized with those in prison and joyfully accepted the confiscation of your property, because you knew that you yourselves had better and lasting possessions [the unshakable kingdom of God]. (Heb. 10:32–34)

The author, then, has diagnosed a problem in the Hebrew church—a lack of brotherly love. Earlier he wrote, "Let us consider how we may spur one another on toward love and good deeds. Let us not give up meeting together, as some are in the habit of doing, but let us encourage one another—and all the more as you see the Day approaching" (Heb. 10:24–25). Because of a certain lessening of first love, a coldness had entered the church. And so the author now commands, "Let *philadelphia* continue."

Some of these believers were not in the habit of assembling together. Yet how can we love one another when we do not get together? When we come together, we get to know the needs of others so that we may respond to them. If we love, we will come together. When people do not go to church, it is due to a lack of love for God and his people. Love always seeks the presence of the beloved.

The church of the Hebrews was urged to do everything to promote brotherly love. They were to strive to maintain the love and unity of the Spirit. They did not create it, but they had to maintain it. Calvin said that "nothing evaporates more easily than love when everyone looks after himself more than his wife and gives less consideration to others."[1]

---

[1] John Calvin, *The Epistle of Paul to the Hebrews and the First and Second Epistles of St. Peter*, trans. William B. Johnston, ed. David W. Torrance and Thomas F. Torrance (Grand Rapids: Eerdmans, 1994), 204.

As a young boy, I saw true brotherly love manifested in our church in South India. When the Holy Spirit was poured out, all racial and class distinctions disappeared. All were seen as members of the same family. There is nothing more beautiful than Christians loving one another sacrificially.

We also practice such brotherly love every day in the church that I pastor. Let me give one illustration: Recently the Holy Spirit directed a white mother of three children to give one of her kidneys to a young black brother. This young man, who was about to die, now lives and thrives because of the love of God practiced in the church. Brotherly love transcends race, nationality, color, sex, or rank because we all are brothers and sisters, an international group of people belonging to the one family of God, redeemed by the same blood of Jesus Christ. This brotherly love is shown to and through all true people of God, for God's church is local as well as universal.

Paul says we are to consider others better than ourselves (Phil. 2:3-4) and honor one another above ourselves (Rom. 12:10). To the Thessalonian church he wrote, "Now about brotherly love we do not need to write to you, for you yourselves have been taught by God to love each other. And in fact, you do love all the brothers throughout Macedonia. Yet we urge you, brothers, to do so more and more" (1 Thess. 4:9-10). This is the nature of the new covenant. The Holy Spirit teaches us to love one another. Where the Spirit of God is, there is love and unity. If there is no brotherly love in a church, it has ceased being a church of Jesus Christ and has become a synagogue of Satan.

Philoxenia: Love of Strangers

Next, the author exhorts, *"Do not forget to entertain strangers, for by so doing some people have entertained angels without knowing it"* (Heb. 13:2). "Strangers" especially refers to believers visiting us from far places.

Abraham was a stranger in a strange land (Heb. 11:13). Yet we see his love for strangers in Genesis 18. Notice, he invited the three visitors even before they sought any help:

Brotherly Love

> Abraham looked up and saw three men standing nearby. When he saw them, he hurried from the entrance of his tent to meet them and bowed low to the ground. He said, "If I have found favor in your eyes, my lord, do not pass your servant by. Let a little water be brought, and then you may all wash your feet and rest under this tree. Let me get you something to eat, so that you can be refreshed and then go on your way—now that you have come to your servant." (Gen. 18:2-5)

Abraham gave these strangers lodging, food, fellowship, water, milk, bread, curds, and meat. While they ate, he stood and served them. He did not know two were angels and one was the Son of God in human form. He entertained angels unawares and received a blessing, the promise of a son (Isaac) to come through Sarah.

Lot also unknowingly entertained angels. When two of them visited Sodom, Lot sought them out and gave them food and lodging. In turn, the angels blessed him and his family by delivering them from the destruction of Sodom (Gen. 19:1-29). In Judges 13, Manoah entertained a heavenly visitor unawares, the Son of God in human form, and God blessed him and all Israel with a deliverer, Samson. Rahab entertained the two spies who came to Jericho, giving them lodging and providing for their needs. As a result, she and her family experienced divine deliverance from the destruction of Jericho (Josh. 2; 6:22-25).

God sent Elijah to the widow of Zarephath, who received him, gave him lodging and food, and in turn received the blessing of Elijah raising her son from the dead (1 Kings 17:8-24). Elisha met a Shunammite woman whose rich husband built and furnished an upper room so that Elisha could stay there. In turn, God blessed this barren woman with a child and later raised him from the dead (2 Kings 4:8-37).

Entertaining strangers played an important role in the spread of Christianity in the first centuries of the church. Jesus himself was entertained by Simon Peter (Mark 1:29), Levi (Mark 2:15), Simon the leper (Mark 14:3), and Mary and Martha (Luke 10:38). When Jesus sent the apostles and disciples to declare the gospel, he told them, "Do not take any silver, any bag, any extra clothing or sandals, or a staff. Stay in homes that are open to you, eating and drinking what they give you" (cf. Matt. 10:9-13; Mark 6:8-11; Luke 10:4-9). In fact, the New Testament uses the terms "receive" and "send on his way" as technical terms for receiving and sending out missionaries.

In his letter to Philemon, Paul wrote, "Prepare a guest room for me" (v. 22). Paul expected to visit Philemon and stay in his home. In Acts 21 we see Paul staying with disciples at Tyre, Ptolemais, Caesarea, and Jerusalem. After Paul's shipwreck, Publius, the pagan governor of Malta, entertained Paul and those with him (Acts 28:7).

We always receive a blessing when we open our homes for believers who come to us from far and near. Paul's words to the Romans give us a principle to inspire us to entertain strangers: "I long to see you so that I may impart to you some spiritual gift to make you strong—that is, that you and I may be mutually encouraged by each other's faith" (Rom. 1:11–12). Oh, the beauty, the wonder, and the strength of mutual fellowship! We are built up and edified by God's gifts given to each other. In the same letter Paul wrote, "I know that when I come to you, I will come in the full measure of the blessing of Christ" (Rom. 15:29).

It was particularly important for believers to show hospitality to strangers because the inns of those days were not suited for believers to lodge in as they traveled. They were expensive, dangerous, filled with immorality, unhygienic, and uncomfortable. So Christians would offer their own homes to traveling believers. William Lane comments about such *philoxenia*: "For Christians, a delight in the guest/host relationship reflects the expectation that God will play a significant role in the ordinary exchange between guests and hosts. This lends to hospitality a sacramental quality." God's people getting together is a sacrament. The Didache instructed believers to "invite the traveler into the family and provide whatever was necessary, even to the extent of making provision for the next leg of the journey."[2]

The New Testament is full of exhortations about the care of visitors. Paul wrote, "I commend to you our sister Phoebe, a servant of the church in Cenchrea. I ask you to receive her in the Lord in a way worthy of the saints and to give her any help she may need from you, for she has been a great help to many people, including me" (Rom. 16:1–2). Paul gave similar instructions about Timothy (1 Cor. 16:10–11), as well as Zenas the lawyer and

---

2   Lane, *Hebrews 9–13*, 512.

Apollos (Titus 3:13). He commended the household of Stephanas for giving such care to him: "You know that the household of Stephanas were the first converts in Achaia, and they have devoted themselves to the service of the saints. I urge you, brothers, to submit to such as these and to everyone who joins in the work, and labors at it. I was glad when Stephanas, Fortunatus and Achaicus arrived, because they have supplied what was lacking from you. For they refreshed my spirit and yours also. Such men deserve recognition" (1 Cor. 16:15–18).

Such hospitality should be characteristic of every leader in the church. If you are a pastor, you should be known as a lover of hospitality (1 Tim. 3:2). Paul urges us all to practice hospitality (Rom. 12:13), and Peter says we must do so without grumbling (1 Pet. 4:9). Hospitality ought to be a delight.

Hospitality and brotherly love are aspects of true worship. Look at Hebrews 13:16: "And do not forget to do good and to share with others, for with such sacrifices God is pleased." We are the New Testament royal priests and these are acceptable sacrifices we have to offer.

Do you want to receive a blessing by entertaining angels unawares? Then practice hospitality. Let us open our houses to those in need, especially to believers who come to worship with us, yet are strangers to us. Let us invite visitors in to eat and fellowship with us for the spiritual benefit of both guest and host. A student once went to a church that preached the word of God faithfully. At one point the pastor preached on the subject of hospitality for several weeks, yet no one reached out to this stranger in their midst. What is the use of preaching without practicing it? Let us practice love for strangers by practicing hospitality in the name of the Lord, for brotherly love demonstrated in sacrificial hospitality is acceptable worship of God.

Philodesmia: Love for Prisoners

"*Remember those in prison as if you were their fellow prisoners, and those who are mistreated as if you yourselves were suffering*" (Heb. 13:3). The term "prisoner" refers to people who have lost their freedom because of their faith in Jesus. They cannot visit the church, so we must remember them by doing helpful things for them.

First-century prisons were cold, terrible places. Prisoners were dependent on friends and family for food, drink, medicine, and clothing. They needed reading materials, the ministry of the word, and the fellowship of God's people. The writer means that we who are not confined in prison are to sympathize with prisoners by first imagining what we would need if we were in their place, and then helping them with tangible support.

When one suffers, all suffer; when one rejoices, all rejoice (1 Cor. 12:26). We are brothers and sisters in the family of God, and this spiritual relationship is greater than all other relationships and loyalties. Thus, the Hebrews writer speaks of "our brother Timothy" being released from prison (Heb. 13:23). Our "elder brother," Jesus Christ, is a high priest who sympathizes with us in all our sufferings and comes to our aid. Hebrews 10:34 spoke about how the Hebrew Christians had sympathized with prisoners before and taken care of them. Now the author is admonishing them to once again remember the prisoners, feel their pain, and do something about it.

We see many examples of this *philodesmia* in the New Testament. When Peter was in prison, the church was praying for him. The Lord heard the prayer and sent an angel to deliver Peter from that prison (Acts 12:5–19). When Paul was in prison, the Philippian church sent gifts with Epaphroditus to help him (Phil. 4:18). Paul said that their gifts were "a fragrant offering, an acceptable sacrifice, pleasing to God." Elsewhere, Paul writes as a prisoner of the Lord to request the prayers of the Ephesian church (Eph. 6:19–20). Onesiphorus was not afraid to identify with Paul when he was imprisoned in Rome. As he was about to die, Paul remembered how Onesiphorus had helped him: "May the Lord show mercy to the household of Onesiphorus, because he often refreshed me and was not ashamed of my chains. On the contrary, when he was in Rome, he searched hard for me until he found me. May the Lord grant that he will find mercy from the Lord on that day! You know very well in how many ways he helped me in Ephesus" (2 Tim. 1:16–18). The imprisoned Paul ended his letter to the Colossian church: "Remember my chains" (Col. 4:18). In Acts 16 we see the Philippian jailer ministering to Paul and Silas by washing their wounds and feeding them.

Like the Hebrew Christians, we also must remember all who are ill-treated for Jesus' sake and help them. In the Western world today there are not too many believers imprisoned for their faith, although we may see more of them in the days to come. But even now there are thousands of Christian prisoners in other parts of the world who need our prayers and material help. In Western countries we can also minister to unbelieving prisoners, especially through evangelism.

The author says to remember *"those who are mistreated as if you yourselves were suffering"* (Heb. 13:3). We live in bodies that are subject to pain and suffering. We may not be suffering now, but the time will come when we need help. We should sow love now so that we may receive a rich harvest when our time of need comes. The body of Christ will remember us and, above all, the Lord will not forsake us.

Transformed to Love

At one time we had no genuine love and concern for others, but now we are God's people, transformed by grace and delivered from the kingdom of self into the unshakable kingdom of God. Now we are to work hard to help all people, especially those in the household of faith. Therefore, may we help those in need, especially fellow believers in Christ, so that on the last day we will hear from our Lord, "Come, you who are blessed by my Father; take your inheritance, the kingdom prepared for you since the creation of the world. For I was hungry and you gave me something to eat, I was thirsty and you gave me something to drink, I was a stranger and you invited me in, I needed clothes and you clothed me, I was sick and you looked after me, I was in prison and you came to visit me" (Matt. 25:34–36).

If you are an unbeliever, may God transform you even this day into a saint, a shining star, a servant of God's people, seeking to please God in all you do. And may all who are people of God rejoice in this great salvation and love one another ever more deeply. Love gives, serves, and joyfully lays down its life for its brothers. Let us, therefore, love one another as Christ loved us and gave himself in death for our eternal salvation.

37

Christian Marriage

Marriage should be honored by all, and the marriage bed kept pure, for God will judge the adulterer and all the sexually immoral.

Hebrews 13:4

In the first three verses of Hebrews 13 we learned that we are to love our brothers and sisters in the church, strangers who come to us from afar, and prisoners who cannot come to us for aid. The fourth verse describes our duty to love our spouses in Christian marriage and gives us the biblical view of sexuality.

Human sexuality is to be expressed in the state of marriage only, and married Christians are to oppose all evils, including fornication and adultery, that destroy and stain marriage. Marriage is good, and sex is good in marriage because God is the Creator of both. Thus, all who oppose marriage and sexual relations within marriage are opposing God. Satan is the destroyer of all that is good, including marriage. Therefore, God will and must judge all who destroy his institution of marriage by practicing fornication, adultery, homosexuality, and all other sexual perversions.

Hebrews 12:14 declares that God's people must actively pursue holiness, without which no one shall see the Lord. In this study we will examine how to have holiness in marriage by looking at the biblical view of marriage and sex and the judgment God promises to those who destroy marriage.

Marriage

The Puritan Thomas Becon defined marriage as a "high, holy, and blessed order of life, ordained not of man, but of God, . . . wherein one man and one woman are coupled and knit together in one flesh and body in the fear and love of God, by the free, loving, hearty, and good consent of them both, to the intent that they both may dwell together as one flesh and body, of one will and mind, in all honesty, virtue and godliness, and spend their lives in equal partaking of all such things as God shall send them with thanksgiving."[1] One man and one woman freely enter into this estate. Thus, the Bible opposes polygamy and polyandry. Christian marriage is monogamous for life.

In Christian marriage, a *virgin* man and a *virgin* woman pledge publicly to live together in the state of marriage. Such emphasis on virginity may be shocking to the modern world, but it is the biblical standard.

Marriage is a covenant of companionship, a publicly sworn promise by a man and woman to each other that brings them into a union intended to provide them with a multi-dimensional life of companionship. The Scriptural purpose of marriage is not just procreation, as Roman Catholics teach. There are several purposes: first, companionship; second, to prevent sexual immorality; and, third, procreation. The Bible says children are not a curse to be avoided through ingenious technology or aborted through murder, but a blessing and gift from God to be received with thanksgiving.

Christians should marry only true Christians (1 Cor. 7:39; 2 Cor. 6:14). Yet we are not to marry within certain degrees of affinity and consanguinity, which would be incest. The problem mentioned in 1 Corinthians 5 was that a man was living with his father's wife.

Many post-apostolic fathers taught unbiblical views of sexuality. This was also true in medieval times when the church became unduly influenced by the Greek idea that matter is evil and, therefore, sexual love was considered evil even in marriage. Leland

---

1 Quoted by Leland Ryken, *Worldly Saints: The Puritans as They Really Were* (Grand Rapids: Zondervan, 1986), 49.

Ryken tells us that the church father Origen "had himself castrated before he was ordained. Tertullian claimed that 'marriage and adultery . . . are not intrinsically different.'" The Roman Catholic church prohibited clergy from marrying from the fifth century on and glorified virginity and celibacy. In medieval times some theologians interpreted the parable of the sower in this way: the Christian who brought forth fruit thirtyfold was compared to those who were married; the one who was fruitful sixtyfold was compared to those who were widowed; and the Christian who brought forth fruit one hundredfold was compared to those who practiced celibacy and virginity. Ambrose taught that "married people ought to blush at the state in which they are living," so the church prohibited sex for married people for up to five days in a week. "Bishop Gregory of Nyssa claimed that Adam and Eve had originally been created without sexual desire." Later, the medieval theologian Erasmus praised married couples who lived without sex.[2]

But the biblical view of marriage and sexuality opposes these nonsensical ideas of the church and churchmen. Paul commands bishops to be the husbands of but one wife (1 Tim. 3:2; Titus 1:6) and teaches that marital sexual relations are ongoing debts to be paid to one another. Because each one's body belongs to the other, one partner cannot "deprive [the] other except by mutual consent and for a time" (1 Cor. 7:3–5). For example, a man cannot just go away on a trip without permission from his wife, nor can a wife go without permission from her husband. Each spouse has veto power, according to the Bible. Owe no man anything (Rom. 13:8), including one's sexual obligation to one's spouse.

God said it was not good for man to be alone, so he created woman as his crowning act of creation, and instituted and solemnized marriage in paradise (Gen. 2:18, 21–24). Marriage is not an evolutionary idea, invented by clever men. God is the author of it, and he created man, male and female, for this purpose. A. W. Pink says, "Man is *advantaged* by having a wife,"[3] and I would add "by having a *wise* wife." Such a marriage is a great blessing till death. If marriage is not sweet, it is because of our sin. God hates

---

2   This paragraph summarizes and quotes material from Ryken, *Worldly Saints*, 40–42.
3   Pink, *Exposition of Hebrews*, 1124.

divorce and opposes it (Mal. 2:16). Divorce is permitted for only two reasons, adultery and desertion, both of which destroy the covenant between husband and wife.

Except for salvation, marriage is the most momentous and precious of earthly events in our lives. Pink declares, "Far, far better to remain single unto the end of our days, than to enter into the marriage state *without* the Divine benediction upon it."[4] Before we marry, we must seek the mind and will of God most earnestly.

God the Father honored marriage by creating man and woman and performing the first marriage—that of Adam and Eve in Eden. Jesus also honored marriage. Born of the virgin Mary, who was married to Joseph, Jesus performed the miracle of turning water into wine at the wedding in Cana (John 2:1–11). He often spoke of great marriage feasts in his parables. The Holy Spirit honors marriage by revealing that Christian marriage reflects the marriage of Christ and the church (Eph. 5:22–33), and by depicting the church as the bride of the Lamb (Rev. 21:9).

Choosing a proper mate is of supreme importance for Christian marriage. We should pay attention to the following considerations:

1. The prospective spouse should be a true Christian, born of God, not someone who is a Christian only in word but not in life.
2. Do not look for someone who just has material riches or social position.
3. Do not focus only on whether a person is highly educated or a professional.
4. Look for someone who is industrious, sufficiently intelligent, and above all, delights to serve God and others.
5. Look for someone of good character. The book of Proverbs gives much instruction on the ideal character of a Christian wife. A woman should look for the same characteristics in a husband: "A wife of noble character is her husband's crown, but a disgraceful wife is like decay in his bones. . . . He who finds a wife finds what is good and receives favor from the Lord. . . . Houses and wealth are inherited from parents, but a prudent wife is from the Lord. . . . A wife of noble character who can find? She is worth far more than rubies" (Prov. 12:4; 18:22; 19:14; 31:10).
6. Do not just look for a pretty face. Unlike man, God does not look at the outward appearance, but at the heart. When you look for a spouse, look for a person of heart beauty: "Your

---

4   Ibid., 1125.

beauty should not come from outward adornment, such as braided hair and the wearing of gold jewelry and fine clothes. Instead, it should be that of your inner self, the unfading beauty of a gentle and quiet spirit, which is of great worth in God's sight" (1 Pet. 3:3–4).
7. He or she should be a person of good reputation, not notorious for open sin.
8. He or she should be a person of good speech: "Out of the abundance of the heart the mouth speaketh" (Matt. 12:34, KJV). He or she should be a person who edifies others by speaking wisdom from the word of God.
9. He or she should be a person who is modest in dress, not a vain person.
10. He or she should have godly friends; we can tell much about people by the company they keep.
11. He or she should be a person of humble countenance (Isa. 3:9).

In Christian marriage, all our attitudes and actions must be regulated by Christ's holy, sacrificial, and enduring love. The loving and wise leadership of the husband depicts Christ's love for the church, while the loving and respectful submission of the wife depicts the church's love for Christ. If we do not follow this pattern, there will be serious consequences. Pink writes, "When the wife refuses to submit to the husband, the children are sure to defy their parents—sow the wind, reap the whirlwind."[5]

Since Christians are saved sinners, there is no perfection possible in marriage here on earth. Therefore we must be patient with each other, forgive and overlook sins, and pray for more divine love. Above all, we must keep our eyes on the cross. One Puritan declared, "Look not for perfection in your [marriage]. God reserves that for another state where marriage is not needed."[6]

The first word in Hebrews 13:4 in the Greek is *timios*, which means precious or honorable. God commands that marriage should be held as precious and honorable. God himself sees marriage as precious; not only did he author it, but he also honors it. *Timios* is used to describe precious stones, precious jewels, the precious blood of Christ, and the precious promises of God in his word. *Timios* is also used for "honor" (Acts 5:34), but it is used more often to mean "precious" or "costly." In other

---

5 Ibid., 1132.
6 Ryken, *Worldly Saints*, 51.

words, marriage is to be valued most highly. Marriage is like a very precious Ming-dynasty vase that we must handle carefully. We must not break it or lose it through carelessness, self-centeredness, or an unforgiving attitude.

Divorce destroys this very precious state called marriage. Therefore, we must do everything in our power every day to promote marriage. We must love one another, pray for one another, serve one another, forgive one another, communicate with one another, and spend time together. We must love those things that promote marriage, hate everything that seeks to destroy it, and always thank God for enriching us with our God-chosen spouses. If we are single, it is proper to pray that God will enrich us in the future by bringing us into this precious and honorable estate of marriage.

The post-apostolic fathers despised marriage and the medieval church dishonored it, but the text says marriage should be honored by all. Therefore, the Roman Catholic church should honor marriage and permit her priests to marry. Asceticism is not superior to marriage, and marriage is not defiling; in fact, it is asceticism that often leads to defilement. We also must note that Christ's relation to the church is illustrated not by asceticism, but by the state of marriage. To dishonor marriage is to sin against God who instituted it.

Marriage should be promoted by the church and state, and laws should promote marriage, not destroy it. In all circumstances, whether in sickness, in poverty, in old age, in middle age, when one is away or when one is home, marriage is to be honored and valued, for this is the will of God.

Sexual Relations in Marriage

The second imperative in Hebrews 13:4 is that the marriage bed be kept pure and undefiled. Sex is God's creation, and all that God has created is good. The Bible teaches us that sex is to be enjoyed within marriage only. Virgins are to marry and enjoy sexual relations in the covenant of marriage. Our bodies belong to God and we are to use them for God's purposes. Both single and married people are to take care of their bodies, for our bodies are a trust from God to us. As stewards, we have no authority to abuse our bodies, whether through obesity or anorexia or engaging in fornication. It is the job of single people to preserve their bodies in purity and holiness for their future spouses. Any sexual relationship outside of marriage is a sin against God, against one's future spouse, and against oneself.

Sexual relations in marriage are not defiling, but edifying and God-glorifying. In marriage, sexual relations are an ongoing obligation of each spouse. So Paul exhorts married people not to defraud each other (1 Cor. 7:3–5). Having entered into a covenant of marriage, we must be diligent to pay up our debts. Failure to do this may bring about sexual immorality.

Yet there have been people in the history of Christianity who taught that married couples should abstain from sexual relations so they could live more holy lives. For instance, Montanists emphasized virginity as part of a state of perfection. But such teaching is of the devil, and Paul writes that those who forbid marriage are heretics (1 Tim. 4:1–3). The writer exhorts, "Let the marriage bed be kept pure" (*hē koítē amíantos*), not by refraining from sexual relations in marriage, but by refraining from promiscuity and marital unfaithfulness. Thus, Ambrose was terribly wrong when he said that married people ought to blush at the state in which they are living. No, they ought to rejoice and praise the Lord for his gift of sexuality to be exercised in marriage. Erasmus was terribly wrong when he praised a married couple living without sexual relations. The Roman Catholic church is terribly wrong when it prevents clergy from marrying. The medieval church was terribly wrong when it prohibited sex for married people up to five days a week. Such ungodly thinking occurs when we rely not on the Bible but on human philosophy.

Plutarch uses the verb without the alpha privative (*miaínein tēn koitēn*, "marriage bed defiled") to refer to violations of conjugal relations.[7] It is for such a sin that Reuben, Jacob's son, lost his preeminence as firstborn son: "Reuben, you are my firstborn, my might, the first sign of my strength, excelling in honor, excelling in power. Turbulent as the waters, you will no longer excel, for you went up onto your father's bed, onto my couch and defiled it" (Gen. 49:3–4; see also Gen. 35:22).

---

7   Dods, "Epistle to the Hebrews," in vol. 4 of *Expositor's Greek Testament*, 375–376.

God's Judgment

Because God honors marriage, he will also judge all who oppose it: *"For God will judge the adulterer and all the sexually immoral"* (Heb. 13:4). This latter part of the verse gives the reason for the previous directives. If we do anything that violates the sanctity of marriage, God will punish us. Marriage is a closed system—closed to a third party, whether man, woman, or beast.

The Greeks were very permissive. They did not have a closed system in marriage; they had wives, concubines, and prostitutes. But that is not biblical marriage. God commands, "What therefore God hath joined together, let not man put asunder" (Matt. 19:6, KJV). If people destroy a marriage, neither the church nor the family nor the judge nor the community nor the state may punish the guilty party, but the all-seeing God surely will. He will punish such people in this life and on the last day.

Even in this life we experience great problems when marriages are destroyed. Such problems include sexually transmitted diseases, emotional disturbances, economic deprivation, damaged children, and generational troubles. When we violate God's prohibition against adultery, we sin against God, our spouse, and our family.

God will judge those who dishonor him. Concerning the man who was living with his father's wife, Paul directed, "Hand this man over to Satan for the destruction of the flesh" (1 Cor. 5:5, NRSV). Fornication is sexual immorality outside of God's institution of marriage, and God will judge all fornicators. So the writer says in Hebrews 12:16, "See that no one is sexually immoral," and Paul exhorts, "Flee from sexual immorality" (1 Cor. 6:18). We must flee, as Joseph did in Egypt, telling Potiphar's wife, "How then could I do such a wicked thing and sin against God?" (Gen. 39:9). God is watching us!

Christian singles are to keep their bodies in purity for their future spouses. If you fornicate, you defile your body and incur divine judgment, and when you marry, you bring that defilement into your marriage. This can bring about sexual frustration and unhappiness. The biblical counsel is to be a virgin before marriage and to practice fidelity in marriage.

God will judge all adulterers. Adultery is sexual immorality within marriage by engaging in sex in violation of the marriage covenant. That is what David did, and he was severely punished. God is watching and he will punish. In Hebrews 13:4 there is emphasis in the Greek text on the word "God" because it appears last. People may not judge, but God himself surely will, because all sin is ultimately against God. The writer has emphasized God's sure judgment throughout his epistle: "Just as man is destined to die once, and after that to face judgment. . . . Since that time he waits for his enemies to be made his footstool. . . . For we know him who said, 'It is mine to avenge; I will repay,' and again, 'The Lord will judge his people.' It is a dreadful thing to fall into the hands of the living God . . . for our 'God is a consuming fire'" (Heb. 9:27; 10:13, 30–31; 12:29).

Paul speaks about this judgment of God as well: "Do you not know that the wicked will not inherit the kingdom of God? Do not be deceived: Neither the sexually immoral nor idolaters nor adulterers nor male prostitutes nor homosexual offenders nor thieves nor the greedy nor drunkards nor slanderers nor swindlers will inherit the kingdom of God" (1 Cor. 6:9–10). John tells us where such people end up: "Outside are . . . the sexually immoral" (Rev. 22:15).

God will judge us now and on the last day at the final judgment. All shall be summoned, and all shall appear.

A Wonderful Conclusion

As Christians, we must not conform to the standards of this world, but must be counter-cultural, standing against the corrupt culture of this world. We must be different, for we are the light of the world and the salt of the earth.

Today's sexual culture is a stinking, open sewer in which anything goes, whether pornography, phone sex, or dalliances on the Internet. Virginity is despised, adultery is glorified, fornication is exciting, homosexuality is taught in grade school as something desirable, marriage is spoken against, motherhood is vilified, lesbianism is promoted, men are belittled, divorce is easy and normal, incest is okay, sex with minors is stimulating, bestiality is fun, and extra-marital affairs are spicy.

Jesus had a different standard: "Anyone who looks at a woman lustfully has already committed adultery with her in his heart" (Matt. 5:28). Modern man may mock God and his standard, but God's judgment has come and is surely coming: "*God will judge the adulterer and all the sexually immoral*" (Heb. 13:4).

Yet there is a wonderful conclusion that gives us great hope. God has good news for all fornicators, adulterers, homosexuals, and all sinners of every type. Jesus Christ, our great high priest, offered a bloody sacrifice that cleanses us from all our sins. In Hebrews 1:3 we read, "After he had provided purification for sins, he sat down at the right hand of the Majesty in heaven." We also read, "So Christ was sacrificed once to take away the sins of many people. . . . But when this priest had offered for all time one sacrifice for sins, he sat down at the right hand of God" (Heb. 9:28; 10:12). In Hebrews 8:12 God graciously proclaims: "For I will forgive their wickedness and will remember their sins no more." And after listing the sins of those who will not inherit the kingdom of God, Paul concludes, "That is what some of you were. But you were washed, you were sanctified, you were justified in the name of the Lord Jesus Christ and by the Spirit of our God" (1 Cor. 6:11).

What must we do to be saved? Repent truly, confess wholly, and believe savingly on this Jesus Christ, who provided purification for sins by his once-for-all sacrifice. Confess him as your Lord and live as his obedient servant. God himself makes us a new creation. God takes dirty, rotten sinners and makes them virgins, holy and undefiled, as pure as fresh snow.

I was gloriously surprised the other day when I read what God says to his wretched, sinful people: "I will build you up again and you will be rebuilt, O Virgin Israel" (Jer. 31:4). God cleanses all our sins and makes us pure virgins. We see the same adjective used in Jeremiah 31:21: "Set up road signs; put up guide posts. Take note of the highway, the road that you take. Return, O Virgin Israel." Read Isaiah 1:18 as well and glory in what God counsels: "Come now, let us reason together. . . . Though your sins are like scarlet, they shall be as white as snow; though they are red as crimson, they shall be like wool."

Our God turns prostitutes like Rahab into virgins. He cleanses us from all our sins and makes us new creations through the power of the blood of Christ. Are you having troubles in your marriage? It is because of your sins. Repent, confess, and forsake your sins, and he will forgive you and make your marriage new and exciting. He will pour out a mighty stream of divine love into your marriage so that once again it will reflect Christ's love for the church. "If we walk in the light, as he is in the light, we have fellowship with one another, and the blood of Jesus, his Son, purifies us from all sin. If we claim to be without sin, we deceive ourselves and the truth is not in us. If we confess our sins, he is faithful and just and will forgive us our sins and purify us from all unrighteousness" (1 John 1:7–9).

Christ is cleansing his people thoroughly. Paul writes, "Husbands, love your wives, just as Christ loved the church and gave himself up for her to make her holy, cleansing her by the washing with water through the word, and to present her to himself as a radiant church, without stain or wrinkle or any other blemish, but holy and blameless" (Eph. 5:25–27). God himself will make us sparkle like precious jewels by the blood of Jesus Christ. Praise be to God the Father, God the Son, and God the Holy Spirit for his great plan of salvation!

38

Key to Happiness: Greed or God?

> [5]*Keep your lives free from the love of money and be content with what you have, because God has said, "Never will I leave you; never will I forsake you."* [6]*So we say with confidence, "The Lord is my helper; I will not be afraid. What can man do to me?"*
>
> Hebrews 13:5–6

The great nineteenth-century English Baptist preacher C. H. Spurgeon said that, although people confessed many sins to him, he had never heard anyone confessing the sin of covetousness. It appears that the West largely has exchanged Christianity for the religion of Mammon (i.e., materialism). Yet Jesus said that no one can serve two masters (Matt. 6:24). Western man used to say, "In God we trust," but now he trusts in money and the pleasure it can buy. He seeks security in money, and lots of it. He does not know that riches deceive (Matt. 13:22).

Hebrews 13:5–6 opposes covetousness and materialism. These verses tell us that our lives must be free from the love of money and that we are to be content with what we presently have. The key to true contentment and real happiness is not greed but the God of the Scriptures. Augustine did not say, "Our hearts are restless until they find more money," but, "until they find rest in God." I would clarify further, "until they find rest in the cross of Christ." Only Christ can give rest to all who come to him.

Jesus was poor, yet he was the happiest man who ever lived. The key to his happiness was not gold but God the Father. Paul was also poor, yet he learned to be content in Christ. I pray that we will pay attention to this passage and also learn to be content. Jesus can deliver us from the anxiety we experience due to our thirst for material things. May we, therefore, drink the water of life from Jesus, for all who drink from the well of this world will thirst again. Let us love God, not gold, with all our heart, mind, soul, and strength.

The author has already exhorted us in light of the doctrine he expounded in the first twelve chapters to love our brothers, strangers, prisoners, and our spouses. Now he tells us to love God, not money. In Hebrews 13:5-6 we see the commands of God, the comfort of God, and the confession of faith that we make in light of God's word.

The Commands of God: Do Not Love Money

The first command the author gives is, "*Keep your lives free from the love of money*" (Heb. 13:5). Money and capitalism in themselves are not evil; it is the *love of money* that is condemned here. Jesus said in the Sermon on the Mount that "pagans run after all these things" (Matt. 6:32). In other words, those who are without God and without hope in the world actively pursue the things of the world. Jesus rebuked the Pharisees for loving money more than God (Luke 16:13-15). They stored up treasures on earth where rust, moth, thieves, fire, and inflation destroyed them. The rich man of Luke 16 took no time to read the Scriptures and find the way of salvation; instead, he trusted in his wealth. But his wealth failed him—when he died he went to hell and to a life of everlasting torment. The rich fool of Luke 12 told himself during his time of prosperity, "You have plenty of good things laid up for many years. Take life easy; eat, drink and be merry" (Luke 12:19). He had no thought for God or his eternal salvation. He was a fool because he denied God and trusted in his goods. But God demanded the fool's life that very night.

You may have heard the question, "How much are you worth?" This reduces man to a sum of money. Jesus says, "Watch out! Be on your guard against all kinds of greed; a man's life does not consist in the abundance of his possessions" (Luke 12:15). The unbeliever finds his security and happiness in money. To

Key to Happiness: Greed or God?

him, more money should assure more happiness. But the truth is, a rich unbeliever lives in anxiety and misery. His is a life of pseudo-happiness. The worries of life and the deceitfulness of riches eventually destroy him.

A covetous man is never happy. He is always searching for another thousand or million or billion dollars. Like the people of Laodicea, he boasts, "I am rich; I have acquired wealth and do not need a thing." He does not realize he is "wretched, pitiful, poor, blind and naked" (Rev. 3:17).

Covetousness is an inordinate desire to have more of something than God in his sovereign wisdom has been pleased to give. The covetous man worships creation rather than the Creator and lusts after honors, wealth, power, pleasure, and knowledge. Paul calls this covetous greed "idolatry" (Col. 3:5). It is worship of the false god of materialism. Greed seeks happiness in stuff and always grasps for more, saying, "Old is no good. New is better. More and bigger and newer is better still."

Love of money is an addiction, and the one who loves money may do many wrong things to gain more. He may cheat others or commit fraud and perjury. Such a person is envious, quarrelsome, and full of hatred and violence. He always wants to make another dollar no matter what it takes. Whoever loves money never has money enough. A covetous person is a slave to the lust of the flesh, the lust of the eyes, and the boasting of things. He is always unhappy. He cannot endure hearing about others having more than he has. The covetous man lusts for his neighbor's wife and property. He is ever violating the tenth commandment: "Thou shalt not covet."

The psalmist understood the utter foolishness of trusting in money rather than God to save us:

> [The wicked] trust in their wealth and boast of their great riches. . . . [But] no man can redeem the life of another or give to God a ransom for him. . . . [Therefore] do not be overawed when a man grows rich, when the splendor of his house increases; for he will take nothing with him when he dies, his splendor will not descend with him. Though while he lived he counted himself blessed—and men praise you when you prosper—he will join the generation of his fathers, who will never see the light of life. A man who has riches without understanding is like the beasts that perish. (Ps. 49:6–7, 16–20)

Elsewhere the psalmist exhorts, "Though your riches increase, do not set your heart on them" (Ps. 62:10).

Wealth is uncertain. Solomon says, "Cast but a glance at riches, and they are gone, for they will surely sprout wings and fly off to the sky like an eagle" (Prov. 23:5). Paul tells us, "The love of money is a root of all kinds of evil" (1 Tim. 6:10). Those who trust in their wealth become arrogant even as they are deceived into thinking that their money can redeem them. Covetous people thereby reject God and cannot enter into his kingdom. But even poor people can suffer from covetousness. For example, in the United States many people incur great debt with their credit cards, thinking that more stuff will make them happy. They try to buy happiness on credit, but what they really are bringing upon themselves is trouble.

God commands us to keep our lives free from the love of money. This also applies to ministers. Paul says they are not to be lovers of money (1 Tim. 3:3), and Peter says they should be "not greedy for money, but eager to serve" (1 Pet. 5:2). Yet many false ministers use religion to increase their wealth by preaching what people want to hear. They are spiritual prostitutes. Jesus exhorts us three times in Matthew 6 not to worry, for our heavenly Father knows that we need food and clothing, and he will provide them through our faithful labor.

The Bible gives many examples of covetous people, whose lives are revealed to us for our rebuke, correction, learning, and warning. Because Balaam loved the wages of wickedness, he was killed (Num. 22–25; 31:8). Achan was a greedy man who stole silver and gold that belonged to God. Because of his greed, he and his family were also killed (Josh. 7). Gehazi was not interested in the double portion of the Spirit. He loved money, clothes, olive groves, vineyards, flocks, and herds, and he lied to obtain them. He wanted to be rich and famous, but instead he became a leper, and his children after him (2 Kings 5). What a tragedy! Gehazi could have ministered to the people of Israel in place of Elisha; instead he now serves as a warning to pastors who are tempted to prostitute themselves for money.

As king of Israel, Ahab had everything he needed. But he was a covetous man and desired the vineyard of Naboth. He got it, but in due time God killed him and his entire family (1 Kings 21).

David was a married man with many wives. But he became covetous and took Bathsheba, Uriah's wife, violating the sixth, seventh, eighth, ninth, and tenth commandments. As a result, God severely punished David and his family (2 Sam. 11–12). Adam and Eve had everything in paradise. Yet they became covetous and ate the forbidden fruit, thinking that they could become free of God, be wise, and live a life of pleasure. They were driven out of God's presence and died, plunging the world into sin and death (Gen. 3).

We also read about Judas, one of the apostles of Jesus Christ, who sold Christ for thirty pieces of silver. Judas was a covetous thief who loved money more than Jesus and his salvation. But Judas lost his money, hanged himself, and went to hell. Jesus called him a son of perdition (John 17:12, KJV). Ananias and Sapphira loved money, power, and position. They lied to the Holy Spirit and the Holy Spirit killed them (Acts 5). Demas was a fellow minister of Paul who served with him for many years. But at the end of his life Paul wrote: "Demas, because he loved this world, has deserted me and has gone to Thessalonica" (2 Tim. 4:10). Demas became a covetous man, a lover of money, and eventually abandoned Paul, God, and the gospel. Ministers, watch out for covetousness.

What should we do? Flee covetousness and the love of money! God commands that our character and conduct must be free from the love of money, that we might save ourselves from destruction.

The Commands of God: Be Content

The second command is, "Be content with what you have" (Heb. 13:5). As God's children, we have a heavenly Father who knows all our needs. Jesus taught us to pray, "Give us this day our daily bread." He is Jehovah Jireh, which means "Jehovah sees our needs and provides." He who gave us existence will also give us all things necessary to sustain that existence. He feeds the birds and beautifies the lilies of the field; how much more will he take care of us, the crown of his creation! We are God's portion, his own treasure.

Jesus said, "Do not worry about your life" (Matt. 6:25). Covetousness is a child of unbelief, but contentment is a child of faith in God. A. W. Pink says, "Contentment is a tranquility of soul, a being satisfied with what God has apportioned."[1] It is the opposite of a grasping spirit.

The psalmist says, "The boundary lines have fallen for me in pleasant places; surely I have a delightful inheritance" (Ps. 16:6). We have God as our inheritance and treasure. What more can we want? Contentment is being happy in Jesus, who came that we may have life and have it more abundantly. In him we are blessed with every spiritual blessing in heavenly places. In Jesus we lack nothing.

It is sinful to be discontented. Discontentment questions both the sovereignty and the goodness of God. Pink says, "Discontent corrodes the strings of the heart."[2] A discontented person is characterized by worry. He cannot sing and rejoice as Paul and Silas did in the Philippian jail in the middle of the night (Acts 16:25). But a content man gives thanks to God the Father in the name of Jesus Christ always and for all things. Pink asks believers: "Didst thou give thyself to Christ for temporal, or for eternal comforts? Didst thou enter upon religion to save thine estate or thy soul?"[3] Paul says, "Godliness with contentment is great gain. . . . If we have food and clothing, we will be content with that" (1 Tim. 6:6, 8).

The unbeliever seeks contentment in riches and material circumstances. The Stoics sought contentment in self-sufficiency, irrespective of circumstances. We Christians enjoy contentment in Christ's sufficiency and grace, not in changing circumstances.

Paul speaks about this in Philippians 4. He had learned to be content in all circumstances—in extreme poverty or in extreme plenty. He knew how to be abased and how to abound. God was teaching him as he experienced divine trials. Finally, he arrived at the state of contentment and he gives us the secret: "I can do everything through him who gives me strength" (Phil. 4:13). Paul was content even in prison while chained between two soldiers. He had learned the secret from the mouth of Jesus: "My grace is sufficient for you" (2 Cor. 12:9). So he writes, "In all things God works for the good of those who love him, who have been called according to his purpose. . . . If God is for us, who can be

---

1 Pink, *Exposition of Hebrews*, 1147.
2 Ibid., 1145.
3 Ibid., 1145.

against us?" (Rom. 8:28, 31). He saves us, and no one can destroy us. Vital union with Jesus Christ is the secret of contentment. Jesus proclaims, "I am the vine; you are the branches" (John 15:5). Branches receive everything they need from the vine.

We are commanded to *"be content with what you have."* What we have is what God gives us through our own industry. God enables us to obtain wealth, but we must work six days a week, and always try to work smarter and harder. We do not believe in asceticism; poverty is not a virtue! Paul tells the thief who now believes in Christ to steal no longer, but to work with his hands, that he may have something to give to those in need (Eph. 4:28). Elsewhere the apostle says that he who does not work shall not eat (2 Thess. 3:10) and that he who does not provide for his family is worse than an unbeliever (1 Tim. 5:8). Sadly, many men today live off their wives. Such laziness is a serious sin. A lazy person is a rebel who opposes God's law that says we must work six days. God gives us daily bread by giving us health and the ability to work with our hands. The Lord is our shepherd, and we shall lack nothing because we work with our hands. Our hands are for work, not for handouts.

God provides. But he does not provide for lazy people who oppose God's plan for obtaining wealth. Be content with what God has provided as a reward for your six days of labor. What God prohibits here is covetousness and love for money, not labor for money. Money is not evil; we cannot live without it. Even Jesus used money. Paul tells us in Romans 12:11 to be "not slothful in business" (KJV). So we are to acquire money by labor, use it profitably, invest it wisely, and give it away generously. But we must never trust in money; we are to trust in Jesus Christ alone. Job says, "If I have put my trust in gold or said to pure gold, 'You are my security,' if I have rejoiced over my great wealth, the fortune my hands had gained . . . then these also would be sins to be judged, for I would have been unfaithful to God on high" (Job 31:24–28).

The Comfort of God

"God has said, 'Never will I leave you; never will I forsake you'" (Heb. 13:5). God is our sufficiency. We can obey these commands to not be covetous and to be content because of God's promise. We are not relying on the word of a man or an angel, but on the word of God Almighty.

In the Greek text there are five negatives in this verse. We could say it this way: "He will never, never, never, never, never fail us nor forsake us." The last verse of the hymn, "How Firm a Foundation," reflects the same truth:

> The soul that on Jesus has leaned for repose
> I will not, I will not desert to his foes.
> That soul, though all hell shall endeavor to shake,
> I will never, no, never, no, never forsake.

These five negatives tell us that God can be trusted. God is always with his people, as he was with the Israelites in the wilderness, in the pillar of fire and cloud. He is the good shepherd who gives his life for his sheep. He never abandons them; rather, he cares for them and brings them all safely home without losing even one. He provides them with manna, water, guidance, protection, and comfort.

What is the greatest comfort God gives to his people? It is his very presence. That God is with us is the greatest reality in the world. When Jacob left his home and went to Aram, God told this lonely man, "I am with you and will watch over you wherever you go, and I will bring you back to this land. I will not leave you until I have done what I have promised you" (Gen. 28:15). God told the Israelites the same thing: "Be strong and courageous. Do not be afraid or terrified . . . for the Lord your God goes with you; he will never leave you nor forsake you" (Deut. 31:6).

God also told Joshua: "I will never leave you nor forsake you. . . . Be strong and courageous. Do not be terrified; do not be discouraged, for the Lord your God will be with you wherever you go" (Josh. 1:5, 9). At the end of his life, David said to Solomon, "God is with you. He will not fail you or forsake you" (1 Chron. 28:20). Jesus told his disciples, "Surely I am with you always, to the very end of the age" (Matt. 28:20). Jesus also told them he would not leave them as orphans, but would send another Comforter to be with them forever (John 14:16–18). That Comforter, the Holy Spirit, has now come and is with us always to guide us, empower us, and gift us with all grace. Though our parents or friends may forsake us, God will never leave us nor forsake us. Note God's language to his people: "Can a mother forget the baby at her breast and have no compassion on the child she has borne? Though she may forget, I will not forget you! See, I have engraved you on the palms of my hands; your walls are ever before me" (Isa. 49:15–16). God sees us every day. He knows all our problems and helps us. Therefore we do not have to be greedy or put our trust in money.

Paul was content and comforted because he knew that God was with him in every situation, even when he was in prison or the open sea. There were times when his friends and fellow ministers abandoned him: "You know that everyone in the province of Asia has deserted me. . . . Demas, because he loved this world, has deserted me and has gone to Thessalonica" (2 Tim. 1:15, 4:10). In his time of great need, no one was there: "At my first defense, no one came to my support, but everyone deserted me" (2 Tim. 4:16). Yet Paul was not alone: "But the Lord stood at my side and gave me strength" (2 Tim. 4:17).

Why should we be greedy and covetous when God is with us every moment of our lives? Moses told God, "If your Presence does not go with us, do not send us up from here" (Exod. 33:15). We need God and his presence, for in him we have all things. The key to our Christian pilgrimage to the city of the living God is God's presence with us. "Let us fix our eyes on Jesus, the author and perfecter of our faith" (Heb. 12:2).

Our Confession of Faith

Finally, we are to make a confession of faith in light of this truth: *"So we say with confidence, 'The Lord is my helper; I will not be afraid. What can man do to me?'"* (Heb. 13:6). Based on God's spoken and written word, which promises his presence with us, we can confidently and courageously confess our faith in God. God's word guaranteeing his presence with us enables us to be courageous. The author here quotes Psalm 118:6–7: "The LORD is with me; I will not be afraid. What can man do to me? The LORD is with me; he is my helper. I will look in triumph on my enemies."

The author uses the word, *tharrountas*, from *tharreō*, which is translated "with confidence" in Hebrews 13:6. We find it also in

Matthew 9:2, where Jesus speaks to the paralytic, "Take heart!" God is telling us, "Cheer up! Rejoice! Fear not, for I am with you and I will help you. I will save you and deliver you. I will never fail you nor forsake you."

Jesus says, "I have told you these things, so that in me you may have peace. In this world you will have trouble. But *take heart!* I have overcome the world" (John 16:33, italics added). Christ has defeated the world and set us free from the dominion of the world, sin, Satan, hell, and death.

Why should we take heart? Our first confession is, *"The Lord is my helper"* (Heb. 13:6). The word "helper" is *boēthos*, which comes from *boētheia*. It means to run to help in response to the cry of those in danger. We cry out to God, and he runs to rescue us out of our troubles.

The word was used by the Syro-Phoenician woman who cried out to Jesus in a loud voice, "Jesus, help me! My daughter is demonized," and she was helped (Matt. 15:21–28). In the will of his Father, the Son became incarnate to help us. He taught truth, performed miracles, overcame temptation, suffered the death of the cross, rose from the dead, ascended to heaven, and is now seated on the throne as King of kings and Lord of lords to help us. He sent the Holy Spirit, gave us the Bible, and raised up ministers to help us. Our God is looking after us.

The author used this word earlier to speak about Jesus Christ: "Because he himself suffered when he was tempted, he is able to help those who are being tempted. . . . Let us then approach the throne of grace with confidence, so that we may receive mercy and find grace to help us in our time of need" (Heb. 2:18; 4:16). Cry out to God, and he will run to your aid to help you.

Our second confession is, *"I will not be afraid."* Hebrews 2:14–15 tells us that our fear is based on fear of death. By his death, Jesus Christ destroyed death and set us free from both the fear of death and death itself. That is why we can say, "I will not be afraid."

If God is with us, we need not fear. God came to Abraham and said, "Do not be afraid, Abram. I am your shield, your very great reward" (Gen. 15:1). And Paul says in great jubilation, "Neither death nor life . . . nor anything else in all creation, will be able to separate us from the love of God that is in Christ Jesus our Lord"

(Rom. 8:38–39). We do not fear because of our inseparable vital union with Jesus.

Our final confession is, "What can man do to me?" The expected answer is, "Nothing!" Why should we fear weak, sinful, mortal men? Our life is hidden with Christ in God (Col. 3:3). Now Christ is our life. We are invincible and indestructible. Man may slander us, sue us, beat us up, fire us from work, confiscate our property, evict us, put us into prison, kill us, or cut us in two; yet neither death nor life nor anything else in all creation is able to separate us from God's love for us in Christ. We are united with Christ— we died with him, were buried with him, were raised with him, and are seated with him in heaven. We are in him, and he is in us. Before a man can destroy us, he must destroy our God.

Conclusion

God the Father, God the Son, and God the Holy Spirit are all with us. Moreover, God's people are with us. Yet this was not true of Jesus. His own disciple Judas betrayed him, Peter denied him three times, and all his disciples abandoned him in his hour of need. Even his heavenly Father abandoned him, so that he cried out, "My God, my God, why hast thou forsaken me?" God poured out his just wrath, which was due us, upon Christ, so that God may be just in justifying us sinners. Jesus said, "Foxes have holes and birds of the air have nests, but the Son of Man has no place to lay his head" (Matt. 8:20). But there was one place he did lay his head: it was the cross. And because of his suffering, we shall never be abandoned. God says he will never, never, never, never, never fail us nor forsake us, which means he is with us always—in our pain, in our suffering, in our problems, in our troubles, in our persecution, in our darkness, and in the hour of our death. Let every man abandon us; God is with us and we shall never lack his help.

> Heaven and earth may pass away,
> but Jesus never fails.

If you have not repented and savingly trusted in Jesus, you are trusting in money or something else to save you. You are a covetous and unhappy man. Only Christians can be truly content with what they have, with what God has provided. The key to happiness is not greed or gold; it is God's presence and his present help. So work hard, make money, and enjoy God's good life. Distribute generously and store up for yourselves treasure in heaven, which is indestructible. May God help us not to be greedy but to be content because God is with us, he is our helper, and he will never fail nor forsake us.

39
The Christian Minister

⁷Remember your leaders, who spoke the word of God to you. Consider the outcome of their way of life and imitate their faith. ⁸Jesus Christ is the same yesterday and today and forever. . . . ¹⁷Obey your leaders and submit to their authority. They keep watch over you as men who must give an account. Obey them so that their work will be a joy, not a burden, for that would be of no advantage to you.

Hebrews 13:7-8, 17

On October 4, 2007, President George W. Bush declared his creed to reporter Elie Nakouzi for Al-Arabiya television: "I believe in an almighty God, and I believe that all the world, whether they be Muslim, Christian, or any other religion, prays to the same God. That is what I believe. I believe that Islam is a great religion that preaches peace."[1]

In this politically correct statement, President Bush denied the biblical revelation that the true God is the Father of our Lord Jesus Christ, that all the gods of the nations are idols, that Christianity preaches a Savior who alone is the way, the truth, and the life, that no one can come to the Father except through Christ, and that God has given us eternal life in the Son. Politicians rarely speak absolute truth, especially concerning the way of salvation.

A Christian minister, however, is charged by God to preach only truth. Paul declares, "If we or an angel from heaven should preach a gospel other than the one we preached to you, let him

---

1   http://www.whitehouse.gov/news/releases/2007/10/print/20071005-5.html (Accessed October 2007).

be eternally condemned!" (Gal. 1:8). We have no freedom to speak like President Bush, but must preach the gospel of our Lord Jesus Christ. We are not ashamed of the gospel, for it alone is the power of God unto salvation to everyone who believes.

Earlier in this chapter the author spoke about love for brothers, strangers, prisoners, spouses, and love for God instead of money. Now he speaks about love for ministers: first, living ministers; then, ministers who have died; and, finally, the chief minister, our Lord Jesus Christ.

Living Christian Ministers

First, we want to examine who a true Christian minister is, because not everyone who calls himself a minister is one. A Christian minister is called, anointed, and appointed by the Lord Jesus Christ. Paul declares that Christian ministers are gifts to the church, given by God to prepare his people for the works of service to build up the body of Christ (Eph. 4:11–13). Jesus states that Christian ministers are to feed the sheep of Christ by the word of God. Thus, they must love Jesus more than anyone or anything else in the world. Jesus asked Peter, "Do you truly love me more than these?" (John 21:15). If we do not love Christ above all else, we are not called, anointed, and appointed ministers of Christ.

Jesus calls believers "my sheep," for he bought us with his own shed blood. Ministers are appointed by the Holy Spirit to oversee and shepherd these people who are bought with God's own blood (Acts 20:28). They are to preach the whole counsel of God to them. They have no freedom to pick and choose what to say from the Scripture. Ministers are to feed, guide, discipline, and protect God's people from all heretics and heresies. God appoints them as watchmen to warn the people of danger. If they fail to preach the gospel, they will be held accountable by God for the destruction of his people (Jer. 6:17, 23:1–4).

Jesus says that the faithful and wise servant whom the master has appointed to take care of his household must provide food in a timely manner to his people (Matt. 24:45). This food is the word of God. If a minister preaches a different gospel, a different Spirit, or a different Jesus, he is a false minister and a servant of Satan (2 Cor. 11:4, 13). We see such ministers all around us today. Galatians 1 says that the test of a minister is whether he preaches the apostolic gospel faithfully. If he does not, he is condemned to hell.

Ministers are to be given double honor, especially those who preach and teach the gospel (1 Tim. 5:17). We are to respect hardworking ministers who admonish us and to hold them in the highest regard in love (1 Thess. 5:12–13). Ministers are to have unimpeachable moral qualities, intellectual abilities to teach the word of God, and good management skills. They must not be lovers of money; rather, they must love Jesus and his people. Their children should not be wild and unbelieving, but must respect and obey their parents, and be believers and examples to the people of God (1 Tim. 3).

The authority of the minister comes directly from his Chief Shepherd (Matt. 28:18–20; 1 Pet. 5:2–4). Jesus Christ assigns to the minister a certain number of people to care for, oversee, and shepherd. He must do so willingly and give Christ an accounting of his service. When Jesus comes again, he will grant to every such pastor a crown of glory.

"Obey Your Leaders"

The writer tells the people of this church, "Obey your leaders" (Heb. 13:17). It is the will of God for each church to have a plurality of elders, who are also known as bishops and pastors (Acts 14:23; Heb.13:7, 17, 24). The word *peithesthe*, "obey," is also used in James 3:3: "We put bits into the mouths of horses to make them obey us."

Note that we are to obey godly leaders alone. Pastors who fail to preach the gospel, to watch over themselves and the people of God, and to be examples to God's flock are not godly, authentic ministers, and we should run away from such false shepherds, saying, "We must obey God rather than men!" (Acts 5:29).

We must test those who claim to be pastors by the litmus test of the gospel of Christ. John writes, "Dear friends, do not believe every spirit, but test the spirits to see whether they are from God, because many false prophets have gone out into the world" (1 John 4:1). Paul warns, "I urge you, brothers, to watch out for those who cause divisions and put obstacles in your way that are contrary to the teaching you have learned. Keep away from them. For such people are not serving our Lord Christ, but their own appetites. By smooth talk and flattery they deceive the minds of naïve people" (Rom. 16:17–18). The evangelical world is full of naïve, emotional people who want ministers to tickle their ears and entertain them. But John says, "If anyone comes to you and does not bring this teaching, do not take him into your house or welcome him" (2 John 10). We have a responsibility to test the preacher and see whether he is preaching the apostolic doctrine. Jesus said, "My sheep listen to my voice" (John 10:27). And if people do not have ears to hear the gospel of Jesus Christ, then they are not his sheep. Eventually they will manifest themselves as goats.

We are to hear the voice of the Chief Shepherd through authentic preachers; therefore, ministers are to preach the Bible truth so that we may be transformed to do God's will. They should not preach psychology, politics, philosophy, poetry, or global warming and cooling, but only the gospel of God. A true pastor who preaches the gospel is a gift of Christ, anointed and appointed by the Holy Spirit to minister the word of God.

We are to obey our leaders in the church. Anarchy is always evil. We see God's kingdom rule in families, the state, and the church: children are to obey their parents, people are to submit to the laws of the state, and God's people are to submit to the Chief Shepherd and his appointed undershepherds. Ministers themselves are to submit to Jesus Christ.

The author is not *suggesting* obedience. *"Obey your leaders"* is a command, a present imperative in the Greek. We are to run away from false ministers who preach a different gospel, and obey the true ministers who preach the gospel of Jesus Christ. We assert the truth that "all Scripture is God-breathed and is useful for teaching, rebuking, correcting and training in righteousness, so that the man of God may be thoroughly equipped for every good work" (2 Tim. 3:16–17). Refusal to receive the minister and his word shows a rejection of Jesus and God the Father (Matt. 10:40). We cannot believe in Jesus and reject the ministry of his servants, who are to be held in the highest regard and given double honor. John Stott says that double honor means both honor and honorarium, if needed.² We must give respect as well as remuneration.

The importance of obeying godly church leaders is stressed throughout the Scriptures. Paul writes, "You know that the household of Stephanas were the first converts in Achaia, and they have devoted themselves to the service of the saints. I urge you, brothers, to submit to such as these and to everyone who joins in the work, and labors at it" (1 Cor. 16:15–16). In the Old Testament theocracy, God appointed Joshua as the shepherd, telling him, "Whoever rebels against your word and does not obey your words, whatever you may command them, will be put to death" (Josh. 1:18). Today, of course, we do not put people to death in the church, but God will deal severely with any person who refuses to submit to the true minister of the gospel.

"Submit to Their Authority"

Not only does the author say we must obey our leaders, but he also says we must *"submit to their authority"* (Heb. 13:17). Again, it is a present imperative, meaning we are to do so continuously. "Submit" means to come under or yield to. It speaks about military subordination. The author is saying we must submit to their teaching especially because of the heresies mentioned in Hebrews 13:9.

A. W. Pink writes about Christian ministers, "The heavier the burden they bear, the more honour they deserve. . . . The more labour anyone undertakes for our sake and the more difficulty and danger he incurs for us, the greater are our obligations to him."³

The next sentence in Hebrews 13:17 begins with the word "for" in the Greek: *"[For] they keep watch over you as men who must give an account."* Why should we obey and submit to our leaders? Because they watch over our souls. True ministers watch over the spiritual, eternal welfare of their flock. They (and no one else, as the Greek text implies) bear that heavy responsibility.

False shepherds are hirelings who have no interest in the sheep. But true shepherds care for the sheep. Like the good shepherd,

---

2   John Stott, *Guard the Truth* (Downers Grove, IL: InterVarsity Press, 1996), 137.
3   Pink, *Exposition of Hebrews*, 1243.

they lay down their lives for their sheep. The Greek word for "watch over" is *agrupneō*. It means they lose sleep watching over God's people in prayer and the ministry of the word.

A clear illustration of such constant watchful care is found in the testimony of Jacob the shepherd: "This was my situation: The heat consumed me in the daytime and the cold at night, and sleep fled from my eyes" (Gen. 31:40). Luke 2:8 also speaks about shepherds watching the sheep at night.

True ministers labor constantly by feeding, counseling, disciplining, and protecting the people of God under their care. They do not tickle people's ears to please them, but speak as the voice of God. Ministry is a continuous task, especially when heretics and heresies abound. Paul warned the elders of the Ephesian church, "I know that after I leave, savage wolves will come in among you and will not spare the flock. Even from your own number men will arise and distort the truth in order to draw away disciples after them" (Acts 20:29–30). Later Paul speaks of several leaders who abandoned the faith (see 1 Tim. 1:19–20; 2 Tim. 1:15; 2:17–18; 4:9).

Ministers Are Responsible to God

"They keep watch over you as men who must give an account" (Heb. 13:17). Christian ministers are not sovereign rulers with absolute authority. They are only undershepherds who must render an account to Christ, the Chief Shepherd, on that day (cf. 1 Pet. 5:2–4). They will be judged on the basis of their performance: Did they preach the gospel of Christ or a false gospel? Did they feed God's sheep or abuse them? Every minister will hear from the Master on that day either, "Depart from me, you evildoer," or, "Good and faithful servant, enter into the joy of your Lord."

Ministers must give an account ultimately to God. They have to please the Lord of the church who builds his church through such God-called, God-anointed, and God-appointed undershepherds. We are to submit to and obey such true ministers so that they may do their work of pastoring with joy, not pain. There is joy in serving Jesus, yet there is also severe pain in ministry.

What happens if people cause ministers to groan and sigh? It will be unprofitable for them: *"Obey them so that their work will be a joy, not a burden, for that would be of no advantage to you"* (Heb. 13:17). The Greek text says it will be detrimental, a great loss, hurtful, even affecting our eternal salvation. Behavior that brings pain to the ministers could indicate that those who engage in it are not truly saved. John Calvin warns, "We cannot be troublesome or disobedient to our pastors without hazarding our own salvation."[4]

Christian Ministers Who Have Died

"Remember your leaders, who spoke the word of God to you. Consider the outcome of their way of life and imitate their faith" (Heb. 13:7). This is speaking about those who had founded the church but had apparently since died, and are now with Christ in the city of the living God. What is the church to do concerning them?

"Remember your leaders." The word for leaders, *hēgoumenoi*, is also used of high state officials, political and military leaders, and princes. Stephen used it in Acts 7:10 to refer to Pharaoh appointing Joseph as *ruler* of Egypt.

But here we are encouraged to remember the past leaders in the church that we may be inspired by their teaching, holy lives, perseverance, and triumphant deaths. These people did not abandon the gospel to go back to the shadow of the Levitical priesthood of Judaism. So the author exhorts, "Do not be unthankful and do not forget these leaders. They lived lives of faith and joined the list of the heroes of faith that we should emulate."

These leaders should be honored primarily because they *"spoke the word of God to you"* (Heb. 13:7). Preaching the word of God is the unique ministry and responsibility of a true preacher. His mission is to declare, "Thus saith the Lord." Any minister who does not preach the word of God is an agent of Satan. Such false ministers abound today. Instead of feeding, guiding, disciplining, and protecting the sheep, they entertain them and tickle their ears with new teachings alien to the gospel. They do so to get more money or to become powerful and famous.

---

4 Ibid., 1244.

The word of God is the word of salvation (Heb. 2:3). Therefore, if a minister is not preaching God's word, he is not preaching salvation. God's word alone is the word of life. Faith comes by hearing this word of God preached. And so ministers are to guard the deposit of the gospel and to preach it faithfully for the eternal salvation of God's elect.

"Consider the outcome of their way of life" (Heb. 13:7). As we study carefully the lives and sermons of ministers of old who lived and died by faith, we will be inspired to also live by faith. Doing so is a medicine that will cure us of the temptation of abandoning Christianity. For example, consider the words of Paul, who wrote at the end of his life, "For I am already being poured out like a drink offering, and the time has come for my departure. I have fought the good fight, I have finished the race, I have kept the faith. Now there is in store for me the crown of righteousness, which the Lord, the righteous Judge, will award to me on that day—and not only to me, but also to all who have longed for his appearing" (2 Tim. 4:6–8). Paul and those like him are heroes of faith who encourage us to run the race with perseverance that we may also win Christ's benediction and approbation. Though they have died, they still speak to us through their writings.

Finally, we are told to *"imitate their faith"* (Heb. 13:7). Consider and emulate the lives of true Christian ministers in word and deeds so that when you die, others may also consider your life and imitate you.

The Ever-Living Minister

Finally, let us consider the ever-living minister, the Lord Jesus Christ: *"Jesus Christ is the same yesterday and today and forever"* (Heb. 13:8). This is perhaps the most well-known verse in this epistle.

The author wrote about ministers who died and those who were still living but would also die. We must obey them and submit to them when they preach the word of salvation, and we must emulate them. Yet we cannot emulate them in everything because they are not perfect. The only perfect minister is Jesus Christ, who came to minister and give his life as a ransom for many (Matt. 20:28). He is the Good Shepherd whose sheep hear his voice. He died for our sins as our substitute and mediator. He alone made purification for our sins by the shedding of his blood as the Lamb of God. As both priest and victim, he makes every elect sinner perfect to approach God with confidence. Through him we have come to the city of the living God to worship God in spirit and in truth. Jesus died once and was buried, but he was raised from the dead to die no more.

Godly pastors have died, and they shall continue to die. It is appointed for all men once to die (Heb. 9:27). But the Good Pastor lives forever. Jesus is our perfect example and we are to emulate him wholly. He is trustworthy and we can always depend on him. He is for us, with us, and in us. He goes before us, feeds us, guides us, guards us from all harm, and shall bring us all safely home to God our Father. He is the final and perfect revelation of God to us. Thus, it would be sheer folly to abandon Jesus and go back to the shadow of Judaism. He was dependable when he lived on earth yesterday, he is dependable today as he intercedes as our high priest in our behalf before the Father, and he will remain dependable forever.

Friends, parents, pastors, children, and spouses may change, but Jesus is the same forever, and his gospel never changes. The gospel alone is the power of God unto salvation. All other religions are impotent to save because they cannot deal effectively with human depravity. Only Jesus saves, and Jesus never fails. There is no new and improved Jesus. Because he is eternal, he gives us eternal salvation (Heb. 5:9), eternal redemption (Heb. 9:12), and an eternal inheritance (Heb. 9:15), based on God's eternal covenant (Heb. 13:20). He helps us now (Heb. 2:18) and gives us grace now (Heb. 4:16). He intercedes for us now (Heb. 7:25), and his grace is sufficient for us now (2 Cor. 12:9). We can do all things through Christ who strengthens us (Phil. 4:13). He will stand with us now and in the hour of our death.

If you are a Christian minister, I urge you to preach the unchanging gospel of the unchanging Christ. Watch over your people for their spiritual welfare. Remember that you are only an undershepherd; Jesus Christ is the Chief Shepherd. Be always prepared to give him an account of your service. If you are one of God's people, I urge you to obey true ministers and submit to them gladly. Enable them to do their work with great joy, that their ministry may be everlastingly profitable to you. If you are a child, may you also respect, obey, and submit to your leaders—parents, teachers, and pastors—that you may be filled with all the blessings of God.

40
The Christian's Sacrifice

> ⁹*Do not be carried away by all kinds of strange teachings. It is good for our hearts to be strengthened by grace, not by ceremonial foods, which are of no value to those who eat them.* ¹⁰*We have an altar from which those who minister at the tabernacle have no right to eat.* ¹¹*The high priest carries the blood of animals into the Most Holy Place as a sin offering, but the bodies are burned outside the camp.* ¹²*And so Jesus also suffered outside the city gate to make the people holy through his own blood.* ¹³*Let us, then, go to him outside the camp, bearing the disgrace he bore.* ¹⁴*For here we do not have an enduring city, but we are looking for the city that is to come.* ¹⁵*Through Jesus, therefore, let us continually offer to God a sacrifice of praise—the fruit of lips that confess his name.* ¹⁶*And do not forget to do good and to share with others, for with such sacrifices God is pleased.*
>
> Hebrews 13:9–16

Hebrews 13:9–16 speaks about the Christian's sacrifice. From this passage we will examine two points: Christian doctrine and Christian sacrifice. Our sacrifice is directly related to our doctrine.

In Hebrews 13:7 we were asked to remember our leaders who spoke the word of God to us, consider their lives, and imitate their faith. Verse 9 gives us the reason for this exhortation. Some of these Hebrew believers were tempted to forsake the true gospel and go back to the security of Judaism. They were tired of being persecuted and suffering shame for their faith in Christ.

Because the Hebrew believers had no temple, no priest, no altar, no sacrifices, no feasts, no candles, no incense, no sacrificial meals, no lamps, and no bells, they were charged with being impious atheists. After all, how could anyone be godly without such accoutrements? So their Christian faith was now threatened by various "strange teachings" that had nothing to do with Jesus Christ. The clear gospel message was threatened by these variegated ideas.

Today's world is full of diversity, pluralism, and multiculturalism. The assumption is that each religion is equally valid. But only the gospel of Jesus is true, and only Jesus can save. He is "the way and the truth and the life"; no one comes to the Father outside of him (John 14:6). "Salvation is found in no one else, for there is no other name under heaven given to men by which we must be saved" (Acts 4:12). Eternal life is in the Son, and he who does not have the Son does not have life (1 John 5:11–12).

True worship of God must be based on the true doctrine of God; false doctrines produce false worship. All worship other than the worship of God the Father through Jesus Christ by the Holy Spirit is demonic. If we abandon the gospel, we lose Jesus and, with him, all things. But with Jesus, we possess all things. That is why we must remember true ministers and their true gospel, consider their lives, and imitate their true faith. That is why we preach the Bible, not the multifaceted, strange doctrines of man. Such novel teachings of the devil are called cults, and they proliferate in this country. Mindless people, including "Christians," are attracted to these teachings that damn the souls of men. We confess Jesus Christ as Lord by the Holy Spirit, but they are energized by Satan to abandon the true gospel. Yet how can they escape the severe judgment of God if they neglect such a great salvation revealed to us in Jesus Christ?

True Doctrine versus False Teachings

The writer exhorts, *"Do not be carried away by varied and strange teachings"* (Heb. 13:9, NASB). Notice the plural: "teachings." This is in contrast to the teaching, or doctrine, of Jesus Christ. Christians do not have multiple teachings; we have one teaching, one doctrine.

Wherever the true gospel is preached, the devil attacks the message by means of strange doctrines that turn people away to

The Christian's Sacrifice

destruction. This was true in the first century and remains true today. How many churches, as well as cults, preach false doctrine! Such churches are ashamed of preaching the true gospel as it is revealed in Christ. Paul warned the Corinthian church about those who were preaching a different gospel, a different Jesus, and a different spirit. The preachers of this false gospel, whom Paul calls servants of Satan, were masquerading as angels of light (2 Cor. 11:3-4, 13-15). He saw such teachers in the Galatian churches as well: "I am astonished that you are so quickly deserting the one who called you by the grace of Christ and turning to a different gospel—which is really no gospel at all. Evidently some people are throwing you into confusion and are trying to pervert the gospel of Christ. But even if we or an angel from heaven should preach a gospel other than the one we preached to you, let him be eternally condemned!" (Gal. 1:6-8).

Paul said to the elders of the church of Ephesus, "Keep watch over yourselves and all the flock of which the Holy Spirit has made you overseers. Be shepherds of the church of God, which he bought with his own blood. I know that after I leave, savage wolves will come in among you and will not spare the flock. Even from your own number men will arise and distort the truth in order to draw away disciples after them" (Acts 20:28-30). I have seen such false people, both coming into the church from outside and rising up from within the church. They are not shepherds. These false teachers have only one purpose: to destroy the flock. Jesus said, "The thief comes only to steal and kill and destroy" (John 10:10). Elsewhere, Paul warns, "The Spirit clearly says that in later times some will abandon the faith and follow deceiving spirits and things taught by demons. Such teachings come through hypocritical liars, whose consciences have been seared as with a hot iron" (1 Tim. 4:1-2). We see such liars of all denominational stripes on television, deceiving those who are not people of God. No true child of God will be misled by such people. Jesus says that his sheep will follow him because they know his voice, "but they will never follow a stranger; in fact, they will run away from him because they do not recognize a stranger's voice" (John 10:5).

The Hebrews writer is warning us to distinguish between the doctrine of Jesus Christ and the doctrines of demons. Why are some people blown away by "strange teachings" that contradict the gospel of our Lord? Because they are not rooted in the gospel. They refuse to exercise their minds; they are centered in their feelings. These people do not want to think; they just want to feel good. They come to church to be entertained. They do not understand that they are being dragged away from truth into error and death everlasting. They are sensualists who are interested only in novelty, like the Athenians who always wanted to hear something new. They do not devote themselves to the apostles' doctrine, although it is the very foundation of the church. If the word is preached to such people, Satan comes and steals the seed of it from their minds. They are like tumbleweeds: when a little breeze comes, they break off and tumble along from teaching to teaching, from church to church, from cult to cult.

Paul likens such people to infants who are "tossed back and forth by the waves, and blown here and there by every wind of teaching and by the cunning and craftiness of men in their deceitful scheming" (Eph. 4:14). In fact, they look for ministers who provide entertainment rather than preach the gospel truth as it is found in Jesus. About such teachers Jude says, "These men are blemishes at your love feasts, eating with you without the slightest qualm—shepherds who feed only themselves. They are clouds without rain, blown along by the wind" (Jude 12). False preachers are chaff—lightweight nothings. It is Christ who gives us gravity, glory, and weight. Their only purpose is to move money from our pockets to theirs, so they can buy bigger rings, larger mansions, and better cars. Such teachers are found throughout the church world today. They may have great fun, but they refuse to preach the gospel.

How many people today want variety instead of the same old gospel! We enjoy variety in everything else; why not in the gospel? Indeed, such thinking is not new; in the wilderness God's people began to long for the leeks, onions, melons, and fish of Egypt, telling Moses, "We are sick and tired of this manna from heaven" (Num. 11). Variety in some things may be good, but variety in doctrine can kill us. The word of God alone is the word of life. The word alone is Spirit that raises the dead (John 6:63).

What about you? Do you want to hear something that will entertain you—some leeks and melons, fish and onions? May God give us a great hunger for the word of God and for the apostolic doctrine—a great love for Jesus.

Those who hunger for variety are lured away into novel teachings that destroy their souls. Eventually some want to go back to externalism, ceremonialism, sacerdotalism, and various dietary laws. Even today many people are leaving the evangelical world to join such churches. They think icons, vestments, lights, smells, frescoes, and cathedrals will give them more dignity. But we have dignity in Christ. God sent Jesus so that he may bring many sons to glory. He called us, justified us, and will glorify us. Jesus Christ alone gives us glory.

Those who are mindless will go back to that which cannot edify them. This is what the author has been warning his readers about throughout this epistle: "How much more severely do you think a man deserves to be punished who has trampled the Son of God under foot, who has treated as an unholy thing the blood of the covenant that sanctified him, and who has insulted the Spirit of grace?" (Heb. 10:29). The Hebrews were tempted to go back to the worship of the temple, the altar, the sacrifices, and special sacrificial meals. They wanted to go back to the security of Judaism, away from the stigma and persecution of Christianity. But by going back, they were abandoning the true salvation that is in Jesus alone.

Strengthening Our Hearts by Grace

The writer warns, *"It is good for our hearts to be strengthened by grace, not by ceremonial foods"* (Heb. 13:9). Foods cannot save anyone, nor can smells, bells, ceremonies, and vestments. Think of the Reformers and Puritans, who all came out of ceremonialism into the marvelous light of the gospel.

Paul warned the Colossians about being led astray by those who insisted on special foods and regulations:

> Therefore do not let anyone judge you by what you eat or drink, or with regard to a religious festival, a New Moon celebration or a Sabbath day. These are a shadow of the things that were to come; the reality, however, is found in Christ.... Since you died with Christ to the basic principles of this world, why, as though you still belonged to it, do you submit to its rules: "Do not

handle! Do not taste! Do not touch!"? These are all destined to perish with use, because they are based on human commands and teachings. Such regulations indeed have an appearance of wisdom, with their self-imposed worship, their false humility and their harsh treatment of the body, but they lack any value in restraining sensual indulgence. (Col. 2:16–17, 20–23)

He also says, "The kingdom of God is not a matter of eating and drinking, but of righteousness, peace and joy in the Holy Spirit" (Rom. 14:17). Only Jesus Christ can bring us to God by the forgiveness of our sins.

The author has already spoken about the futility of the sacrificial system to cleanse us from our sins: "The Holy Spirit was showing by this that the way into the Most Holy Place had not yet been disclosed as long as the first tabernacle was still standing. This is an illustration for the present time, indicating that the gifts and sacrifices being offered were not able to clear the conscience of the worshiper. They are only a matter of food and drink and various ceremonial washings—external regulations applying until the time of the new order" (Heb. 9:8–10). The new order has come in Jesus Christ. Life and forgiveness have come. The blood of Jesus cleanses us from all our sins.

"Food does not bring us near to God" (1 Cor. 8:8). Food can strengthen our bodies, but it is useless to strengthen our hearts. We need abounding grace, grace that is sufficient for our every need, grace that is greater than all our sins, grace by which we are saved. Where do we obtain this grace? We cannot find it in Judaism, in cults, or in mindless modern churches. For this grace we have to go out to Jesus Christ, who was crucified on Calvary's cross. The Jews considered Jesus an unholy blasphemer, so they put him to death outside the gate of the city. But he is the Holy One, and it was his own people who were unholy. They were like the Israelites in the wilderness. Because they worshiped the golden calf, Israel and their camp became unholy, and God refused to meet with Moses inside the camp. Moses had to go outside the camp to meet with God (Exod. 33).

The blood of the sin offerings sprinkled on the mercy seat in the Holy of Holies did not truly sanctify anyone. The blood of bulls and goats pointed to the sanctifying blood of the coming One, Jesus Christ, who was crucified outside the gates of Jerusalem, not because he was unholy, but because his people were. He alone is the Holy One who makes us holy: *"And so Jesus also suffered outside the city gate to make the people holy through his own blood. Let us, then, go to him outside the camp, bearing the disgrace he bore"* (Heb. 13:12–13). As true Christians, we must go outside—out from Judaism and everything else—to Jesus, the Holy One.

We Have a Priest, an Altar, and Food

The writer says, *"We have an altar from which those who minister at the tabernacle have no right to eat"* (Heb. 13:10). Earlier he declared that we have a high priest (Heb. 8:1). Never think that Christians are irreligious. We have an altar and a high priest, and we have sacrifices to offer to God by which he is well pleased.

The altar stands for sacrifice. Jesus as the high priest offered himself in sacrifice to atone for our sins once for all. His sacrifice is unrepeatable, effectual for all time for all who come to him. He tells us, "Come unto me, all you sinners, and I will give you rest" —the rest that is found in the forgiveness of sins and communion with God. No tradition or ceremony of this world, whether secular or religious, can cleanse our consciences and forgive our sins. "Come unto me," Jesus says. "I alone can give you a clean conscience." Heed the call of God: *"Come, all you who are thirsty, come to the waters; and you who have no money, come, buy and eat! Come, buy wine and milk without money and without cost"* (Isa. 55:1).

Not only do we have a high priest and an altar, but we also have food that will satisfy our souls and strengthen our hearts. Jesus declares, *"I am the living bread that came down from heaven. If anyone eats of this bread, he will live forever. This bread is my flesh, which I will give for the life of the world. . . . I tell you the truth, unless you eat the flesh of the Son of Man and drink his blood, you have no life in you. Whoever eats my flesh and drinks my blood has eternal life, and I will raise him up at the last day. For my flesh is real food and my blood is real drink."* (John 6:51, 53–55)

But how can we eat the flesh and drink the blood of Jesus? He tells us: *"I am the bread of life. He who comes to me will never go hungry, and he who believes in me will never be thirsty"*

(John 6:35). Jesus is asking us to eat his flesh and drink his blood by believing in his person and his atoning sacrifice for our sins.

Let us come to Jesus and live! May we come to Jesus and be strengthened by grace in our inner being. We read that when he came to his own, his own did not receive him. But that is not the whole story: "Yet to all who received him, to those who believed in his name, he gave the right to become children of God" (John 1:12). We also read, "Whoever believes in the Son has eternal life" (John 3:36). Jesus admonished the unbelieving Jews, "You diligently study the Scriptures because you think that by them you possess eternal life. These are the Scriptures that testify about me, yet you refuse to come to me to have life" (John 5:39-40). Let us come to Jesus and have life!

We need grace to be strengthened in our inner being. That grace comes through the sacrifice of Christ on the cross. So we are told, "Let us then approach the throne of grace with confidence, so that we may receive mercy and find grace to help us in our time of need" (Heb. 4:16). God gives us an abundance of grace so that we can do everything he wants us to do (2 Cor. 9:8). Jesus told Paul, "My grace is sufficient for you" (2 Cor. 12:9). In other words, he was telling Paul that he would not heal his problem, but would give him sufficient grace to live with it. God's grace is always sufficient to help us meet all the challenges of life, including death itself. Neither death nor life can separate us from the love of God.

What we need is grace—more grace, sufficient grace, abundant grace—that flows from the cross of Christ to us. Paul committed the Ephesian elders "to God and to the word of his grace" (Acts 20:32). He also tells us of "the grace of God that brings salvation" (Titus 2:11). Peter exhorts, "Grow in the grace and knowledge of our Lord and Savior Jesus Christ" (2 Pet. 3:18), and James says, "He gives us more grace" (James 4:6).

We Must Go Out to Him

Let us, then, go outside to Jesus, who is the Holy One, our atonement and high priest, the source of all grace, and our holy altar and food. Let us leave the obsolete shadow that is passing away and is impotent to save, and go to Jesus, bearing proudly

The Christian's Sacrifice

the shame of Christ as Moses did (Heb. 11:26). The reproach of the cross of Christ is of greater worth than all the treasures of this world.

Let us get out of the worldliness and out of all churches that refuse to preach Jesus Christ and him crucified. Let us, rather, go to a church that preaches the gospel of God's grace, for what fellowship is there between light and darkness, between life and death? Jesus tells us to deny ourselves, take up the cross, and follow him. He did not come to make us rich and famous, but to make us sons of glory, fit to live in the world to come.

Let us flee the City of Destruction and follow Jesus to the City of God. Let us join Abraham, Moses, Peter, Paul, Stephen, James, and all the holy martyrs in bearing the stigma of Christ proudly. We are marching to the heavenly Zion. Earthly Jerusalem cannot save us. There is no abiding city here. The security of this world is just a mirage. This world is Sodom, about to be burned. Jesus alone will take us to the abiding city, the unshakable kingdom of God. May we seek earnestly the kingdom of God and his righteousness, and all these things will be added unto us (Matt. 6:33).

Paul speaks about how he went outside to Jesus:

> If anyone else thinks he has reasons to put confidence in the flesh, I have more: circumcised on the eighth day, of the people of Israel, of the tribe of Benjamin, a Hebrew of Hebrews; in regard to the law, a Pharisee; as for zeal, persecuting the church; as for legalistic righteousness, faultless. But whatever was to my profit I now consider loss for the sake of Christ. What is more, I consider everything a loss compared to the surpassing greatness of knowing Christ Jesus my Lord, for whose sake I have lost all things. I consider them rubbish, that I may gain Christ and be found in him, not having a righteousness of my own that comes from the law, but that which is through faith in Christ—the righteousness that comes from God and is by faith. (Phil. 3:4–9)

We may have everything inside the City of Destruction, but we will never have Christ. We are fools if we stay inside the structures of this world, where there is no Christ. So Paul says elsewhere, "May I never boast except in the cross of our Lord Jesus Christ, through which the world has been crucified to me, and I to the world" (Gal. 6:14).

May we, therefore, love Jesus and his word, that we will not be blown away by diverse and strange teachings, but trust solely in Christ. Then we will go to the city of the living God and dwell eternally with God in the new heaven and the new earth.

Christian Doctrine Leads to Christian Sacrifice

"Through Jesus, therefore, let us continually offer to God a sacrifice of praise—the fruit of lips that confess his name" (Heb. 13:15). The result of true Christian doctrine is true Christian worship. Our worship and sacrifices are a response to God's free gift of salvation to us. The psalmist asked, "How can I repay the LORD for all his goodness to me? I will lift up the cup of salvation and call on the name of the LORD" (Ps. 116:12–13). Because God saved us, we now offer the sacrifice of praise to him.

Jesus Christ is the Prophet, Priest, and King, and we are prophets, priests, and kings in him. He sacrificed himself once for all, and his sacrifice is always effectual for all who trust in him for salvation. Now, in him, we have sacrifices to offer to God throughout our life.

The Greek text says, "Through him [who is the high priest], we offer our sacrifice of praise" (Heb. 13:15). Our sacrifice will not be accepted unless it is offered in the name of his beloved Son. He is our high priest; we function as priests under his authority. Without him we are nothing and can do nothing. In him and through him we can do all things. So when we come to the church to worship, and the Holy Spirit enables us to sing praises in the name of our great high priest, that praise goes to the very presence of God. It is not just wasted energy. Praise is sacrifice. Christ died for us, and because of this we offer sacrifices of praise to God through Christ.

All Christians are priests—old and young, male and female, Jews and Gentiles, rich and poor. We do not believe in the clergy worshiping apart from the laity, but in the priesthood of all believers. We are the temple of God, and we are also priests. As priests, we have something to offer because of the great salvation achieved by the Father at the cost of his Son: we now offer spiritual sacrifices acceptable to God through Jesus Christ. Peter tells us, "As you come to him, the living Stone—rejected by men but chosen by God and precious to him—you also, like living stones, are being built into a spiritual house to be a holy priesthood, offering spiritual sacrifices acceptable to God through Jesus Christ. . . . You are a chosen people, a royal priesthood, a holy nation, a people belonging to God, that you may declare the praises of him who called you out of darkness into his wonderful light" (1 Pet. 2:4–5, 9).

What is the purpose of salvation? That we may declare God's praises. Salvation gives springs to our feet, and the Holy Spirit performs glossal surgery so that we open our mouths and sing praises to God. If a person is not born again, he will not worship God. We must examine ourselves to see whether we are born of God.

The Sacrifices of Praise

As priests, then, what sacrifices do we offer? First, let us note what we do not do offer. Sacerdotalist churches re-crucify Christ at every mass. We do not do that. Christ the high priest offered himself once for all, and the benefit of his sacrifice accrues to us daily.

The writer says, *"Through Jesus, therefore, let us continually offer to God a sacrifice of praise"* (Heb. 13:15). Christ has given us the privilege of worshiping God; therefore, we look forward to every opportunity to come together and praise God.

Our praise is the thank offering we give to God. We thank God for saving us from our sins, from his wrath, and from eternal damnation. Christ died for our sins and was raised for our justification. He is now bringing many sons to glory, and we look forward to singing God's praises for all eternity.

God planned our salvation, Christ accomplished it, and the Holy Spirit applied this redemption to each one of us. Thus, we praise God, as ancient Israel did after they were delivered from Egypt. The Egyptians were drowned, but the Israelites came out of the Red Sea alive and singing, "I will sing to the LORD, for he is highly exalted. The horse and its rider he has hurled into the sea. The LORD is my strength and my song; he has become my salvation. He is my God, and I will praise him, my father's God, and I will exalt him. The LORD is a warrior; the LORD is his name" (Exod. 15:1–3).

The Fruit of Our Lips

"The sacrifice of praise" means the sacrifice consisting in praise to God. It is further defined as *"the fruit of lips that confess his name"* (Heb. 13:15). This fruit is created by the Spirit of God, for out of the abundance of the heart the mouth speaks (Matt. 12:34). As we meditate on the doctrine of our eternal salvation, we will joyfully sing God's praises. We will sing about God—his nature and his works, particularly the wonderful work of redemption. We will eagerly tell others about the incarnation, death, burial, and resurrection of Christ, which brought about our eternal salvation.

In some churches, people sit as an audience, saying nothing. In true worship, however, the people of God are engaged not only in listening but also in singing and speaking out as the Spirit of God comes upon them. Such is the fruit of our lips that is created by the Spirit.

Hosea speaks of this offering of praise: "Return, O Israel, to the LORD your God. Your sins have been your downfall! Take words with you and return to the LORD. Say to him: 'Forgive all our sins and receive us graciously, that we may offer the fruit of our lips'" (Hosea 14:1–2). Isaiah prophesied about it also when he revealed God's words to sinful Israel: "I have seen his ways, but I will heal him; I will guide him and restore comfort to him, creating praise on the lips of the mourners in Israel. Peace, peace, to those far and near. . . . And I will heal them" (Isa. 57:18–19).

God has healed us and forgiven our sins. Now he creates praise on our lips. God has declared peace to those who are far and peace to those who are near. The cross brings us peace and the cross brings us near. Nearer to God we cannot be. We express our gratitude by praising him with the praises he himself has created.

Such worship results from the ministry of the Holy Spirit. We are not sufficient in ourselves to worship God properly; we need the Spirit and his gifts. Paul writes, "Do not get drunk on wine, which leads to debauchery. Instead, be filled with the Spirit. Speak to one another with psalms, hymns and spiritual songs. Sing and make music in your heart to the Lord, always giving thanks to God the Father for everything, in the name of our

Lord Jesus Christ" (Eph. 5:18–20). When the Spirit of God falls upon us, he creates praise within us, and all of a sudden we want to sing and make music to the Lord. That is why it is so refreshing to come into the house of God. Paul says, "What then shall we say, brothers? When you come together, everyone has a hymn, or a word of instruction, a revelation, a tongue or an interpretation. All of these must be done for the strengthening of the church" (1 Cor. 14:26). This is worship. When the Holy Spirit comes upon us, one will have a psalm, another a hymn, another an instruction, another a tongue, and so on.

In Acts 2:4 we are told that the Holy Spirit created praises upon the lips of the early disciples. When the Holy Spirit came upon these people at first, they spoke in other tongues, as the Spirit gave them utterance. What were they saying? The crowd reported, "We hear them declaring the wonders of God in our own tongues!" (Acts 2:11). I believe the disciples were talking about what had happened in their recent history: the death, burial, and resurrection of Christ. They had seen him ascend into the presence of God; now they were singing his praise.

What is the reason for our worship? Christ Jesus, God's Son, lives forevermore as the Sovereign Lord of the universe. No other religion has a Savior who died and rose again and is seated as the Sovereign Lord of the universe on the right hand of God the Father.

We are told to worship continually: *"Through Jesus, therefore, let us continually offer to God a sacrifice of praise"* (Heb. 13:15). The psalmist says, "I will extol the LORD at all times; his praise will always be on my lips" (Ps. 34:1). What are we speaking about—Jesus Christ or something else? "I will extol the Lord *at all times"*—in the morning, at noon, and in the evening, when I am young and when I am old, when I am sick and when I am well. True Christians are continually singing God's praises, telling others how he saved us and gave us eternal life, healed us from all our diseases and forgave all our sins. "Praise the LORD, O my soul, and forget not all his benefits" (Ps. 103:2).

Paul exhorts us, "Be joyful always; pray continually; give thanks in all circumstances, for this is God's will for you in Christ Jesus" (1 Thess. 5:16–18). Elsewhere he describes himself and his Christian companions as "dying, and yet we live on;

beaten, and yet not killed; sorrowful, yet always rejoicing; poor, yet making many rich; having nothing, and yet possessing everything" (2 Cor. 6:9–10). This is true charismatic, Holy-Spirit-filled life.

My mother worked hard all the time; hers was not an easy life. But sick or well, in bad times and good, she always praised the Lord. A true Christian is born of God, filled with the Holy Spirit, and always rejoicing in God.

When Paul and Silas were stripped, beaten up, and put in stocks in the innermost cell of the prison, what did they do? "About midnight Paul and Silas were praying and singing hymns to God, and the other prisoners were listening to them" (Acts 16:25). Here they were in chains, with their backs furrowed, and experiencing intense pain from the beatings they had suffered. Yet the Holy Spirit came upon them and created praise on their lips.

Why do we murmur and complain? God's people must sing his praises, especially when we have trouble. In fact, that is the very time when we cannot afford not to praise. Let us *continually* offer the sacrifice of praise.

Confessing His Name

The author says our praise is *"the fruit of lips that confess his name"* (Heb. 13:15). Evangelism is worship; it is a sacrifice of praise. We must confess Christ's name especially to those who have not heard of him.

Paul says, "I am not ashamed of the gospel, because it is the power of God for the salvation of everyone who believes: first for the Jew, then for the Gentile" (Rom. 1:16). True Christians are not ashamed of the gospel; rather, we are confident and happy to say that Jesus is the Savior of the world and that Jesus saves sinners like us. Yes, we were blind but now we see; we were lost, but now we are found; we were dead, but now we are alive.

No one confesses the name of Christ except by the Holy Spirit (1 Cor. 12:3). Jesus himself says, "Whoever acknowledges me before men, I will also acknowledge him before my Father in heaven. But whoever disowns me before men, I will disown him before my Father in heaven" (Matt. 10:32–33).

When a person wins the lottery, he will speak about it to everyone he meets. But we have received something far greater than millions of dollars. By his supreme sacrifice in our place on the cross, Jesus Christ has given us eternal life. He is the only Savior; that is why we are not ashamed of Jesus. Confessing Christ, therefore, is worship, a sacrifice we Christians gladly make.

Doing Good and Sharing

The writer next tells us, "*And do not forget to do good and to share with others, for with such sacrifices God is pleased*" (Heb. 13:16). Years ago, when my family came into the evangelical church that believed in the gospel and the Holy Spirit, I saw people regularly helping one another. If a brother was sick, others would fast, pray, and take care of that person. If someone needed a new roof, they would come and put on a new one. If someone had fields, members of the church would come and help with the harvest. I recognized that this is how God's church should act, loving and sharing with one another as a family.

We sacrifice, then, not only with words but also with deeds, particularly done on behalf of God's people. How can we not help when our brother has no food, clothing, or other necessities! We are the body of Christ, and the Bible says, "If one part suffers, every part suffers with it; if one part is honored, every part rejoices with it" (1 Cor. 12:26). The church is not a place where autonomous people come together, disconnected from everyone else, and walk away when the service is done without talking to others. We are the family of God, the people of God. We are connected to one another, and Jesus Christ is our head. There is no discrimination between black and white, rich or poor. We are all bought with a price, the precious blood of Jesus Christ. Let us, therefore, make sure that we do good and share with others.

God wants us to share. Jesus spoke about such sacrificial sharing in Matthew 25:35–40. Elsewhere, he said that if we have two tunics, and another person has none, we are to give him one. I remember watching my father take his supper and walk a mile to the home of a brother in the church because he knew this man did not have food. He was happier to give it to this other man and see him eat than to eat it himself.

The early church shared when the Holy Spirit came upon them: "All the believers were together and had everything in common. Selling their possessions and goods, they gave to anyone as he had need. . . . All the believers were one in heart and mind. No one claimed that any of his possessions was his own, but they shared everything they had" (Acts 2:44–45; 4:32). In Acts 9 we read, "In Joppa there was a disciple named Tabitha (which, when translated, is Dorcas), who was always doing good and helping the poor. About that time she became sick and died, and her body was washed and placed in an upstairs room. . . . All the widows stood around [Peter], crying and showing him the robes and other clothing that Dorcas had made while she was still with them" (vv. 36–39). When you die, will people come to your funeral because you sowed into their lives, saying, "He did this for me," or, "She helped me"?

James tells us, "Religion that God our Father accepts as pure and faultless is this: to look after orphans and widows in their distress" (Jas. 1:27). God is interested in widows and orphans, and he especially wants those who confess the name of Christ to look after them. Paul encourages us: "Let us not become weary in doing good, for at the proper time we will reap a harvest if we do not give up. Therefore, as we have opportunity, let us do good to all people, especially to those who belong to the family of believers" (Gal. 6:9–10). When we become weary, God will fill us with the Holy Spirit, giving us new vitality, energy, grace, and competence.

When we share, God blesses us. When Paul was in prison, the Macedonian churches shared with him out of their deep poverty, and, in turn, God met their needs. Paul wrote: "I have received full payment and even more; I am amply supplied, now that I have received from Epaphroditus the gifts you sent. They are a fragrant offering, an acceptable sacrifice, pleasing to God. And my God will meet all your needs according to his glorious riches in Christ Jesus" (Phil. 4:18–19). Jesus tells us, "Give, and it will be given to you. A good measure, pressed down, shaken together and running over, will be poured into your lap. For with the measure you use, it will be measured to you" (Luke 6:38). I have been receiving such blessings throughout my life. As I give to others, God gives back to me.

The Christian's Sacrifice

Worship Is All of Life

Finally, the writer says, *"For with such sacrifices God is pleased"* (Heb. 13:16). Worship is not what we do just on Sundays: it is all of life, lived for the glory of God as a response to what God has done for us. Enoch lived such a life that pleased God (Heb. 11:5). Jesus said, "I always do what pleases him" (John 8:29). What is the chief end of man? To glorify God and enjoy him forever. God by his grace works in us that we may work out what is pleasing to him (Heb. 13:20–21).

All of life, then, is a sacrifice to God. Paul exhorts, "Offer your bodies as living sacrifices, holy and pleasing to God—this is your spiritual act of worship" (Rom. 12:1). Elsewhere, he teaches, "So whether you eat or drink or whatever you do, do it all for the glory of God" (1 Cor. 10:31).

May God help us all to come to Jesus in repentance and faith, that he may save us and lead us into that unshakable kingdom to which by faith we have already come, the enduring city where God dwells with his people. In thanksgiving to God for our eternal salvation, may we as God's priests offer to him the sacrifices that consist in praise and good deeds of service to God's people, that God may be well pleased with our sacrifices and tell us on that day, "Thou good and faithful servant, enter into the joy of your Lord."

41
Living the Resurrection Life

[20]*May the God of peace, who through the blood of the eternal covenant brought back from the dead our Lord Jesus, that great Shepherd of the sheep, [21]equip you with everything good for doing his will, and may he work in us what is pleasing to him, through Jesus Christ, to whom be glory for ever and ever. Amen.*

Hebrews 13:20-21

Today billions of people refuse to believe in Jesus and his resurrection. Jesus himself prophesied that very few would believe in him. In this passage, the writer directly refers to the resurrection of Jesus, saying, "God . . . through the blood of the eternal covenant brought back from the dead our Lord Jesus" (Heb. 13:20). The writer has already made reference to it indirectly several times before: "The Son is the radiance of God's glory and the exact representation of his being, sustaining all things by his powerful word. After he had provided purification for sins, he sat down at the right hand of the Majesty in heaven" (Heb. 1:3; see also Heb. 8:1; 10:12; 12:2). Jesus went through the heavens and arrived in the presence of God as high priest to intercede in our behalf.

This whole epistle rests on the death and resurrection of our Lord. Let us, then, examine the resurrection of Christ and the resurrection life he gives us.

The Resurrection Proofs

All four gospels record the historical truth of Christ's death and resurrection. Jesus himself predicted his death and resurrection many times (e.g., Mark 8:31; 9:9–10; 10:32–34; John 2:18–22). He was not resuscitated; he was resurrected, never to die again. He is the only one who has been so raised in the history of the universe. Jesus conquered death, hell, and Satan for our salvation.

Mary Magdalene saw and heard the risen Christ. If someone were to make up a resurrection story, he would have not put the words into the mouth of Mary Magdalene, because no court of law at that time would accept a woman's testimony, particularly that of a woman with a sinful past. In fact, Mary did not expect to see a risen Christ and was confused when she met him in the garden (John 20). So what is reported in the gospels has the ring of truth.

As Jesus himself had predicted, he rose from the dead on the third day according to the Scriptures and appeared to many at different times. During the forty days he was with the apostles, even Thomas stopped doubting and confessed, "My Lord and my God!" (John 20:28). Paul says the risen Lord was seen by over five hundred people at one time, many of whom were still living when Paul wrote his first epistle to the Corinthians (1 Cor. 15:3–8). He appeared also to Saul of Tarsus, the brilliant Jew and dedicated enemy of Christianity. Having been convinced of Christ's resurrection, Saul became the apostle of the risen Christ, eventually suffering martyrdom for his faith.

Dr. James Boice says that the resurrection of Jesus is proof of the existence of God because God is the only adequate cause for this unique miracle.[1] The resurrection of Christ is also the seal and proof of the deity of Jesus. During his time on earth, Jesus claimed several times to be equal with God (e.g., John 5:17–18; 10:30–38; 14:7–11). Had he not been raised, his claim would have been false. His resurrection from the dead is proof that Jesus Christ is God, as the Father declared (Rom. 1:4).

Christ's resurrection is also the seal and proof of our justification. "He was delivered over to death for our sins and was raised to life

---

1   Boice, *God the Redeemer*, 223–224.

for our justification" (Rom. 4:25). God raised Jesus from the dead because he accepted the Son's sacrificial death of atonement, solving our sin problem forever. The resurrection is the Father's signature to the truth that the atonement was acceptable to the holy and righteous God.

The resurrection is also the seal and proof of our sanctification and eternal life. We are raised with Christ to live a new life by the power of Christ's resurrection. The resurrection proves once and for all that death is not the end of life. Death has been defeated for those who have been united with Christ by faith.

Finally, the resurrection of Christ is the proof of eternal judgment. The billions of people who do not believe in the resurrection of Jesus Christ will believe the truth of the resurrection on the day he himself will judge them (Acts 17:31; Heb. 9:27). Being judged by the risen Jesus will be the final proof to unbelievers.

The Resurrection Benefits

How does the historical resurrection of Jesus benefit those who believe in him? Jesus said, "I am the resurrection and the life. He who believes in me will live, even though he dies; and whoever lives and believes in me will never die" (John 11:25–26). A dead Christ can never give a person eternal life. But praise be to God, God has raised Jesus from the dead, and he gives eternal life to everyone who believes in him.

"May the God of peace, who through the blood of the eternal covenant brought back from the dead our Lord Jesus, that great Shepherd of the sheep, equip you with everything good for doing his will, and may he work in us what is pleasing to him, through Jesus Christ, to whom be glory for ever and ever. Amen" (Heb. 13:20–21). This passage teaches us how we benefit from this resurrection life. The resurrection is not just a theoretical assertion that has no enduring effects. We need God's resurrection power to live our daily lives, to die in faith, and to be brought into the very presence of God. A close look at these verses highlights the benefits we receive through Christ's resurrection.

1. *"May the God of peace . . ."* (Heb. 13:20). By nature we were enemies at war with God. But God devised and executed a salvation

plan to bring about a peaceful relationship with us. Paul says that "God was reconciling the world to himself in Christ, not counting men's sins against them" (2 Cor. 5:19). On his own initiative, God made Christ "who had no sin to be sin for us, so that in him we might become the righteousness of God" (2 Cor. 5:21).

God the Father is both the author and the giver of peace; it is his idea, power, and plan. Through the cross of Christ, this peace was secured for us (Eph. 2:14–17). Paul writes, "Therefore, since we have been justified through faith, we have peace with God through our Lord Jesus Christ" (Rom. 5:1). And because we have peace with God, we have peace within ourselves and can live at peace with others. We who were enemies have been reconciled to God and made his children. God is no longer our Judge. Now he is our heavenly Father, and we are his adopted sons in Jesus Christ. Have you experienced this rest of peace through the risen Christ?

2. "God . . . brought back from the dead our Lord Jesus, that great Shepherd of the sheep" (Heb. 13:20). The Father brought Jesus up from the dead. Death had no power to keep the sinless Christ in the grave. "The soul who sins is the one who will die" (Ezek. 18:20), but Christ did not sin. By his death he destroyed death for us. The resurrection of Christ is the Father's signature certifying that he fully accepts Christ's atoning sacrifice in our place. Now our sins can be forgiven once for all. Death could not keep him down because he is the Holy One (Acts 2:24, 27).

The writer of Hebrews may have been thinking of Isaiah 63:11, which reads in the Septuagint, "Where is the one who brought up out of the sea the shepherd of the sheep?" Isaiah was speaking about how God brought the shepherd Moses and his people out of the judgment of the Red Sea. But in Hebrews the author is speaking about how God brought the great Shepherd of the sheep up from death itself.

He may also have been thinking of Zechariah 9:11: "As for you, because of the blood of my covenant with you, I will free your prisoners from the waterless pit." God the Father brought Jesus Christ out of the waterless pit of death because Christ's bloody atonement was acceptable to him. And, notice, Christ did not come up alone. In him, all his elect sheep are brought out from the dead. Because he lives, we also live forever. Jesus has vanquished death and given us eternal life.

Living the Resurrection Life

3. The basis and guarantee of our own resurrection is *"the blood of the eternal covenant"* (Heb. 13:20). God raised Jesus from the dead because of the blood he shed on the cross when he, as our great high priest, offered himself to God in our place for our eternal salvation. The basis for our resurrection is the death of Christ, and the blood of Christ sealed and confirmed this new and eternal covenant of grace, which saves and enriches his people.

The cause of our resurrection is Christ's acceptable sacrifice. "But we see Jesus, who was made a little lower than the angels, now crowned with glory and honor because he suffered death, so that by the grace of God he might taste death for everyone" (Heb. 2:9). Without the shedding of Christ's blood, eternal death would be the final word. We all would live hopeless lives. But, thank God, death is not the last word. There has been a bloody atonement. The Son of God died, and God accepted his death as ours. By raising Jesus from the dead, the holy Father declared death was conquered and Satan defeated.

4. Jesus Christ is *"that great Shepherd of the sheep"* (Heb. 13:20). Christ is greater than Moses, Joshua, David, and all human shepherds. The Son of God is the chief Shepherd and Bishop of our souls, the Creator and Sustainer of the universe, the King of kings and the Lord of lords.

He is the good Shepherd because he loved us and gave his life for us. He is the chief Shepherd who appointed undershepherds over all his flock. All human shepherds must give an account to the chief Shepherd. The flock is his flock; he purchased them by his blood. He died for them and he lives for them.

As the great Shepherd, Christ cares for his sheep. Not even one will be lost, but all will be regenerated, justified, adopted, sanctified, glorified, and brought into God's presence to enjoy eternal communion with him. No wolf, bear, or devil can harm us when Jesus is our good Shepherd. He comforts us and we lack nothing. He loves us and calls us by name. Evil shepherds kill their sheep, but the good Shepherd laid down his life for us. And because he is raised from the dead, we shall also be raised up on the last day by him, as our great Shepherd promised three times: "And this is the will of him who sent me, that I shall lose none of all that he has given me, but raise them up at the last day. For my Father's will is that everyone who looks to the Son and believes in him shall have eternal life, and I will raise him up at the last day.... No one can come to me unless the Father who sent me draws him, and I will raise him up at the last day" (John 6:39, 40, 44).

5. *"May the God of peace . . . equip you with everything good"* (Heb. 13:20–21). God our Father gives us everything we need to live a holy life. We can never excuse our sin by claiming that God does not enable us to resist temptations. It is his responsibility to equip us and make us fit to do his will, and he does so by repairing all of our weaknesses, setting right every broken bone, and giving us the health and fitness to do the will of God. He gives us good hearts, minds, wills, and affections, and puts his Holy Spirit within us to enlighten our minds and enable us to will God's will. God makes us new creations to do his will with delight.

6. God equips us with everything good *"for [the purpose of] doing his will"* (Heb. 13:21). Although God has the responsibility to equip us and make us able to do his will, we also have a responsibility in this process of sanctification: we must do the will of God. We are able to do so because the Father makes us able. Those who are truly saved will seek out the will of God and do it.

The incarnate Jesus Christ always did the will of God the Father (John 8:29). God has given us a book, the Bible, in our own language, wherein his will is revealed. God's people eagerly read God's word to discover his will, and that is where Jesus himself discovered God's will. What is God's will? To love God with all our heart, mind, soul, and strength, and to love our neighbor as ourselves (Matt. 22:36–40).

7. *"May he work in us what is pleasing to him"* (Heb. 13:21). Not only does God save and equip us, but he also works in us to will and to do his good pleasure. God works in us so that it becomes our nature to do his will. This is one of the chief blessings of the new covenant.

God works in us to do what gives both him and us pleasure, because what gives pleasure to God is that which also gives Christians pleasure. We are happy when we do the will of God but miserable when we do our own thing. Sanctification means God works in us as we work out his will (Phil. 2:12–13). We are raised from the dead to be servants of God. "For Christ's love compels us, because we are convinced that one died for all, and therefore all died. And he died for all, that those who live should no longer live for themselves, but for him who died for them and was raised again" (2 Cor. 5:14–15).

Therefore, both we and God are active. For example, Paul writes, "He who has been stealing must steal no longer, but must work, doing something useful with his own hands, that he may have something to share with those in need" (Eph. 4:28). That is the type of radical change God expects from us because he equips us and works in us. "How much more, then, will the blood of Christ, who through the eternal Spirit offered himself unblemished to God, cleanse our consciences from acts that lead to death, so that we may serve the living God!" (Heb. 9:14). God works in us that we may work for him.

Philippians 3:9–11 shows the connection between the resurrection and our present life. Verse 9 speaks about justification, verse 10 speaks about sanctification, and verse 11 speaks about glorification. Therein, Paul expresses his desire to gain Christ "and be found in him, not having a righteousness of my own that comes from the law, but that which is through faith in Christ—the righteousness that comes from God and is by faith. I want to know Christ and the power of his resurrection and the fellowship of sharing in his sufferings, becoming like him in his death, and so, somehow, to attain to the resurrection from the dead." We need his power to live a life of suffering. Without the resurrection power, we simply cannot deal with the problems that we as Christians face.

God works in us, and we work out by his resurrection power. "Dear friends, if our hearts do not condemn us, we have confidence before God and receive from him anything we ask, because we obey his commands and do what pleases him" (1 John 3:21–22). We cannot live the Christian life through sheer will power or positive thinking. We must have an alien power, the resurrection power of Jesus Christ that comes to us by faith. We are raised with him to live a new life (Rom. 6:4). We live the Christian life by the power of the Holy Spirit, who raised Jesus from the dead.

Paul writes, "To this end I labor, struggling with all his energy, which so powerfully works in me" (Col. 1:29). If you are a Christian, he equips you and works in you, and you are able to work out the good pleasure of God. Paul says elsewhere, "Now to him who is able to do immeasurably more than all we ask or imagine, according to his power that is at work within us . . ." (Eph. 3:20). The Holy Spirit works within every person who trusts in Jesus Christ alone for his salvation. We are not merely to draw upon our education and skills. We are to draw upon nothing less than the power with which God raised Jesus Christ from the dead, the incomparably great power for us who believe (Eph. 1:19).

We receive this power through Jesus Christ. We are who we are and we do whatever we do through the merits of Jesus Christ. By grace are we saved and by grace we live forevermore. That grace flows to us from Christ.

8. *"To [him] be glory for ever and ever. Amen"* (Heb. 13:21). Our entire salvation is the result of the Father's eternal plan. We live for his exclusive and endless glory. Ephesians 1 highlights God's grace: "to the praise of his glorious grace" (v. 6); "in order that we, who were the first to hope in Christ, might be for the praise of his glory" (v. 12); "[The Holy Spirit] is a deposit guaranteeing our inheritance until the redemption of those who are God's possession, to the praise of his glory" (v. 14). The glory is God's alone! To him be glory forever!

The Resurrection Life

The resurrection of Jesus Christ is not merely a historical fact; it is the power that enables us to live a victorious Christian life. More than that, the resurrection of Christ has secured for us an eternal future of victory. Paul reminds us, "If only for this life we have hope in Christ, we are to be pitied more than all men" (1 Cor. 15:19). Then he triumphantly concludes, "But Christ has indeed been raised from the dead, the firstfruits of those who have fallen asleep" (v. 20).

Do you believe in the resurrection of Jesus Christ in history? Do you believe that the Father raised him from the dead because of his perfect atonement? If so, rejoice forevermore and live for his glory. He works in us to make us able to work out his will for his glory and our eternal delight. There is no other way to happiness.

We have nothing to fear, not even death. An account of D. L. Moody's death illustrates this point:

> [It was in 1899] the great evangelist Dwight L. Moody died, but his death was triumphant both for himself and for his family. Moody had been declining for some time, and the family had taken turns being with him. On the morning of his death, his son, who was standing by the bedside, heard him exclaim, "Earth is receding; heaven is opening; God is calling." "You are dreaming, Father," the son said. Moody answered, "No, Will, this is no dream. I have been within the gates. I have seen the children's faces." For awhile it seemed as if Moody were reviving, but he began to slip away again. He said, "Is this death? This is not bad; there is no valley. This is bliss. This is glorious." By this time his daughter was present, and she began to pray for his recovery. He said, "No, no, Emma, don't pray for that. God is calling. This is my coronation day. I have been looking forward to it." Shortly after that Moody was received into heaven. At the funeral the family and friends joined in a joyful service. They spoke. They sang hymns. They heard the words proclaimed: "O death, where is thy sting? O grave, where is thy victory? The sting of death is sin; and the strength of sin is the law. But thanks be to God, who giveth us the victory through our Lord Jesus Christ." (1 Cor. 15:55–57 KJV)[2]

A Christian's death is victory! But if you have not confessed Jesus as your King and Savior, remember that the writer to the Hebrews has also described him as a consuming fire (Heb. 12:29). There will be severe punishment for those who despise the blood of Jesus Christ. God is angry at sinners every day and hates all who do wrong (Ps. 7:11; 5:5).

Jesus is the great Shepherd of the sheep, not of goats. The Bible says that everyone who calls upon the name of the Lord will be saved. May we become his sheep by trusting in his atonement and resurrection, that he may raise us up victorious on the last day.

---

2   Boice, *God the Redeemer*, 229–230.

Select Bibliography

Alford, Henry. "Prolegomena and Hebrews." Vol. 4, part 1 in *Alford's Greek Testament: An Exegetical and Critical Commentary*. Grand Rapids: Guardian Press, 1976.

Boice, James M. *God the Redeemer*. Foundations of the Christian Faith, vol. 2. Downers Grove, IL: InterVarsity Press, 1978.

Bowman, George M. *Don't Let Go! An Exposition of Hebrews*. Phillipsburg, NJ: Presbyterian and Reformed, 1982.

Brown, Raymond. *The Message of Hebrews: Christ Above All*. The Bible Speaks Today series. Edited by John R.W. Stott. Downers Grove, IL: InterVarsity Press, 1982.

Bruce, F. F. *The Epistle to the Hebrews*. The New International Commentary on the New Testament, rev. ed. Grand Rapids: Eerdmans, 1990.

Dods, Marcus. "The Epistle to the Hebrews" in *The Expositor's Greek Testament*, vol. 4. Edited by W. Robertson Nicoll. Grand Rapids: Eerdmans, reprinted 1970.

Ellingworth, Paul. *The Epistle to the Hebrews*. The New International Greek Testament Commentary series. Edited by I. Howard Marshall and W. Ward Gasque. Grand Rapids: Eerdmans, 2000.

Frame, John M. *Salvation Belongs to the Lord: An Introduction to Systematic Theology*. Phillipsburg, NJ: Presbyterian and Reformed, 2006.

Guthrie, Donald. *The Letter to the Hebrews: An Introduction and Commentary*. Tyndale New Testament Commentaries, vol. 15. Grand Rapids: Eerdmans, 2000.

Hendriksen, William, and Simon J. Kistemaker. *Thessalonians, the Pastorals and Hebrews*. New Testament Commentary. Grand Rapids: Baker Books, 1995.

Hughes, Philip Edgcumbe. *A Commentary on the Epistle to the Hebrews*. Grand Rapids: Eerdmans, 1977.

Hughes, R. Kent. *Hebrews: An Anchor for the Soul*. 2 vols. Wheaton, IL: Good News Publishers, 1993.

Jones, Hywel R. *Let's Study Hebrews*. Edinburgh: Banner of Truth Trust, 2002.

Kistemaker, Simon J. *Exposition of the Epistle to the Hebrews*. New Testament Commentary. Grand Rapids: Baker Books, 1995.

Lane, William L. *Hebrews 1–8*. Word Biblical Commentary, vol. 47a. Nashville: Nelson, 1991.

———. *Hebrews 9–13*. Word Biblical Commentary, vol. 47b. Nashville: Nelson, 1991.

MacArthur, John, Jr. *Hebrews*. The MacArthur New Testament Commentary. Chicago: Moody Press, 1983.

Morris, Leon. "Hebrews." In vol. 12 of *The Expositor's Bible Commentary: Hebrews through Revelation*. Edited by Frank E. Gaebelein. Grand Rapids: Zondervan, 1981.

Murray, John. *The Covenant of Grace*. Phillipsburg, NJ: Presbyterian and Reformed, 1988.

Newell, William R. *Hebrews Verse by Verse*. Chicago: Moody Press, 1947.

Owen, John. *Hebrews*. The Crossway Classic Commentaries. Edited by Alister McGrath and J.I. Packer. Wheaton, IL: Crossway Books, 1998.

Pink, Arthur W. *An Exposition of Hebrews*. Grand Rapids: Baker Books, 1970.

Piper, John. Resources on Hebrews. http://www.desiringgod.org/ResourceLibrary/ScriptureIndex/26/.

Robertson, A. T. *The Fourth Gospel* and *The Epistle to the Hebrews*. Word Pictures in the New Testament, vol. 5. Nashville: Broadman Press, 1932.

Stibbs, Alan M. *So Great Salvation: The Meaning and Message of the Letter to the Hebrews*. The Christian Student's Library. Exeter, Devon: The Paternoster Press, 1970.

Vos, Geerhardus. *The Teaching of the Epistle to the Hebrews*. Philadelphia: The Theological Seminary of the Reformed Episcopal Church, 1944.

Westcott, Brooke Foss. *The Epistle to the Hebrews: The Greek Text with Notes and Essays*. Grand Rapids: Eerdmans, 1952.

Grace and Glory Ministries

Grace and Glory Ministries is an extension of Grace Valley Christian Center. We are committed to the teaching of God's infallible word. It is our mission to proclaim the whole gospel to the whole world for the building up of the whole body of Christ.

For more information on the ministries of Grace Valley Christian Center, please visit:

http://www.gracevalley.org

To obtain additional copies of this book, please e-mail:

gvcc@gracevalley.org